S0-BDM-233

Commercial Pilot Test Guide 1996–1998

FAA Practical & Computer-Based Airmen Knowledge

Capt. Douglas S. Carmody, CFII

McGraw-Hill

New York   San Francisco   Washington, D.C.   Auckland   Bogotá   Caracas   Lisbon   London   Madrid   Mexico City
Milan   Montreal   New Delhi   San Juan   Singapore   Sydney   Tokyo   Toronto

SOMERSET COUNTY LIBRARY
6022 GLADES PIKE, SUITE 120
SOMERSET, PA 15501-4309
(814) 445-5907

Other books in the McGraw-Hill Pilot Test Guide Series

Private Pilot Test Guide 1996–1998 FAA Practical & Computer-Based Airmen Knowledge   by Douglas S. Carmody, CFII

McGraw-Hill

A Division of The McGraw-Hill Companies

©1996 by The McGraw-Hill Companies, Inc.

Printed in the United States of America. All rights reserved. The publisher takes no responsibility for the use of any materials or methods described in this book, nor for the products thereof.

pbk 1 2 3 4 5 6 7 8 9 BBC/BBC 9 0 0 9 8 7 6

Product or brand names used in this book may be trade names or trademarks. Where we believe that there may be proprietary claims to such trade names or trademarks, the name has been used with an initial capital or it has been capitalized in the style used by the name claimant. Regardless of the capitalization used, all such names have been used in an editorial manner without any intent to convey endorsement of or other affiliation with the name claimant. Neither the author nor the publisher intends to express any judgment as to the validity or legal status of any such proprietary claims.

Library of Congress Cataloging-in-Publication Data
Carmody, Douglas S.
    Commercial pilot test guide, 1996–1998 : FAA practical & computer
-based airmen knowledge / by Douglas S. Carmody.
      p.   cm.
    Includes index.
    ISBN 0-07-011519-2 (pbk.)
    1. Aeronautics—Examinations, questions, etc. 2. Air pilots-
-Licenses—United States. I. Title.
TL546.5.C37 1995
629.132'52'076—dc20   95-39911
                                                                  CIP

McGraw-Hill books are available at special quantity discounts to use as premiums and sales promotions, or for use in corporate training programs. For more information, please write to the Director of Special Sales, McGraw-Hill, 11 West 19th Street, New York, NY 10011. Or contact your local bookstore.

Acquisitions editor: Shelley IC. Chevalier
Editorial team: Laura J. Bader, Editor
                        Susan W. Kagey, Managing Editor
                        Lori Flaherty, Executive Editor
                        Joann Woy, Indexer
Production team: Katherine G. Brown, Director
                        Janice Ridenour, Computer Artist
                        Wanda S. Ditch, Desktop Operator
                        Lori L. White, Proofreading
Design team: Jaclyn J. Boone, Designer   0115192
                        Katherine Lukaszewicz, Associate Designer   AV2

DEDICATION

For Bonny, Caroline, and Mary Catherine

ACKNOWLEDGMENTS

This book would not have been possible without the generous help and support of the following people: Shirley Kumpf for tireless typing and retyping. Thanks Shirley! John Cellini, who thought this book was a good idea. Chris Goodall, whose advice has proven invaluable. Finally, all the pilots and students I've had the opportunity to fly with. Their experience and knowledge has been a valued resource.

Contents

Part II   Oral Test Questions

How to Use This Book

Thank you for purchasing McGraw-Hill's *Commercial Pilot Test Guide 1996-1998: FAA Practical & Computer-Based Airmen Knowledge*. This book will help prepare you for the FAA Practical Test and the Computer-Based Airmen Knowledge Test (previously known as the written exam). Whether you are flying an airplane, balloon, rotorcraft or sailplane, this study guide will help you achieve the highest score possible!

QUESTIONS

The book is organized to make your studying easier and more effective. Each section of the test is broken down into easy-to-absorb subject areas. All the test questions relate to the applicant who seeks a commercial pilot certificate. Any question requiring a problem-solving process is considered to be academic in nature and is not predicated on any commercial operator's operating specifications, procedures, or policies. The Fundamentals of Instruction subject matter is included in this book for use by lighter-than-air applicants. The instrument approach charts and IFR en route charts are included for use by airship applicants.

The guide is divided into two parts. The first part contains study guide material and the computer-based questions. The second part contains the oral questions. All the figures referenced by test questions appear in Appendix B, which follows the index. These pages are perforated for easy removal so you don't have to flip back and forth. All the questions in this book are the actual FAA test questions. That's a real confidence booster when you take the computer exam.

The oral and practical questions were compiled by interviewing hundreds of students, instructors, and designated examiners. Remember, however, that this book is a test *guide*. It is not a substitute for study or hard work. No amount of rote memorization can replace working with a competent instructor.

Using the guide is easy. First, read all the study guide information thoroughly. Then read each question completely, followed by the correct answer. Once you have read all the questions and their respective answers, go back and cover the answers with a piece of paper to test your retention. It's that simple! A word of caution: This study process will work even if you *do not* know the material! If you are weak in a subject area, it is imperative that you get competent ground instruction.

TESTING

The Commercial Pilot Computer-Based Airmen Knowledge Test may be taken at any one of the several FAA approved "instant results" testing centers. Check with your flight school for an accurate list.

SCORING AND SUBJECT KNOWLEDGE CODES

After you take the test, the computer will grade it and assign a test score and list the questions you missed, referencing the subject matter knowledge codes. The subject matter knowledge codes are matched to the corresponding subject matter knowledge areas published in an appendix of this test book. You should review those subject areas you missed until you are satisfied you know the material. You should be aware that a subject matter code on your computer test results appears only once even though you might have missed more than one question in that subject area. Therefore, the number of subject matter codes may not represent the number of questions missed on the test.

TEST-TAKING POINTERS

When taking the test, keep the following points in mind:

1. Answer each question in accordance with the latest regulations and procedures.

2. Read each question carefully before looking at the possible answers. You should clearly understand the problem before attempting to solve it.

3. After formulating an answer, determine which of the alternatives most nearly corresponds with that answer. The answer chosen should completely resolve the problem.

4. From the answers given, it might appear that there is more than one possible answer; however, there is only one answer that is correct and complete. The other answers are either incomplete or are derived from popular misconceptions.

5. If a certain question is difficult for you, it is best to proceed to other questions. After you answer the less-difficult questions, return to those that gave you difficulty.

6. When solving a calculator problem, select the answer nearest your solution. The problem has been checked with various types of calculators; therefore, if you have solved it correctly, your answer will be closer to the correct answer than to any of the other choices.

RETESTING AFTER FAILURE (FAR SECTION 61.49)

An applicant for a Computer-Based Knowledge Test or practical test who fails that test may not apply for retesting until 30 days after the date the test was failed. However, in the case of a first failure, the applicant may apply for retesting before the 30 days have expired provided the applicant presents a logbook or training record endorsement from an authorized instructor who has given the applicant remedial instruction and finds the applicant competent to pass the test.

Good luck and fly safe,
Captain Douglas S. Carmody

ALL COMMERCIAL APPLICANTS (airplane, rotorcraft, glider, or lighter-than-air) must answer the following questions:

5001–5012, 5018, 5020, 5022, 5026, 5028, 5031, 5032, 5043–5047, 5052, 5056, 5063, 5064, 5073, 5075, 5080, 5082, 5085, 5092–5103, 5105, 5121, 5122, 5124, 5125, 5301–5354, 5356, 5357, 5359–5381, 5391, 5393, 5399–5433, 5439, 5442–5450, 5477, 5478, 5490–5506, 5532–5538, 5551–5554, 5559, 5560, 5564–5570, 5572, 5574, 5576, 5577, 5581–5585, 5587, 5588, 5601, 5604, 5605, 5678, 5746–5760

Rotorcraft applicants (both helicopter and gyroplanes) must additionally answer the following questions:

5021, 5025, 5051, 5058, 5059–5062, 5065, 5068, 5070, 5072, 5074, 5076, 5086, 5087, 5091, 5104, 5106, 5116, 5118–5120, 5123, 5126–5130, 5137, 5141, 5144, 5145, 5147, 5150, 5168, 5169, 5186, 5187, 5189, 5190, 5240–5267, 5298, 5299, 5358, 5507–5523, 5528–5531, 5539–5550, 5556–5558, 5561, 5591–5600, 5606–5611, 5616–5618, 5632, 5634–5639, 5644, 5645, 5667–5677, 5679–5734, 5744, 5745, 5761–5763

Glider pilots must additionally answer the following questions:

5013–5015, 5033, 5034, 5038, 5053, 5054, 5079, 5084, 5151, 5155, 5158–5160, 5167, 5181, 5182, 5192, 5197–5199, 5201, 5202, 5206, 5216, 5218, 5219, 5222, 5225–5227, 5231–5233, 5239, 5273–5297, 5355, 5358, 5386–5391, 5394–5397, 5437, 5612, 5613, 5616–5619, 5634–5643, 5738–5743, 5745, 5765–5820

Balloon (lighter-than-air) pilots must additionally answer the following questions:

5020, 5035–5037, 5040, 5042, 5048, 5052, 5057, 5059, 5062, 5081, 5091, 5298, 5299, 5480, 5507–5515, 5539–5550, 5555–5558, 5561–5563, 5571, 5573, 5578–5580, 5586, 5589, 5590–5600, 5603, 5606–5611, 5761, 5821–5877

Airplane applicants must additionally answer the following questions:

5013–5017, 5019, 5023–5025, 5033, 5034, 5039, 5051, 5055, 5059–5062, 5065–5067, 5069–5071, 5074, 5076–5079, 5088–5091, 5104, 5106–5117, 5123, 5126–5136, 5138–5140, 5142, 5143, 5146, 5148, 5150–5167, 5169–5177, 5179–5239, 5268–5271, 5276, 5298, 5299, 5355, 5358, 5382–5385, 5434–5436, 5438, 5440, 5441, 5451–5476, 5479, 5481–5489, 5507–5531, 5538–5550, 5556–5558, 5561, 5575, 5591–5600, 5602, 5606–5611, 5614–5639, 5647–5666, 5735, 5744, 5745, 5761–5764

MILITARY COMPETENCY EXAM APPLICANTS must be able to answer the following questions:

For airplane category:

5001, 5002, 5018–5028, 5031–5034, 5039, 5043–5047, 5049–5052, 5055, 5056, 5059–5067, 5069–5071, 5073–5080, 5082, 5083, 5085, 5088–5117, 5120–5136, 5138–5140, 5142, 5143, 5146, 5148, 5150

For rotorcraft category:

5001, 5018, 5020–5023, 5025–5029, 5031, 5032, 5043–5056, 5058–5068, 5070, 5072–5075, 5077, 5078, 5080–5083, 5085, 5086, 5089, 5091–5105, 5116, 5120–5130, 5137, 5141, 5144, 5145, 5147, 5150

Part I

Study Guide and Computer-Based Test Questions

1

NTSB Part 830

STUDY GUIDE

Although unpleasant to contemplate, pilots need to know what is required of them if they have an accident. NTSB 830 deals with aircraft accidents and incidents. The easiest way to understand this section is to memorize what constitutes an aircraft accident. A memory aid that has worked well with my students is to use the title of the section, NTSB 830.

N—Notify

T—The

S—Safety

B—Board

8—If one of 8 things occur:

1. An aircraft accident or any of the following listed incidents occur:

2. Flight control system malfunction or failure

3. Inability of any required flight crewmember to perform normal flight duties as a result of injury or illness

4. Failure of structural components of a turbine engine excluding compressor and turbine blades and vanes

5. Inflight fire

6. Aircraft collision in flight

7. Damage to property, other than the aircraft, estimated to exceed $325,000 for repair (including materials and labor) or fair market value in the event of total loss, whichever is less

8. For large multiengine aircraft (more than 12,000 pounds maximum certificated takeoff weight):
   • Inflight failure of electrical systems that requires the sustained use of an emergency bus powered by a backup source such as a battery, auxiliary power unit, or air-driven generator to retain flight control or essential instruments
   • Inflight failure of hydraulic systems that results in sustained reliance on the sole remaining hydraulic or mechanical system for movement of flight control surfaces
   • Sustained loss of the power or thrust produced by two or more engines
   • An evacuation of an aircraft in which an emergency egress system is utilized
   • Overdue aircraft believed to have been involved in an accident

3—Three items define an accident:

1. Death
2. Serious injury
3. Aircraft receives substantial damage

0—"Zero" time to report. In other words, you must notify the NTSB immediately if any of the above items occur.

COMPUTER-BASED QUESTIONS

5001. Notification to the NTSB is required when there has been substantial damage

A. that requires repairs to landing gear.

B. to an engine caused by engine failure in flight.

C. that adversely affects structural strength or flight characteristics.

5001. "C" is the correct answer. According to NTSB 830.2 and 830.5, the "Operator of an aircraft shall immediately and by the most expeditious means available, notify the nearest NTSB Field Office when an aircraft accident occurs." An aircraft accident is defined as "an occurrence associated with the operation of an aircraft which takes place between the time any person boards the aircraft with intention of flight and all such persons have disembarked, and in which any person suffers death or serious injury or in which *the aircraft receives substantial damage which adversely affects the structural strength, performance or flight characteristics of the aircraft.*"
Reference NTSB 830

FAA subject matter knowledge code G10, G11

5002. NTSB 830 requires an immediate notification as a result of which incident?

A. Engine failure for any reason during flight.

B. Damage to the landing gear as a result of a hard landing.

C. Any required flight crewmember being unable to perform flight duties because of illness.

5002. "C" is the correct answer. According to NTSB 830.2 and 830.5, "The operator of an aircraft shall immediately, and by the most expeditious means available, notify the nearest NTSB Field Office of the inability of any required flight crewmember to perform normal flight duties as a result of injury or illness."
Reference NTSB 830

FAA subject matter knowledge code G10, G11

5003. Which incident would require that the nearest NTSB field office be notified immediately?

A. Inflight fire.

B. Ground fire resulting in fire equipment dispatch.

C. Fire of the primary aircraft while hangared that results in damage to other property of more than $50,000.

5003. "A" is the correct answer. According to NTSB 830.5(a)(4), "The operator of an aircraft shall immediately and by the most expeditious means available notify the nearest NTSB Field Office when an *in flight* fire occurs." Notice that the rule states inflight fire, thus B and C are incorrect.
Reference NTSB 830

FAA subject matter knowledge code G11

5004. While taxiing for takeoff, a small fire burned the insulation from a transceiver wire. What action would be required to comply with NTSB 830?

A. No notification or report is required.

B. A report must be filed with the avionics inspector at the nearest FAA field office within 48 hours.

C. An immediate notification must be filed by the operator of the aircraft with the nearest NTSB field office.

5004. "A" is the correct answer because the rule is for *inflight fires* only.
Reference NTSB 830

FAA subject matter knowledge code G11

5005. During flight, a fire, which was extinguished, burned the insulation from a transceiver wire. What action is required by regulations?

A. No notification or report is required.

B. A report must be filed with the avionics inspector at the nearest FAA field office within 48 hours.

C. An immediate notification by the operator of the aircraft to the nearest NTSB field office.

5005. "C" is the correct answer because this fire occurred *in flight* requiring in an immediate notification by the operator of the aircraft to the nearest NTSB field office.

Reference NTSB 830

FAA subject matter knowledge code G11

5006. When should notification of an aircraft accident be made to the NTSB if there was substantial damage and no injuries?

A. Immediately.

B. Within 10 days.

C. Within 30 days.

5006. "A" is the correct answer. Remember, according to the NTSB, an aircraft accident occurs if the aircraft receives substantial damage.

Reference NTSB 830

FAA subject matter knowledge code G10, G11

5007. The operator of an aircraft that has been involved in an incident is required to submit a report to the nearest field office of the NTSB

A. within 7 days.

B. within 10 days.

C. only if requested to do so.

5007. "C" is the correct answer. The only time a written report should be submitted to the NTSB following an incident is if they request it.

Reference NTSB 830

FAA subject matter knowledge code G10, G13

5008. Within how many days of an accident is an accident report required to be filed with the nearest NTSB field office?

A. 2 days.

B. 7 days.

C. 10 days.

5008. "C" is the correct answer. According to the NTSB, the operator has 10 days to file a report following an accident. However, notification of the NTSB following an accident has to be immediate.

Reference NTSB 830

FAA subject matter knowledge code G10, G13

2

FAR Part 1

FEDERAL AVIATION REGULATIONS

A commercial pilot must have a thorough and complete understanding of the Federal Aviation Regulations. To make it easier to understand and remember, I have divided the regulations on the written test into six sections (study guides): FAR Parts 1, 61, 71, 91, 125, and 135.

In each study guide I have only listed those parts of the regulation that pertain to the question you will be asked on the computer-based test. Although this process allows you to earn a high score on the exam, it is not a substitute for in-depth knowledge or study of the regulations.

STUDY GUIDE

FAR 1.1—Definitions and abbreviations are probably one of the most overlooked and underutilized resources available to you. Numerous test questions, both oral and written, can be answered directly from this section. Read FAR section 1.1 thoroughly, then answer the following questions.

Category: (1) As used with respect to the certification, ratings, privileges, and limitations of airmen, means a broad classification of aircraft. Examples include airplane, rotorcraft, glider, and lighter-than-air, and

(2) As used with respect to the certification of aircraft, means a grouping of aircraft based on intended use or operating limitations. Examples include transport, normal, utility, acrobatic, limited, restricted, and provisional.

Commercial operator means a person who, for compensation or hire, engages in the carriage by aircraft in air commerce of persons or property, other than as an air carrier or foreign air carrier under the authority of part 375 of this title. Where it is doubtful that an operation is for "compensation or hire," the test applied is whether the carriage by air is merely incidental to the person's other business or is, in itself, a major enterprise for profit.

Operate, with respect to aircraft, means use, cause to use, or authorize to use aircraft for the purpose (except as provided in § 91.13 of this chapter) of air navigation including the piloting of aircraft, with or without the right of legal control (as owner, lessee, or otherwise).

Operational control, with respect to a flight means the exercise of authority over initiating, conducting, or terminating a flight.

V_F means design flap speed.

V_{LE} means maximum landing gear extended speed.

V_S means the stalling speed or the minimum steady flight speed at which the airplane is controllable.

V_{S1} means the stalling speed or the minimum steady flight speed obtained in a specific configuration.

COMPUTER-BASED QUESTIONS

5009. What designated airspace associated with an airport becomes inactive when the control tower at that airport is not in operation?

A. Class D, which then becomes Class C.

B. Class D, which then becomes Class E.

C. Class B.

5009. "B" is the correct answer. Class D airspace only exists when the tower is operating. It becomes Class E when the tower is closed.

Reference FAR 1.1

FAA subject matter knowledge code A01

5010. Regulations that refer to commercial operators relate to that person who

A. is the owner of a small scheduled airline.

B. for compensation or hire, engages in the carriage by aircraft in air commerce of persons or property, as an air carrier.

C. for compensation or hire, engages in the carriage by aircraft in air commerce of persons or property, other than as an air carrier.

5010. "C" is the correct answer. FAR 1.1 defines a commercial operator as a "person who, for compensation or hire, engages in the carriage by aircraft in air commerce of persons or property, other than an air carrier."

Reference FAR 1.1

FAA subject matter knowledge code A01

5011. Regulations that refer to operate relate to that person who

A. acts as pilot in command of the aircraft.

B. is the sole manipulator of the aircraft controls.

C. causes the aircraft to be used or authorizes its use.

5011. "C" is the correct answer. According to the definition, operate means use, cause to use, or authorize to use aircraft.

Reference FAR 1.1

FAA subject matter knowledge code A01

5012. Regulations that refer to the operational control of a flight are in relation to

A. the specific duties of any required crewmember.

B. acting as the sole manipulator of the aircraft controls.

C. exercising authority over initiating, conducting, or terminating a flight.

5012. "C" is the correct answer. Operational control means the exercise of authority over initiating, conducting, or terminating a flight.

Reference FAR 1.1

FAA subject matter knowledge code A01

5013. Which is the correct symbol for the stalling speed or the minimum steady flight speed in a specified configuration?

A. V_S.

B. V_{S1}.

C. V_{SO}.

5013. "B" is the correct answer. V_{S1} is the stalling speed or the minimum steady flight speed obtained in a specified configuration.

Reference FAR 1.1

FAA subject matter knowledge code A02

5014. Which is the correct symbol for the stalling speed or the minimum steady flight speed at which the airplane is controllable?

A. V_S.

B. V_{S1}.

C. V_{SO}.

5014. "A" is the correct answer. V_S is the stalling speed or the minimum steady flight speed at which the airplane is controllable.

Reference FAR 1.2

FAA subject matter knowledge code A02

5015. FAR 1 defines V_F as

A. design flap speed.

B. flap operating speed.

C. maximum flap extended speed.

5015. "A" is the correct answer. V_F is the design flap speed.
Reference FAR 1.2
FAA subject matter knowledge code A02

5016. FAR 1 defines V_{LE} as

A. maximum landing gear extended speed.

B. maximum landing gear operating speed.

C. maximum leading edge flaps extended speed.

5016. "A" is the correct answer. V_{LE} means maximum landing gear *extended* speed.
Reference FAR 1.2
FAA subject matter knowledge code A02

5017. If the operational category of an airplane is listed as utility, it would mean that this airplane could be operated in which of the following maneuvers?

A. Limited aerobatics, excluding spins.

B. Limited aerobatics, including spins.

C. Any maneuver except aerobatics or spins.

5017. "B" is the correct answer. Airplanes certified in the utility category can do all normal category maneuvers plus limited aerobatics including spins.
Reference FAR 23.3(b)
FAA subject matter knowledge code A10

3

FAR Part 61

STUDY GUIDE

§ 61.3 Requirement for certificates, rating, and authorizations.

(a) Pilot certificate. No person may act as pilot in command or in any other capacity as a required pilot flight crewmember of a civil aircraft of United States registry unless he has in his personal possession a current pilot certificate issued to him under this part.

§ 61.19 Duration of pilot and flight instructor certificates.

(c) Any pilot certificate (other than a student pilot certificate) issued under this part is issued without a specific expiration date.

§ 61.23 Duration of medical certificates.

(b) A second-class medical certificate expires at the end of the last day of
    (1) The 12th month after the month of the date of examination shown on the certificate, for operations requiring a commercial pilot certificate or an air traffic control tower operator certificate; and
    (2) The 24th month after the month of the date of examination shown on the certificate, for operations requiring only a private, recreational, or student pilot certificate.

(c) A third-class medical certificate expires at the end of the 24th month after the month of the date of examination shown on the certificate, for operations requiring a private, recreational, or student pilot certificate.

§ 61.31 General limitations.

(a) Type ratings required. A person may not act as pilot in command of any of the following aircraft unless he holds a type rating for that aircraft:
    (1) A large aircraft (except lighter-than-air).
    (2) A helicopter, for operations requiring an airline transport pilot certificate.
    (3) A turbojet powered airplane.
    (4) Other aircraft specified by the Administrator.

(c) Category and class rating: Carrying another person or operating for compensation or hire. Unless he holds a category and class rating for that aircraft, a person may not act as pilot in command of an aircraft that is carrying another person or is operated for compensation or hire.

(e) High performance airplanes. A person holding a private or commercial pilot certificate may not act as pilot in command of an airplane that has more than 200 horsepower, or that has a retractable landing gear, flaps and a controllable propeller, unless he has received flight instruction from an authorized flight instructor who has certified in his logbook that he is competent to pilot an airplane that has more than 200 horsepower, or that has a retractable landing gear, flaps, and a controllable propeller, as the case may be.

§ 61.51 Pilot logbooks.

(a) The aeronautical training and experience used to meet the requirements for a certificate or rating, or the recent flight experience requirements of this part must be shown by a reliable record. The logging of other flight time is not required.

(c) Logging of pilot time
   (3) Second-in-command flight time. A pilot may log as second in command time all flight time during which he acts as second in command of an aircraft on which more than one pilot is required under the type certification of the aircraft, or the regulations under which the flight is conducted.

§ 61.56 Flight review.

(c) No person may act as pilot in command of an aircraft unless, since the beginning of the 24th calendar month before the month in which that pilot acts as pilot in command that person has
   (1) Accomplished a flight review given in an aircraft for which that pilot is rated by an appropriately rated instructor certificated under this part or other person designated by the Administrator; and
   (2) A logbook endorsed by the person who gave the review certifying that the person has satisfactorily completed the review.

(d) A person who has, within the period specified in paragraph (c) of this section, satisfactorily completed a pilot proficiency check conducted by the FAA, an approved pilot check airman, or a U.S. Armed Force, for a pilot certificate, rating, or operating privilege, need not accomplish the flight review required by this section.

§ 61.57 Recent flight experience: Pilot in command.

(c) General experience. No person may act as pilot in command of an aircraft carrying passengers, nor of an aircraft certificated for more than one required pilot flight crewmember, unless within the preceding 90 days, he has made three takeoffs and three landings as the sole manipulator of the flight controls in an aircraft of the same category and class and, if a type rating is required, of the same type.

(d) Night experience. No person may act as pilot in command of an aircraft carrying passengers during the period beginning 1 hour after sunset and ending 1 hour before sunrise (as published in the American Air Almanac) unless, within the preceding 90 days, he has made at least three takeoffs and three landings to a full stop during that period in the category and class of aircraft to be used.

(e) Instrument
   (1) Recent IFR experience. No pilot may act as pilot in command under IFR, nor in weather conditions less than the minimums prescribed for VFR, unless he has within the past 6 calendar months
   (i) In the case of an aircraft other than a glider, logged at least 6 hours of instrument time under actual or simulated IFR conditions, at least 3 of which were in flight in the category of aircraft involved, including at least six instrument approaches, or passed an instrument competency check in the category of aircraft involved.

§ 61.60 Change of address.

The holder of a pilot or flight instructor certificate who has made a change in his permanent mailing address may not after 30 days from the date he moved, exercise the privileges of his certificate unless he has notified in writing the

Department of Transportation, Federal Aviation Administration, Airman Certification Branch, Box 25082, Oklahoma City, OK 73125, of his new address.

§ 61.69 Glider towing: Experience and instruction requirements.

No person may act as pilot in command of an aircraft towing a glider unless he meets the following requirements:

(a) He holds a current pilot certificate (other than a student or recreational pilot certificate) issued under this part.

(b) He has an endorsement in his pilot logbook from a person authorized to give flight instruction in gliders, certifying that he has received ground and flight instruction in gliders and is familiar with the techniques and procedures essential to the safe towing of gliders, including airspeed limitations, emergency procedures, signals used, and maximum angles of bank.

§ 61.83 Eligibility requirements: Student pilots.

To be eligible for a student pilot certificate, a person must

(a) Be at least 14 years of age for a student pilot certificate limited to the operation of a glider or free balloon.

§ 61.87 Solo flight requirements for student pilots.

(m) Flight instructor endorsements. No student pilot may operate an aircraft in solo flight unless that student's pilot certificate and logbook have been endorsed for the specific make and model aircraft to be flown by an authorized flight instructor certificated under this part, and the student's logbook has been endorsed, within the 90 days prior to the student operating in solo flight, by an authorized flight instructor certificated under this part who has flown with the student.

COMMERCIAL PILOTS

§ 61.123 Eligibility requirements: General.

To be eligible for a commercial pilot certificate, a person must

(c) Hold at least a valid second-class medical certificate issued under part 67 of this chapter, or, in the case of a glider or free balloon rating, certify that he has no known medical deficiency that makes him unable to pilot a glider or a free balloon, as appropriate.

§ 61.129 Airplane rating: Aeronautical experience.

(a) The applicant must hold an instrument rating (airplane), or the commercial pilot certificate that is issued is endorsed with a limitation prohibiting the carriage of passengers for hire in airplanes on cross-country flights of more than 50 nautical miles, or at night.

§ 61.189 Flight instructor records.

(b) The record required by this section (part 61) shall be retained by the flight instructor separately or in his logbook for at least 3 years.

§ 61.195 Flight instructor limitations.

The holder of a flight instructor certificate is subject to the following limitations:

(a) Hours of instruction. He may not conduct more than 8 hours of flight instruction in any period of 24 consecutive hours.

COMPUTER-BASED QUESTIONS

5018. Commercial pilots are required to have a current and appropriate pilot certificate in their personal possession when

A. piloting for hire only.

B. carrying passengers only.

C. acting as pilot in command.

5018. "C" is the correct answer. FAR 61.3 states that no person may act as pilot in command or in any other capacity as a required pilot flight crewmember of a civil aircraft unless he has in his personal possession a current pilot certificate and an appropriate current medical certificate.
Reference FAR 61.3
FAA subject matter knowledge code A20

5019. Which of the following are considered aircraft class ratings?

A. Transport, normal, utility, and acrobatic.

B. Airplane, rotorcraft, glider, and lighter-than-air.

C. Single-engine land, multiengine land, single-engine sea, and multiengine sea.

5019. "C" is the correct answer. Class includes single-engine land, single-engine sea, multiengine land, and multiengine sea.
Reference FAR 61.5(c)
FAA subject matter knowledge code A20

5020. Does a commercial pilot certificate have a specific expiration date?

A. No, it is issued without an expiration date.

B. Yes, it expires at the end of the 24th month after the month in which it was issued.

C. No, but commercial privileges expire if a flight review is not satisfactorily completed each 12 months.

5020. "A" is the correct answer. Only student pilot and flight instructor certificates are issued with an expiration date.
Reference FAR 61.19(c)
FAA subject matter knowledge code A20

5021. A second-class medical certificate issued to a commercial pilot on April 10, this year, permits the pilot to exercise which of the following privileges?

A. Commercial pilot privileges through April, next year.

B. Commercial pilot privileges through April, two years later.

C. Private pilot privileges through, but not after March 31, next year.

5021. "A" is the correct answer. A second-class medical certificate expires at the end of the last day of the 12th month after the month of the date of examination shown on the certificate for operations requiring a commercial pilot certificate. It expires at the end of the last day of the 24th month after the month of the date of examination shown on the certificate for private pilot or student pilot operations.
Reference FAR 61.23(b)
FAA subject matter knowledge code A20

5022. When is the pilot in command required to hold a category and class rating appropriate to aircraft being flown?

A. All solo flights.

B. Flight tests given by the FAA.

C. Flights for compensation or hire.

5022. "C" is the correct answer. Unless holding a category and class rating for that aircraft, a person may not act as pilot in command of an aircraft that is carrying another person or is operated for compensation or hire.
Reference FAR 61.31(c)
FAA subject matter knowledge code A20

5023. Unless otherwise authorized, the pilot in command is required to hold a type rating while operating any

A. aircraft that is certificated for more than one pilot.

B. aircraft of more than 12,500 pounds maximum certificated takeoff weight.

C. multiengine aircraft having a gross weight of more than 6000 pounds.

5023. "B" is the correct answer. FAR 61.31 states that a person may not act as pilot in command of a large aircraft (over 12,500 pounds) unless they hold a type rating for that aircraft. "A" is incorrect because no regulation requires a type rating just because two pilots are required. "C" is also incorrect because multiengine airplanes do not require a type rating unless they weight over 12,500 pounds.
Reference FAR 61.31
FAA subject matter knowledge code A20

5024. To act as pilot in command of an airplane that is equipped with a retractable landing gear, if no pilot-in-command time in such an airplane was logged prior to November 1, 1973, a person is required to

A. hold a multiengine airplane class rating.

B. make at least six takeoffs and landings in such an airplane within the preceding six months.

C. receive flight instruction in such an airplane and obtain a logbook endorsement of competency.

5024. "C" is the correct answer. This is commonly referred to as a *high-performance signoff*. A person holding a private or commercial pilot certificate may *not* act as pilot in command of an airplane that has more than 200 horsepower, or that has retractable landing gear, flaps, and a controllable propeller, unless he has received flight instruction from an authorized flight instructor who has certified in his logbook that he is competent to pilot a high-performance airplane. "A" is incorrect because retractable landing gear is also available on single-engine airplanes. "B" is incorrect because no such requirement exists.
Reference FAR 61.31

FAA subject matter knowledge code A20

5025. What flight time may a pilot log as second in command?

A. All flight time while acting as second in command in aircraft requiring more than one pilot.

B. Only that flight time during which the second in command is the sole manipulator of the controls.

C. All flight time while acting as second in command regardless of aircraft crew requirements.

5025. "A" is the correct answer. A pilot may log as second-in-command time all flight time during which he acts as second in command of an aircraft that requires more than one pilot under the type certification of the aircraft, or the regulation under which the flight is conducted. Numerous pilots misinterpret this regulation while building multiengine flight time. Just because you are in the right seat of a twin does not mean you can log that flight time. "C" is incorrect. "B" is also incorrect, because being sole manipulator is not stated in the regulation.
Reference FAR 61.51

FAA subject matter knowledge code A20

5026. What flight time must be shown, in a reliable record, by a pilot exercising the privileges of a commercial certificate?

A. Flight time showing aeronautical training and experience to meet requirements for a certificate or rating.

B. All flight time flown for compensation or hire.

C. Flight time necessary to meet the recent flight experience requirements while flying for compensation or hire.

5026. "A" is the correct answer. The regulation states that the aeronautical training and experience used to meet the requirement for a certificate or rating, or the recent flight experience requirements of FAR 61.51 must be shown by a reliable record. "B" and "C" are incorrect because they limit the logging of flight time to time flown for compensation or hire. Nowhere is that listed as a requirement.
Reference FAR 61.51

FAA subject matter knowledge code A20

5027. If a pilot does not meet the recency of experience requirements for night flight and official sunset is 1800 CST, the latest time passengers should be carried is

A. 1759 CST.

B. 1829 CST.

C. 1859 CST.

5027. "C" is the correct answer. No person may act as pilot in command of an aircraft carrying passengers during the period beginning 1 hour after official sunset and ending 1 hour before official sunrise as published in the American Air Almanac unless they meet the night experience requirements. "A" and "B" are incorrect because they do not meet this 1 hour requirement.
Reference FAR 61.57

FAA subject matter knowledge code A20

5028. Prior to carrying passengers at night, the pilot in command must have accomplished the required takeoffs and landings in

A. any category aircraft.

B. the same category and class of aircraft to be used.

C. the same category, class, and type of aircraft to be used.

5028. "B" is the correct answer. According to the regulation, no person may act as pilot in command during the period beginning 1 hour after sunset and ending 1 hour before sunrise unless, within the preceding 90 days, he or she has made at least three takeoffs and landings to a full stop during that period in the *category* and *class* of aircraft to be used. "A" is incorrect because the regulation specifies class. "C" is also incorrect because the type of aircraft is not stated in the regulation.
Reference FAR 61.57

FAA subject matter knowledge code A20

5029. To act as pilot in command of a gyroplane carrying passengers, what must the pilot do in that gyroplane to meet recent daytime flight experience requirements?

A. make nine takeoffs and landings in the preceding 30 days.

B. make three takeoffs and landings to a full stop in the preceding 90 days.

C. make three takeoffs and landings in the preceding 90 days

5029. "C" is the correct answer. It is the same as airplanes in that no person may act as pilot in command carrying passengers unless within the preceding 90 days he has made three takeoffs and landings in the same category and class.

Reference FAR 61.57c

FAA subject matter knowledge code A20

5030. No pilot may act as pilot in command of an airship under IFR nor in weather conditions less than the minimums prescribed for VFR unless that pilot has, within the past 6 months, completed at least

A. three instrument approaches and logged 3 hours.

B. six instrument flights under actual IFR conditions.

C. six instrument approaches and logged 6 hours instrument time, or passed an instrument competency check in an airship.

5030. "C" is the correct answer. No pilot may act as pilot in command under IFR, nor in weather conditions less than the minimums prescribed for VFR, unless he has within the past 6 calendar months, in the case of an aircraft other than a glider, logged at least 6 hours of instrument time under actual or simulated conditions, at least 3 of which were in flight in the category of aircraft involved, including at least six instrument approaches, or passed an instrument competency check in the category of aircraft involved.

Reference FAR 61.57(e)(1)(i)

FAA subject matter knowledge code A20

5031. To act as pilot in command of an aircraft under FAR 91, a commercial pilot must have satisfactorily accomplished a flight review or completed a proficiency check within the preceding

A. 6 months.

B. 12 months.

C. 24 months.

5031. "C" is the correct answer. A commercial pilot, or any pilot for that matter, must remain current. The regulation allows a pilot to complete either a biennial flight review, a proficiency check, or a wings program to satisfy this requirement. The actual regula-

tion states that "no person may act as pilot in command of an aircraft unless, within the preceding 24 calendar months they have satisfactorily completed a flight review, a pilot proficiency check, or one or more phases of an FAA sponsored pilot proficiency award program." "A" and "B" do not specify 24 months.

Reference FAR 61.56

FAA subject matter knowledge code A20

5032. Pilots who change their permanent mailing address and fail to notify the FAA Airmen Certification Branch of this change are entitled to exercise the privileges of their pilot certificate for a period of

A. 30 days.

B. 60 days.

C. 90 days.

5032. "A" is the correct answer. Probably one of the most ignored regulations, it can have dire consequences. Remember if you move, you have a month (30 days) to notify the FAA.

Reference FAR 61.60

FAA subject matter knowledge code A20

5033. To act as a pilot in command of an airplane towing a glider, a certificated airplane pilot is required to have

A. a logbook record of having made at least three flights as sole manipulator of the controls of a glider being towed by an airplane.

B. a logbook endorsement for receipt of ground and flight instruction in gliders and familiarity with techniques and procedures for glider towing.

C. at least a Private Pilot Certificate with a glider rating, and made and logged at least three flights as pilot or observer in a glider being towed by an airplane.

5033. "B" is the correct answer. You must have logged ground and flight instruction in gliders and glider towing. No person may act as pilot in command of an aircraft towing a glider unless he has an endorsement in his logbook from a person authorized to give flight instruction in gliders, certifying that the pilot has received ground and flight instruction in gliders and is familiar with the techniques and procedures essential to the safe towing of gliders. "A" and "C" are incorrect because neither mention "Familiarity with techniques and procedures for glider towing."

Reference FAR 61.69

FAA subject matter knowledge code A21

5034. To act as pilot in command of an airplane towing a glider, the tow pilot is required to have a pilot certificate and

A. a glider rating, and pass a written test on the techniques and procedures essential for safe towing of gliders.

B. a logbook record of having made at least three flights in a glider, and be familiar with the techniques and procedures essential for safe towing of gliders.

C. have received and logged ground and flight instruction in gliders, and be familiar with the techniques and procedures essential for safe towing of gliders.

5034. "C" is the correct answer. Again, you must have logged ground and flight instruction in gliders and glider towing. No person may act as pilot in command of an aircraft towing a glider unless he has an endorsement in his logbook from a person authorized to give flight instruction in gliders, certifying that the pilot has received ground and flight instruction in gliders and is familiar with the techniques and procedures essential to the safe towing of gliders. "A" and "C" are incorrect because neither mention "Familiarity with techniques and procedures for glider towing."
Reference FAR 61.69
FAA subject matter knowledge code A21

5035. What is the minimum age requirement for a person to be issued a student pilot certificate limited to gliders or free balloons?

A. 14 years of age.

B. 15 years of age.

C. 16 years of age.

5035. "A" is the correct answer. A person must be at least 14 years of age to hold a student pilot certificate limited to the operation of a glider or free balloon.
Reference FAR 61.83(a)
FAA subject matter knowledge code A22

5036. To operate a free balloon in solo flight, a student pilot must have a logbook endorsement of competence by an authorized instructor within the preceding

A. 30 days.

B. 60 days.

C. 90 days.

5036. "C" is the correct answer. A student pilot may not operate an aircraft in solo flight unless his student pilot certificate is endorsed, and unless within the preceding 90 days his pilot logbook has been endorsed by an authorized flight instructor.
Reference FAR 61.87(m)
FAA subject matter knowledge code A22

5037. To exercise the privileges of a commercial pilot certificate with a lighter-than-air category, free balloon class rating, the minimum medical requirement is a

A. second-class medical certificate when carrying passengers for hire.

B. statement by the pilot certifying he has no known medical deficiency that would make him unable to act as pilot.

C. statement from any designated medical examiner certifying the pilot has no medical deficiencies.

5037. "B" is the correct answer. In the case of a glider or free balloon rating, the commercial pilot must certify "that he has no known medical deficiency that makes him unable to pilot a glider or a free balloon, as appropriate."
Reference FAR 61.123(c)
FAA subject matter knowledge code A24

5038. The medical requirements to exercise the privileges of a commercial pilot certificate with a glider rating is at least a

A. valid second-class medical certificate.

B. medical statement from a designated medical examiner on file with the nearest FAA district office.

C. statement by the pilot certifying he has no known medical deficiency that makes him unable to pilot a glider.

5038. "C" is the correct answer. In the case of a glider or free balloon rating, the commercial pilot must certify "that he has no known medical deficiency that makes him unable to pilot a glider or a free balloon, as appropriate."
Reference FAR 61.123(c)
FAA subject matter knowledge code A24

5039. What limitation is imposed on a newly certificated commercial airplane pilot if that person does not hold an instrument pilot rating?

A. The carrying of passengers or property for hire on cross-country flights at night is limited to a radius of 50 nautical miles.

B. The carrying of passengers for hire on cross-country flights is limited to 50 nautical miles for night flights, but not limited for day flights.

C. The carrying of passengers for hire on cross-country flights is limited to 50 nautical miles and the carrying of passengers for hire at night is prohibited.

5039. "C" is the correct answer. Without an instrument rating, a commercial pilot certificate is very limited. The commercial pilot applicant must hold an instrument rating (airplane), or the commercial pilot certificate that is issued is endorsed with a limitation prohibiting the carriage of passengers for hire in airplanes on cross-country flights of more than 50 nautical miles, or at night. "A" and "B" are incorrect because without an instrument rating no night flying for hire is allowed.
Reference FAR 61.129
FAA subject matter knowledge code A24

5040. A commercial pilot who gives flight instruction in lighter-than-air category aircraft must keep a record of such instruction for a period of

A. 1 year.

B. 2 years.

C. 3 years.

5040. "C" is the correct answer. The records required by this section (FAR 61) shall be retained by the flight instructor separately or in his logbook for at least 3 years.
Reference FAR 61.189(b)
FAA subject matter knowledge code A26

5041. What is the maximum amount of flight instruction an authorized instructor may give in any 24 consecutive hours?

A. 4 hours.

B. 6 hours.

C. 8 hours.

5041. "C" is the correct answer. An instructor may not conduct more than 8 hours of flight instruction in any 24 consecutive hour period.
Reference FAR 61.195(a)
FAA subject matter knowledge code A26

5042. A student pilot may not operate a balloon in initial solo flight unless that pilot has

A. received a minimum of 5 hours of dual instruction in a balloon.

B. a valid student pilot certificate and logbook endorsed by an authorized flight instructor.

C. made at least 10 free balloon flights under the supervision of an authorized instructor.

5042. "B" is the correct answer. No student pilot may operate an aircraft in solo flight unless that student's pilot certificate and logbook have been endorsed for the specific make and model aircraft to be flown by an authorized flight instructor. "A" and "C" are obviously incorrect since the regulation does not specify any specific amount of time or flights.
Reference FAR 61.87(m)
FAA subject matter knowledge code A22

4

Airspace

STUDY GUIDE

Controlled Airspace

Class A Airspace. Generally, that airspace from 18,000 ft msl up to and including FL600. Unless otherwise authorized, all persons must operate their aircraft under IFR. Class A airspace is not specifically charted.

Class B Airspace. Generally, that airspace from the surface to 10,000 ft msl surrounding the nation's busiest airports in terms of IFR operations or passenger enplanements. Regardless of weather conditions, an ATC clearance is required prior to operating within Class B airspace.

Class C Airspace. Generally, that airspace from the surface to 4000 ft above the airport elevation (charted in msl) surrounding those airports that have an operational control tower, are serviced by a radar approach control, and that have a certain number of IFR operations or passenger enplanements. Class C airspace is charted on sectional charts, IFR en route low-altitude charts, and terminal area charts where appropriate.

Class D Airspace. Generally, that airspace from surface to 2500 ft above the airport elevation (charted in msl) surrounding those airports that have an operational control tower.

Class E Airspace. Generally, if the airspace is not Class A, Class B, Class C, or Class D, and it is controlled airspace, it is Class E airspace. Except for 18,000 ft msl, Class E airspace has no defined vertical limit, but rather it extends upward from either the surface or a designated altitude to the overlying or adjacent controlled airspace. There are Class E airspace areas beginning at either 700 or 1200 ft agl used to transition to/from the terminal or en route environment.

§ 71.75 Extent of Federal airways.

(1) Each Federal airway includes that airspace extending upward from 1200 ft above the surface of the earth to, but not including, 18,000 ft msl, except that Federal airways for Hawaii have no upper limits.

COMPUTER-BASED QUESTIONS

5043. Excluding Hawaii, the vertical limits of the Federal low altitude airways extend from

A. 700 ft agl up to, but not including, 14,500 ft msl.

B. 1200 ft agl up to, but not including, 18,000 ft msl.

C. 1200 ft agl up to, but not including, 14,500 ft msl.

5043. "B" is the correct answer. Each Federal airway includes that airspace extending upward from 1200 ft above the surface of the earth to, but not including, 18,000 ft msl. "A" and "C" are incorrect because they don't extend up to, but not including, 18,000 ft msl.
Reference FAR 71.75(c)(1)
FAA subject matter knowledge code A22

5044. One of the major differences between Class D airspace and Class E airspace is that Class D airspace

A. is located at tower-controlled airports and Class E airspace is at uncontrolled airports.

B. always begins at 700 ft agl, while Class E always begins at 1200 ft above the surface.

C. begins at the surface, while Class E always begins at an altitude of 700 ft or 1200 ft above the surface.

5044. "A" is the correct answer. Class D airspace surrounds those airports with an operating control tower. Class E is airspace at uncontrolled airports. "B" is incorrect because Class D begins at the surface. "C" is incorrect because Class E does not always begin at 700 ft or 1200 ft agl.
Reference Aeronautical Information Manual, paragraph 3-14
FAA subject matter knowledge code A01

5045. The Continental Control Area

A. does not exist anymore.

B. extends upward from 10,000 ft msl.

C. extends upward from 14,500 ft msl.

5045. "A" is the correct answer. The Continental Control Area was abolished with the introduction of airspace reclassification. From 14,500 ft msl to the base of Class A airspace (18,000 ft) is now called Class E airspace.
Reference FAR 71.9
FAA subject matter knowledge code A60

5046. Within the contiguous United States, the vertical limit of Class D airspace normally extends from the surface upward to

A. infinity.

B. but not including the base of Class A airspace.

C. 2500 ft agl or indicated within a square depicted within that airspace on aeronautical charts.

5046. "C" is the correct answer. Generally, Class D airspace extends from the surface to 2500 ft above the airport elevation charted in msl. On charts, the ceiling is shown in a bracket [ ]. "A" is incorrect because Class D does have a ceiling. "B" is incorrect because the base of Class A is not the ceiling for Class D airspace.
Reference Aeronautical Information Manual, paragraph 3-14
FAA subject matter knowledge code J08

5047. Which is true regarding Class E airspace?

A. The basic VFR minimums are greater than those associated with Class D airspace.

B. Class E airspace may start at the surface, but usually begins at an altitude of 700 ft or 1200 ft above the surface.

C. Class E airspace begins at the surface and extends upward to FL600.

5047. "B" is the correct answer. Class E airspace extends upward from the surface or upward from 700 ft or more above the surface, or from 1200 ft or more above the surface.
Reference Aeronautical Information Manual, paragraph 3-15
FAA subject matter knowledge code A60

5

FAR Part 91

FAR 91: GENERAL OPERATING AND FLIGHT RULES STUDY GUIDE

§ 91.3 Responsibility and authority of the pilot in command.

(a) The pilot in command of an aircraft is directly responsible for, and is the final authority as to, the operation of that aircraft.

§ 91.21 Portable electronic devices.

(a) No person may operate, nor may any operator or pilot in command of an aircraft allow the operation of, any portable electronic device on any of the following U.S. registered civil aircraft.

(1) Aircraft operated by a holder of an air carrier operating certificate or an operating certificate, or

(2) Any other aircraft while it is operated under IFR.

§ 91.23 Truth-in-leasing clause requirement in leases and conditional sales contracts.

(c) No person may operate a large civil aircraft of U.S. registry that is subject to a lease or contract of conditional sale to which paragraph (a) of this section applies, unless

(1) The lessee or conditional buyer, or the registered owner if the lessee is not a citizen of the United States, has mailed a copy of the lease or contract that complies with the requirements of paragraph (a) of this section, within 24 hours of its execution.

§ 91.103 Preflight action.

Each pilot in command shall, before beginning a flight, become familiar with all available information concerning that flight. This information must include

(a) For a flight under IFR or a flight not in the vicinity of an airport, weather reports and forecasts, fuel requirements, alternatives available if the planned flight cannot be completed, and any known traffic delays of which the pilot in command has been advised by ATC.

(b) For any flight, runway lengths at airports of intended use, and the following takeoff and landing distance information.

(1) For civil aircraft for which an approved Airplane or rotorcraft Flight Manual containing takeoff and landing distance data is required, the takeoff and landing distance data contained therein.

§ 91.105 Flight crewmembers at stations.

(a) During takeoff and landing, and while en route, each required flight crewmember shall

(2) Keep the safety belt fastened while at the crewmember station.

§ 91.107 Use of safety belts, shoulder harnesses, and child restraint systems.

(1) No pilot may take off a U.S.-registered civil aircraft (except a free balloon that incorporates a basket or gondola, or an airship type certificated before November 2, 1987) unless the pilot in command of that aircraft ensures that each person on board is briefed on how to fasten and unfasten that person's safety belt and, if installed, shoulder harness.

(3) Each person on board a U.S.-registered civil aircraft must occupy an approved seat or berth with a safety belt and, if installed, shoulder harness, properly secured about him or her during movement on the surface, takeoff, and landing.

§ 91.111 Operating near other aircraft.

(c) No person may operate an aircraft, carrying passengers for hire, in formation flight.

§ 91.113 Right-of-way rules: Except water operations.

(d) Converging. When aircraft of the same category are converging at approximately the same altitude (except head-on, or nearly so), the aircraft to the other's right has the right-of-way.

(f) Overtaking. Each aircraft that is being overtaken has the right-of-way and each pilot of an overtaking aircraft shall alter course to the right to pass well clear.

(g) Landing. Aircraft, while on final approach to land or while landing, have the right-of-way over other aircraft in flight or operating on the surface, except that they shall not take advantage of the rule to force an aircraft off the runway surface which has already landed and is attempting to make way for an aircraft on final approach. When two or more aircraft are approaching an airport for the purpose of landing, the aircraft at the lower altitude has the right-of-way, but it shall not take advantage of this rule to cut in front of another which is on final approach to land or to overtake that aircraft.

§ 91.117 Aircraft speed.

(a) Unless otherwise authorized by the Administrator, no person may operate an aircraft below 10,000 ft msl at an indicated airspeed of more than 250 knots (288 mph).

(b) Unless otherwise authorized or required by ATC, no person may operate an aircraft at or below 2500 ft above the surface within 4 nautical miles of the primary airport of a Class C or Class D airspace area at an indicated airspeed of more than 200 knots (230 mph).

(c) No person may operate an aircraft in the airspace underlying a Class B airspace area designated for an airport or in a VFR corridor designated through such a Class B airspace area at an indicated airspeed of more than 200 knots (230 mph).

§ 91.131 Operations in Class B airspace.

(a) Operating rules. No person may operate an aircraft within a Class B airspace area except in compliance with § 91.129 and the following rules:

(b) Pilot requirements.

(i) The pilot in command holds at least a private pilot certificate; or

(ii) The aircraft is operated by a student pilot or recreational pilot who seeks private pilot certification and has met the requirements of § 61.95 of this chapter.

§ 91.151 Fuel requirements for flight in VFR conditions.

(a) No person may begin a flight in an airplane under VFR conditions unless there is enough fuel to fly to the first point of intended landing and, assuming normal cruising speed

(1) During the day, to fly after that for at least 30 minutes; or

(2) At night, to fly after that for at least 45 minutes.

(b) No person may begin a flight in a rotorcraft under VFR conditions unless there is enough fuel to fly to the first point of intended landing and, assuming normal cruising speed, to fly after that for at least 20 minutes.

§ 91.155 Basic VFR weather minimums.

Airspace	Flight visibility	Distance from clouds
Class A	Not applicable	Not applicable
Class B	3 statute miles	Clear of clouds
Class C	3 statute miles	500 ft below 1000 ft above 2000 ft horizontal
Class D	3 statute miles	500 ft below 1000 ft above 2000 ft horizontal
Class E		
Less than 10,000 ft msl	3 statute miles	500 ft below 1000 ft above 2000 ft horizontal
At or above 10,000 ft msl	5 statute miles	1000 ft below 1000 ft above 1 statute mile horizontal
Class G		
1200 ft or less above the surface (regardless of msl altitude)		
Day, except as provided in § 91.155(b)	1 statute mile	Clear of clouds
Night, except as provided in § 91.155(b)	3 statute miles	500 ft below 1000 ft above 2000 ft horizontal
More than 1200 ft above the surface but less than 10,000 ft msl		
Day	1 statute mile	500 ft below 1000 ft above 2000 ft horizontal
Night	3 statute miles	500 ft below 1000 ft above 2000 ft horizontal
More than 1200 ft above the surface and at or above 10,000 ft msl	5 statute miles	1000 ft below 1000 ft above 1 statute mile horizontal

§ 91.157 Special VFR weather minimums.

(b) Special VFR operations may only be conducted

(1) With an ATC clearance;

(2) Clear of clouds;

(3) Except for helicopters, when flight visibility is at least 1 statute mile; and

(4) Except for helicopters, between sunrise and sunset unless

(i) The person being granted the ATC clearance meets the applicable requirements for instrument flight under part 61 of this chapter;

(ii) The aircraft is equipped as required in § 91.205(d).

(c) No person may take off or land an aircraft (other than a helicopter) under special VFR

(1) Unless ground visibility is at least 1 statute mile; or

(2) If ground visibility is not reported, unless flight visibility is at least 1 statute mile.

§ 91.159 VFR cruising altitude or flight level.

Each person operating an aircraft under VFR in level cruising flight more than 3000 ft above the surface shall maintain the appropriate altitude or flight level prescribed below.

(a) When operating below 18,000 ft msl and

(1) On a magnetic course of 0 degrees through 179 degrees, any odd thousand-ft msl altitude + 500 ft (such as 3500, 5500, or 7500); or

(2) On a magnetic course of 180 degrees through 359 degrees, any even thousand-ft msl altitude + 500 ft (such as 4500, 6500, or 8500).

§ 91.167 Fuel requirements for flight in IFR conditions.

(a) No person may operate a civil aircraft in IFR conditions unless it carries enough fuel to

(1) Complete the flight to the first airport of intended landing;

(2) Fly from that airport to the alternate airport; and

(3) Fly after that for 45 minutes at normal cruising speed or, for helicopters, fly after that for 30 minutes at normal cruising speed.

§ 91.171 VOR equipment check for IFR operations.

(a) No person may operate a civil aircraft under IFR using the VOR system of radio navigation unless the VOR equipment of that aircraft has been checked.

(b) Except as provided in paragraph (c) of this section, each person conducting a VOR check under paragraph (a)(2) of this section shall

(1) Use, at the airport of intended departure, an FAA-operated or approved test signal or a test signal radiated by a certificated and appropriately rated radio repair station or, outside the United States, a test signal operated or approved by an appropriate authority to check the VOR equipment (the maximum permissible indicated bearing error is plus or minus 4 degrees.

§ 91.177 Minimum altitudes for IFR operations.

(a) Operation of aircraft at minimum altitudes. Except when necessary for takeoff or landing, no person may operate an aircraft under IFR below

(i) In the case of operations over an area designated as a mountainous area in § 95, an altitude of 2000 ft above the highest obstacle within a horizontal distance of 4 nautical miles from the course to be flown; or

(ii) In any other case, an altitude of 1000 ft above the highest obstacle within a horizontal distance of 4 nautical miles from the course to be flown.

§ 91.205 Powered civil aircraft with standard category U.S. airworthiness certificates: Instrument and equipment requirements.

(b) Visual flight rules (day). For VFR flight during the day, the following instruments and equipment are required:

(1) Airspeed indicator.

(2) Altimeter.

(3) Magnetic direction indicator.

(4) Tachometer for each engine.

(5) Oil pressure gauge for each engine using pressure system.

(6) Temperature gauge for each liquid-cooled engine.

(7) Oil temperature gauge for each air-cooled engine.

(8) Manifold pressure gauge for each altitude engine.

(9) Fuel gauge indicating the quantity of fuel in each tank.

(10) Landing gear position indicator, if the aircraft has a retractable landing gear.

(11) If the aircraft is operated for hire over water and beyond power-off gliding distance from shore, approved flotation gear readily available to each occupant and at least one pyrotechnic signaling device.

(c) Visual flight rules (night). For VFR flight at night, the following instruments and equipment are required:

(1) Instruments and equipment specified in paragraph (b) of this section.

(2) Approved position lights.

(3) An approved aviation red or aviation white anticollision light system on all U.S.-registered civil aircraft.

(4) If the aircraft is operated for hire, one electric landing light.

(5) An adequate source of electrical energy for all installed electrical and radio equipment.

(6) One spare set of fuses, or three spare fuses of each kind required, that are accessible to the pilot in flight.

§ 91.207 Emergency locator transmitters.

(c) Batteries used in the emergency locator transmitters required by paragraphs (a) and (b) of this section must be replaced (or recharged, if the batteries are rechargeable)

(1) When the transmitter has been in use for more than 1 cumulative hour.

§ 91.209 Aircraft lights.

No person may during the period from sunset to sunrise

(a) Operate an aircraft unless it has lighted position lights.

§ 91.211 Supplemental oxygen.

(a) General. No person may operate a civil aircraft of U.S. registry

(1) At cabin pressure altitudes above 12,500 ft (msl) up to and including 14,000 ft (msl) unless the required minimum flightcrew is provided with and uses supplemental oxygen for that part of the flight at those altitudes that is of more than 30 minutes duration.

(2) At cabin pressure altitudes above 14,000 ft (msl) unless the required minimum flightcrew is provided with and uses supplemental oxygen during the entire flight time at those altitudes; and

(3) At cabin pressure altitudes above 15,000 ft (msl) unless each occupant of the aircraft is provided with supplemental oxygen.

§ 91.215 ATC transponder and altitude reporting equipment and use.

(b) All airspace. Unless otherwise authorized or directed by ATC, no person may operate an aircraft in the airspace described in this section, unless that aircraft is equipped with an operable coded radar beacon transponder having either Mode 3/A 4096 code capability, replying to Mode 3/A interrogations with the code specified by ATC, or a Mode S capability, replying to Mode 3/A interrogations with the code specified by ATC and intermode and Mode S interrogations in accordance with the applicable provisions specified in TSO C-112. This requirement applies to

(1) All aircraft in Class A, Class B, and Class C airspace area.

§ 91.303 Aerobatic flight.

No person may operate an aircraft in aerobatic flight

(e) Below an altitude of 1500 ft above the surface; or

(f) When flight visibility is less than 3 statute miles.

§ 91.309 Towing: Gliders.

(a) No person may operate a civil aircraft towing a glider unless

(2) The towing aircraft is equipped with a tow-hitch of a kind, and installed in a manner, that is approved by the Administrator;

(3) The towline used has breaking strength not less than 80 percent of the maximum certificated operating weight of the glider and not more than twice this operating weight. However, the towline used may have a breaking strength more than twice the maximum certificated operating weight of the glider if

(i) A safety link is installed at the point of attachment of the towline to the glider with a breaking strength not less than 80 percent of the maximum certificated operating weight of the glider and not greater than twice this operating weight.

§ 91.311 Towing: Other than under § 91.309.

No pilot of a civil aircraft may tow anything with that aircraft (other than under § 91.309) except in accordance with the terms of a certificate of waiver issued by the Administrator.

§ 91.313 Restricted category civil aircraft: Operating limitations.

(c) No person may operate a restricted category civil aircraft carrying persons or property for compensation or hire.

§ 91.315 Limited category civil aircraft: Operating limitations.

No person may operate a limited category civil aircraft carrying persons or property for compensation or hire.

Subpart E—Maintenance, Preventive Maintenance, and Alterations

§ 91.403 General.

(a) The owner or operator of an aircraft is primarily responsible for maintaining that aircraft in an airworthy condition, including compliance with part 39 of this chapter (Airworthiness Directives).

§ 91.407 Operation after maintenance, preventive maintenance, rebuilding, or alteration.

(a) No person may operate any aircraft that has undergone maintenance, preventive maintenance, rebuilding, or alteration unless

(1) It has been approved for return to service by a person authorized under § 43.7 of this chapter, and

(2) The maintenance record entry required by § 43.9 or § 43.11, as applicable, of this chapter has been made.

(b) No person may carry any person (other than crewmembers) in an aircraft that has been maintained, rebuilt, or altered in a manner that may have appreciably changed its flight characteristics or substantially affected its operation in flight until an appropriately rated pilot with at least a private pilot certificate flies the aircraft, makes an operational check of the maintenance performed or alteration made, and logs the flight in the aircraft records.

§ 91.409 Inspections.

No person may operate an aircraft unless, within the preceding 12 calendar months, it has had

(1) An annual inspection in accordance with part 43 of this chapter and has been approved for return to service by a person authorized by § 43.7 of this chapter; or

(2) An inspection for the issuance of an airworthiness certificate in accordance with part 21 of this chapter.

(b) No person may operate an aircraft carrying any person for hire, and no person may give flight instruction for hire in an aircraft which that person provides, unless within the preceding 100 hours of time in service the aircraft has received an annual or 100 hour inspection and been approved for return to service in accordance with part 43 of this chapter. The 100 hour limitation may be exceeded by not more than 10 hours while en route to reach a place where the inspection can be done. The excess time used to reach a place where the inspection can be done must be included in computing the next 100 hours of time in service.

§ 91.413 ATC transponder tests and inspections.

(a) No persons may use an ATC transponder that is specified in § 91.215(a), 121.345(c), 127.123(b), or 135.143(c) of this chapter unless, within the preceding 24 calendar months, the ATC transponder has been tested and inspected and found to comply with appendix F of part 43 of this chapter.

§ 91.417 Maintenance records.

(a) The records must include

(ii) The current status of life-limited parts of each airframe, engine, propeller, rotor, and appliance.

§ 91.421 Rebuilt engine maintenance records.

(b) Each manufacturer or agency that grants zero time to an engine rebuilt by it shall enter in the new record

(2) Each change made as required by airworthiness directives.

COMPUTER-BASED QUESTIONS

5048. Which person is directly responsible for the prelaunch briefing of passengers for a balloon flight?

A. Crew chief.

B. Safety officer.

C. Pilot in command.

5048. "C" is the correct answer. The pilot in command of an aircraft is directly responsible for, and is the final authority as to, the operation of that aircraft. This includes the duty of briefing the passengers prior to launching.
Reference FAR 91.3

FAA subject matter knowledge code A26

5049. The required preflight action relative to alternatives available, if the planned flight cannot be completed, is applicable to

A. IFR flights only.

B. any flight not in the vicinity of an airport.

C. any flight conducted for hire or compensation.

5049. "B" is the correct answer. Each pilot in command shall, before beginning a flight, become familiar with all available information concerning that flight. For a flight under IFR, or not in the vicinity of an airport, this information must include weather reports and available alternatives if the planned flight cannot be completed. "A" is incorrect because the regulation does not limit the preflight action to only IFR flights. "C" limits the preflight action to flights for compensation or hire, which is obviously wrong.
Reference FAR 91.103

FAA subject matter knowledge code B08

5050. Before beginning any flight under IFR, the pilot in command must become familiar with all available information concerning that flight. In addition, the pilot must

A. be familiar with all instrument approaches at the destination airport.

B. list an alternate airport on the flight plan and confirm adequate takeoff and landing performance at the destination airport.

C. be familiar with the runway lengths at airports of intended use, and the alternatives available if the flight cannot be completed.

5050. "C" is the correct answer. Each pilot in command shall, before beginning a flight, become familiar with all available information concerning that flight. For flights under IFR, this must include weather reports and forecasts, fuel requirements, alternatives available if the flight cannot be completed as planned, and any known traffic delays. He must also be familiar with runway lengths at airports of intended use, and the following takeoff and landing distance information: for civil aircraft for which an approved airplane or rotorcraft flight manual containing takeoff and landing distance data is required, the takeoff and landing distance data contained therein. "A" and "B" are incorrect. Although good to know, they do not list everything the pilot in command must be familiar with.
Reference FAR 91.103(a)

FAA subject matter knowledge code B08

5051. Required flight crewmembers' seatbelts must be fastened

A. only during takeoff and landing.

B. while the crewmembers are at their stations.

C. only during takeoff and landing when passengers are aboard the aircraft.

5051. "B" is the correct answer. During takeoff and landing, and while en route, each required flight crewmember shall keep the safety belt fastened while at the crewmember station.
Reference FAR 61.105(a)(2)

FAA subject matter knowledge code B08

5052. The use of seatbelts, with certain exceptions, during takeoffs and landings is

A. required for all occupants.

B. required during commercial operations only.

C. a good operating practice, but not required by regulations.

5052. "A" is the correct answer. Each person on board a U.S.-registered civil aircraft must occupy an approved seat with a safety belt and, if installed, shoulder harness properly secured during takeoff and landings.
Reference FAR 91.107(3)
FAA subject matter knowledge code B08

5053. given:

Glider's maximum certificated   1140 pounds
operating weight
Towline breaking strength   3050 pounds

Which meets the requirement for one of the safety links. A breaking strength of

A. 812 pounds installed where the towline is attached to the towplane.

B. 920 pounds installed where the towline is attached to the glider.

C. 2300 pounds installed where the towline is attached to the glider.

5053. "B" is the correct answer. A safety link must be installed at the point of attachment of the towline to the glider with a breaking strength not less than 80 percent of the maximum certified operating weight of the glider and not greater than twice this operating weight: 80% × 1140 lb = 912 lb, and 2 × 1140 lb = 2280 lb, so "B" is the only correct choice.
Reference FAR 91.309(2)(1)
FAA subject matter knowledge code B12

5054. During aerotow of a glider that weighs 940 pounds, which tow rope tensile strength would require the use of safety links at each end of the rope?

A. 752 pounds.

B. 1500 pounds.

C. 2000 pounds.

5054. "C" is the correct answer. The towline used must have a breaking strength not less than 80 percent of the maximum certified operating weight of the glider and not more than twice this operating weight. "A" and "B" both fit in this definition without using a safety link; 1880 pounds is twice the weight of the glider so "C" is the only answer that is correct.
Reference FAR 91.309(3)
FAA subject matter knowledge code B12

5055. Which is required to operate an aircraft towing an advertising banner?

A. Approval from ATC to operate in a control area.

B. A certificate of waiver issued by the Administrator.

C. A safety link at each end of the towline that has a breaking strength not less than 80 percent of the aircraft's gross weight.

5055. "B" is the correct answer. No pilot of a civil aircraft may tow anything with that aircraft, except in accordance with the terms of a certificate of waiver issued by the Administrator. "A" and "C" are incorrect because they do not address this regulation.
Reference FAR 91.311
FAA subject matter knowledge code B12

5056. Portable electronic devices that may cause interference with the navigation or communication system may not be operated on aircraft being flown

A. along Federal airways.

B. within the United States.

C. in commercial operations.

5056. "C" is the correct answer. No person may operate, nor may any operator or pilot in command of an aircraft allow the operation of, any portable electronic device on an aircraft operated by a holder of an air carrier operating certificate. In simpler terms, if it's a commercial operation, it's not allowed.
Reference FAR 91.21(a)(1)
FAA subject matter knowledge code B07

5057. The use of certain portable electronic devices is prohibited on airships that are being operated under

A. IFR.

B. VFR.

C. DVFR.

5057. "A" is the correct answer. No person may operate or allow to be operated any portable electronic devices on any aircraft while it is operated under IFR regulations.
Reference FAR 91.21(a)(2)
FAA subject matter knowledge code B09

5058. To begin a flight in a rotorcraft under VFR, there must be enough fuel to fly to the first point of intended landing and, assuming normal cruising speed, to fly thereafter for at least

A. 20 minutes.

B. 30 minutes.

C. 45 minutes.

5058. "A" is the correct answer. No person may begin a flight in a rotorcraft under VFR conditions unless there is enough fuel to fly to the first point of intended landing and, assuming normal cruising speed, to fly after that for at least 20 minutes.
Reference FAR 91.151(b)
FAA subject matter knowledge code B09

5059. If weather conditions are such that you are required to designate an alternate airport or IFR flight plan, you should plan to carry enough fuel to arrive at the first airport of intended landing, fly from that airport to the alternate airport, and fly thereafter for

A. 30 minutes at slow cruising speed.

B. 45 minutes at normal cruising speed.

C. 1 hour at normal cruising speed.

5059. "B" is the correct answer. You cannot operate civil aircraft under IFR unless you have enough fuel to fly to the first airport of intended landing, from there to the alternate airport, and then fly 45 minutes at normal cruising speed.
Reference FAR 91.167(a)(3)
FAA subject matter knowledge code B10

5060. A coded transponder equipped with altitude reporting equipment is required for

A. Class A, Class B, and Class C airspace areas.

B. all airspace of the 48 contiguous United States and the District of Columbia at and above 10,000 ft msl (including airspace at and below 2500 ft above the surface).

C. both A and B.

5060. "A" is the correct answer. No person may operate an aircraft in Class A, Class B, or Class C airspace unless that aircraft is equipped with an operable coded radar beacon transponder with altitude reporting capability.
Reference FAR 91.215(b)
FAA subject matter knowledge code B11

5061. In the contiguous United States, excluding the airspace at and below 2500 ft agl, an operable coded transponder equipped with Mode C capability is required in all airspace above

A. 10,000 ft msl.

B. 12,500 ft msl.

C. 14,500 ft msl.

5061. "A" is the correct answer. An operable coded transponder equipped with Mode C capability is required in all airspace above 10,000 ft msl in the con-

tiguous United States, excluding the airspace at and below 2500 ft agl.
Reference FAR 91.215
FAA subject matter knowledge code B11

5062. What is the maximum tolerance (+ or –) allowed for an operational VOR equipment check when using a VOT?

A. 4 degrees.

B. 6 degrees.

C. 8 degrees.

5062. "A" is the correct answer. The VOT maximum tolerance is plus or minus 4 degrees.
Reference FAR 91.171(b)(1)
FAA subject matter knowledge code B10

5063. In accordance with FAR 91, supplemental oxygen must be used by the required minimum flightcrew for that time exceeding 30 minutes while at cabin pressure altitudes of

A. 10,500 ft msl up to and including 12,500 ft msl.

B. 12,000 ft msl up to and including 18,000 ft msl.

C. 12,500 ft msl up to and including 14,000 ft msl.

5063. "C" is the correct answer. No person may operate a civil aircraft at cabin pressure altitudes above 12,500 ft msl up to and including 14,000 ft msl unless the required minimum flightcrew is provided with and uses supplemental oxygen for that part of the flight at those altitudes that is of more than 30 minutes duration.
Reference FAR 91.211(a)(1)
FAA subject matter knowledge code B11

5064. What are the oxygen requirements when operating above 15,000 ft msl?

A. Oxygen must be available for the flightcrew.

B. Oxygen is not required at any altitude in a free balloon.

C. The flightcrew must use and passengers must be provided oxygen.

5064. "C" is the correct answer. No person may operate a civil aircraft at cabin pressure altitudes above 15,000 ft msl unless each occupant of the aircraft is provided with supplemental oxygen.
Reference FAR 91.211(a)(1)
FAA subject matter knowledge code B11

5065. Which is required equipment for powered aircraft during VFR night flights?

A. Anticollision light system.

B. Gyroscopic direction indicator.

C. Gyroscopic bank-and-pitch indicator.

5065. "A" is the correct answer. Although a dark night VFR flight is very similar to instrument flying, only the anticollision light system is required.
Reference FAR 91.205(b)(3)
FAA subject matter knowledge code B11

5066. Which is required equipment for powered aircraft during VFR night flights?

A. Flashlight with red lens if the flight is for hire.

B. A landing light if the flight is for hire.

C. Sensitive altimeter adjustable for barometric pressure.

5066. "B" is the correct answer. Of the choices listed only the landing light is required by regulations if the flight is for hire.
Reference FAR 91.205(b)(4)
FAA subject matter knowledge code B11

5067. Approved flotation gear, readily available to each occupant, is required on each aircraft if it is being flown for hire over water

A. in amphibious aircraft beyond 50 nautical miles from shore.

B. beyond power-off gliding distance from shore.

C. regardless of the distance flown from shore.

5067. "B" is the correct answer. If the aircraft is operated for hire over water and beyond power-off gliding distance from shore, approved flotation gear must be readily available to each occupant and at least one pyrotechnic signaling device must be on board.
Reference FAR 91.20(b)(11)
FAA subject matter knowledge code B11

5068. Which is true with respect to operating limitations of a "restricted" category helicopter?

A. A restricted category helicopter is limited to an operating radius of 25 miles from its home base.

B. A pilot of a restricted category helicopter is required to hold a commercial pilot certificate.

C. No person may operate a restricted category helicopter carrying property or passengers for compensation or hire.

5068. "C" is the correct answer. No person may operate a restricted category civil aircraft carrying persons or property for compensation or hire.
Reference FAR 91.313(c)
FAA subject matter knowledge code B12

5069. The carriage of passengers for hire by a commercial pilot is

A. not authorized in utility category aircraft.

B. not authorized in limited category aircraft.

C. authorized in restricted category aircraft.

5069. "B" is the correct answer. No person may operate a limited category civil aircraft carrying persons or property for hire. "A" is incorrect because you can fly a utility category aircraft for hire. "C" is wrong because a restricted category aircraft is also banned from carrying persons or property for hire.
Reference FAR 91.315
FAA subject matter knowledge code B12

5070. The maximum cumulative time that an emergency locator transmitter may be operated before the rechargeable battery must be recharged is

A. 30 minutes.

B. 45 minutes.

C. 60 minutes.

5070. "C" is the correct answer. Batteries used in ELTs must be recharged after 60 minutes of cumulative use. Remember, if you are in the habit of testing your ELT battery you need to keep a record of the cumulative time so when you reach 1 hour you can recharge the battery.
Reference FAR 91.207(c)(1)
FAA subject matter knowledge code B11

5071. No person may operate a large civil U.S. aircraft that is subject to a lease unless the lessee has mailed a copy of the lease to the FAA Mike Monroney Aeronautical Center within how many hours of its execution?

A. 24.

B. 48.

C. 72.

5071. "A" is the correct answer. The lessee must mail a copy of the lease within 24 hours of its execution.
Reference FAR 91.23(c)(1)
FAA subject matter knowledge code B07

5072. What transponder equipment is required for helicopter operations within Class B airspace?

A. A transponder with 4096 code and Mode C capability.

B. A transponder is required for helicopter operations when visibility is less than 1 mile.

C. A transponder with 4096 code capability is required except when operating at or below 1000 ft agl under the terms of a letter of agreement.

5072. "A" is the correct answer. Helicopters are required to use Mode C in Class B airspace. "B" is incorrect because visibility has nothing to do with transponder requirements. "C" is incorrect because letters of agreement usually are for the individual operators.
Reference FAR 91.215(b)(1)
FAA subject matter knowledge code B11

5073. Which is true with respect to formation flights?

A. Formation flights are authorized when carrying passengers for hire with prior arrangement with the pilot in command of each aircraft in the formation.

B. Formation flights are not authorized when visibilities are less than 3 statute miles.

C. Formation flights are not authorized when carrying passengers for hire.

5073. "C" is the correct answer. No person may operate an aircraft carrying passengers for hire in formation flight.
Reference FAR 91.111(c)
FAA subject matter knowledge code B08

5074. While in flight a helicopter and an airplane are converging at a 90° angle, and the helicopter is located to the right of the airplane. Which aircraft has the right-of-way, and why?

A. The helicopter, because it is to the right of the airplane.

B. The helicopter, because helicopters have the right-of-way over airplanes.

C. The airplane, because airplanes have the right-of-way over helicopters.

5074. "A" is the correct answer. When aircraft of the same category are converging at approximately the same altitude (except head on or nearly so), the aircraft to the other's right has the right-of-way. For the purpose of this question, category means both aircraft are equally maneuverable. For this reason "B" and "C" are clearly incorrect.
Reference FAR 91.113(d)
FAA subject matter knowledge code B08

5075. Two aircraft of the same category are approaching an airport for the purpose of landing. The right-of-way belongs to the aircraft

A. at the higher altitude.

B. at the lower altitude, but the pilot shall not take advantage of this rule to cut in front of or overtake the other aircraft.

C. that is more maneuverable, and that aircraft may move in front of or overtake the other aircraft.

5075. "B" is the correct answer. When two or more aircraft are approaching an airport for the purpose of landing, the aircraft at the lower altitude has the right-of-way, but it shall not take advantage of this rule to cut in front of another aircraft that is on final approach to land or to overtake that aircraft.
Reference FAR 91.113(d)
FAA subject matter knowledge code B08

5076. Airplane A is overtaking airplane B. Which airplane has the right-of-way?

A. Airplane A; the pilot should alter course to the right to pass.

B. Airplane B; the pilot should expect to be passed on the right.

C. Airplane B; the pilot should expect to be passed on the left.

5076. "B" is the correct answer. Each aircraft that is being overtaken has the right-of-way and each pilot of an overtaking aircraft shall alter course to the right to pass well clear.
Reference FAR 91.113(f)
FAA subject matter knowledge code B08

5077. What is the maximum indicated airspeed allowed in the airspace underlying Class B airspace?

A. 156 knots.

B. 200 knots.

C. 230 knots.

5077. "B" is the correct answer. No person may operate an aircraft in the airspace underlying a Class B airspace area at an indicated airspeed of more than 200 knots. Be careful on this question since 200 knots equals 230 mph.
Reference FAR 91.117(c)
FAA subject matter knowledge code B08

5078. Unless otherwise authorized or required by ATC, the maximum indicated airspeed permitted when at or below 2500 ft agl within 4 nautical miles of the primary airport of a Class B, C, or D airspace is

A. 180 knots.

B. 200 knots.

C. 230 knots.

5078. "B" is the correct answer. Unless authorized or required by ATC, no person may operate an aircraft at or below 2500 ft above the surface within 4 nautical miles of the primary airport of a Class C or Class D airspace area at an indicated airspeed of more than 200 knots. The speed limit for Class B airspace is 250 knots, but since that answer isn't one of the choices, "B" is the best choice.
Reference FAR 91.113(d)
FAA subject matter knowledge code B08

5079. What is the minimum altitude and flight visibility required for acrobatic flight?

A. 1500 ft agl and 3 miles.

B. 2000 ft msl and 2 miles.

C. 3000 ft agl and 1 mile.

5079. "A" is the correct answer. No person may operate an aircraft in acrobatic flight below an altitude of 1500 ft above the surface, or when flight visibility is less than 3 statute miles.
Reference FAR 91.303(d)(e)
FAA subject matter knowledge code B08

5080. If not equipped with required position lights, an aircraft must terminate flight

A. at sunset.

B. 30 minutes after sunset.

C. 1 hour after sunset.

5080. "A" is the correct answer. No person may operate an aircraft during the period from sunset to sunrise unless it has lighted position lights.
Reference FAR 91.209(a)
FAA subject matter knowledge code B11

5081. If a free balloon is not equipped for night flight and official sunset is 1730 EST, the latest a pilot may operate that balloon and not violate regulations is

A. 1629 EST.

B. 1729 EST.

C. 1759 EST.

5081. "B" is the correct answer. No person may operate an aircraft during the period from sunset to sunrise unless it has lighted position lights.
Reference FAR 91.209(a)
FAA subject matter knowledge code B11

5082. Which is true regarding VFR operations in Class B airspace?

A. Area navigation equipment is required.

B. Flight under VFR is not authorized unless the pilot in command is instrument rated.

C. Solo student pilot operations are allowed if certain conditions are satisfied.

5082. "C" is the correct answer. Although the student pilot must meet certain training requirements, he can operate in Class B airspace unless that airspace prohibits student operations.
Reference FAR 91.131(b)(2)
FAA subject matter knowledge code B08

5083. The minimum flight visibility for VFR flight increases to 5 miles beginning at an altitude of

A. 14,500 ft msl.

B. 10,000 ft msl if above 1200 ft agl.

C. 10,000 ft msl regardless of height above the ground.

5083. "B" is the correct answer. The flight visibility increases to 5 statute miles if you are more than 1200 ft agl and at or above 10,000 ft msl.
Reference FAR 91.155
FAA subject matter knowledge code B09, J07

5084. When flying a glider above 10,000 ft msl and more than 1200 ft agl, what minimum flight visibility is required?

A. 3 nautical miles.

B. 5 statute miles.

C. 7 statute miles.

5084. "B" is the correct answer. The flight visibility increases to 5 statute miles if you are more than 1200 ft agl and at or above 10,000 ft msl.
Reference FAR 91.155
FAA subject matter knowledge code B09, J07

5085. What is the minimum flight visibility and proximity to cloud requirements for VFR flight at 6500 ft msl in Class C, D, and E airspace?

A. 1 mile visibility; clear of clouds.

B. 3 miles visibility; 1000 ft above and 500 ft below.

C. 5 miles visibility; 1000 ft above and 1000 ft below.

5085. "B" is the correct answer. The cloud clearance and visibility requirements for Class C, D, and E airspace below 10,000 ft msl are 3 miles visibility and at least 1000 ft above, 500 ft below, and 2000 ft horizontally from any clouds.
Reference FAR 91.155
FAA subject matter knowledge code B08

5086. Which minimum flight visibility and distance from clouds is required for a day VFR helicopter flight in Class G airspace at 3500 ft msl over terrain with an elevation of 1900 ft msl?

A. Visibility—3 miles; distance from clouds—1000 ft below, 1000 ft above, and 1 mile horizontally.

B. Visibility—3 miles; distance from clouds—500 ft below, 1000 ft above, and 2000 ft horizontally.

C. Visibility—1 mile; distance from clouds—500 ft below, 1000 ft above, and 2000 ft horizontally.

5086. "C" is the correct answer. The helicopter is at 1600 ft agl but less than 10,000 ft msl. According to the chart listed in FAR 91.155, 1 mile visibility is required plus 500 ft below, 1000 ft above, and 2000 ft horizontally. Thus "C" is the only correct answer.
Reference FAR 91.155
FAA subject matter knowledge code B09

5087. Basic VFR weather minimums require at least what visibility for operating a helicopter within Class D airspace?

A. 1 mile.

B. 2 miles.

C. 3 miles.

5087. "C" is the correct answer. Visibility of 3 miles is required to operate in Class D airspace.
Reference FAR 91.155
FAA subject matter knowledge code B09

5088. When operating an airplane for the purpose of landing or takeoff within Class D airspace under special VFR, what minimum distance from clouds and what visibility are required?

A. Remain clear of clouds, and the ground visibility must be at least 1 statute mile.

B. 500 ft beneath clouds, and the ground visibility must be at least 1 statute mile.

C. Remain clear of clouds, and the flight visibility must be at least 1 statute mile.

5088. "A" is the correct answer. Special VFR operations may only be conducted clear of clouds, and if ground visibility is reported, it must be at least 1 statute mile. If ground visibility is not reported, flight visibility must be at least 1 statute mile. Answer "C" is incorrect because ground visibility has priority, thus answer "A" is more correct.
Reference FAR 91.157(c)
FAA subject matter knowledge code B09

5089. At some airports located in Class D airspace where ground visibility is not reported, takeoffs and landings under special VFR are

A. not authorized.

B. authorized by ATC if the flight visibility is at least 1 statute mile.

C. authorized only if the ground visibility is observed to be at least 3 statute miles.

5089. "B" is the correct answer. If ground visibility is not reported, flight visibility must be at least 1 statute mile.
Reference FAR 91.157(d)(2)
FAA subject matter knowledge code B09

5090. To operate an airplane under special VFR (SVFR) within Class D airspace at night, which is required?

A. The pilot must hold an instrument pilot rating, but the airplane need not be equipped for instrument flight, as long as the weather remains at or above SVFR minimums.

B. The Class D airspace must be specifically designated as a night SVFR area.

C. The pilot must hold an instrument pilot rating and the airplane must be equipped for instrument flight.

5090. "C" is the correct answer. Special VFR operations may only be conducted between sunrise and sunset unless the pilot, being granted the ATC clearance, meets the requirements for instrument flight and the aircraft is equipped for instrument flight.
Reference FAR 91.157(b)(4)(i)(ii)
FAA subject matter knowledge code B09

5091. VFR cruising altitudes are required to be maintained when flying

A. at 3000 ft agl or more, based on true course.

B. more than 3000 ft agl, based on magnetic course.

C. at 3000 ft msl or more, based on magnetic heading.

5091. "B" is the correct answer. Anytime you are flying above 3000 ft agl, you are required to maintain a VFR cruising altitude based on a magnetic course. This helps separate aircraft since heading can vary widely but magnetic courses or ground tracks do not.
Reference FAR 91.159(a)
FAA subject matter knowledge code B08

5092. Except when necessary for takeoff or landing, or unless otherwise authorized by the Administrator, the minimum altitude for IFR flight is

A. 3000 ft over all terrain.

B. 3000 ft over designated mountainous terrain; 2000 ft over terrain elsewhere.

C. 2000 ft above the highest obstacle over designated mountainous terrain; 1000 ft above the highest obstacle over terrain elsewhere.

5092. "C" is the correct answer. In the case of operations over an area of mountainous terrain, an altitude of 2000 ft above the highest obstacle, and in other areas 1000 ft above the highest obstacle, within 4 nautical miles of the course to be flown must be maintained.
Reference FAR 91.177(a)(2)
FAA subject matter knowledge code B10

5093. Who is primarily responsible for maintaining an aircraft in an airworthy condition?

A. The lead mechanic responsible for that aircraft.

B. The pilot in command.

C. The operator or owner of the aircraft.

5093. "C" is the correct answer. The owner or operator is primarily responsible for maintaining an aircraft in an airworthy condition including compliance with airworthiness directives (part 39).
Reference FAR 91.403(a)
FAA subject matter knowledge code B13

5094. Assuring compliance with an airworthiness directive is the responsibility of the

A. pilot in command and the FAA certificated mechanic assigned to that aircraft.

B. pilot in command of that aircraft.

C. owner or operator of that aircraft.

5094. "C" is the correct answer. The owner or operator is primarily responsible for maintaining an aircraft in an airworthy condition including compliance with airworthiness directives (part 39).
Reference FAR 91.403(a)
FAA subject matter knowledge code B13

5095. After an annual inspection has been completed and the aircraft has been returned to service, an appropriate notation should be made

A. on the airworthiness certificate.

B. in the aircraft maintenance records.

C. in the FAA-approved flight manual.

5095. "B" is the correct answer. No person may operate any aircraft that has undergone maintenance unless the maintenance record entry has been made. "A" is incorrect because a mechanic cannot alter or amend an airworthiness certificate. "C" is also incorrect because the airplane flight manual is totally separate from the maintenance logbooks.
Reference FAR 91.405(b)
FAA subject matter knowledge code B13

5096. The validity of the airworthiness certificate is maintained by

A. performance of an annual inspection.

B. performance of an annual inspection and a 100-hour inspection prior to their expiration date.

C. an appropriate return to service statement in the aircraft maintenance records upon the completion of required inspections and maintenance.

5096. "C" is the correct answer. The airworthiness certificate is valid as long as the maintenance, preventive maintenance, and alterations are completed and a return to service statement entry is made in the aircraft's maintenance logbooks.
Reference FAR 91.407
FAA subject matter knowledge code A10

5097. If an aircraft's operation in flight was substantially affected by an alteration or repair, the aircraft documents must show that it was test-flown and approved for return to service by an appropriately rated pilot prior to being operated

A. by any private pilot.

B. with passengers aboard.

C. for compensation or hire.

5097. "B" is the correct answer. No person may carry any person in an aircraft that has been maintained, rebuilt, or altered in any manner that may have appreciably changed its flight characteristics or substantially affected its operation in flight until an appropriately rated pilot with at least a private pilot certificate flies the aircraft, makes an operational check of the maintenance performed or alterations made, and logs the flight in the aircraft records.
Reference FAR 91.407(b)
FAA subject matter knowledge code B13

5098. Which is correct concerning preventive maintenance, when accomplished by a pilot?

A. A record of preventive maintenance is not required.

B. A record of preventive maintenance must be entered in the maintenance records.

C. Records of preventive maintenance must be entered in the FAA-approved flight manual.

5098. "B" is the correct answer. Each person who maintains, performs preventive maintenance, rebuilds, or alters an aircraft part shall make an entry in the aircraft logbooks. This would include a pilot if he performed any preventive maintenance.
Reference FAR 91.407
FAA subject matter knowledge code A15

5099. An aircraft carrying passengers for hire has been on a schedule of inspection every 100 hours of time in service. Under which condition may that aircraft be operated beyond 100 hours without a new inspection?

A. The aircraft may be flown for any flight as long as the time in service has not exceeded 110 hours.

B. The aircraft may be dispatched for a flight of any duration as long as 100 hours has not been exceeded at the time it departs.

C. The 100-hour limitation may be exceeded by not more than 10 hours if necessary to reach a place at which the inspection can be done.

5099. "C" is the correct answer. The 100-hour limitation may be exceeded by no more than 10 hours in order to reach a maintenance facility that can do the inspection. The excess time must be included in computing the next 100 hours of time in service.
Reference FAR 91.409(b)
FAA subject matter knowledge code B13

5100. Which is true concerning required maintenance inspections?

A. A 100-hour inspection may be substituted for an annual inspection.

B. An annual inspection may be substituted for a 100-hour inspection.

C. An annual inspection is required even if a progressive inspection system has been approved.

5100. "B" is the correct answer. An annual inspection may take the place of a 100-hour inspection, but a 100-hour inspection may not be substituted for an annual. "C" is incorrect because a progressive inspection program replaces the requirements for 100-hour or annual inspections.
Reference FAR 91.409(a)(b)(c)
FAA subject matter knowledge code B13

5101. An ATC transponder is not to be used unless it has been tested, inspected, and found to comply with regulations within the preceding

A. 30 days.

B. 12 calendar months.

C. 24 calendar months.

5101. "C" is the correct answer. No person may use an ATC transponder unless, within the preceding 24 calendar months, that ATC transponder has been tested and inspected and found to comply with Appendix F of FAR 43.
Reference FAR 91.413(a)
FAA subject matter knowledge code B13

5102. Aircraft maintenance records must include the current status of the

A. applicable airworthiness certificate.

B. life-limited parts of only the engine and airframe.

C. life-limited parts of each airframe, engine, propeller, rotor, and appliance.

5102. "C" is the correct answer. Aircraft maintenance records must include the current status of life-limited parts of each airframe, engine propeller, rotor, and appliance. "A" is incorrect because the airworthiness certificate is not required to be in the aircraft's maintenance records. "B" is incorrect because it does not go into enough detail.
Reference FAR 91.417(a)(2)(ii)
FAA subject matter knowledge code B13

5103. Which is true relating to airworthiness directives?

A. Airworthiness directives are advisory in nature and generally are not addressed immediately.

B. Noncompliance with airworthiness directives renders an aircraft unairworthy.

C. Compliance with airworthiness directives is the responsibility of maintenance personnel.

5103. "B" is the correct answer. The owner or operator is primarily responsible for maintaining that aircraft in an airworthy condition. This includes compliance with part 39, which addresses airworthiness directives. "A" is incorrect because airworthiness directives are regulatory, not advisory. "C" is incorrect because the regulation clearly states that the "owner or operator is primarily responsible."
Reference FAR 91.403
FAA subject matter knowledge code B13

5104. A new maintenance record being used for an aircraft engine rebuilt by the manufacturer must include previous

A. operating hours of the engine.

B. annual inspections performed on the engine.

C. changes as required by airworthiness directives.

5104. "C" is the correct answer. Each manufacturer or agency that grants zero time to an engine rebuilt by it shall enter, in the new record, each change made as required by airworthiness directives.
Reference FAR 91.421(b)(2)
FAA subject matter knowledge code B13

5105. If an ATC transponder installed in an aircraft has not been tested, inspected, and found to comply with regulations within a specified period, what is the limitation on its use?

A. Its use is not permitted.

B. It may be used when outside controlled airspace.

C. It may be used for VFR flight but not for IFR flight.

5105. "A" is the correct answer. No person may use an ATC transponder unless, within the preceding 24 calendar months, that ATC transponder has been tested and inspected and found to comply with Appendix F of FAR 43.
Reference FAR 91.413(a)
FAA subject matter knowledge code B13

6

FAR Part 125

STUDY GUIDE

FAR 125—Certification and Operations: Airplanes Having a Seating Capacity of 20 or More Passengers

§ 125.1

Part 125 applies to operations of aircraft that seat 20 or more passengers or have a maximum payload capacity of 6000 pounds or more and are not being operated under FAR parts 121, 129, 135, or 137.

§ 125.3

A request for deviation authority must be submitted to the nearest Flight Standards District Office not less than 60 days prior to the date of intended operations. This deviation authority will be issued as a Letter of Deviation Authority by the Administrator.

§ 125.7

The certificate holder must display a true copy of the certificate in each of its aircraft.

§ 125.11

No certificate holder may conduct any operation which results directly or indirectly from any person's holding out to the public to furnish transportation.

(b) No person is eligible for a certificate of operations specifications under part 125, if that person holds only the appropriate operating certificate and/or operations specifications necessary to conduct operations under parts 121, 129, or 135.

§ 125.23

Each person operating an airplane in operations under part 125, shall comply with the applicable rules of part 91 while operating inside the United States.

§ 125.281

No person may serve as pilot in command unless that person holds at least a commercial pilot certificate, an appropriate category, class, and type rating, and an instrument rating. Required flight time is 1200 hours as a pilot, including 500 hours of cross-country flight time, 100 hours of night flight time, and 75 hours of actual or simulated instrument flight time, of which at least 50 hours were actual flight.

§ 125.283

No person may act as second in command unless that person holds at least a commercial pilot certificate with appropriate category and class ratings and an instrument rating.

§ 125.285

A required pilot crewmember must have three takeoffs and landings within the preceding 90 days in that type airplane or an approved visual simulator.

COMPUTER-BASED QUESTIONS

5106. Which of these operations could fall under the jurisdiction of FAR 125?

A. Operations in U.S.-registered civil airplanes having a seating capacity of more than 10 but less than 20 passenger seats.

B. Scheduled commercial operations (not an air carrier) using an airplane having a seating capacity of 20 or more passenger seats.

C. Nonscheduled commercial operations (not an air carrier) using an airplane having a maximum payload of 6000 pounds or more.

5106. "C" is the correct answer. FAR 125 applies to the operations of aircraft that seat 20 or more passengers or have a maximum payload capacity of 6000 pounds or more and are not being operated under FAR parts 121, 129, 135, or 137. "A" is incorrect because the seating capacity is too low. "B" is incorrect because scheduled operations are not conducted under FAR 125.

Reference FAR 125.1(a)

FAA subject matter knowledge code D30

5107. FAR 125 could apply to which of these operations?

A. Nonscheduled commercial operations (not an air carrier) using an airplane having a maximum payload of less than 6000 pounds.

B. Nonscheduled commercial operations (not an air carrier) using an airplane having a seating capacity of 20 or more passenger seats.

C. U.S.-registered civil airplanes operating outside the United States by persons who are not U.S. citizens.

5107. "B" is the correct answer. FAR 125 applies to the operations of aircraft that seat 20 or more passengers or have a maximum payload capacity of 6000 pounds or more and are not being operated under FAR parts 121, 129, 135, or 137. "A" is incorrect because FAR 125 applies to payloads in excess of

6000 pounds. "C" is incorrect because foreign operations are not allowed by FAR 125.

Reference FAR 125.3

FAA subject matter knowledge code D30, D37

5108. To obtain relief from any specified section of FAR 125, an operator holding a FAR 125 certificate should request

A. an "authorization waiver" from the FAA district office holding that certificate.

B. an appropriate waiver from the Administrator for Aviation Standards.

C. a "letter of deviation authority" from the nearest Flight Standards District Office.

5108. "C" is the correct answer. A request for deviation authority must be submitted to the nearest Flight Standards District Office. This deviation authority will be issued as a letter of deviation authority by the Administrator. "A" and "B" are incorrect because these requests are not addressed by FAR 125.

Reference FAR 125.3

FAA subject matter knowledge code D30

5109. A FAR 125 certificate holder must display a true copy of the

A. FAR 125 "letter of deviation authority."

B. address of its principal operations base in each of its aircraft.

C. FAR 125 certificate in each of its aircraft.

5109. "C" is the correct answer. The certificate holder must display a true copy of the certificate in each of its aircraft.

Reference FAR 125.7

FAA subject matter knowledge code D30

5110. No person is eligible for a certificate to operate under FAR 125 if that person

A. conducts pilot training under FAR 61.

B. conducts ferry flights under FAR 135.

C. "holds out" to the public to furnish transportation.

5110. "C" is the correct answer. No certificate holder may conduct any operation that results directly or indirectly from any person's holding out to the public to furnish transportation. *Holding out* means to advertise.

Reference FAR 125.11(b)

FAA subject matter knowledge code D30

5111. No person is eligible to operate under FAR 125 if that person already holds an appropriate operating certificate under

A. FAR 103.

B. FAR 121 or FAR 135.

C. FAR 141.

5111. "B" is the correct answer. No person is eligible for a certificate or operations specifications under this part if the person holds the appropriate operating certificate and/or operations specifications necessary to conduct operations under FAR parts 121, 129, or 135. "A" is incorrect because FAR 103 prescribes rules governing the operation of ultralight vehicles. "C" is incorrect because it pertains to pilot schools.

Reference FAR 125.11(a)

FAA subject matter knowledge code D30

5112. Each person operating an airplane inside the United States under FAR 125 shall also operate under

A. FAR 91.

B. FAR 121.

C. FAR 135.

5112. "A" is the correct answer. Each person operating an airplane in operations under part 125, shall comply with the applicable rules of part 91 while operating inside the United States.

Reference FAR 125.23

FAA subject matter knowledge code B07

5113. No person may serve as pilot in command of an airplane under FAR 125 operations unless that person

A. holds at least an airline transport pilot certificate and a type rating for the airplane to be flown.

B. holds at least a commercial pilot certificate, an appropriate category, class, and type rating, and an instrument rating.

C. has logged at least 700 hours of flight time as pilot, including 100 hours of night flight time.

5113. "B" is the correct answer. No person may serve as pilot in command unless that person holds at least a commercial pilot certificate, an appropriate category, class (A through D), and type rating, and an instrument rating.

Reference FAR 125.781

FAA subject matter knowledge code D38

5114. To act as second in command under a FAR 125 operation, a person is required to hold at least a

A. U.S. commercial pilot certificate or commercial pilot certificate issued on the basis of a valid foreign senior commercial pilot license.

B. commercial pilot certificate with appropriate category, class, and instrument rating.

C. commercial pilot certificate with appropriate category and class.

5114. "B" is the correct answer. No person may act as second in command unless that person holds at least a commercial pilot certificate with appropriate category A through D class ratings and an instrument rating.

Reference FAR 125.283

FAA subject matter knowledge code D38

5115. Select the pilot action listed below that meets the recent experience requirement for a person to serve as pilot in command of an airplane for a FAR 125 operation.

A. Passed a written test within the preceding 6 calendar months covering FAR parts 61, 91, and 135, and the operations specifications and manual of the certificate holder.

B. Completed three takeoffs and three landings within the preceding 90 days in an approved visual simulator.

C. Passed a written equipment test, in at least one of the aircraft operated, within the preceding 6 calendar months.

5115. "B" is the correct answer. A pilot must have three takeoffs and landings within the preceding 90 days in that type airplane or an approved visual simulator.

Reference FAR 125.285

FAA subject matter knowledge code O38

7

FAR Part 135

STUDY GUIDE

FAR 135—Air Taxi Operators and Commercial Operators

§ 135.1 Applicability.

(a) Except as provided in paragraph (b) of the section, this part prescribes rules governing

(1) Air taxi operations conducted under the exemption authority of part 298 of this title;

(2) The transportation of mail by aircraft conducted under a postal service contract awarded under § 5402(c) of title 39, U.S.C.;

(3) The carriage in air commerce of persons or property for compensation or hire as a commercial operator (not an air carrier) in aircraft having a maximum seating capacity of less than 20 passengers or a maximum payload capacity of less than 6000 pounds, or the carriage in air commerce of persons or property in common carriage operations solely between points entirely within any state of the United States in aircraft having a maximum seating capacity of 30 seats or less or a maximum payload capacity of 7500 pounds or less.

(b) This part does not apply to

(1) Student instruction;

(2) Nonstop sightseeing flights that begin and end at the same airport and are conducted within a 25 statute mile radius of that airport;

(4) Aerial work operations, including;

(i) Crop dusting, seeding, spraying, and bird chasing;

(iii) Aerial photography or survey;

(vi) Powerline or pipeline patrol, or similar types of patrol approved by the Administrator.

(6) Nonstop flights conducted within a 25 statute mile radius of the airport of takeoff carrying persons for the purpose of intentional parachute jumps;

(7) Helicopter flights conducted within a 25 statute mile radius of the airport of takeoff if

(i) Not more than two passengers are carried in the helicopter in addition to the required flightcrew;

(ii) Each flight is made under VFR during the day;

(iv) The operator notifies the FAA Flight Standards District Office responsible for the geographic area concerned at least 72 hours before each flight and furnishes any essential information that the office requests;

(v) The number of flights does not exceed a total of six in any calendar year.

§ 135.21 Manual requirements.

Each certificate holder shall prepare and keep current a manual setting forth the certificate holder's procedures and policies acceptable to the Administrator.

(d) A copy of the manual, or appropriate portions of the manual, and ground operations personnel by the certificate holder and furnished to
    (1) its flight crewmembers.
    Each employee of the certificate holder to whom a manual or appropriate portions of it are furnished under paragraph (d)(1) of this section shall keep it up to date with the changes and additions furnished to them.

§ 135.23 Manual contents.

(e) Procedures for ensuring that the pilot in command knows that required airworthiness inspections have been made and that the aircraft has been approved for return to service in compliance with applicable maintenance requirements.

§ 135.33 Area limitations on operations.

(a) No person may operate an aircraft in a geographical area that is not specifically authorized by appropriate operations specifications issued under this part.
(b) No person may operate an aircraft in a foreign country unless that person is authorized to do so by that country.

§ 135.85 Carriage of persons without compliance with the passenger-carrying provisions of this part.

The following persons may be carried aboard an aircraft without complying with the passenger-carrying requirements of this part:
    A person necessary for the safe handling of animals on the aircraft.

§ 135.87 Carriage of cargo including carry-on baggage.

No person may carry cargo, including carry-on baggage in or on any aircraft unless
    (1) For cargo, it is properly secured by a safety belt or other tie-down having enough strength to eliminate the possibility of shifting under all normally anticipated flight and ground conditions, or for carry-on baggage, it is restrained so as to prevent its movement during air turbulence.

§ 135.89 Pilot requirements: Use of oxygen.

(a) Unpressurized aircraft. Each pilot of an unpressurized aircraft shall use oxygen continuously when flying
    (1) At altitudes above 10,000 ft through 12,000 ft msl for that part of the flight at those altitudes that is of more than 30 minutes duration, and
    (2) Above 12,000 ft msl.

§ 135.93 Autopilot: Minimum altitudes for use.

(a) Except as provided in paragraphs (b), (c), and (d) of this section, no person may use an autopilot at an altitude above the terrain which is less than 500 ft or less than twice the maximum altitude loss specified in the approved Aircraft Flight Manual or equivalent for a malfunction of the autopilot, whichever is higher.

§ 135.105 Exception to second-in-command requirement: Approval for use of autopilot system.

No certificate holder may use any person, nor may any person serve, as a pilot in command under this section of an aircraft operated by a commuter air

SOMERSET COUNTY LIBRARY
6022 GLADES PIKE, SUITE 120
SOMERSET, PA 15501-4300
(814) 445-5907

carrier in passenger-carrying operations unless that person has at least 100 hours pilot-in-command flight time in the make and model of aircraft to be flown and has met all other applicable requirements of this part.

§ 135.107 Flight attendant crewmember requirement.

No certificate holder may operate an aircraft that has a passenger seating configuration, excluding any pilot seat, of more than 19 unless there is a flight attendant crewmember on board the aircraft.

§ 135.117 Briefing of passengers before flight.

(a) Before each takeoff each pilot in command of an aircraft carrying passengers shall ensure that all passengers have been orally briefed on
(1) Smoking;
(2) Use of seat belts;
(3) The placement of seat backs in an upright position before takeoff and landing;
(4) Location and means for opening the passenger entry door and emergency exits;
(5) Location of survival equipment;
(6) If the flight involves extended overwater operation, ditching procedures and the use of required flotation equipment;
(7) If the flight involves operations above 12,000 ft msl, the normal and emergency use of oxygen; and
(8) Location and operation of fire extinguishers.

(c) The oral briefing required by paragraph (a) of this section shall be given by the pilot in command or a crewmember.

(e) The oral briefing required by paragraph (a) shall be supplemented by printed cards which must be carried in the aircraft in locations convenient for the use of each passenger. The cards must
(1) Be appropriate for the aircraft on which they are to be used;
(2) Contain a diagram of, and method of operating, the emergency exits; and
(3) Contain other instructions necessary for the use of emergency equipment on board the aircraft.

Aircraft and Equipment

§ 135.149 Equipment requirements: General.

No person may operate an aircraft unless it is equipped with

(c) For turbojet airplanes, in addition to two gyroscopic bank-and-pitch indicators (artificial horizons) for use at the pilot stations, a third indicator that is installed in accordance with the instrument requirements prescribed in § 121.305(j) of this chapter.

§ 135.171 Shoulder harness installation at flight crewmember stations.

No person may operate a turbojet aircraft or an aircraft having a passenger seating configuration, excluding any pilot seat, of 10 seats or more unless it is equipped with an approved shoulder harness installed for each flight crewmember station.

§ 135.181 Performance requirements: Aircraft operated over-the-top or in IFR conditions.

(d) A person may operate an aircraft over-the-top under conditions allowing
(2) For single-engine aircraft, descent under VFR if its engine fails.

§ 135.183 Performance requirements: Land aircraft operated over water.

No person may operate a land aircraft carrying passengers over water unless

(a) It is operated at an altitude that allows it to reach land in the case of engine failure.

(d) It is a helicopter equipped with helicopter flotation devices.

VFR/IFR Operating Limitations and Weather Requirements

§ 135.203 VFR: Minimum altitudes.

Except when necessary for takeoff and landing, no person may operate under VFR

(a) An airplane
   (1) During the day, below 500 ft above the surface or less than 500 ft horizontally from any obstacle, or
   (2) At night, at an altitude less than 1000 ft above the highest obstacle within a horizontal distance of 5 miles from the course intended to be flown or, in designated mountainous terrain, less than 2000 ft above the highest obstacle within a horizontal distance of 5 miles from the course intended to be flown.

(b) A helicopter over a congested area at an altitude less than 300 ft above the surface.

§ 135.205 VFR: Visibility requirements.

No person may operate an airplane under VFR in uncontrolled airspace when the ceiling is less than 1000 ft unless flight visibility is at least 2 miles.

(b) No person may operate a helicopter under VFR in Class G airspace at an altitude of 1200 ft or less above the surface or within the lateral boundaries of the surface areas of Class B, Class C, Class D, or Class E airspace designated for an airport unless the visibility is at least
   (1) During the day—½ mile; or
   (2) At night—1 mile.

§ 135.211 VFR: Over-the-top carrying passengers: Operating limitations.

No person may operate an aircraft under VFR over-the-top carrying passengers, unless

(b) It is operated under conditions allowing
   (1) For multiengine aircraft, descent or continuation of the flight under VFR if its critical engine fails; or
   (2) For single-engine aircraft, descent under VFR if its engine fails.

Flight Crewmember Requirements

§ 135.243 Pilot-in-command qualifications.

No certificate holder may use a person, nor may any person serve, as pilot in command of an aircraft under IFR unless that person
   (1) Holds at least a commercial pilot certificate with appropriate category and class ratings and, if required, an appropriate type rating for that aircraft; and
   (2) Has had at least 1200 hours of flight time as a pilot, including 500 hours of cross-country flight time, 100 hours of night flight time, and 75 hours of actual or simulated instrument time at least 50 hours of which were in actual flight; and
   (3) For an airplane, holds an instrument rating or an airline transport pilot certificate with an airplane category rating.
   (4) For helicopter operations conducted VFR over-the-top, holds a helicopter instrument rating, or an airline transport pilot certificate with a category and class rating for that aircraft, not limited to VFR.

COMPUTER-BASED QUESTIONS

5116. FAR 135 applies to which operation?

A. Aerial work including crop dusting and spraying.

B. Carrying weekend skiers for hire to another state.

C. Student instruction for hire at an approved school.

5116. "B" is the correct answer. FAR 135 applies to the carriage in air commerce of persons or property for compensation or hire as a commercial operator (not an air carrier) in aircraft having a maximum seating capacity of less than 20 persons or a maximum payload capacity of less than 6000 pounds. "A" is incorrect because crop dusting is not covered by FAR 135. "C" is incorrect because FAR 141 applies to approved flight schools.
Reference FAR 135.1
FAA subject matter knowledge code E01

5117. When operating an airplane with a maximum payload capacity of 7500 pounds or less as a scheduled commercial operator (not an air carrier) in common carriage solely between points within a state, the operation is governed by the provisions of

A. FAR 121.

B. FAR 133.

C. FAR 135.

5117. "C" is the correct answer. FAR 135 applies to the carriage in air commerce of persons or property for compensation or hire as a commercial operator (not an air carrier) in aircraft having a maximum seating capacity of less than 20 passengers or a maximum payload capacity of less than 6000 pounds, or the carriage in air commerce of persons or property in common carriage operations solely between points entirely within any state of the United States in aircraft having a maximum seating capacity of 30 seats or less or a maximum payload capacity of 7500 pounds or less.
Reference FAR 135.1(a)(3)
FAA subject matter knowledge code E01

5118. A helicopter is being operated for hire with two passengers aboard. If the flight remains within a 25 mile radius of the departure point, the operation could be conducted, with certain stipulations, under

A. FAR 91.

B. FAR 97.

C. FAR 135.

5118. "A" is the correct answer. FAR 135 does not apply to helicopter flights conducted within a 25 statute mile radius of the airport of takeoff, if not more than two passengers are carried and each flight is made under VFR during the day.
Reference FAR 135.1(b)(7)
FAA subject matter knowledge code E01

5119. May a helicopter be operated for hire with passengers aboard and not be subject to the rules of FAR 135?

A. Yes, by notifying the FAA 72 hours before each flight.

B. Yes, for sightseeing operations within 50 miles of the flight's origin.

C. No, all flights for hire must comply with FAR 135.

5119. "A" is the correct answer. The operator must notify the FAA Flight Standards District Office responsible for the geographic area concerned at least 72 hours before each flight and furnish any essential information that the office requests. The number of flights cannot exceed a total of six in any calendar year.
Reference FAR 135.1(b)(7)
FAA subject matter knowledge code E01

5120. FAR 135 applies to which operations?

A. Nonstop sightseeing flights that begin and end at the same airport and are conducted within a 25 statute mile radius of that airport.

B. Aerial operations for compensation, such as aerial photography, pipeline patrol, rescue, and crop dusting.

C. Commercial operations (not an air carrier) in an aircraft with less than 20 passenger seats and a maximum payload capacity of less than 6000 pounds.

5120. "C" is the correct answer. FAR 135 applies to the carriage in air commerce of persons or property for compensation or hire as a commercial operator (not an air carrier) in aircraft having a maximum seating capacity of less than 20 persons or a maximum payload capacity of less than 6000 pounds. "A" and "B" are incorrect because FAR 135 specifically exempts sightseeing flights and survey flights.
Reference FAR 135.1
FAA subject matter knowledge code E01

5121. Under FAR 135 operations, who is responsible for keeping copies of the ATCO manual up to date with approved changes or additions?

A. Supervising FAA district office and the certificate holder.

B. Each district office employee responsible for that manual.

C. Each employee of the certificate holder who is furnished a manual.

5121. "C" is the correct answer. Each employee of the certificate holder to whom a manual is furnished shall keep it up to date with the changes and additions furnished to them.
Reference FAR 135.21
FAA subject matter knowledge code E01

5122. For FAR 135 operations, which document(s) contain(s) procedures that explain how the pilot in command knows that the required return-to-service conditions have been met?

A. Daily flight log and operation specifications.

B. Certificated holder's manual.

C. Mechanical deviation summary guide.

5122. "B" is the correct answer. The certificated holder's manual must include procedures for ensuring that the pilot in command knows that required airworthiness inspections have been made and that the aircraft has been approved for return to service in compliance with applicable maintenance requirements.
Reference FAR 135.23
FAA subject matter knowledge code E01

5123. For FAR 135 operations, which document specifically authorizes a person to operate an aircraft in a particular geographic area?

A. Letter of authorization.

B. Operations specifications.

C. Air taxi operating certificate.

5123. "B" is the correct answer. No person may operate an aircraft in a geographical area that is not specifically authorized by appropriate operations specifications issued under this part (FAR 135).
Reference FAR 135.33(a)
FAA subject matter knowledge code E01

5124. An aircraft may be operated in a foreign country by a FAR 135 operator if authorized to do so by

A. that country.

B. the supervising district office.

C. the FAA International Field Office in that country.

5124. "A" is the correct answer. No person may operate an aircraft in a foreign country unless that person is authorized to do so by that country.
Reference FAR 135.33(b)
FAA subject matter knowledge code E01

5125. In accordance with FAR 135, what period of time is the minimum flightcrew required to use supplemental oxygen while cruising at 13,500 ft msl for 3 hours, 45 minutes in an unpressurized aircraft?

A. 1 hour, 30 minutes.

B. 2 hours, 30 minutes.

C. 3 hours, 45 minutes.

5125. "C" is the correct answer. Each pilot of an unpressurized aircraft shall use oxygen continuously when flying at altitudes above 10,000 ft msl through 12,000 ft msl for that part of the flight at those altitudes that is more than 30 minutes duration and above 12,000 ft msl.
Reference FAR 135.89(a)
FAA subject matter knowledge code E02

5126. Which person may be carried aboard an aircraft without complying with the passenger-carrying requirements of FAR 135?

A. A crewmember or employee of another certificate holder.

B. A member of the U.S. diplomatic corps on an official courier mission.

C. An individual who is necessary for the safe handling of animals on the aircraft.

5126. "C" is the correct answer. A person necessary for the safe handling of animals may be carried aboard an aircraft without complying with the passenger-carrying requirement of FAR 135.
Reference FAR 135.85(b)
FAA subject matter knowledge code E02

5127. For FAR 135 operations, what restrictions must be observed regarding the carrying of cargo in the passenger compartment?

A. Cargo must be carried directly above the seated occupants in overhead bins.

B. Cargo must be properly secured by a seatbelt or other approved tie-down.

C. Cargo must be separated from seated passengers by a partition capable of withstanding specified stresses.

5127. "B" is the correct answer. No person may carry cargo, including carry-on baggage, in or on any aircraft unless it is properly secured by a safety belt or other tie-down having enough strength to eliminate the possibility of shifting under all normally anticipated flight and ground conditions, or for carry-on baggage, it is restrained so as to prevent its movement during air turbulence.
Reference FAR 135.87(c)(1)
FAA subject matter knowledge code E02

5128. Under FAR 135, which is a requirement governing the carriage of carry-on baggage?

A. Carry-on baggage must be stowed ahead of all seated occupants.

B. All carry-on baggage must be restrained so that its movement is prevented during turbulence.

C. Any piece of carry-on baggage, regardless of size, must be properly secured by a seatbelt or tie-down device.

5128. "B" is the correct answer. No person may carry cargo, including carry-on baggage, in or on any aircraft unless it is properly secured by a safety belt or other tie-down having enough strength to eliminate the possibility of shifting under all normally anticipated flight and ground conditions, or for carry-on baggage, it is restrained so as to prevent its movement during air turbulence.
Reference FAR 135.87(c)(1)
FAA subject matter knowledge code E02

5129. In accordance with FAR 135, what period of time is the minimum flightcrew required to use supplemental oxygen while cruising at 12,500 ft msl for 1 hour, 50 minutes in an unpressurized aircraft?

A. 55 minutes.

B. 1 hour, 20 minutes.

C. 1 hour, 50 minutes.

5129. "C" is the correct answer. Each pilot of an unpressurized aircraft shall use oxygen continuously when flying at altitudes above 10,000 ft msl through 12,000 ft msl for that part of the flight at those altitudes that is more than 30 minutes duration and above 12,000 ft msl.
Reference FAR 135.89(a)
FAA subject matter knowledge code E02

5130. In accordance with FAR 135, what use of supplemental oxygen is required, if any, of a pilot when cruising at 12,500 ft msl in an unpressurized aircraft?

A. Supplemental oxygen is not required at that altitude.

B. Supplemental oxygen is to be used during the entire flight while at that altitude.

C. Supplemental oxygen is required for that portion of the flight that is more than 60 minutes in duration while at that altitude.

5130. "B" is the correct answer. Each pilot of an unpressurized aircraft shall use oxygen continuously when flying at altitudes above 10,000 ft msl through 12,000 ft msl for that part of the flight at those altitudes that is more than 30 minutes duration and above 12,000 ft msl.
Reference FAR 135.89(a)
FAA subject matter knowledge code E02

5131. For FAR 135 operations, the airplane flight manual specified a maximum altitude loss of 75 ft for malfunction of the autopilot under cruise conditions. What is the lowest altitude above the terrain the autopilot may be used during en route operations?

A. 500 ft.

B. 1000 ft.

C. 1500 ft.

5131. "A" is the correct answer. No person may use an autopilot at an altitude above the terrain that is less than 500 ft or less than twice the maximum loss specified in the approved Aircraft Flight Manual or equivalent for a malfunction of the autopilot, whichever is higher. In this question, twice the maximum loss specified would be 150 ft, so 500 ft would be the correct answer.
Reference FAR 135.93(a)
FAA subject matter knowledge code E02

5132. A commuter air carrier certificate holder plans to assign a pilot as pilot in command of an airplane to be used in passenger-carrying operations. Which experience requirement must that pilot meet if the airplane is to be flown with an autopilot and no second in command?

A. 150 hours as pilot in command in category and type.

B. 100 hours in category, class, and type.

C. 100 hours as pilot in command in make and model.

5132. "C" is the correct answer. No certificate holder may use any person, nor may any person serve as pilot in command of an aircraft operated by a commercial air carrier in passenger-carrying operations unless that person has at least 100 hours pilot-in-command flight time in the make and model of aircraft to be flown.

Reference FAR 135.105(a)

FAA subject matter knowledge code E02

5133. For FAR 135 operations, in which airplanes is a flight attendant crewmember required?

A. Any airplane being operated in commuter air carrier service with a gross weight in excess of 12,500 pounds, regardless of the seating capacity.

B. All turbine-engine-powered airplanes having a total seating capacity of 19 or more.

C. Any airplane having a passenger seating configuration, excluding any pilot seat, of 20 or more.

5133. "C" is the correct answer. No certificate holder may operate an aircraft that has a passenger seating configuration, excluding any pilot seat, of more than 19 unless there is a flight attendant crewmember on board the aircraft. "A" is incorrect because the regulation does not address aircraft weight. "B" is tempting because it has the correct number of seats, but the regulation makes no differentiation between turbine and non-turbine-powered aircraft.

Reference FAR 135.107

FAA subject matter knowledge code E02

5134. The oral preflight briefing required on FAR 135 passenger-carrying airplanes shall be

A. substituted by printed cards carried in locations convenient for use by each passenger in aircraft with nine seats or less.

B. conducted by the pilot in command or a crewmember and supplemented by printed cards for the use of each passenger.

C. presented in person by the pilot in command while another flight crewmember demonstrates the operation of emergency equipment.

5134. "B" is the correct answer. Before each takeoff, each pilot in command of an aircraft carrying passengers shall ensure that all passengers have been orally briefed. This oral briefing shall be supplemented by printed cards that must be carried in the aircraft in locations convenient for the use of each passenger.

Reference FAR 135.117(c)(e)

FAA subject matter knowledge code E02

5135. In which aircraft, operating under FAR 135, is a third gyroscopic pitch-and-bank indicator required?

A. All turbojet airplanes.

B. All transport category airplanes.

C. All airplanes where a pilot in command and second in command is required.

5135. "A" is the correct answer. No person may operate a turbojet aircraft unless a third gyroscopic bank-and-pitch indicator (artificial horizon) is installed for use by the pilots.

Reference FAR 135.149(c)

FAA subject matter knowledge code E03

5136. For which airplanes, under FAR 135 operations, must each flight crewmember station have a shoulder harness installed?

A. All airplanes operated in commuter air carrier service.

B. Any airplane being operated under FAR 135, regardless of weight and seating configuration.

C. All airplanes having a passenger seating configuration, excluding any pilot seat, of 10 seats or more.

5136. "C" is the correct answer. No person may operate a turbojet aircraft or an aircraft having a passenger seating configuration, excluding any pilot seat, of 10 seats or more unless it is equipped with an approved shoulder harness installed for each flight crewmember station.

Reference FAR 135.171(a)

FAA subject matter knowledge code E03

5137. While en route over water with passengers aboard, a helicopter is required by FAR 135 to

A. have a visibility of at least, during the day—½ mile; or at night—1 mile.

B. be operated at an altitude 1½ times the altitude needed to reach shore in the event of an engine failure.

C. be equipped with flotation devices.

5137. "C" is the correct answer. No person may operate a land helicopter carrying passengers over water unless it is equipped with flotation devices.

Reference FAR 135.183(d)

FAA subject matter knowledge code E03

5138. To operate an airplane over water with passengers aboard, except for takeoff and landing, what is the minimum altitude requirement (FAR 135)?

A. There is no minimum altitude if flotation devices are aboard.

B. There is no minimum altitude requirement under FAR 135.

C. An altitude that allows land to be reached in the event of an engine failure.

5138. "C" is the correct answer. No person may operate a land aircraft carrying passengers over water unless it is operating at an altitude that allows it to reach land in the case of engine failure.
Reference FAR 135.183(a)
FAA subject matter knowledge code E03

5139. A pilot is en route over designated mountainous terrain at night in an airplane under VFR. Under FAR 135, what is the minimum altitude requirement above the highest obstacle within 5 miles of the course to be flown?

A. 1000 ft.

B. 1500 ft.

C. 2000 ft.

5139. "C" is the correct answer. No person may operate any airplane under VFR at night in designated mountainous terrain less than 2000 ft above the highest obstacle within a horizontal distance of 5 miles from the course intended to be flown.
Reference FAR 135.203(a)(2)
FAA subject matter knowledge code E04

5140. A pilot is en route at night in an airplane under VFR. Under FAR 135, what is the minimum altitude requirement above the highest obstacle within 5 miles of the course to be flown?

A. 500 ft.

B. 1000 ft.

C. 1500 ft.

5140. "B" is the correct answer. No person may operate an airplane at night at an altitude less than 1000 ft above the highest obstacle within a horizontal distance of 5 miles from the course intended to be flown.
Reference FAR 135.203(a)(2)
FAA subject matter knowledge code E04

5141. Under FAR 135, except for takeoffs and landings, a helicopter operating under VFR over a congested area is required to be operated at least

A. 300 ft agl.

B. 500 ft agl.

C. 700 ft agl.

5141. "A" is the correct answer. No person may operate a helicopter under VFR over a congested area at an altitude less than 300 ft above the surface.
Reference FAR 135.203(b)
FAA subject matter knowledge code E04

5142. Except for takeoffs and landings, what is the minimum altitude requirement to operate an airplane under FAR 135 during day VFR?

A. 1500 ft agl.

B. 1000 ft agl.

C. 500 ft agl.

5142. "C" is the correct answer. No person may operate an airplane under VFR during the day below 500 ft above the surface or less than 500 ft horizontally from any obstacle.
Reference FAR 135.203(a)(1)
FAA subject matter knowledge code E04

5143. Except for takeoffs and landings, what is the minimum horizontal distance from any obstacle required for an airplane under FAR 135 during day VFR?

A. 1500 ft.

B. 1000 ft.

C. 500 ft.

5143. "C" is the correct answer. No person may operate an airplane under VFR during the day below 500 ft above the surface or less than 500 ft horizontally from any obstacle.
Reference FAR 135.203(a)(1)
FAA subject matter knowledge code E04

5144. What is the minimum visibility requirement for FAR 135 helicopter VFR operations in Class G airspace at less than 1200 ft agl?

A. Day—½ mile; night—1 mile.

B. Day—½ mile; night—½ mile.

C. Day—1 mile; night—1 mile.

5144. "A" is the correct answer. No person may operate a helicopter within Class G airspace at an altitude of 1200 ft or less above the surface unless the visibility is at least ½ mile during the day and 1 mile at night.
Reference FAR 135.205(b)
FAA subject matter knowledge code E04

5145. What is the minimum visibility requirement for FAR 135 helicopter VFR operations in Class D airspace?

A. Day—½ mile; night—½ mile.

B. Day—½ mile; night—1 mile.

C. Day—1 mile; night—1 mile.

5145. "B" is the correct answer. No person may operate a helicopter under VFR within Class D airspace unless the visibility is at least ½ mile during the day and 1 mile at night.
Reference FAR 135.205(b)
FAA subject matter knowledge code E04

5146. Under FAR 135, what is the minimum visibility requirement for airplane VFR operations in Class G airspace when the ceiling is less than 1000 ft?

A. Day—½ mile; night—1 mile.

B. Day—2 miles; night—3 miles.

C. Day—2 miles; night—2 miles.

5146. "C" is the correct answer. No person may operate an airplane under VFR in Class G airspace unless flight visibility is at least 2 miles. The rule is the same day or night, so "A" and "B" are incorrect.
Reference FAR 135.205
FAA subject matter knowledge code E04

5147. To operate a helicopter VFR over-the-top while carrying passengers, what operating limitations, in part, are required by FAR 135 operations?

A. Two appropriately rated pilots must be aboard; autopilot not authorized.

B. Weather conditions that allow descent under VFR in the event of an engine failure.

C. The helicopter must be certificated for IFR flight and the pilot in command must hold an airline transport pilot certificate.

5147. "B" is the correct answer. No person may operate an aircraft under VFR over-the-top carrying passengers unless it is operated under conditions allowing descent under VFR if its engine fails.
Reference FAR 135.211b
FAA subject matter knowledge code E04

5148. To operate an airplane VFR over-the-top while carrying passengers, what operating limitations, in part, are required by FAR 135 operations?

A. Two appropriately rated pilots must be aboard; autopilot not authorized.

B. Weather conditions that allow descent under VFR in the event of an engine failure.

C. Radar approach facilities must be in operation at the destination point 1 hour before to 1 hour after ETA.

5148. "B" is the correct answer. No person may operate an aircraft under VFR over-the-top carrying passengers unless it is operated under conditions allowing descent under VFR if its engine fails.
Reference FAR 135.211b
FAA subject matter knowledge code E04

5149. To conduct VFR over-the-top in a helicopter under FAR 135, the pilot in command is required to hold at least a(n)

A. helicopter instrument rating.

B. airline transport pilot certificate with helicopter rating.

C. helicopter instrument rating and a Class I medical certificate.

5149. "A" is the correct answer. For helicopter operations conducted VFR over-the-top the pilot in command must hold a helicopter instrument rating.
Reference FAR 135.243(a)(4)
FAA subject matter knowledge code E05

5150. To act as pilot in command during IFR operations under FAR 135, how many hours of previous instrument time in actual flight is required?

A. At least 50 hours.

B. At least 75 hours.

C. At least 100 hours.

5150. "A" is the correct answer. No person may serve as pilot in command of an aircraft under IFR unless that person has had at least 75 hours of actual or simulated instrument time, at least 50 hours of which were in actual flight.
Reference FAR 135.243(b)(2)
FAA subject matter knowledge code E05

8

Loads and Load Factors

STUDY GUIDE

An airplane is designed and certificated for a certain maximum weight during flight. This weight is referred to as the *maximum certificated gross weight*. It is important that the airplane be loaded within the specified weight limits before flight, because certain flight maneuvers impose an extra load on the airplane structure, which might, particularly if the airplane is overloaded, impose stresses that will exceed the design capabilities of the airplane. Overstressing the airplane can also occur if the pilot engages in maneuvers creating high loads, regardless of how the airplane is loaded. During flight the wings of an airplane support the maximum allowable gross weight of the airplane.

A change in speed during straight flight does not produce any appreciable change in load, but when a change is made in the airplane's flight path, an additional load is imposed on the airplane structure. This is particularly true if a change in direction is made at high speeds with rapid forceful control movements.

According to certain laws of physics, a mass (the airplane in this case) will continue to move in a straight line unless some force intervenes, causing the mass (airplane) to assume a curved path. During the time the airplane is in a curved flight path, it still attempts, because of inertia, to force itself to follow straight flight. This tendency to follow straight flight, rather than curved flight, generates a force known as centrifugal force, which acts toward the outside of the curve.

Anytime the airplane is flying in a curved flight path with a positive load, the load the wings must support is equal to the weight of the airplane plus the load imposed by centrifugal force. A positive load occurs when back pressure is applied to the elevator, causing centrifugal force to act in the same direction as the force of the weight. A negative load occurs when forward pressure is applied to the elevator control, causing centrifugal force to act in a direction opposite to that of the force of the weight.

Curved flight producing a positive load is a result of increasing the angle of attack, and consequently, the lift. Increased lift always increases the position load imposed on the wings. However, the load is increased only at the time the angle of attack is being increased. Once the angle of attack is established, the load remains constant. The loads imposed on the wings in flight are stated in terms of load factor.

Load factor is the ratio of the total load supported by the airplane's wings to the actual weight of the airplane and its contents; that is, the actual load supported by the wings divided by the total weight of the airplane.

Load Factors and Airplane Design

To be certificated by the Federal Aviation Administration, the structural strength (load factor) of airplanes must conform with prescribed standards set forth by Federal Aviation Regulations.

All airplanes are designed to meet certain strength requirements depending on the intended use of the airplane. Classification of airplanes as to strength and operational use is known as the *category* system.

The category of each airplane can be readily identified by a placard or document (airworthiness certificate) in the cockpit that states the operational category or categories in which that airplane is certificated. The categories, maneuvers that are permitted, and maximum safe load factors (limit load factors) specified for these airplanes are as follows:

Category	Permissible maneuvers	Limit load factor
Normal	1. Any maneuver incident to normal flying.	3.8
	2. Stalls (except whip stalls).	
	3. Lazy eights, chandelles, and steep turns in which the angle of bank does not exceed 60°.	
Utility	1. All operations in the normal category.	4.4
	2. Spins (if approved for that airplane).	
	3. Lazy eights, chandelles, and steep turns in which the angle of bank is more than 60°.	
Acrobatic	No restrictions except those shown to be necessary as a result of required flight tests.	6.0

Effect of Turns on Load Factor

In a constant altitude coordinated turn, the load factor (resultant load) is the result of two forces: pull of gravity and centrifugal force. In any airplane at any airspeed, if a constant altitude is maintained during the turn, the load factor for a given degree of bank is the same, and is the resultant of gravity and centrifugal force. For any given angle of bank, the rate of turn varies with the airspeed. If the angle of bank is held constant and the airspeed is increased, the rate of turn decreases; or if the airspeed is decreased, the rate of turn increases. Because of this, there is no change in centrifugal force for any given bank. Therefore, the load factor remains the same.

The load factor increases at a rapid rate after the angle of bank reaches 50°. The wing must produce lift equal to this load factor if altitude is to be maintained.

It should also be noted how rapidly load factor increases as the angle of bank approaches 90°. The 90° banked, constant altitude turn is not mathematically possible. An airplane can be banked to 90°, but a continued coordinated turn is impossible at this bank angle without losing altitude.

The approximate maximum bank for conventional light airplanes is 60°, which produces a load factor of 2.

Effect of Load Factor on Stalling Speed

Any airplane can be stalled at any airspeed. At a given airspeed the load factor increases as angle of attack increases, and the wing stalls because the angle of attack has been increased to a certain angle. There is a direct relationship between the load factor imposed on the wing and its stalling characteristics.

A rule for determining the speed at which a wing will stall is that the stalling speed increases in proportion to the square root of the load factor. To further explain, the load factor produced in a 75° banked turn is 4. Applying the rule, the square root of 4 is 2. This means that an airplane with a normal unaccelerated stalling speed of 50 knots can be stalled at twice that speed or 100 knots by inducing a load factor of 4. Since the load factor squares as the stalling speed doubles, tremendous loads may be imposed on structures by stalling an airplane at relatively high airspeeds.

The maximum speed at which an airplane can be safely stalled is the *design maneuvering speed*. The design maneuvering speed is a valuable reference point for the pilot. When operating below this speed a damaging positive flight load should not be produced because the airplane should stall before the load becomes excessive. Any combination of flight control usage, including full deflection of the controls or gust loads created by turbulence, should not create an excessive air load if the airplane is operated below maneuvering speed. A rule of thumb that can be used to determine the maneuvering speed is approximately 1.7 times the normal stalling speed.

Turbulence should not create an excessive air load if the airplane is operated below maneuvering speed.

Effect of Turbulence on Load Factor

Turbulence in the form of vertical air currents can, under certain conditions, cause severe load stress on an airplane wing. When an airplane is flying at a high speed with a low angle of attack, and suddenly encounters a vertical current of air moving upward, the relative wind changes to an upward direction as it meets the airfoil. This increases the angle of attack of the wing.

If the air current is well defined and travels at a significant rate of speed upward, a sharp vertical gust is produced that has the same effect on the wing as applying sudden sharp back pressure on the elevator control.

Load Factors in Airplane Design

Airplanes designed under the category system are readily identified by a placard in the cockpit that states the operational categories in which the airplane is certificated. The maximum safe load factors (limit load factors) specified for airplanes in the various categories are as follows:

Category	Limit	Load
Normal	3.8	−1.52
Utility (mild acrobatics including spins)	4.4	−1.76
Acrobatic	6.0	−3.0

A safety factor of 50 percent has been added to these limit load factors.

Load Factors in Steep Turns

For any given bank angle, the rate of turn varies with the airspeed; the higher the speed, the slower the rate of turn. This compensates for added centrifugal force, allowing the load factor to remain the same.

Drag

All parts of the airplane that are exposed to the air contribute to the drag, though only the wings provide lift of any significance. For this reason, and certain others related to it, the total drag may be divided into two parts: the wing drag (induced) and the drag of everything but the wings (parasite).

Parasite drag is the sum of pressure and friction drag that is due to the airplane's basic configuration and, as defined, is independent of lift. Induced drag is the undesirable but unavoidable consequence of the development of lift.

While the parasite drag predominates at high speed, induced drag predominates at low speed. For example, if an airplane in a steady flight condition at 100 knots is then accelerated to 200 knots, the parasite drag becomes four times as great, but the power required to overcome that drag is eight times the original value. Conversely, when the airplane is operated in steady flight at twice as great a speed, the induced drag is one-fourth the original value and the power required to overcome that drag is only one-half the original value.

COMPUTER-BASED QUESTIONS

5151. The ratio between the total airload imposed on the wing and the gross weight of an aircraft in flight is known as

A. the load factor, and directly affects stall speed.

B. the aspect load, and directly affects stall speed.

C. the load factor, and has no relation with stall speed.

5151. "A" is the correct answer. Load factor is the ratio of the total load supported by the airplane's wing to the actual weight of the airplane. There is a direct relationship between the load factor imposed on the wing and its stalling characteristics.
Reference Pilot's Handbook of Aeronautical Knowledge (PHOAK), p. 23
FAA subject matter knowledge code H01, H66

5152. Load factor is the lift generated by the wings of an aircraft at any given time

A. divided by the total weight of the aircraft.

B. multiplied by the total weight of the aircraft.

C. divided by the basic empty weight of the aircraft.

5152. "A" is the correct answer. Load factor is the actual load supported by the wings divided by the total weight of the airplane.
Reference PHOAK, p. 23
FAA subject matter knowledge code H01, H66

5153. For a given angle of bank in any airplane, the load factor imposed in a coordinated constant-altitude turn

A. is constant and the stall speed increases.

B. varies with the rate of turn.

C. is constant and the stall speed decreases.

5153. "A" is the correct answer. In an airplane at any airspeed, if a constant altitude is maintained during the turn, the load factor for a given degree of bank is the same, which is the resultant of gravity and centrifugal force. The load supported by the wings increases as the angle of bank increases. The stalling speed increases in proportion to the square root of the load factor.
Reference PHOAK, p. 24
FAA subject matter knowledge code H01, H66

5154. Airplane wing loading during a level coordinated turn in smooth air depends on the

A. rate of turn.

B. angle of bank.

C. true airspeed.

5154. "B" is the correct answer. For any given angle of bank the rate of turn varies with the airspeed. If the angle of bank is held constant and the airspeed is increased, the rate of turn decreases. If the airspeed is decreased, the rate of turn increases. Because of this, there is no change in centrifugal force for any given bank; therefore, the load factor remains the same.
Reference PHOAK, p. 23
FAA subject matter knowledge code H01, H66

5155. In a rapid recovery from a dive, the effects of load factor would cause the stall speed to

A. increase.

B. decrease.

C. not vary.

5155. "A" is the correct answer. A rapid recovery from a dive increases the load factor on the aircraft. Stall speed increases in proportion to the square root of the load factor.
Reference Flight Training Handbook, p. 296
FAA subject matter knowledge code H01, H66

5156. If an aircraft with a gross weight of 2000 pounds was subjected to a 60° constant altitude bank, the total load would be

A. 3000 pounds.

B. 4000 pounds.

C. 12,000 pounds.

5156. "B" is the correct answer. The load factor increases at a rapid rate after the angle of bank reaches 50°. At 60° of bank, the load factor is 2 Gs: 2000 × 2 = 4000 pounds.

Reference PHOAK, p. 25

FAA subject matter knowledge code H01, H66

5157. While maintaining a constant angle of bank and altitude in a coordinated turn, an increase in airspeed

A. decreases the rate of turn resulting in a decreased load factor.

B. decreases the rate of turn resulting in no change in load factor.

C. increases the rate of turn resulting in no change in load factor.

5157. "B" is the correct answer. If the angle of bank is held constant and the airspeed is increased, the rate of turn decreases. Because of this, there is no change in centrifugal force for any given bank. Therefore, the load factor remains the same.

Reference PHOAK, p. 24

FAA subject matter knowledge code H01

5159. While holding the angle of bank constant, if the rate of turn is varied the load factor would

A. remain constant regardless of air density and the resultant lift vector.

B. vary depending on speed and air density provided the resultant lift vector varies proportionately.

C. vary depending on the resultant lift vector.

5159. "A" is the correct answer. If the angle of bank is held constant and the airspeed is increased, the rate of turn decreases. Because of this, there is no change in centrifugal force for any given bank. Therefore, the load factor remains the same. Load factor changes with the angle of bank and is not influenced by air density or the resultant lift vector.

Reference PHOAK, p. 24

FAA subject matter knowledge code H01, H66

5161. In theory, if the airspeed of an airplane is doubled while in level flight, parasite drag becomes

A. twice as great.

B. half as great.

C. four times greater.

5161. "C" is the correct answer. Parasite drag varies proportionately to the square of the airspeed. If the airspeed of an airplane is doubled, the parasite drag quadruples.

Reference Flight Training Handbook, p. 306

FAA subject matter knowledge code H66

5162. As airspeed decreases in level flight below that speed for the maximum lift/drag ratio, total drag of an airplane

A. decreases because of lower parasite drag.

B. increases because of increased induced drag.

C. increases because of increased parasite drag.

5162. "B" is the correct answer. Induced drag changes with speed because of the changes in angle of attack. As the airplane slows to a speed below maximum lift/drag, the wing is inclined to the relative wind at a greater angle and this increases induced drag.

Reference Flight Training Handbook, p. 306

FAA subject matter knowledge code H66

5163. If the airspeed is increased from 90 knots to 135 knots during a level 60° banked turn, the load factor

A. increases, as well as the stall speed.

B. decreases, and the stall speed will increase.

C. remains the same, but the radius of turn increases.

5163. "C" is the correct answer. For any given bank angle, the rate of turn varies with the airspeed; the higher the speed, the slower the rate of turn. This compensates for added centrifugal force, allowing the load factor to remain the same.

Reference Flight Training Handbook, p. 295

FAA subject matter knowledge code H66

5164. Baggage weighing 90 pounds is placed in a normal category airplane's baggage compartment, which is placarded at 100 pounds. If this airplane is subjected to a positive load factor of 3.5 Gs, the total load of the baggage would be

A. 315 pounds and would be excessive.

B. 315 pounds and would not be excessive.

C. 350 pounds and would not be excessive.

5164. "B" is the correct answer. Normal category aircraft are certified for a maximum load limit of 3.8 positive Gs and 1.52 negative Gs. Take the 3.5 Gs and

multiply them by the 90 pounds. That equals 315 pounds, which is within limits.
Reference Flight Training Handbook, p. 285
FAA subject matter knowledge code H66

5165. Refer to Fig. 1. At the airspeed represented by point A, in steady flight, the airplane

A. has its maximum L/D ratio.

B. has its minimum L/D ratio.

C. is developing its maximum coefficient of lift.

5165. "A" is the correct answer. At point A in Fig. 1, the total drag curve is at its lowest point. This is the point where the aircraft is operating at the best lift/drag ratio or L/D_{max}.
Reference Flight Training Handbook, p. 269
FAA subject matter knowledge code H66

5166. At an airspeed represented by point B in Fig. 1, in steady flight the pilot can expect to obtain the airplane's maximum

A. endurance.

B. glide range.

C. coefficient of lift.

5166. "B" is the correct answer. Point B represents the airspeed that results in the maximum ratio of lift to drag. This point provides the maximum glide range and the best power-off glide speed.
Reference Flight Training Handbook, p. 269
FAA subject matter knowledge code H66

5604. Why should flight speeds above V_{NE} be avoided?

A. Excessive induced drag results in structural failure.

B. Design limit load factors might be exceeded if gusts are encountered.

C. Control effectiveness is so impaired that the aircraft becomes uncontrollable.

5604. "B" is the correct answer. Flight speeds above V_{NE} should be avoided because design limit load factors may be exceeded if gusts are encountered.
Reference Flight Training Handbook, pp. 299–300
FAA subject matter knowledge code H66

5605. Maximum structural cruising speed is the maximum speed at which an airplane can be operated during

A. abrupt maneuvers.

B. normal operations.

C. flight in smooth air.

5605. "B" is the correct answer. Maximum structural cruising speed is the maximum speed at which an airplane can be operated during normal operations.
Reference PHOAK, p. 65
FAA subject matter knowledge code H03

5741. Which is the best technique for minimizing the wing load factor when flying in severe turbulence?

A. Change power settings, as necessary, to maintain constant airspeed.

B. Control airspeed with power, maintain wings level, and accept variations of altitude.

C. Set power and trim to obtain an airspeed at or below maneuvering speed, maintain wings level, and accept variations of airspeed and altitude.

5741. "C" is the correct answer. When flying in severe turbulence remember to maintain constant attitude; let the aircraft "ride the waves." Trying to maintain a constant altitude increases stress on the aircraft. Don't change power settings; maintain settings for the recommended turbulence penetration airspeed.
Reference Aeronautical Information Manual, paragraph 7–26
FAA subject knowledge code J25

9

Weight and Balance

STUDY GUIDE

During your oral exam, the examiner is going to ask you to perform a weight and balance problem. This is fairly straightforward, but I have observed a few students attempting to use the sample problem weight and balance numbers from the pilot's operating handbook to calculate the actual weight and balance. These numbers are SAMPLES ONLY! The actual airplane weight is NOT listed. Even if someone has penciled a number beside the sample, do not use it!! The actual weight of the airplane can only be found in the weight and balance paperwork for that particular airplane. Match up the "N" number and the serial number before proceeding with the assigned problem. I recommend that you use the sample form to help you calculate your problem, but only after you get the most current weights for your airplane. Remember, most training airplanes are getting old and have had radios and other equipment replaced or deleted. Each time that happens a new weight and balance form is completed. The old form will have "superseded" written on it. Use the most current form.

Weight and balance control should be a matter of concern to all pilots. The airplane owner or operator should make certain that up-to-date information is available in the airplane for the pilot's use, and should ensure that appropriate entries are made in the airplane records when repairs or modifications have been accomplished. Weight changes must be accounted for and proper notations made in weight and balance records. Without such information the pilot has no foundation on which to base the necessary calculations and decisions.

Terms and Definitions

The pilot needs to be familiar with the terms used in working the problems related to weight and balance.

- *Arm* (moment arm) is the horizontal distance in inches from the reference datum line to the center of gravity of an item. The algebraic sign is plus (+) if measured aft of the datum and minus (–) if measured forward of the datum.

- *Center of gravity* (CG) is the point about which an airplane would balance if it were possible to suspend it at that point. It is the mass center of the airplane, or the theoretical point at which the entire weight of the airplane is assumed to be concentrated. It is expressed in percent of MAC (mean aerodynamic chord) or in inches from the reference datum.

- *Center of gravity limits* are the specified forward and aft points within which the CG range must be located during flight. These limits are indicated on pertinent airplane specifications.

- *Center of gravity range* is the distance between the forward and aft CG limits indicated on pertinent airplane specifications.

- *Datum* (reference datum) is an imaginary vertical plane or line from which all measurements of arm are taken. The datum is established by the manufacturer. Once the datum has been selected, all moment arms and the location of the CG are measured from this point.

- *Delta*, expressed by the symbol Δ, indicates a change of values. As an example, Δ CG indicates a change (or movement) of the CG.

- *Moment* is the product of the weight of an item multiplied by its arm. Moments are expressed in pound-inches (lb-in.). Total moment is the weight of the airplane multiplied by the distance between the datum and the CG.

- *Moment index* (index) is a moment divided by a constant such as 100, 1000, or 10,000. The purpose of using a moment index is to simplify weight and balance computations of airplanes where heavy items and long arms result in large, unmanageable numbers.

- *Mean aerodynamic chord* (MAC) is the average distance from the leading edge to the trailing edge of the wing.

- *Standard weights* have been established for numerous items involved in weight and balance computations, such as gasoline = 6 lb/U.S. gal, and oil = 7.5 lb/U.S. gal.

- *Useful load* is the weight of the pilot, copilot, passengers, baggage, usable fuel, and drainable oil. It is the empty weight subtracted from the maximum allowable gross weight.

- *Empty weight* consists of the airframe, engines, and all items of operating equipment that have fixed locations and are permanently installed in the airplane. It includes optional and special equipment, fixed ballast, hydraulic fluid, unusable (residual) fuel, and undrainable (residual) oil.

Basic Principles of Weight and Balance Computations

The following method of computation can be applied to any object or vehicle where weight and balance information is essential. By determining the weight of the empty airplane and adding the weight of everything loaded on the airplane, a total weight can be determined.

The point where the airplane will balance can be determined by locating the CG. A safe zone within which the balance point (CG) must fall is called the CG range. The extremities of the range are called the forward CG limits and aft CG limits.

The distance from the datum to any component part of the airplane, or any object loaded on the airplane, is called the arm. When the object or component is located aft of the datum it is measured in positive inches; if it is located forward of the datum it is measured in negative inches (minus inches).

Important Formulas to Remember

$$\text{Weight} \times \text{Arm} = \text{Moment}$$

$$\text{CG} = \frac{\text{Total moments}}{\text{Total weight}}$$

Change of Weight

In many instances the pilot must be able to solve problems that involve the shifting, addition, or removal of weight. The most satisfactory solution to this problem is to relocate baggage, or passengers, or both. There are some standardized and simple calculations that can help make these determinations.

Weight Shifting

When weight is shifted from one location to another, the total weight of the airplane does not change. The total moments, however, do change in relation and proportion to the direction and distance the weight is moved. When weight is moved forward, total moments decrease; when weight is moved aft, total moments increase. If the airplane weight, CG, and total moments are known, the new CG (after the weight shift) can be determined by dividing the new total moments by the total airplane weight.

To determine the new total moments, find out how many moments are gained or lost when the weight is shifted. By adding the moment change to the original moment (or subtracting if the weight has been moved forward instead of aft), the new total moments can be determined. The new CG can then be determined by dividing the new moments by the total weight.

A simple solution may be obtained by using a computer or electronic calculator. This can be done because the CG shifts a distance that is proportional to the distance the weight has shifted.

Example: (Note $\Delta =$ change)

$$\text{Weight to be shifted} = \frac{\text{Total weight} \times \Delta CG}{\text{distance weight is shifted}}$$

Weight Addition or Removal

In many instances the weight and balance of the airplane change when weight is added or removed. A new CG must be calculated and checked against the limitations to determine if the new CG is within limits. First, determine the weight and balance with all items loaded except fuel. Second, determine the weight and balance, including the fuel. These calculations provide an indication of how fuel consumption affects balance.

The addition or removal of cargo causes a CG change, which should be calculated before flight. These problems can be solved by calculations involving total moments. However, a shortcut formula that can be adapted to the aeronautical computer can be used to simplify computations:

$$\text{Weight added (or removed)} = \frac{\Delta CG}{\text{Distance between weight and old CG}}$$

Example:

$$\text{Airplane total weight} = 6860 \text{ lb}$$

$$CG = -80.0 \text{ in. aft of datum}$$

What is the location of the CG if 140 pounds of baggage are added to station 150 (150 in. aft of datum)?

Solution:

1. Use the added weight formula:

$$\frac{\text{Added weight}}{\text{New total weight}} = \frac{\Delta CG}{\text{Distance between weight station and old CG}}$$

$$\frac{140 \text{ lb}}{6860 \text{ lb} + 140 \text{ in.}} = \frac{\Delta CG}{150 \text{ lb} + -80 \text{ in.}}$$

$$\frac{140}{7000} = \frac{\Delta CG}{70}$$

$$CG = 1.4 \text{ inches aft}$$

2. Add CG to the old CG

New CG = 80.0 in. + 1.4 in. = 81.4 in.

COMPUTER-BASED QUESTIONS

5632. When computing weight and balance, the empty weight includes the weight of the airframe, engines, and all items of operating equipment permanently installed. Empty weight also includes

A. the unusable fuel, hydraulic fluid, and undrainable oil or, in some aircraft, all of the oil.

B. all usable fuel, maximum oil, hydraulic fluid, but does not include the weight of pilot, passenger, or baggage.

C. all usable fuel and oil, but does not include any radio equipment or instruments that were installed by someone other than the manufacturer.

5632. "A" is the correct answer. Empty weight consists of the airframe, engines, and all items of operating equipment that have fixed locations and are permanently installed in the airplane. It includes optional and special equipment, fixed ballast, hydraulic fluid, unusable (residual) fuel, and undrainable (residual) oil.

Reference PHOAK, p. 76
FAA subject matter knowledge code H04

5633. If all index units are positive when computing weight and balance, the location of the datum would be at the

A. centerline of the main wheels.

B. nose, or out in front of the airplane.

C. centerline of the nose or tailwheel, depending on the type of airplane.

5633. "B" is the correct answer. The distance from the datum to any component part of the airplane, or any object loaded on the airplane, is called the arm. When the object or component is located aft of the datum it is measured in positive inches; if it is located forward of the datum it is measured in negative inches.

Reference PHOAK, p. 77
FAA subject matter knowledge code H04

5634. The CG of an aircraft can be determined by which of the following methods?

A. Dividing total arms by total moments.

B. Multiplying total arms by total weight.

C. Dividing total moments by total weight.

5634. "C" is the correct answer.

$$CG = \frac{\text{Total moments}}{\text{Total weight}}$$

Reference PHOAK, p. 78
FAA subject matter knowledge code H04

5635. The CG of an aircraft may be determined by

A. dividing total arms by total moments.

B. dividing total moments by total weight.

C. multiplying total weight by total moments.

5635. "B" is the correct answer.

$$CG = \frac{\text{Total moments}}{\text{Total weight}}$$

Reference PHOAK, p. 78
FAA subject matter knowledge code H04

5636. Given:

Weight A = 155 pounds at 45 inches aft of datum
Weight B = 165 pounds at 145 inches aft of datum
Weight C = 95 pounds at 185 inches aft of datum

Based on this information, where would the CG be located aft of datum?

A. 86.0 inches.

B. 116.8 inches.

C. 125.0 inches.

5636. "B" is the correct answer.

Remember: Weight × Arm = Moment, and

$$\frac{\text{Total moments}}{\text{Total weight}} = CG.$$

$$155 \times 45 = 6975$$

$$165 \times 145 = 23,925$$

$$95 \times 185 = 17,575$$

$$\frac{(6975 + 23{,}925 + 17{,}575)}{(155 + 165 + 95)} = \frac{48{,}475}{415} = 116.8 \text{ in.}$$

Reference PHOAK, p. 86
FAA subject matter knowledge code H04

5637. Given:

Weight A = 140 pounds at 17 inches aft of datum
Weight B = 120 pounds at 110 inches aft of datum
Weight C = 85 pounds at 210 inches aft of datum

Based on this information, the CG would be located how far aft of datum?

A. 89.11 inches.

B. 96.89 inches.

C. 106.92 inches.

5637. "B" is the correct answer.

Remember: Weight × Arm = Moment, and

$$\frac{\text{Total moments}}{\text{Total weight}} = \text{CG}.$$

$$140 \times 17 = 2380$$
$$120 \times 110 = 13{,}200$$
$$85 \times 210 = 17{,}850$$

$$\frac{(2380 + 13{,}200 + 17{,}850)}{(140 + 120 + 85)} = \frac{33{,}430}{345} = 96.89 \text{ in.}$$

Reference PHOAK, pp. 76–86
FAA subject matter knowledge code H04

5638. Given:

Weight A = 135 pounds at 15 inches aft of datum
Weight B = 205 pounds at 117 inches aft of datum
Weight C = 85 pounds at 195 inches aft of datum

Based on this information, the CG would be located how far aft of datum?

A. 100.2 inches.

B. 109.0 inches.

C. 121.7 inches.

5638. "A" is the correct answer.

Remember: Weight × Arm = Moment, and

$$\frac{\text{Total moments}}{\text{Weight}} = \text{CG}.$$

$$135 \times 15 = 2025$$
$$205 \times 117 = 23{,}985$$
$$85 \times 195 = 16{,}575$$

$$\frac{(2025 + 23{,}985 + 16{,}575)}{(135 + 205 + 85)} = \frac{42{,}585}{425} = 100.2 \text{ in.}$$

Reference PHOAK, pp. 76–86
FAA subject matter knowledge code H04

5639. Given:

Weight A = 175 pounds at 135 inches aft of datum
Weight B = 135 pounds at 115 inches aft of datum
Weight C = 75 pounds at 85 inches aft of datum

Based on this information, the CG would be located how far aft of datum?

A. 91.76 inches.

B. 111.67 inches.

C. 118.24 inches.

5639. "C" is the correct answer.

Remember: Weight × Arm = Moment, and

$$\frac{\text{Total moments}}{\text{Weight}} = \text{CG}.$$

$$175 \times 135 = 23{,}625$$
$$135 \times 115 = 15{,}525$$
$$75 \times 85 = 6375$$

$$\frac{(23{,}625 + 15{,}525 + 6375)}{(175 + 135 + 75)} = \frac{45{,}525}{385} = 118.24 \text{ in.}$$

Reference PHOAK, pp. 76–86
FAA subject matter knowledge code H04

5640. Refer to Fig. 36.

Given:

	Weight	Arm	Moment
Empty	610	96.47	?
Pilot (forward seat)	150	?	?
Passenger (aft seat)	180	?	?
Radio and batteries	10	23.2	?
Total	?	?	?

The CG is located at station

A. 33.20.

B. 59.55.

C. 83.26.

5640. "C" is the correct answer.

	Weight	Arm	Moment
Empty	610	96.47	58,846.7
Pilot (forward seat)	150	43.8	6570.0
Passenger (aft seat)	180	74.7	13,446.0
Radio and batteries	10	23.2	232.0
Total	950	238.17	79,094.7

Remember: $\dfrac{\text{Total moments}}{\text{Total weight}} = \text{CG}$

$$\dfrac{79094.7}{950} = 83.26$$

Reference PHOAK, pp. 76–86
FAA subject matter knowledge code N21

5641. Refer to Fig. 36.

Given:

	Weight	Arm	Moment
Empty	612	96.47	?
Pilot (forward seat)	170	?	?
Passenger (aft seat)	160	?	?
Radio and batteries	10	23.2	?
Ballast	20	14.75	?
Total	?	?	?

The CG is located at station

A. 81.24.

B. 82.63.

C. 83.26.

5641. "A" is the correct answer.

	Weight	Arm	Moment
Empty	612	96.47	59,039.6
Pilot (forward seat)	170	43.8	7446
Passenger (aft seat)	160	74.7	11,952
Radio and batteries	10	23.2	232
Ballast	20	14.74	294.8
Total	972	252.91	78,964.4

Remember: $\dfrac{\text{Total moments}}{\text{Total weight}} = \text{CG}$

$$\dfrac{78,964.4}{972} = 81.24$$

Reference PHOAK, pp. 76–86
FAA subject matter knowledge code H04

5642. Refer to Fig. 36.

Given:

	Weight	Arm	Moment
Empty	605	96.47	?
Pilot (forward seat)	120	?	?
Passenger (aft seat)	160	?	?
Radio and batteries	20	23.2	?
Ballast	40	14.75	?
Total	?	?	?

The CG is located at station

A. 79.77.

B. 80.32.

C. 81.09.

5642. "C" is the correct answer.

	Weight	Arm	Moment
Empty	605	96.47	58,364.4
Pilot (forward seat)	120	43.8	5256.0
Passenger (aft seat)	160	74.7	11,952.0
Radio and batteries	20	23.2	464.0
Ballast	40	14.75	590.0
Total	945	252.92	76,626.4

Remember: $\dfrac{\text{Total moments}}{\text{Total weight}} = \text{CG}$

$$\dfrac{76,626.4}{945} = 81.09$$

Reference PHOAK, pp. 76–86
FAA subject matter knowledge code H04

5643. Given:

	Weight	Arm	Moment
Empty	957	29.07	?
Pilot (forward seat)	140	−45.30	?
Passenger (aft seat)	170	+1.60	?
Ballast	15	−45.30	?
Total	?	?	?

The CG is located at station

A. −6.43.

B. +16.43.

C. +27.38.

5643. "B" is the correct answer.

Remember: Weight × Arm = Moment, and

$$\dfrac{\text{Total moments}}{\text{Total weight}} = \text{CG}$$

	Weight	Arm	Moment
Empty	957	29.07	27,819.9
Pilot (forward seat)	140	−45.30	−6342.0
Passenger (aft seat)	170	1.60	272.0
Ballast	15	−45.30	−679.5
Total	1282	−59.93	21,070.4

$$\frac{\text{Total moments}}{\text{Total weight}} = CG$$

$$\frac{21,070.4}{1282} = 16.43$$

Reference PHOAK, pp. 76–86

FAA subject matter knowledge code H04

5644. Refer to Fig. 37.

Given:

	Weight	Moment
Gyroplane (oil included)	1315	150.1
Pilot	140	?
Passenger	150	?
27 gal of fuel	162	?
Total	?	?

The CG is located

A. outside the CG envelope; the maximum gross weight is exceeded.

B. outside the CG envelope; the maximum gross weight and the gross weight moment are exceeded.

C. within the CG envelope; neither maximum gross weight nor gross weight moment is exceeded.

5644. "C" is the correct answer.

	Weight	Moment
Gyroplane (oil included)	1315	150.1
Pilot	140	7.2
Passenger	150	12.6
27 gal of fuel	162	17.8
Total	1767	187.7

These figures are within the CG envelope.

Reference PHOAK, pp. 76–86

FAA subject matter knowledge code H04

5645. Refer to Fig. 37.

Given:

	Weight	Moment
Gyroplane (oil included)	1315	154.0
Pilot	145	?
Passenger	153	?
27 gal of fuel	162	?
Total	?	?

The CG is located

A. outside the CG envelope; the maximum gross weight is exceeded.

B. outside the CG envelope; but the maximum gross weight is not exceeded.

C. within the CG envelope; neither maximum gross weight nor gross weight moment is exceeded.

5645. "B" is the correct answer.

	Weight	Moment
Gyroplane (oil included)	1315	154.0
Pilot	145	7.4
Passenger	153	12.8
27 gal of fuel	162	17.6
Total	1775	191.8

These figures are outside the CG envelope; but the maximum gross weight is not exceeded.

Reference PHOAK, p. 76–86

FAA subject matter knowledge code H04

5646. Given:

Total weight	4137 pounds
CG location station	67.8
Fuel consumption	13.7 gph
Fuel CG station	68.0

After 1 hour, 30 minutes of flight time, the CG would be located at station

A. 67.69.

B. 68.79.

C. 70.78.

5646. "A" is the correct answer.

Find the weight change:

$$12.7 \text{ gph} \times 1.5 \text{ hr} = 19.05 \text{ gal}$$

$$19.05 \text{ gal} \times 6.0 \text{ lb} = 114.3 \text{ lb}$$

New weight:

$$4137 \text{ lb} - 114.3 \text{ lb} = 4022.7 \text{ lb}$$

The CG change is $68.0 - 67.8 = 0.2$

Use the formula from the study guide:

$$\frac{114.3}{4022.7} = \frac{CG \text{ change}}{}$$

$$\begin{array}{r} 67.80000 \\ - .00568 \\ \hline 67.79432 \text{ New CG} \end{array}$$

Reference PHOAK, p. 83

FAA subject matter knowledge code H04

5647. An aircraft is loaded with a ramp weight of 3650 pounds and having a CG of 94.0, approximately how much baggage would have to be moved from the rear baggage area at station 180 to the forward baggage area at station 40 in order to move the CG to 92.0?

A. 52.14 pounds.

B. 62.24 pounds.

C. 78.14 pounds.

5647. "A" is the correct answer. Use the formula from the study guide:

$$\text{Weight to be shifted} = \frac{3650 \times 2.0}{140} = \frac{7300}{140} = 52.14 \text{ lb}$$

Reference PHOAK, p. 83

FAA subject matter knowledge code H04

5648. An airplane is loaded to a gross weight of 4800 pounds, with three pieces of luggage in the rear baggage compartment. The CG is located 98 inches aft of datum, which is 1 inch aft of limits. If luggage that weighs 90 pounds is moved from the rear baggage compartment (145 inches aft of datum) to the front compartment (45 inches aft of datum), what is the new CG?

A. 96.13 inches aft of datum.

B. 95.50 inches aft of datum.

C. 99.87 inches aft of datum.

5648. "A" is the correct answer.

$$\Delta CG = \frac{\text{Distance shifted} \times \text{weight shifted}}{\text{total weight}}$$

$$\Delta CG = (145 - 45) \times \left(\frac{90}{4800}\right)$$

$$\Delta CG = 1.875 \text{ inches}$$

If the weight moves forward, so does the CG: 98.0 – 1.875 = 96.13 in.

Reference PHOAK, p. 83

FAA subject matter knowledge code H04

5649. Given:

Total weight	3037 pounds
CG location station	68.8
Fuel consumption	12.7 gph
Fuel CG station	68.0

After 1 hour, 45 minutes of flight time, the CG would be located at station

A. 68.77.

B. 68.83.

C. 69.77.

5649. "B" is the correct answer. Use the same procedure as you did to answer question 5646.

Reference PHOAK, p. 83

FAA subject matter knowledge code H04

5650. Refer to Fig. 38.

Given:

Empty weight (oil included)	1271 pounds
Empty weight moment (in.-lb/1000)	102.04
Pilot and copilot	400 pounds
Rear seat passenger	140 pounds
Cargo	100 pounds
Fuel	37 gal

Is the airplane loaded within limits?

A. Yes, the weight and CG is within limits.

B. No, the weight exceeds the maximum allowable.

C. No, the weight is acceptable, but the CG is aft of the aft limit.

5650. "A" is the correct answer.

Step 1:

Item	Weight (lb)	Moment (lb-in./1000)
Empty	1271	102.04
Pilot and copilot	400	36.0
Aft passengers	140	18.0
Cargo	100	11.5
Fuel (37.0 gal)	222	20.0
Total	2133	187.54

Step 2:

Move vertically until you reach the loaded airplane scale of 2133. Then move horizontally to the 187.54 point. The weight and CG are within limits.

Reference PHOAK, p. 83

FAA subject matter knowledge code H04

5651. Refer to Fig. 38.

Given:

Empty weight (oil included)	1271 pounds
Empty weight moment (in.-lb/1000)	102.04
Pilot and copilot	260 pounds
Aft passengers	120 pounds
Cargo	60 pounds
Fuel	37 gal

Under these conditions, the CG is located

A. within the CG envelope.

B. on the forward limit of the CG envelope.

C. within the shaded area of the CG envelope.

5651. "A" is the correct answer.

Step 1:

Item	Weight (lb)	Moment (lb-in./1000)
Empty	1271	102.04
Pilot and copilot	260	23.3
Aft passenger	120	15.0
Cargo	60	6.8
Fuel (37.0 gal)	222	20.0
Total	1933	167.14

Step 2:

On the CG graph, move vertically until you reach the loaded airplane scale of 1933. Now move horizontally until you reach 167.14. The weight and CG are within limits.

Reference PHOAK, p. 85

FAA subject matter knowledge codes H04

5652. Refer to Fig. 38.

Given:

Empty weight (oil included)	1271 pounds
Empty weight moment (in.-lb/1000)	102.04
Pilot and copilot	360 pounds
Cargo	340 pounds
Fuel	37 gal

Will the CG remain within limits after 30 gallons of fuel have been used in flight?

A. Yes, the CG will remain within limits.

B. No, the CG will be located aft of the aft CG limit.

C. Yes, but the CG will be located in the shaded area of the CG envelope.

5652. "A" is the correct answer.

Step 1:

Item	Weight (lb)	Moment (lb-in./1000)
Empty	1271	102.04
Pilot and copilot	360	32.8
Cargo	340	39.5
Fuel (37.0 gal)	222	20.0
Total	2193	194.34

Step 2:

On the CG graph, move vertically until you reach the loaded aircraft weight of 2193. Now move across to 194.34. The CG is within limits.

Reference PHOAK, p. 82

FAA subject matter knowledge code H04

5677. Refer to Fig. 39.

Given:

	Weight	Arm (in.)	Moment (in.-lb)
Empty	1700	+6	+10,200
Pilot weight	200	−31	?
Oil (8 qt, all usable)	?	+1	?
Fuel (50 gal, all usable)	?	+2	?
Baggage	30	−31	?
Total	?	?	?

If the datum line is located at station O, the CG is located approximately

A. 1.64 inches aft of datum.

B. 1.64 inches forward of datum.

C. 1.66 inches forward of datum.

5677. "A" is the correct answer.

	Weight	Arm (in.)	Moment (in.-lb)
Empty	1700	6	10,200
Pilot	200	−31	−6200
Oil (8 qt, all usable)	15	1	15
Fuel (50 gal, all usable)	300	2	600
Baggage	30	−31	−930
Total	2245	−53	3685

Remember, $\dfrac{\text{Total moments}}{\text{Total weight}} = \text{CG}$.

$\dfrac{3685}{2245} = 1.64$ inches aft of datum.

Reference PHOAK, p. 82

FAA subject matter knowledge code H10

5678. Refer to Fig. 40.

Given:

Basic weight (oil included)	830 pounds
Basic weight moment (in.-lb/1000)	104.8
Pilot weight	175 pounds
Passenger weight	160 pounds
Fuel	19.2 gal

The CG is located

A. well aft of the aft CG limit.

B. within the CG envelope.

C. forward of the forward CG limit.

5678. "A" is the correct answer. Remember, Weight × Arm = Moment.

Item	Weight (lb)	Arm (in.)	Moment (in.lb/1000)
Aircraft	830	126 0	= 104.8
Pilot	175	79.0	= 13.8
Passenger	160	79.0	= 12.6
Fuel (19.2 gal × 6)	115.2	108.6	= 12.5
Total	1280.2		143.7

The values fall aft of the CG.
Reference PHOAK, p. 81
FAA subject matter knowledge code H04

5679. Given:

	WT	LNG. ARM	LNG. MOM	LAT. ARM	LAT. MOM
Empty weight	1700	116.1	?	+0.2	—
Fuel (75 gal at 6.8 ppg)	?	110.0	?	—	—
Oil	12	179.0	?	—	—
Pilot (right seat)	175	65.0	?	+12.5	?
Passenger (left seat)	195	104.0	?	–13.3	?
Totals	?	?	?	?	?

Determine the longitudinal and lateral CG respectively.

A. 109.35" and –0.04".

B. 110.43" and +0.02".

C. 110.83" and –0.02".

5679. "C" is the correct answer.

	LNG. WT	LNG. ARM	LNG. MOM	LAT. ARM	LAT. MOM	LAT. WT
Empty weight	1700	116.1	197,370	+0.2	+340	1700
Fuel (75 gal at 6.8 ppg)	510	110.0	56,100			
Oil	12	179.0	2148			
Pilot (right seat)	175	65.0	11,375	+12.5	+2188	175
Passenger (left seat)	195	104.0	20,280	–13.3	–2594	195
Totals	2592		287,273		–66	2070

Now, calculate the CG using the formula

$$CG = \frac{\text{Total moment}}{\text{Total weight}}$$

Longitudinal: $\frac{287,273}{2592} = 110.83$ inches

Lateral: $\frac{-66}{2070} = -0.03188$ inch

Reference PHOAK, p. 81
FAA subject matter knowledge code H04

5680. A helicopter is loaded in such a manner that the CG is located aft of the aft allowable CG limit. Which is true about this situation?

A. In case of an autorotation, sufficient aft cyclic control may not be available to flare properly.

B. This condition would become more hazardous as fuel is consumed, if the main fuel tank is located aft of the rotor mast.

C. If the helicopter should pitch up due to gusty winds during high-speed flight, there may not be sufficient forward cyclic control available to lower the nose.

5680. "C" is the correct answer. The pilot will recognize this condition after coming to a hover following a vertical takeoff. The helicopter will have a tail-low attitude, and an excessive forward displacement of the cyclic stick will be required to maintain a hover in a no-wind condition, if a hover can be maintained at all. If flight is continued in this condition, the pilot may find it impossible to fly in the upper allowable airspeed range due to insufficient forward cyclic displacement to maintain a nose-low attitude. This particular condition may become quite dangerous if gusty or rough air accelerates the helicopter to a higher airspeed than forward cyclic control will allow. The nose will start to rise and full forward cyclic stick may not be sufficient to hold it down or to lower it once it rises.
Reference Basic Helicopter Handbook, p. 44
FAA subject matter knowledge code H76

5681. A helicopter is loaded in such a manner that the CG is located forward of the allowable CG limit. Which is true about this situation?

A. This condition would become less hazardous as fuel is consumed if the fuel tank is located aft of the rotor mast.

B. In case of engine failure and the resulting autorotation, sufficient cyclic control may not be available to flare properly to land.

C. Should the aircraft pitch up during cruise flight due to gusty winds, there may not be enough forward cyclic control available to lower the nose.

5681. "B" is the correct answer. Flight under this condition should not be continued since the possibility of running out of rearward cyclic control increases rapidly as fuel is consumed, and the pilot may find it impossible to decelerate sufficiently to bring the helicopter to a stop. Also, in case of engine failure and the resulting autorotation, sufficient cyclic control may not be available to flare properly for the landing.

Reference Basic Helicopter Handbook, p. 44

FAA subject matter knowledge code H76

5682. With respect to using the weight information given in a typical aircraft owner's manual for computing gross weight, it is important to know that if items have been installed in the aircraft in addition to the original equipment, the

A. allowable useful load is decreased.

B. allowable useful load remains unchanged.

C. maximum allowable gross weight is increased.

5682. "A" is the correct answer. It must be stressed that the empty weight and moment given in most manufacturers' handbooks are for the basic airplane prior to the installation of additional optional equipment. When the owner adds such items as radio navigation equipment, autopilot, deicers, etc., the empty weight and the moment are changed. These changes must be recorded in the airplane's weight and balance data and used in all computations.

Reference Flight Training Handbook, p. 304–305

FAA subject matter knowledge code H66

10

Advanced Aircraft Systems

STUDY GUIDE

Engine Operation

Knowledge of a few general principles of engine operation can help you obtain increased dependability and efficiency from the engine and, in many instances, this knowledge can help you avoid engine failure.

Ignition System

The function of the ignition system is to provide a spark to ignite the fuel/air mixture in the cylinder. The magneto ignition system is used on most modern aircraft engines because it produces a hotter spark at high engine speeds. Also, it does not depend on an external source of energy such as the electrical system.

It is important to turn the ignition switch to BOTH for flight and completely OFF when shutting down the engine after flight. If the magneto switch ground wire is disconnected the magneto is ON even though the ignition switch is in the OFF position.

Mixture Control

A *mixture control* in the cockpit is provided to change the fuel flow to the engine to compensate for varying air densities as the airplane changes altitude. As the airplane climbs and the atmospheric pressure decreases, there is a corresponding decrease in the weight of air passing through the induction system. The volume of air, however, remains constant, and since it is the volume of airflow that determines the pressure drop at the throat of the venturi, the carburetor tends to meter the same amount of fuel to this thin air as to the more dense air at sea level. Therefore, the mixture becomes richer as the airplane gains altitude. The mixture control prevents this by decreasing the rate of fuel discharge to compensate for the decrease in air density. However, the mixture must be enriched when descending from altitude.

If the fuel/air mixture is too rich (that is, too much fuel in terms of the weight of air), excessive fuel consumption, rough engine operation, and appreciable loss of power occur. Because of excessive fuel, a cooling effect takes place which causes below normal temperatures in the combustion chambers. This cooling results in spark plug fouling.

Carburetor Heat

The carburetor heater is an anti-icing device that preheats the air before it reaches the carburetor. Use of carburetor heat tends to reduce the output of the engine and increase the operating temperature. Therefore, the heat should not be used when full power is required (as during takeoff) or during normal engine operation except to check for the presence of or to remove carburetor ice.

Detonation

When the fuel/air mixture is subjected to a combination of excessively high temperature and high pressure within the cylinder, the spontaneous combustion point of the gaseous mixture is reached. When this critical detonation point is reached, normal progressive combustion is replaced by a sudden explosion, or instantaneous combustion.

Preignition

Preignition is defined as ignition of the fuel prior to normal ignition, or ignition before the electrical arcing occurs at the spark plugs. Preignition can be caused by excessively hot exhaust valves, carbon particles, or spark plug electrodes heated to an incandescent or glowing state. In most cases these local "hot spots" are caused by the high temperatures encountered during detonation.

Oil System

Proper lubrication of the engine is essential to the extension of engine life and prevention of excessive maintenance. Lubricating oil serves two purposes: (1) it furnishes a coating of oil over the surfaces of the moving parts, preventing direct metal-to-metal contact and the generation of heat, and (2) it absorbs and dissipates, through the oil cooling system, part of the engine heat produced by the internal combustion process.

Controllable-Pitch Propellers

The pitch on these propellers can be changed in flight; they are thus referred to as controllable-pitch propellers. These propeller systems vary from a simple two-position propeller to more complex automatic constant-speed propellers.

An airplane equipped with a controllable-pitch propeller has two controls: a throttle control and a propeller control. The throttle controls the power output of the engine that is registered on the manifold pressure gauge. The propeller control regulates the engine rpm, and in turn the propeller rpm. The rpm is registered on the tachometer.

When both manifold pressure and rpm need to be changed, avoid engine overstress by making power adjustments in the proper order. When power settings are being decreased, reduce manifold pressure before rpm. When power settings are being increased, increase rpm first, then manifold pressure.

The Airspeed Indicator

The following is a description of the standard color-code markings on airspeed indicators used on single-engine light airplanes:

- Flap operating range—the white arc.
  - ~Power-off stalling speed with the wing flaps and landing gear in the landing position—the lower limit of the white arc.
  - ~Maximum flaps extended speed—the upper limit of the white arc.

- Normal operating range—the green arc.
  ~Power-off stalling speed with the wing flaps and landing gear retracted—
    the lower limit of the green arc.
  ~Maximum structural cruising speed—the upper limit of the green arc.
- Caution range—the yellow arc.
- Never-exceed speed—the red line.
- Maneuvering speed is not marked on the face of the airspeed indicator.

COMPUTER-BASED QUESTIONS

5168. For gyroplanes with constant-speed propellers, the first indication of carburetor icing is usually

A. a decrease in engine rpm.

B. a decrease in manifold pressure.

C. engine roughness followed by a decrease in engine rpm.

5168. "B" is the correct answer. A decrease in manifold pressure is usually the first indication of carburetor icing.
Reference Air & Space 18A Gyroplane Flight Manual
FAA subject matter knowledge code H02

5169. Before shutdown, while at idle, the ignition key is momentarily turned OFF. The engine continues to run with no interruption; this

A. is normal because the engine is usually stopped by moving the mixture to idle cutoff.

B. should not normally happen and indicates a dangerous situation.

C. is an undesirable practice, but indicates that nothing is wrong.

5169. "B" is the correct answer. An engine that continues to run after the key is switched OFF may have a broken ground wire. This is a dangerous situation because the propeller is "hot" even with the ignition OFF.
Reference PHOAK, p. 23
FAA subject matter knowledge code H02

5170. Leaving the carburetor heat on while taking off

A. leans the mixture for more power on takeoff.

B. decreases the takeoff distance.

C. increases the ground roll.

5170. "C" in the correct answer. Use of carburetor heat tends to reduce the output of the engine. This results in an increase in the ground roll during takeoff. "B" is obviously incorrect because reduced engine output does not increase performance. "A" is also incorrect because adding carburetor heat enriches the mixture.
Reference PHOAK, p. 43
FAA subject matter knowledge code H01

5171. A way to detect a broken magneto primary grounding lead is to

A. idle the engine and momentarily turn the ignition off.

B. add full power, while holding the brakes, and momentarily turn off the ignition.

C. run on one magneto, lean the mixture, and look for a rise in manifold pressure.

5171. "A" is the correct answer. This check should be done in accordance with the manufacturer's procedures. Reduce the throttle to idle and then momentarily turn the ignition OFF, then back to BOTH. The engine should begin to stop. If it continues to run normally even with the ignition switch off, then the ground wire is broken or disconnected. "B" is incorrect because it causes unnecessary stress on the engine. "C" is incorrect because the mixture has nothing to do with the ignition system.
Reference PHOAK, p. 40
FAA subject matter knowledge code H02

5172. Fouling of spark plugs is more apt to occur if the aircraft

A. gains altitude with no mixture adjustment.

B. descends from altitude with no mixture adjustment.

C. throttle is advanced very abruptly.

5172. "A" is the correct answer. As the altitude increases, the density of air entering the carburetor decreases. The volume of air, however, remains the same. Since volume of airflow determines the pressure drop at the throat of the venturi, the carburetor meters the same amount of fuel to this thin air as it does to the denser sea level air. This too-rich fuel/air mixture causes a rough engine and power loss. Be-

cause of excessive fuel, a cooling effect takes place that causes below normal temperatures in the cylinders. This results in fouled spark plugs.
Reference PHOAK, p. 42
FAA subject matter knowledge code H02

5173. The most probable reason an engine continues to run after the ignition switch has been turned off is

A. carbon deposits glowing on the spark plugs.

B. a magneto ground wire is in contact with the engine casing.

C. a broken magneto ground wire.

5173. "C" is the correct answer. If the magneto switch ground wire is broken or disconnected, the engine continues to run even with the ignition turned OFF.
Reference PHOAK, p. 40
FAA subject matter knowledge code H02

5174. If the ground wire between the magneto and the ignition switch becomes disconnected, the engine

A. will not operate on one magneto.

B. cannot be started with the switch in the BOTH position.

C. could accidentally start if the propeller is moved with fuel in the cylinder.

5174. "C" is the correct answer. If the magneto switch ground wire is disconnected, the magneto is ON even if the ignition switch is in the OFF position. The engine could fire if the propeller is moved.
Reference PHOAK, p. 40
FAA subject matter knowledge code H02

5175. For internal cooling, reciprocating aircraft engines are especially dependent on

A. a properly functioning cowl flap augmenter.

B. the circulation of lubricating oil.

C. the proper freon/compressor output ratio.

5175. "B" is the correct answer. Lubricating oil absorbs and dissipates part of the heat produced by the internal combustion process.
Reference PHOAK, p. 45
FAA subject matter knowledge code H02

5176. The pilot controls the air/fuel mixture with the

A. throttle.

B. manifold pressure.

C. mixture control.

5176. "C" is the correct answer. The mixture control is used to adjust the fuel/air mixture entering the combustion chamber.
Reference PHOAK, p. 42
FAA subject matter knowledge code H53

5177. Which airspeed would a pilot be unable to identify by the color coding of an airspeed indicator?

A. The never-exceed speed.

B. The power-off stall speed.

C. The maneuvering speed.

5177. "C" is the correct answer. Maneuvering speed is not marked on the face of the airspeed indicator. Both "A" and "B" can be found on the airspeed indicator.
Reference PHOAK, p. 63
FAA subject matter knowledge code H03

5178. Which statement is true about magnetic deviation of a compass?

A. Deviation varies over time as the agonic line shifts.

B. Deviation varies for different headings of the same aircraft.

C. Deviation is the same for all aircraft in the same locality.

5178. "B" is the correct answer. Deviation depends, in part, on aircraft heading. Deviation is additional compass errors caused by magnetic disturbances from magnetic fields produced by metals and electrical accessories in the aircraft.
Reference PHOAK, p. 71
FAA subject matter knowledge code H03

5183. Which statement best describes the operating principle of a constant-speed propeller?

A. As throttle setting is changed by the pilot, the propeller governor causes pitch angle of the propeller blades to remain unchanged.

B. A high blade angle, or increased pitch, reduces the propeller drag and allows more engine power for takeoffs.

C. The propeller control regulates the engine rpm and in turn the propeller rpm.

5183. "C" is the correct answer. The propeller control regulates the engine rpm and in turn the propeller rpm.
Reference PHOAK, p. 48
FAA subject matter knowledge code H02

5184. In aircraft equipped with constant-speed propellers and normally aspirated engines, which procedure should be used to avoid placing undue stress on the engine components?

A. When power is being decreased, reduce the rpm before reducing the manifold pressure.

B. When power is being increased, increase the rpm before increasing the manifold pressure.

C. When power is being increased or decreased, the rpm should be adjusted before the manifold pressure.

5184. "B" is the correct answer. To avoid engine overstress, make power adjustments in the proper order. When power settings are being decreased, reduce manifold pressure before rpm. When power is being increased, increase rpm first, then increase manifold pressure.
Reference PHOAK, p. 48
FAA subject matter knowledge code H02

5185. Detonation may occur at high power settings when

A. the fuel mixture instantaneously ignites instead of burning progressively and evenly.

B. an excessively rich fuel mixture causes an explosive gain in power.

C. the fuel mixture is ignited too early by hot carbon deposits in the cylinder.

5185. "A" is the correct answer. Detonation is a sudden explosion of fuel in a small area of the piston top instead of the fuel/air mixture burning progressively and evenly. Detonation occurs when there are excessively high engine temperatures. This can be caused by too lean a mixture or the incorrect grade of fuel.
Reference PHOAK, p. 44
FAA subject matter knowledge code H02

5186. The uncontrolled firing of the fuel/air charge in advance of normal spark ignition is known as

A. instantaneous combustion.

B. detonation.

C. preignition.

5186. "C" is the correct answer. Preignition is hot spots caused by carbon deposits or extremely hot exhaust valves igniting the fuel/air mixture prematurely.
Reference Flight Training Handbook, p. 22
FAA subject matter knowledge code H51

5187. Fuel/air ratio is the ratio between the

A. volume of fuel and volume of air entering the cylinder.

B. weight of fuel and weight of air entering the cylinder.

C. weight of fuel and weight of air entering the carburetor.

5187. "B" is the correct answer. The mixture control is used to adjust the fuel/air mixture entering the cylinders. This mixture must have a specific ratio in order to burn efficiently. This fuel/air ratio is the ratio of the weight of fuel and weight of air entering the cylinder. Answer "A" is incorrect because the fuel/air mixture is not measured by volume. Answer "C" is incorrect because the fuel/air mixture occurs in the carburetor, not while entering the carburetor.
Reference Flight Training Handbook, p. 19
FAA subject matter knowledge code H02

5188. The mixture control can be adjusted, which

A. prevents the fuel/air mixture from becoming too rich at higher altitudes.

B. regulates the amount of airflow through the carburetor's venturi.

C. prevents the fuel/air mixture from becoming lean as the airplane climbs.

5188. "A" is the correct answer. Carburetors are normally calibrated at sea level pressure to meter the correct amount of fuel with the mixture control in a full rich position. As altitude increases, air density decreases and the mixture becomes too rich. The mixture control allows the pilot to adjust the fuel/air mixture to compensate for this condition. "B" is incorrect because the mixture control does not regulate air. "C" is also incorrect because the fuel/air mixture becomes too rich, not too lean.
Reference PHOAK, pp. 41–42
FAA subject matter knowledge code H51

5189. Which statement is true concerning the effect of the application of carburetor heat?

A. It enriches the fuel/air mixture.

B. It leans the fuel/air mixture.

C. It has no effect on the fuel/air mixture.

5189. "A" is the correct answer. Application of carburetor heat causes hot air to enter the carburetor. This hot air is less dense than the ambient air, causing a slight reduction in engine performance. This

less dense air mixed with the same amount of fuel causes a richer mixture.
Reference PHOAK, p. 42
FAA subject matter knowledge code H02

5190. Detonation occurs in a reciprocating aircraft engine when

A. there is an explosive increase of fuel caused by a too-rich fuel/air mixture.

B. the spark plugs receive an electrical jolt caused by a short in the wiring.

C. the unburned charge in the cylinders is subjected to instantaneous combustion.

5190. "C" is the correct answer. Detonation is a sudden explosion of fuel in a small area of the piston top instead of the fuel/air mixture burning progressively and evenly. Detonation occurs when there are excessively high engine temperatures. This can be caused by too lean a mixture or the incorrect grade of fuel. Answer "A" is incorrect because a too-rich mixture burns cooler (remember, excess fuel is used to cool the engine). "B" is also incorrect because a short might cause preignition but not the excess heat required for detonation.
Reference PHOAK, p. 44
FAA subject matter knowledge code H02

5298. The best power mixture is that fuel/air ratio at which

A. cylinder head temperatures are the coolest.

B. the most power can be obtained for any given throttle setting.

C. a given power can be obtained with the highest manifold pressure or throttle setting.

5298. "B" is the correct answer. The fuel/air ratio of the combustible mixture delivered to the engine is controlled by the mixture control. The best power mixture is that fuel/air ratio at which the most power can be obtained for any given power setting.
Reference Flight Training Handbook, p. 46
FAA subject matter knowledge code H02

5299. Detonation can be caused by

A. too lean a mixture.

B. low engine temperatures.

C. using a higher grade fuel than recommended.

5299. "A" is the correct answer. Operation with an excessively lean mixture (that is, too little fuel in terms of the weight of air) results in rough engine

operation, detonation, overheating, and a loss of power.
Reference PHOAK, p. 42
FAA subject matter knowledge code H02

5300. What effect, if any, would a change in ambient temperature or air density have on gas turbine engine performance?

A. As air density decreases, thrust increases.

B. As temperature increases, thrust increases.

C. As temperature increases, thrust decreases.

5300. "C" is the correct answer. An increase in air temperature causes a decrease in thrust.
Reference Flight Training Handbook, p. 306
FAA subject matter knowledge code T17

5606. Applying carburetor heat

A. does not affect the mixture.

B. leans the fuel/air mixture.

C. enriches the fuel/air mixture.

5606. "C" is the correct answer. Use of carburetor heat tends to reduce the power output of the engine by enriching the fuel/air mixture.
Reference PHOAK, p. 43
FAA subject matter knowledge code H02

5607. An abnormally high engine oil temperature indication may be caused by

A. a defective bearing.

B. the oil level being too low.

C. operating with an excessively rich mixture.

5607. "B" is the correct answer. Starting a flight with an insufficient oil supply can lead to serious consequences. The airplane engine burns off a certain amount of oil during operation, and beginning a flight when the oil level is low usually results in an insufficient supply of oil before the flight terminates. This may be indicated by abnormally high oil temperature indications.
Reference PHOAK, p. 46
FAA subject matter knowledge code H02

5608. What will occur if no leaning is done with the mixture control as the flight altitude increases?

A. The volume of air entering the carburetor decreases and the amount of fuel decreases.

B. The density of air entering the carburetor decreases and the amount of fuel increases.

C. The density of air entering the carburetor decreases and the amount of fuel remains constant.

5608. "C" is the correct answer. As the airplane climbs and the atmospheric pressure decreases, there is a corresponding decrease in the weight of air passing through the induction system. The volume of air, however, remains constant, and since it is the volume of airflow that determines the pressure drop at the throat of the venturi, the carburetor tends to meter the same amount of fuel to this thin air as to the more dense air at sea level. Therefore, the mixture becomes richer as the airplane gains altitude.
Reference PHOAK, p. 42
FAA subject matter knowledge code H02

5609. Unless adjusted, the fuel/air mixture becomes richer with an increase in altitude because the amount of fuel

A. decreases, while the volume of air decreases.

B. remains constant, while the volume of air decreases.

C. remains constant, while the density of air decreases.

5609. "C" is the correct answer. As the airplane climbs and the atmospheric pressure decreases, there is a corresponding decrease in the weight of air passing through the induction system. The volume of air, however, remains constant, and since it is the volume of airflow that determines the pressure drop at the throat of the venturi, the carburetor tends to meter the same amount of fuel to this thin air as to the more dense air at sea level. Therefore, the mixture becomes richer as the airplane gains altitude.
Reference PHOAK, p. 42
FAA subject matter knowledge code H02

5610. The basic purpose of adjusting the fuel/air mixture control at altitude is to

A. decrease the fuel flow to compensate for decreased air density.

B. decrease the amount of fuel in the mixture to compensate for increased air density.

C. increase the amount of fuel in the mixture to compensate for the decrease in pressure and density of the air.

5610. "A" is the correct answer. As altitude increases, the weight of air decreases, even though the volume of air entering the carburetor remains the same. To compensate for this difference, the mixture control is used to adjust the fuel/air mixture entering the combustion chamber.
Reference PHOAK, pp. 41–42
FAA subject matter knowledge code H02

5611. At high altitudes, an excessively rich mixture causes the

A. engine to overheat.

B. fouling of spark plugs.

C. engine to operate smoother even though fuel consumption is increased.

5611. "B" is the correct answer. If the fuel/air mixture is too rich (that is, too much fuel in terms of the weight of air), excessive fuel consumption, rough engine operation, and appreciable loss of power occur because of excessive fuel, and a cooling effect takes place. This cooling causes below-normal temperatures in the combustion chambers, resulting in spark plug fouling.
Reference PHOAK, p. 42
FAA subject matter knowledge code H02

5653. Frequent inspections should be made of aircraft exhaust manifold heating systems to minimize the possibility of

A. exhaust gases leaking into the cockpit.

B. a power loss due to back pressure in the exhaust system.

C. a cold-running engine due to the heat withdrawn by the heater.

5653. "A" is the correct answer. Most heaters in light aircraft work by blowing air over the manifold. Use of these heaters while exhaust fumes are escaping through manifold cracks and seals is responsible for several nonfatal and fatal aircraft accidents from carbon monoxide poisoning every year.
Reference PHOAK, p. 249
FAA subject matter knowledge code J31

5654. To establish a climb after takeoff in an aircraft equipped with a constant-speed propeller, the output of the engine is reduced to climb power by decreasing manifold pressure and

A. increasing rpm by decreasing propeller blade angle.

B. decreasing rpm by decreasing propeller blade angle.

C. decreasing rpm by increasing propeller blade angle.

5654. "C" is the correct answer. A controllable-pitch propeller permits the pilot to select the blade angle that results in the most efficient performance for a particular flight condition. A low blade angle or decreased pitch reduces the propeller drag and allows

more engine power for takeoffs. When both manifold pressure and rpm need to be changed, the pilot can further avoid engine overstress by making power adjustments in the proper order. When power settings are being decreased, reduce manifold pressure before rpm.
Reference PHOAK, p. 48
FAA subject matter knowledge code H51

5667. To develop maximum power and thrust, a constant-speed propeller should be set to a blade angle that produces a

A. large angle of attack and low rpm.

B. small angle of attack and high rpm.

C. large angle of attack and high rpm.

5667. "B" is the correct answer. A controllable-pitch propeller permits the pilot to select the blade angle that results in the most efficient performance for a particular flight condition. A low blade angle or decreased pitch reduces the propeller drag and allows more engine power for takeoffs.
Reference PHOAK, p. 48
FAA subject matter knowledge code H02

5668. For takeoff, the blade angle of a controllable-pitch propeller should be set at a

A. small angle of attack and high rpm.

B. large angle of attack and low rpm.

C. large angle of attack and high rpm.

5668. "A" is the correct answer. A controllable-pitch propeller permits the pilot to select the blade angle that results in the most efficient performance for a particular flight condition. A low blade angle or decreased pitch reduces the propeller drag and allows more engine power for takeoffs.
Reference PHOAK, p. 48
FAA subject matter knowledge code H02

5748. Pilots are encouraged to turn on the aircraft rotating beacon

A. just prior to taxi.

B. anytime they are in the cockpit.

C. anytime an engine is in operation.

5748. "C" is the correct answer. The FAA has a voluntary pilot safety program—Operation Lights On—to enhance the see-and-avoid concept. Pilots are encouraged to turn on their anticollision lights anytime their engine(s) are running, day or night.
Reference Aeronautical Information Manual, paragraph 4-72
FAA subject matter knowledge code J13

5766. During preflight in cold weather, crankcase breather lines should receive special attention because they are susceptible to clogging by

A. congealed oil from the crankcase.

B. moisture from the outside air that has frozen.

C. ice from crankcase vapors that have condensed and subsequently frozen.

5766. "C" is the correct answer. Crankcase breather lines should receive extra care during preflight because they can be clogged by ice from crankcase vapors that have condensed and subsequently frozen.
Reference Flight Training Handbook
FAA subject matter knowledge code L52

5767. Which is true regarding preheating an aircraft during cold weather operations?

A. The cabin area as well as the engine should be preheated.

B. The cabin area should not be preheated with portable heaters.

C. Hot air should be blown directly at the engine through the air intakes.

5767. "A" is the correct answer. When preheating an aircraft during cold weather operations it is advisable for the pilot to heat the cabin area as well as the engine(s).
Reference CFI Examination Handbook, p. 37
FAA subject matter knowledge code L52

5768. If necessary to take off from a slushy runway, the freezing of landing gear mechanisms can be minimized by

A. recycling the gear.

B. delaying gear retraction.

C. increasing the airspeed to V_{LE} before retraction.

5768. "A" is the correct answer. The freezing of landing gear mechanisms can be minimized by recycling the gear.
Reference Flight Training Handbook
FAA subject matter knowledge code L52

5793. The spoilers should be in what position when operating in a strong wind?

A. Extended during both a landing roll or ground operations.

B. Retracted during both a landing roll or ground operations.

C. Extended during a landing roll, but retracted during ground operations.

5793. "A" is the correct answer. The spoilers should remain out (extended) during ground operations in strong wind conditions.
Reference Soaring Flight Manual
FAA subject matter knowledge codes N20

5794. Which is true regarding the assembly of a glider for flight?

A. It may be accomplished by the pilot.

B. It is not required by regulations for a glider pilot to know this.

C. It must be accomplished under the supervision of an FAA maintenance inspector.

5794. "A" is the correct answer. A certified pilot is authorized to assemble a glider for flight.
Reference Soaring Flight Manual
FAA subject matter knowledge code N29

5795. Is it good operating practice to release from a low-tow position?

A. No. The towline may snap back and strike the towplane.

B. No. The tow ring may strike and damage the glider after release.

C. Yes. Low-tow position is the correct position for releasing from the towplane.

5795. "B" is the correct answer. This is not a good operating practice because the tow ring could fly back and damage the glider after release.
Reference Soaring Flight Manual
FAA subject matter knowledge code N04

5796. To signal the glider pilot during an aerotow to release immediately, the tow pilot

A. fishtails the towplane.

B. rocks the towplane's wings.

C. alternately raises and lowers the towplane's pitch attitude.

5796. "B" is the correct answer. Rocking the towplane's wing is the signal to release immediately.
Reference Soaring Flight Manual
FAA subject matter knowledge code N30

5807. Which is true regarding the use of glider tow hooks?

A. The use of a CG hook for auto or winch tows allows the sailplane greater altitude for a given line length.

B. The use of a CG hook for aerotows allows better directional control at the start of the launch than the use of a nose hook.

C. The use of a nose hook for an auto or winch launch reduces structural loading on the tail assembly compared to the use of a CG hook.

5807. "A" is the correct answer. The use of a CG hook for auto or winch tows allows the sailplane greater altitude for a given line length.
Reference Soaring Flight Manual
FAA subject matter knowledge code N31

5825. What should a pilot do if a small hole is seen in the balloon fabric during inflation?

A. Continue the inflation and make a mental note of the location of the hole for later repair.

B. Instruct a ground crewmember to inspect the hole, and if under 5 inches in length, continue the inflation.

C. Consult the flight manual to determine if the hole is within acceptable damage limits established for the balloon being flown.

5825. "C" is the correct answer. If a small hole is seen in the fabric of a balloon during inflation, the pilot should consult the flight manual to determine if the hole is within acceptable damage limits established for the balloon being flown.
Reference Ballooning Flight Manual
FAA subject matter knowledge code O01

5826. Propane is preferred over butane for fuel in hot air balloons because

A. it has a higher boiling point.

B. it has a lower boiling point.

C. butane is very explosive under pressure.

5826. "B" is the correct answer. Propane is preferred over butane for fuel in hot air balloons because it has a lower boiling point.
Reference Ballooning Flight Manual
FAA subject matter knowledge code O21

5827. On a balloon equipped with a blast valve, the blast valve is used for

A. climbs only.

B. emergencies only.

C. control of altitude.

5827. "C" is the correct answer. A blast valve on a balloon is used to control altitude.
Reference Ballooning Flight Manual
FAA subject matter knowledge code O22

5832. While in flight, ice begins forming on the outside of the fuel tank in use. This would most likely be caused by

A. water in the fuel.

B. a leak in the fuel line.

C. vaporized fuel instead of liquid fuel being drawn from the tank into the main burner.

5832. "C" is the correct answer. While in flight, if ice begins forming on the outside of the fuel tank in use it is likely to be caused by vaporized fuel instead of liquid fuel being drawn from the tank into the main burner.
Reference Ballooning Flight Manual
FAA subject matter knowledge code O21

5834. When landing a free balloon, what should the occupants do to minimize landing shock?

A. Be seated on the floor of the basket.

B. Stand back-to-back and hold onto the load ring.

C. Stand with knees slightly bent facing the direction of movement.

5834. "C" is the correct answer. When landing a free balloon, occupants should stand with knees slightly bent facing the direction of movement.
Reference Ballooning Flight Manual
FAA subject matter knowledge code O40

5835. One means of vertical control on a gas balloon is

A. by using the rip panel rope.

B. valving gas or releasing ballast.

C. opening and closing the appendix.

5835. "B" is the correct answer. One means of vertical control on a gas balloon is by valving gas or releasing ballast.
Reference Ballooning Flight Manual
FAA subject matter knowledge code P04

5839. What action is most appropriate when an envelope overtemperature condition occurs?

A. Turn the main burner OFF.

B. Land as soon as practical.

C. Throw all unnecessary equipment overboard.

5839. "B" is the correct answer. When an envelope overtemperature condition occurs you should land as soon as practical.
Reference Ballooning Flight Manual
FAA subject matter knowledge code O40

5840. Which is the proper way to detect a fuel leak?

A. Sight.

B. Use of smell and sound.

C. Check fuel pressure gauge.

5840. "B" is the correct answer. The use of smell and sound is the proper way to detect a fuel leak.
Reference Ballooning Flight Manual
FAA subject matter knowledge code O02

5841. What is the weight of propane?

A. 4.2 pounds per gallon.

B. 6.0 pounds per gallon.

C. 7.5 pounds per gallon.

5841. "A" is the correct answer. Propane weighs 4.2 pounds per gallon.
Reference Ballooning Flight Manual
FAA subject matter knowledge code O02

5843. Why is it considered a good practice to blast the burner after changing fuel tanks?

A. To check for fuel line leaks.

B. It creates an immediate source of lift.

C. To ensure the new tank is functioning properly.

5843. "C" is the correct answer. It is a good practice to blast the burner after changing fuel tanks because it ensures the new tank is functioning properly.
Reference Ballooning Flight Manual
FAA subject matter knowledge code O23

5844. For what reason is methanol added to the propane fuel of hot air balloons?

A. As a fire retardant.

B. As an anti-icing additive.

C. To reduce the temperature.

5844. "B" is the correct answer. Methanol is added to the propane fuel of hot air balloons as an anti-icing additive.
Reference Ballooning Flight Manual
FAA subject matter knowledge code O21

5845. To respond to a small leak around the stem of a Rego blast valve in a single-burner balloon, one should

A. turn off the fuel system and make an immediate landing.

B. continue operating the blast valve, making very small quick blasts until a good landing field appears.

C. continue operating the blast valve, making long infrequent blasts and opening the handle slightly to reduce leakage until a good landing field appears.

5845. There is no correct answer to this question. However, do make a selection.
Reference Ballooning Flight Manual
FAA subject matter knowledge code O20

5846. Which action would be appropriate if a small leak develops around the stem of the tank valve, and no other tanks have sufficient fuel to reach a suitable landing field?

A. Warm the tank valve leak with your bare hand.

B. Turn the leaking tank handle to the full-open position.

C. Turn off the tank, then slowly reopen to reseat the seal.

5846. "B" is the correct answer. If a small leak develops around the stem of the tank valve, and no other tanks have sufficient fuel to reach a suitable landing field, you should turn the leaking tank handle to the full-open position.
Reference Ballooning Flight Manual
FAA subject matter knowledge code O21

5847. Why should propane lines be bled after use?

A. Fire may result from spontaneous combustion.

B. The propane may expand and rupture the lines.

C. If the temperature is below freezing, the propane may freeze.

5847. "B" is the correct answer. Propane lines should be bled after use because the propane may expand and rupture the lines.
Reference Ballooning Flight Manual
FAA subject matter knowledge code O23

5848. The purpose of the preheating coil as used in hot air balloons is to

A. prevent ice from forming in the fuel lines.

B. warm the fuel tanks for more efficient fuel flow.

C. vaporize the fuel for more efficient burner operation.

5848. "C" is the correct answer. The purpose of the preheating coil as used in hot air balloons is to vaporize the fuel for more efficient burner operation.
Reference Ballooning Flight Manual
FAA subject matter knowledge code O22

5849. The best way to determine burner Btu availability is the

A. burner sound.

B. tank quantity.

C. fuel pressure gauge.

5849. "C" is the correct answer. The best way to determine burner Btu availability is the fuel pressure gauge.
Reference Ballooning Flight Manual
FAA subject matter knowledge code O21

5850. The practice of allowing the ground crew to lift the balloon into the air is

A. a safe way to reduce stress on the envelope.

B. unsafe because it can lead to a sudden landing at an inopportune site just after lift-off.

C. considered to be a good operating practice when obstacles must be cleared shortly after lift-off.

5850. "B" is the correct answer. The practice of allowing the ground crew to lift the balloon into the air is unsafe because it can lead to a sudden landing at an inopportune site just after lift-off.
Reference Ballooning Flight Manual
FAA subject matter knowledge code O40

5857. One characteristic of nylon rope is that it

A. is flexible.

B. does not stretch.

C. splinters easily.

5857. "A" is the correct answer. One characteristic of nylon rope is that it is flexible.
Reference Ballooning Flight Manual
FAA subject matter knowledge code O01

5858. Why is nylon rope good for tethering a balloon?

A. It does not stretch under tension.

B. It is not flexible and therefore can withstand greater tension without breaking.

C. It stretches under tension but recovers to normal size when tension is removed, giving it excellent shock absorbing qualities.

5858. "C" is the correct answer. Nylon rope is good for tethering a balloon because it stretches under tension but recovers to normal size when tension is removed, giving it excellent shock absorbing qualities.
Reference Ballooning Flight Manual
FAA subject matter knowledge code O01

5859. One advantage nylon rope has over manila rope is that it

A. does not stretch.

B. is nearly three times as strong.

C. does not tend to snap back if it breaks.

5859. "B" is the correct answer. One advantage nylon rope has over manila rope is that it is nearly three times as strong.
Reference Ballooning Flight Manual
FAA subject matter knowledge code O01

5860. A pilot should be aware that drag ropes constructed of hemp or nylon

A. should be a maximum of 100 ft long and used only in gas balloons.

B. can be considered safe because they do not conduct electricity.

C. can conduct electricity when contacting power lines carrying 600 volts or more current if they are not clean and dry.

5860. There is no correct answer, but do make a selection.
Reference Ballooning Flight Manual
FAA subject matter knowledge code O30

5864. Superheat is a term used to describe the condition that exists

A. when the surrounding air is at least 10°F warmer than the gas in the envelope.

B. when the sun heats the envelope surface to a temperature at least 10°F greater than the surrounding air.

C. relative to the difference in temperature between the gas in the envelope and the surrounding air caused by the sun.

5864. "C" is the correct answer. The term *superheat* is used to describe the condition that exists relative to the difference in temperature between the gas in the envelope and the surrounding air caused by the sun.
Reference Ballooning Flight Manual
FAA subject matter knowledge code O03

5865. How does the pilot know when pressure height has been reached?

A. Liquid in the gas and air manometers falls below the normal level.

B. Liquid in the gas manometer falls and liquid in the air manometer rises above normal levels.

C. Liquid in the gas manometer rises and liquid in the air manometer falls below normal levels.

5865. "C" is the correct answer. When pressure height has been reached, liquid in the gas manometer rises and liquid in the air manometer falls below normal levels.
Reference Ballooning Flight Manual
FAA subject matter knowledge code P01

11

Aerodynamics

STUDY GUIDE

Newton's Laws of Motion and Force

Newton's first law states, in part, that

> A body at rest tends to remain at rest and a body in motion tends to remain moving at the same speed and in the same direction.

Newton's second law implies that

> When a body is acted upon by a constant force, its resulting acceleration is inversely proportional to the mass of the body and is directly proportional to the applied force.

Newton's third law states that

> Whenever one body exerts a force on another, the second body always exerts on the first a force that is equal in magnitude but opposite in direction.

Bernoulli's Principle of Pressure

Bernoulli stated that an increase in the speed of movement of flow would cause a decrease in a fluid's pressure. This is exactly what happens to air passing over the curved top of an airplane wing.

Airfoil Design

The construction of the wing to provide actions greater than its weight is done by shaping the wing so that advantage can be taken of air's response to certain physical laws and thus develop two actions from the air mass: a positive-pressure lifting action from the air mass below the wing, and a negative-pressure lifting action from lowered pressure above the wing.

Forces on an Airfoil

Air through which the wing moves creates a force, the components of which are referred to as *lift* and *drag*. The resultant force, or *force vector*, is resolved trigonometrically into these components of lift and drag, perpendicular and parallel, respectively, to the direction of the undisturbed "relative wind." The drag of a wing is a rearward force that acts opposite to the direction of the airplane's forward motion.

Angle of Attack and Lift

Angle of attack must not be confused with an airplane's attitude in relation to the earth's surface. In a very real sense the angle of attack is what flight in airplanes is all about. By changing the angle of attack the pilot can control lift, airspeed, and drag. The angle of attack of an airfoil directly controls the distribution of pressure below and above it.

When the angle of attack increases to approximately 18° to 20°, the air can no longer flow smoothly over the top wing surface. Because the airflow cannot make such a great change in direction so quickly, it becomes impossible for the air to follow the contour of the wing. This is the stalling or critical angle of attack.

One of the most important things a pilot should understand about angle of attack is that for any given airplane the stalling or critical angle of attack remains constant regardless of weight, dynamic pressure, bank angle, or pitch attitude.

Basic Propeller Principles

Every fixed-pitch propeller must be a compromise, because it can be efficient at only a given combination of airspeed and rpm. The efficiency of any machine is the ratio of the useful power output to the actual power input. Propeller efficiency is the ratio of thrust horsepower to brake horsepower. Twisting, or variations in the geometric pitch of the blades, permits the propeller to operate with a relatively constant angle of attack along its length when in cruising flight. To put it another way, propeller blades are twisted to change the blade angle in proportion to the differences in speed of rotation along the length of the propeller, thereby keeping thrust more nearly equalized along this length. Since an airplane's propeller rotates clockwise, as viewed from the cockpit, the slipstream strikes the vertical tail surface on the left side, pushing the tail to the right and yawing the nose of the airplane to the left.

Wing Form

The rectangular wing has a tendency to stall first at the wingroot and provides adequate stall warning, adequate aileron effectiveness, and is usually quite stable.

Forces Acting on the Airplane

First, we should define these forces in relation to straight and level, unaccelerated flight. *Thrust* is the forward force produced by the power plant and propeller. It opposes or overcomes the force of drag. *Drag* is a rearward, retarding force, and is caused by disruption of airflow by the wing, fuselage, and other protruding objects. Drag opposes thrust and acts rearward parallel to the relative wind.

Weight is the combined load of the airplane, the crew, the fuel, and the cargo or baggage. Weight pulls the airplane downward because of the force of gravity. It opposes lift and acts vertically downward through the airplane's center of gravity.

Lift opposes the downward force of weight, is produced by the dynamic effect of the air acting on the wing, and acts perpendicular to the flight path through the wing's center of lift. Anytime the *flight path* of the airplane is not horizontal, lift, weight, thrust, and drag vectors must each be broken down into two components:

1. The sum of *all upward* forces (not just lift) equals the sum of *all downward* forces (not just weight).

2. The sum of *all forward* forces (not just thrust) equals the sum of *all backward* forces (not just drag).

Basic Concepts of Stability

- *Static stability* is the initial tendency that the airplane displays after its equilibrium is disturbed.
- *Negative static stability* is the initial tendency of the airplane to continue away from the original state of equilibrium after being disturbed.
- *Positive static stability* is the initial tendency of the airplane to return to the original state of equilibrium after being disturbed.
- *Neutral static stability* is the initial tendency of the airplane to remain in a new condition after its equilibrium has been disturbed.
- *Dynamic stability* is the overall tendency that the airplane displays after its equilibrium is disturbed.
- *Longitudinal stability* is the quality that makes an airplane stable about its lateral axis. It involves the pitching motion as the airplane's nose moves up and down in flight. A longitudinally unstable airplane has a tendency to dive or climb, or even stall.

Thrust

Most pilots are aware that an airplane stalls at a slower speed with the power on than with the power off. (Induced airflow over the wings from the propeller contributes to this.)

Lift

Lift is proportional to the square of the airplane's velocity. For example, an airplane traveling at 200 knots has four times the lift as the same airplane traveling at 100 knots, if the angle of attack and other factors remain constant. Therefore, it may be concluded that for every angle of attack there is a corresponding indicated airspeed required to maintain altitude in steady, unaccelerated flight.

Lift and drag vary directly with the density of the air. Density is affected by several factors: pressure, temperature, and humidity. At an altitude of 18,000 ft the density of the air is one-half the density of air at sea level. In order to maintain its lift at a higher altitude, an airplane must fly at a greater true airspeed for any given angle of attack. At low speeds, during which the wing affects a lesser amount of air, a larger angle of attack is needed to deflect the air a larger amount. The angle of attack at various speeds must be such that the deflection of air is adequate for the amount of lift needed.

Ground Effect

The reduction of the wingtip vortices due to ground effect alters the spanwise lift distribution and reduces the induced angle of attack and induced drag. Therefore, the wing requires a lower angle of attack in ground effect to product the same lift coefficient. If a constant angle of attack is maintained, an increase in lift coefficient results. The reduction in induced flow due to ground effect causes a significant reduction in *induced drag*. The airplane leaving ground effect

1. requires an increase in angle of attack to maintain the same lift coefficient
2. experiences an increase in induced drag and thrust required
3. experiences a decrease in stability and a nose-up change in moment
4. produces a reduction in static source pressure and an increase in indicated airspeed

Forces in Turns

To compensate for the added lift that would result if the airspeed were increased during a turn, the angle of attack must be decreased, or the angle of bank increased, if a constant altitude is to be maintained.

Climbing Flight

When transitioning from level flight to a climb, the forces acting on the airplane go through definite changes. The first change, an increase in lift, occurs when back pressure is applied to the elevator control. This initial change is a result of the increase in the angle of attack that occurs when the airplane's pitch attitude is being raised. This results in a climbing attitude. When the inclined flight path and the climb speed are established, the angle of attack and the corresponding lift again stabilize at approximately the original value. The vertical component of lift decreases as the bank angle increases. The angle of attack must be progressively increased to produce sufficient vertical lift to support the airplane's weight. The horizontal component of lift is proportional to the angle of bank; that is, it increases or decreases, respectively, as the angle of bank increases or decreases.

Effect of Load Distribution

Generally speaking, an airplane becomes less controllable, especially at slow flight speeds, as the center of gravity is moved further aft. The recovery from a stall in any airplane becomes progressively more difficult as its center of gravity moves aft. This is particularly important in spin recovery, as there is a point in rearward loading of any airplane at which a "flat" spin will develop. A flat spin is one in which centrifugal force, acting through a center of gravity located well to the rear, pulls the tail of the airplane away from the axis of the spin, making it impossible to get the nose down and recover. The airplane, thus, becomes less and less stable as the center of gravity is moved rearward.

Range Performance

The maximum *range* condition is obtained at the maximum lift/drag ratio (L/D_{max}). It is important to note that for a given airplane configuration, the maximum lift/drag ratio occurs at a particular angle of attack and lift coefficient, and is unaffected by weight or altitude.

HELICOPTERS: STUDY GUIDE

Auxiliary Rotor

The force that compensates for torque and keeps the fuselage from turning in the direction opposite to the main rotor is produced by means of an auxiliary rotor located on the end of the tail boom. This auxiliary rotor, generally referred to as a *tail rotor*, or antitorque rotor, produces thrust in the direction opposite to torque reaction developed by the main rotor.

Gyroscopic Precession

The spinning main rotor of a helicopter acts like a gyroscope. Gyroscopic precession is the resultant action or deflection of a spinning object when a force is applied to the object. This action occurs approximately 90° in the direction of rotation from the point where the force is applied.

The movement of the cyclic pitch control in a two-bladed rotor system increases the angle of attack of one rotor blade, resulting in a greater lifting force being applied at this point in the plane of rotation. This same control movement simultaneously decreases the angle of attack of the other blade a like amount, thus decreasing the lifting force applied at this point in the plane of rotation. The blade with the increased angle of attack tends to rise; the blade with the decreased angle of attack tends to lower. However, because of the gyroscopic precession property, the blades do not rise or lower to maximum deflection until a point approximately 90° later in the plane of rotation.

Dissymmetry of Lift

Dissymmetry of lift is created by horizontal flight or by wind during hovering flight, and is the difference in lift that exists between the advancing blade half of the disc area and the retreating blade half of the disc area.

Coning

Coning is the upward bending of the blades caused by the combined forces of lift and centrifugal force.

Coriolis Effect

When a rotor blade of a three-bladed rotor system flaps upward, the center of mass of that blade moves closer to the axis of rotation and blade acceleration takes place. Conversely, when the blade flaps downward, its center of mass moves further from the axis of rotation and blade deceleration takes place. This is the Coriolis effect. The acceleration and deceleration actions (often referred to as leading, lagging, or hunting) of the rotor blades are absorbed by dampers or the blade structure itself, depending on the design of the rotor system.

Translating Tendency

The entire helicopter has a tendency to move in the direction of tail rotor thrust (to the right) when hovering. This movement is often referred as *translating tendency*. To counteract this drift, the rotor mast in some helicopters is rigged slightly to the left side so that the tip-path plane has a built-in tilt to the left, thus producing a small sideward thrust. In other helicopters, drift is overcome by rigging the cyclic pitch system to give the required amount of tilt to the tip-path plane.

Load Factor

The load factor is the actual load on the rotor blades at any time divided by the normal load or gross weight. The load factor is relatively small in banks up to 30°. Above 30° of bank, the apparent increase in gross weight soars. If the weight of the helicopter is 1600 pounds, the weight supported by the rotor in a 30° bank at a constant altitude would be 1856 pounds.

Controls

The capability for tail rotors to produce thrust to the left (negative pitch angle) is necessary because, during autorotation, the drag of the transmission tends to yaw the nose to the left—in the same direction that the main rotor is turning.

Clutch

Because of the much greater weight of a helicopter rotor in relation to the power of the engine than the weight of a propeller in relation to the power of the engine in an airplane, it is necessary to have the rotor disconnected from the engine to relieve the starter load. For this reason, it is necessary to have a clutch between the engine and rotor. The clutch allows the engine to be started and gradually assume the load of driving the heavy rotor system.

Freewheeling Unit

The freewheeling coupling provides for autorotative capabilities by automatically disconnecting the rotor system from the engine when the engine stops or slows below the equivalent of rotor rpm.

Fully Articulated Rotor Systems

Fully articulated rotor systems generally consist of three or more rotor blades. In a fully articulated rotor system, each rotor blade is attached to the rotor hub by a horizontal hinge, called the flapping hinge, that permits the blades to flap up and down.

Each rotor blade is also attached to the hub by a vertical hinge, called a drag or lag hinge, that permits each blade, independent of the others, to move back and forth in the plane of the rotor disc. This movement is called dragging, lead-lag, or hunting.

The blades of a fully articulated rotor can also be feathered, that is, rotated about their spanwise axis.

Semirigid Rotor Systems

In a semirigid rotor system, the rotor blades are rigidly interconnected to the hub, but the hub is free to tilt and rock with respect to the rotor shaft. The rotor flaps as a unit; that is, as one blade flaps up, the other blade flaps down an equal amount.

Collective pitch control changes the pitch of each blade simultaneously and an equal amount, either increasing the pitch of both or decreasing the pitch of both. Thus, a semirigid rotor system can flap and feather as a unit.

Performance

The performance of the helicopter is dependent on three major factors: density altitude (air density), gross weight, and wind velocity during takeoff, hovering, and landing.

Effect of High-Density Altitudes on Helicopter Performance

High elevations, high temperatures, and high moisture content, all of which contribute to a high-density altitude condition, lessen helicopter performance. Helicopter performance is reduced because the thinner air at high-density altitudes reduces the amount of lift of the rotor blades. Also, the engine does not develop as much power because of the thinner air and the decreased atmospheric pressure.

Effect of Gross Weight on Helicopter Performance

The heavier the gross weight, the greater the power required to hover and for flight in general, and the poorer the performance of the helicopter because less reserve power is available.

Effect of Wind on Helicopter Performance

No-wind conditions increase the amount of power necessary to hover, or require that a lighter load be carried. Thus, no-wind conditions reduce helicopter performance.

Retreating Blade Stall

The stall of a rotor blade limits the high airspeed potential of a helicopter. The airflow over the retreating blade of the helicopter slows down as the forward airspeed of the helicopter increases; the airflow over the advancing blade speeds up as forward airspeed increases. However, the retreating blade must produce the same amount of lift as the advancing blade. Therefore, as the airflow over the retreating blade decreases with forward airspeed, the blade angle of attack must be increased to help equalize lift throughout the rotor disc area. As this increase in angle of attack is continued, the retreating blade will stall at some high forward airspeed.

Ground Resonance

Ground resonance may develop when a series of shocks cause the rotor head to become unbalanced. It occurs only in helicopters possessing three-bladed, fully articulated rotor systems and landing wheels.

Abnormal Vibrations

Abnormal vibrations in the helicopter generally fall into three ranges:
- Low frequency—100 to 400 cycles per minute (cpm)
- Medium frequency—1000 to 2000 cpm
- High frequency—2000 cpm or higher

Low-frequency vibrations

Abnormal vibrations in this category are always associated with the main rotor.

Medium-frequency vibrations

Medium-frequency vibrations are a result of trouble with the tail rotor in most helicopters.

High-frequency vibrations

High-frequency vibrations in most helicopters are associated with the engine. However, any bearings in the engine, transmission, or tail rotor drive shaft that go bad result in vibrations with frequencies directly related to the speed of the engine.

Carburetor Icing

Carburetor icing is a frequent cause of engine failure. The vaporization of fuel, combined with the expansion of air as it passes through the carburetor, causes a sudden cooling of the mixture. Water vapor in the air is "squeezed out" by this cooling, and if the temperature in the carburetor reaches 32°F or below, the moisture is deposited as frost or ice inside the carburetor passages. Even a slight accumulation of this deposit reduces power and may lead to complete engine failure, particularly when the throttle is partly or fully closed.

Rapid Deceleration or Quick Stop

Begin the maneuver at a fast hover speed headed into the wind, at an altitude high enough to avoid danger to the tail rotor during the flare, but low enough to stay out of the height-velocity chart shaded area throughout the performance.

The deceleration is initiated by applying aft cyclic to reduce forward speed. Simultaneously, the collective pitch should be lowered as necessary to counteract any climbing tendency. As collective pitch is lowered, right pedal should be increased to maintain heading, and throttle should be adjusted to maintain rpm.

COMPUTER-BASED QUESTIONS: HELICOPTERS

5671. During the full flare portion of a power-off landing, the rotor rpm tends to

A. remain constant.

B. increase initially.

C. decrease initially.

5671. "B" is the correct answer. Forward speed during autorotative descent permits a pilot to incline the rotor disc rearward, thus causing a flare. The greater volume of air acting on the rotor disc normally increases rotor rpm during the flare.
Reference Basic Helicopter Handbook
FAA subject matter knowledge code H71

5672. Which produces the slowest rotor rpm?

A. A vertical descent with power.

B. A vertical descent without power.

C. Pushing over after a steep climb.

5672. "C" is the correct answer. Assuming a constant collective pitch setting, that is, a constant rotor blade pitch angle, an overall greater angle of attack of the rotor disc (as in a flare) increases rotor rpm; a lessening in overall angle of attack (such as "pushing over" into a descent) decreases rotor rpm.
Reference Basic Helicopter Handbook
FAA subject matter knowledge code H71

5673. If the rpm is low and the manifold pressure is high, what initial corrective action should be taken?

A. Increase the throttle.

B. Lower the collective pitch.

C. Raise the collective pitch.

5673. "B" is the correct answer. The pilot must analyze both the tachometer (rpm indicator) and manifold pressure gauge to determine which control to use and how much. To best illustrate the relationship, a few problems with solutions follow:

Problem: rpm low, manifold pressure high.

Solution: Lowering the collective pitch reduces the manifold pressure, decreases drag on the rotor, and increases the rpm.

Problem: rpm high, manifold pressure low.

Solution: Raising the collective pitch increases the manifold pressure, increases drag on the rotor, and decreases the rpm.
Reference Basic Helicopter Handbook
FAA subject matter knowledge code H73

5674. During climbing flight, the manifold pressure is low and the rpm is high. What initial corrective action should be taken?

A. Increase the throttle.

B. Decrease the throttle.

C. Raise the collective pitch.

5674. "C" is the correct answer. If the rpm is high and the manifold pressure low, raising the collective pitch increases the manifold pressure, increases drag on the rotor, and decreases the rpm.
Reference Basic Helicopter Handbook
FAA subject matter knowledge code H73

5675. During level flight, if the manifold pressure is high and the rpm is low, what initial corrective action should be made?

A. Decrease the throttle.

B. Increase the throttle.

C. Lower the collective pitch.

5675. "C" is the correct answer. When the rpm is low and the manifold pressure high, lowering the collective pitch reduces the manifold pressure, decreases drag on the rotor, and increases the rpm.
Reference Basic Helicopter Handbook
FAA subject matter knowledge code H73

5676. When operating a helicopter in conditions favorable for carburetor icing, the carburetor heat should be

A. adjusted to keep the carburetor air temperature gauge indicating in the green arc at all times.

B. OFF for takeoffs, and adjusted to keep the carburetor air temperature gauge indicating in the green arc at all other times.

C. OFF during takeoffs, approaches, and landings, and adjusted to keep the carburetor air temperature gauge indicating in the green arc at all other times.

5676. "A" is the correct answer. The carburetor heat control should be adjusted so that the carburetor air temperature remains in the green arc.
Reference Basic Helicopter Handbook
FAA subject matter knowledge code H79

COMPUTER-BASED QUESTIONS: AERODYNAMICS

5158. Lift on a wing is most properly defined as the

A. force acting perpendicular to the relative wind.

B. differential pressure acting perpendicular to the chord of the wing.

C. reduced pressure resulting from a laminar flow over the upper camber of an airfoil, which acts perpendicular to the mean camber.

5158. "A" is the correct answer. Lift is produced by the dynamic effect of the air acting on the wing. It acts perpendicular to the relative wind through the wing's center of lift.
Reference Flight Training Handbook, p. 265
FAA subject matter knowledge code H01, H66

5167. Which statement is true relative to changing angle of attack?

A. A decrease in angle of attack increases impact pressure below the wing and decreases drag.

B. An increase in angle of attack decreases impact pressure below the wing and increases drag.

C. An increase in angle of attack increases impact pressure below the wing and increases drag.

5167. "C" is the correct answer. As the angle of attack is increased, more surface area on the bottom of the wing is exposed to the relative wind. This is called impact lift or impact pressure. The larger the angle of attack, the more rearward drag is produced.
Reference Flight Training Handbook, pp. 30–32
FAA subject matter knowledge code H01

5179. Refer to Fig. 2. Select the correct statement regarding stall speeds.

A. Power-off stalls occur at higher airspeeds with the gear and flaps down.

B. In a 60° bank the airplane stalls at a lower airspeed with the gear up.

C. Power-on stalls occur at lower airspeeds in shallower banks.

5179. "C" is the correct answer. Most pilots are aware that an airplane stalls at a slower speed with the power on than with the power off. This is caused by the induced airflow over the wings from the propeller. "A" and "B" are incorrect because airplanes tend to stall at a slower speed with the gear and flaps extended.
Reference Flight Training Handbook, p. 267
FAA subject matter knowledge code H01, H66

5180. Refer to Fig. 2. Select the correct statement regarding stall speeds. The airplane stalls

A. 10 knots higher in a power-on, 60° bank with gear and flaps up than with gear and flaps down.

B. 35 knots lower in a power-off, flaps-up, 60° bank than in a power-off, flaps-down, wings-level configuration.

C. 10 knots higher in a 45° bank, power-on stall than in a wings-level stall.

5180. "A" is the correct answer. According to the chart in Fig. 2, the stalling speed for a power-on, 60° bank with the gear and flaps up is 76 knots. The stalling speed for a power-on, 60° bank with gear and flaps down is 66 knots. The difference is 10 knots.
Reference PHOAK, pp. 24–25
FAA subject matter knowledge code H01, H66

5181. Which is true regarding the use of flaps during level turns?

A. The lowering of flaps increases the stall speed.

B. The raising of flaps increases the stall speed.

C. Raising flaps requires added forward pressure on the yoke or stick.

5181. "B" is the correct answer. The use of flaps permits using a slower approach speed. This is due to lowering the stalling speed. Conversely, raising the flaps increases the stall speed. "A" is obviously incorrect, and "C" is incorrect because raising the flaps requires back pressure on the yoke.
Reference PHOAK, pp. 33–34
FAA subject matter knowledge code H66

5182. One of the main functions of flaps during the approach and landing is to

A. decrease the angle of descent without increasing the airspeed.

B. provide the same amount of lift at a slower airspeed.

C. decrease lift, thus enabling a steeper-than-normal approach to be made.

5182. "B" is the correct answer. The practical effect of flaps is to permit the pilot to use a steeper angle of descent without increasing the airspeed. They also allow increased lift at slower airspeeds. "A" is incorrect because flaps allow you to increase the angle of descent. "C" is incorrect because flaps do not decrease lift.
Reference PHOAK, pp. 33–34
FAA subject matter knowledge code H02

5191. Name the four fundamentals involved in maneuvering an aircraft.

A. Power, pitch, bank, and trim.

B. Thrust, lift, turns, and glides.

C. Straight and level flight, turns, climbs, and descents.

5191. "C" is the correct answer. The four fundamentals involved in maneuvering an aircraft are straight and level flight, turns, climbs, and descents.
Reference Flight Training Handbook, p. 59
FAA subject matter knowledge code H55

5192. To increase the rate of turn and at the same time decrease the radius, a pilot should

A. maintain the bank and decrease airspeed.

B. steepen the bank and increase airspeed.

C. steepen the bank and decrease airspeed.

5192. "C" is the correct answer. At a constant bank angle, an increase in airspeed results in an increase in the turn radius. If the angle of bank is increased, the rate of turn also increases. To increase the rate of turn, you must steepen the bank. To decrease the ra-

dius, you must decrease the airspeed. Thus, "C" is the only correct answer.
Reference Flight Training Handbook, pp. 284–285
FAA subject matter knowledge code H66

5193. Which is correct with respect to rate and radius of turn for an airplane flown in a coordinated turn at a constant altitude?

A. For a specific angle of bank and airspeed, the rate and radius of turn do not vary.

B. To maintain a steady rate of turn, the angle of bank must be increased as the airspeed is decreased.

C. The faster the true airspeed, the faster the rate and larger the radius of turn regardless of the angle of bank.

5193. "A" is the correct answer. It must be remembered that the angle of bank and the airspeed determine the rate and the radius of a turn. If these remain constant, the rate and radius of turn do not vary.
Reference Flight Training Handbook, pp. 284–285
FAA subject matter knowledge code H66

5194. Why is it necessary to increase back elevator pressure to maintain altitude during a turn?

A. To compensate for the loss of the vertical component of lift.

B. To compensate for the loss of the horizontal component of lift and the increase in centrifugal force.

C. To compensate for the rudder deflection and slight opposite aileron throughout the turn.

5194. "A" is the correct answer. To provide a vertical component of lift sufficient to maintain altitude in a turn, an increase in the angle of attack (back elevator pressure) is required.
Reference Flight Training Handbook, p. 284
FAA subject matter knowledge code H66

5195. To maintain altitude during a turn, the angle of attack must be increased to compensate for the decrease in the

A. forces opposing the resultant component of drag.

B. vertical component of lift.

C. horizontal component of lift.

5195. "B" is the correct answer. To provide a vertical component of lift sufficient to maintain altitude in a turn, an increase in the angle of attack (back elevator pressure) is required.
Reference Flight Training Handbook, p. 284
FAA subject matter knowledge code H66

5196. Stall speed is affected by

A. weight, load factor, and power.

B. load factor, angle of attack, and power.

C. angle of attack, weight, and air density.

5196. "A" is the correct answer. The stalling speed of an airplane is not a fixed value for all flight situations. It is affected by weight, load factor, and power. The greater the weight, the greater the stall speed. An increased load factor (steep bank) also increases the stall speed. Increasing the power decreases the stall speed. "B" and "C" are incorrect because angle of attack is a fixed value.
Reference Flight Training Handbook, p. 287
FAA subject matter knowledge code H66

5197. A rectangular wing, as compared to other wing forms, has a tendency to stall first at the

A. wingtip, with the stall progression toward the wingroot.

B. wingroot, with the stall progression toward the wingtip.

C. center trailing edge, with the stall progression outward toward the wingroot and tip.

5197. "B" is the correct answer. The rectangular wing has a tendency to stall first at the wingroot and provides adequate aileron effectiveness as the stall progresses from the wingroot to the wingtips.
Reference Flight Training Handbook, p. 265
FAA subject matter knowledge code H66

5198. By changing the angle of attack of a wing, the pilot can control the airplane's

A. lift, airspeed, and drag.

B. lift, airspeed, and CG.

C. lift and airspeed, but not drag.

5198. "A" is the correct answer. In a very real sense the angle of attack is what flight in airplanes is all about. By changing the angle of attack the pilot can control lift, airspeed, and drag.
Reference Flight Training Handbook, p. 263
FAA subject matter knowledge code H66

5199. The angle of attack of a wing directly controls the

A. angle of incidence of the wing.

B. amount of airflow above and below the wing.

C. distribution of pressures acting on the wing.

5199. "C" is the correct answer. The angle of attack of an airfoil directly controls the distribution of pressure below and above the wing.
Reference Flight Training Handbook, p. 263
FAA subject matter knowledge code H66

5200. In theory, if the angle of attack and other factors remain constant and the airspeed is doubled, the lift produced at the higher speed is

A. the same as at the lower speed.

B. two times greater than at the lower speed.

C. four times greater than at the lower speed.

5200. "C" is the correct answer. Lift is proportional to the square of the airplane's velocity. For example, an airplane traveling at 200 knots has four times the lift as the same airplane traveling at 100 knots, if the angle of attack and other factors remain constant.
Reference Flight Training Handbook, p. 270
FAA subject matter knowledge code H01

5201. An aircraft wing is designed to produce lift resulting from relatively

A. negative air pressure below and a vacuum above the wing's surface.

B. a vacuum below the wing's surface and greater air pressure above the wing's surface.

C. higher air pressure below the wing's surface and lower air pressure above the wing's surface.

5201. "C" is the correct answer. Wings are designed to create lift by a positive pressure lifting action from the air mass below the wing, and a negative pressure lifting action from lowered pressure above the wing.
Reference Flight Training Handbook, p. 257
FAA subject matter knowledge code H66

5202. On a wing, the force of lift acts perpendicular to and the force of drag acts parallel to the

A. chord line.

B. flight path.

C. longitudinal axis.

5202. "B" is the correct answer. Air movement of a wing through the air create forces called lift and drag. Lift acts perpendicular to the direction of the relative wind or flight path. Drag is a rearward force that acts opposite to the direction of the airplane's forward motion.
Reference Flight Training Handbook, p. 261
FAA subject matter knowledge code H01

5203. Which statement is true regarding the opposing forces acting on an airplane in steady-state level flight?

A. These forces are equal.

B. Thrust is greater than drag, and weight and lift are equal.

C. Thrust is greater than drag, and lift is greater than weight.

5203. "A" is the correct answer. The four forces acting on an airplane in flight are lift, weight, thrust, and drag. In unaccelerated steady flight, the opposing forces are equal.
Reference PHOAK, p. 61
FAA subject matter knowledge code H66

5204. The angle of attack at which a wing stalls remains constant regardless of

A. weight, dynamic pressure, bank angle, or pitch attitude.

B. dynamic pressure, but varies with weight, bank angle, and pitch attitude.

C. weight and pitch attitude, but varies with dynamic pressure and bank angle.

5204. "A" is the correct answer. One of the most important things a pilot should understand about angle of attack is that, for any given airplane, the stalling angle of attack remains constant regardless of weight, dynamic pressure, bank angle, or pitch attitude.
Reference Flight Training Handbook, p. 264
FAA subject matter knowledge code H66

5205. In light airplanes, normal recovery from spins may become difficult if the

A. CG is too far rearward and rotation is around the longitudinal axis.

B. CG is too far rearward and rotation is around the CG.

C. spin is entered before the stall is fully developed.

5205. "B" is the correct answer. The recovery from a stall in any airplane becomes progressively more difficult as its CG moves aft. This is particularly true in spin recovery. There is a point in rearward loading of any airplane at which a "flat" spin will develop. A *flat spin* is one in which centrifugal force, acting through a CG located well aft, pulls the tail of the airplane out away from the axis of the spin, making it impossible to get the nose down and recover. Answer "A" is incorrect because the spin develops around the CG cen-

ter. Answer "C" is incorrect because an airplane must stall before it can enter a spin.
Reference Flight Training Handbook, p. 303
FAA subject matter knowledge code H66

5206. The inclinometer is mounted on the left side of the instrument panel. A spin to the left would displace the ball in which direction?

A. To the right.

B. No displacement, it remains centered.

C. To the left.

5206. "C" is the correct answer. The ball in the inclinometer is displaced in the same direction as the placement of the inclinometer.
Reference Flight Training Handbook, pp. 156–157
FAA subject matter knowledge code H60

5207. If an airplane is loaded to the rear of its CG range, it tends to be unstable about its

A. vertical axis.

B. lateral axis.

C. longitudinal axis.

5207. "B" is the correct answer. An airplane becomes less and less stable as the CG is moved rearward. This is because when the angle of attack is increased it tends to result in additional increased angle of attack.
Reference Flight Training Handbook, p. 304
FAA subject matter knowledge code H60

5209. An airplane leaving ground effect

A. experiences a reduction in ground friction and requires a slight power reduction.

B. experiences an increase in induced drag and requires more thrust.

C. requires a lower angle of attack to maintain the same lift coefficient.

5209. "B" is the correct answer. An airplane leaving ground effect

1. Requires an increase in angle of attack to maintain the same lift coefficient
2. Experiences an increase in induced drag and requires more thrust
3. Experiences a decrease in stability and a nose up change in moment
4. Produces a reduction in static source pressure and increase in indicated airspeed.

Reference Flight Training Handbook, p. 273
FAA subject matter knowledge code H66

5210. If airspeed is increased during a level turn, what action would be necessary to maintain altitude?

A. The angle of attack and angle of bank must be decreased.

B. The angle of attack must be increased or angle of bank decreased.

C. The angle of attack must be decreased or angle of bank increased.

5210. "C" is the correct answer. To maintain altitude during a level turn while increasing airspeed, the angle of attack must be decreased or the angle of bank increased.
Reference Flight Training Handbook, p. 285
FAA subject matter knowledge code H66

5211. The stalling speed of an airplane is most affected by

A. changes in air density.

B. variations in flight altitude.

C. variations in airplane loading.

5211. "C" is the correct answer. An airplane's stalling speed increases in proportion to the square root of the load factor, so variations in airplane loading is the correct answer. "A" and "B" are incorrect because altitude and air density do not affect the indicated stalling speed.
Reference Flight Training Handbook, p. 296
FAA subject matter knowledge code H66

5212. An airplane stalls at the same

A. angle of attack, regardless of the attitude with relation to the horizon.

B. airspeed, regardless of the attitude with relation to the horizon.

C. angle of attack and attitude with relation to the horizon.

5212. "A" is the correct answer. Angle of attack must not be confused with an airplane's attitude in relation to the earth's surface. When the angle of attack increases to approximately 18° to 20°, the air can no longer flow smoothly over the top wing surface. Because the airflow cannot change direction so quickly, it becomes impossible for the air to follow the contour of the wind. This is the stalling or critical angle of attack.
Reference Flight Training Handbook, p. 263
FAA subject matter knowledge code H60

5213. Refer to Fig. 3. If an airplane glides at an angle of attack of 10°, how much altitude will it lose in 1 mile?

A. 240 ft.

B. 480 ft.

C. 960 ft.

5213. "B" is the correct answer. To find how much altitude an airplane will lose while gliding at a 10° angle of attack, follow these steps. Refer to Fig. 3. The bottom line refers to angle of attack in degrees. Locate the 10° angle of attack on this line. Next, move up the vertical 10° angle of attack line until you intersect the L/D curve. At that point, move to the right and read the bold L/D scale. The L/D ratio of 11:1 means that for every 11 ft the airplane moves horizontally, it will descend 1 ft. To determine the amount of altitude you will lose in 1 mile, divide 5280 ft (1 mile) by the L/D ratio of 11: 5280/11 = 480.
Reference Flight Training Handbook, p. 262
FAA subject matter knowledge code H66

5214. Refer to Fig. 3. How much altitude will this airplane lose in 3 miles of gliding at an angle of attack of 8°?

A. 440 ft.

B. 880 ft.

C. 1320 ft.

5214. "C" is the correct answer. To find how much altitude an airplane will lose while gliding at a 10° angle of attack, follow these steps. Refer to Fig. 3. The bottom line refers to angle of attack in degrees. Locate the 8° angle of attack on this line. Next, move up the vertical 8° angle of attack line until you intersect the L/D curve. At that point, move to the right and read the bold L/D scale. The L/D ratio of 12:1 means that for every 12 ft the airplane moves horizontally, it will descend 1 ft. To determine the amount of altitude you would lose in 1 mile, divide 5280 ft (1 mile) by the L/D ratio of 12: 5280/12 = 440. Multiply 440 × 3 miles = 1320.
Reference Flight Training Handbook, p. 262
FAA subject matter knowledge code H66

5215. Refer to Fig. 3. The L/D ratio at a 2° angle of attack is approximately the same as the L/D ratio for a

A. 9.75° angle of attack.

B. 10.5° angle of attack.

C. 16.5° angle of attack.

5215. "C" is the correct answer. Locate the 2° angle of attack on the bottom horizontal reference line. Move up the vertical 2° angle of attack line until you intersect the L/D curve. Now move right until you reintersect the L/D curve. Move straight down to read a 16.5° angle of attack.
Reference Flight Training Handbook, p. 260
FAA subject matter knowledge code H66

5216. If the same angle of attack is maintained in ground effect as when out of ground effect, lift

A. increases and induced drag decreases.

B. decreases and parasite drag increases.

C. increases and induced drag increases.

5216. "A" is the correct answer. If a constant angle of attack is maintained, an increase in lift results while in ground effect. Ground effect also causes a significant reduction in induced drag.
Reference Flight Training Handbook, p. 276
FAA subject matter knowledge code H66

5217. What performance is characteristic of flight at maximum lift/drag ratio in a propeller-driven airplane?

A. Maximum gain in altitude over a given distance.

B. Maximum range and maximum distance glide.

C. Maximum coefficient of lift and minimum coefficient of drag.

5217. "B" is the correct answer. Operating at the airplane's best L/D (lift/drag) angle allows the airplane to travel the greatest distance over the ground with the least loss of altitude. It also is the maximum range condition. It is important to note that for a given airplane configuration, the maximum L/D ratio occurs at a particular angle of attack and lift coefficient, and is unaffected by weight or altitude.
Reference Flight Training Handbook, pp. 310–311
FAA subject matter knowledge code H60

5218. Which is true regarding the forces acting on an aircraft in a steady-state descent?

A. The sum of all upward forces is less than the sum of all downward forces.

B. The sum of all rearward forces is greater than the sum of all forward forces.

C. The sum of all forward forces is equal to the sum of all rearward forces.

5218. "C" is the correct answer. Anytime the flight path of the airplane is not horizontal, lift, weight, thrust, and drag vectors must be broken down into the two components. The sum of all forward forces (not just thrust) equals the sum of all backward forces (not just drag).
Reference Flight Training Handbook, p. 266
FAA subject matter knowledge code H66

5219. Which is true regarding the force of lift in steady, unaccelerated flight?

A. At lower airspeeds the angle of attack must be less to generate sufficient lift to maintain altitude.

B. There is a corresponding indicated airspeed required for every angle of attack to generate sufficient lift to maintain altitude.

C. An airfoil always stalls at the same indicated airspeed; therefore, an increase in weight requires an increase in speed to generate sufficient lift to maintain altitude.

5219. "B" is the correct answer. For every angle of attack, there is a corresponding indicated airspeed required to maintain altitude in steady, unaccelerated flight.
Reference Flight Training Handbook, p. 270
FAA subject matter knowledge code H66

5220. During the transition from straight and level flight to a climb, the angle of attack is increased and lift

A. is momentarily decreased.

B. remains the same.

C. is momentarily increased.

5220. "C" is the correct answer. During transition from straight and level flight to a climb, the forces acting on the airplane go through definite changes. The first change, an increase in lift, occurs when back pressure is applied to the elevator control. This initial change results in an increased angle of attack and increased lift.
Reference Flight Training Handbook, p. 37
FAA subject matter knowledge code H52

5221. Refer to Fig. 4. What is the stall speed of an airplane under a load factor of 2 Gs if the unaccelerated stall speed is 60 knots?

A. 66 knots.

B. 74 knots.

C. 84 knots.

5221. "C" is the correct answer. Start at the left side of the chart at a load factor of 2. From there, proceed horizontally to the right until you intercept the load factor line. From there proceed vertically until you intercept the stall speed increase line. Now return to the left horizontally until you read 40. That's a 40% increase in stall speed: 40% × 60 = 24 knots; 24 knots + 60 knots = 84 knots.

Reference Flight Training Handbook, p. 288
FAA subject matter knowledge code H66

5222. Refer to Fig. 4. What increase in load factor would take place if the angle of bank were increased from 60° to 80°?

A. 3 Gs

B. 3.5 Gs

C. 4 Gs

5222. "C" is the correct answer. Start at the bottom of the graph. At a 60° bank angle proceed vertically until you intersect the load factor line. Now proceed horizontally and read 2 Gs. Repeat the procedure for 80° of bank. You should come up with 6 Gs: 6 Gs – 2 Gs = 4 Gs.

Reference Flight Training Handbook, p. 288
FAA subject matter knowledge code H66

5223. To generate the same amount of lift as altitude is increased, an airplane must be flown at

A. the same true airspeed regardless of angle of attack.

B. a lower true airspeed and a greater angle of attack.

C. a higher true airspeed for any given angle of attack.

5223. "C" is the correct answer. Lift and drag vary directly with the density of the air. Density is affected by several factors: pressure, temperature, and humidity. At an altitude of 18,000 ft the density of the air has one-half the density of air at sea level. In order to maintain lift at a higher altitude an airplane must fly at a greater (higher) true airspeed for any given angle of attack.

Reference Flight Training Handbook, p. 270
FAA subject matter knowledge code H66

5224. To produce the same lift while in ground effect as when out of ground effect, the airplane requires

A. a lower angle of attack.

B. the same angle of attack.

C. a greater angle of attack.

5224. "A" is the correct answer. The reduction of the wingtip vortices due to ground effect alters the spanwise lift distribution and reduces the induced angle of attack and induced drag. The wing requires a lower angle of attack in ground effect to produce the same lift coefficient.

Reference Flight Training Handbook, p. 272
FAA subject matter knowledge code H66

5225. As the angle of bank is increased, the vertical component of lift

A. decreases and the horizontal component of lift increases.

B. increases and the horizontal component of lift decreases.

C. decreases and the horizontal component of lift remains constant.

5255. "A" is the correct answer. The vertical component of lift decreases as the bank angle increases. The angle of attack must be progressively increased to produce sufficient lift to support the airplane's weight. The horizontal component of lift is proportional to the angle of bank. It increases or decreases as the angle of bank increases or decreases.

Reference Flight Training Handbook, p. 284
FAA subject matter knowledge code H66

5226. If the airplane attitude remains in a new position after the elevator control is pressed forward and released, the airplane displays

A. neutral longitudinal static stability.

B. positive longitudinal static stability.

C. neutral longitudinal dynamic stability.

5226. "A" is the correct answer. Longitudinal stability is the quality that makes an airplane stable about its lateral axis. Neutral static stability is the initial tendency of the airplane to remain in a new condition after its equilibrium has been disturbed. "B" is incorrect because positive static stability is the initial tendency to return to the original state of equilibrium after being disturbed. "C" is incorrect because dynamic stability is the overall tendency that the airplane displays for a period of time after its equilibrium is disturbed.

Reference Flight Training Handbook, pp. 275–277
FAA subject matter knowledge code H66

5227. Longitudinal dynamic instability in an airplane can be identified by

A. bank oscillations becoming progressively steeper.

B. pitch oscillations becoming progressively steeper.

C. trilatitudinal roll oscillations becoming progressively steeper.

5227. "B" is the correct answer. A longitudinally unstable airplane has a tendency to dive or climb progressing into a very steep climb or dive.
Reference Flight Training Handbook, p. 277
FAA subject matter knowledge code H66

5228. Longitudinal stability involves the motion of the airplane controlled by its

A. rudder.

B. elevator.

C. ailerons.

5228. "B" is the correct answer. Longitudinal stability is the quality that makes the airplane stable about its lateral axis. It involves the pitching motion as the airplane's nose moves up and down in flight. This pitching motion is controlled by the elevator. Thus "A" and "C" are incorrect.
Reference Flight Training Handbook, p. 277
FAA subject matter knowledge code H66

5229. What changes in airplane longitudinal control must be made to maintain altitude while the airspeed is being decreased?

A. Increase the angle of attack to produce more lift than drag.

B. Increase the angle of attack to compensate for the decreasing lift.

C. Decrease the angle of attack to compensate for the increasing drag.

5229. "B" is the correct answer. At low speeds, during which the wing affects a lesser amount of air, a larger angle of attack is needed to deflect the air a large amount. The angle of attack at various speeds must be such that the deflection of air is adequate for the amount of lift required.
Reference Flight Training Handbook, p. 31
FAA subject matter knowledge code H52

5230. If the airplane attitude initially tends to return to its original position after the elevator control is pressed forward and released, the airplane displays

A. positive dynamic stability.

B. positive static stability.

C. neutral dynamic stability.

5230. "B" is the correct answer. Positive static stability is the initial tendency of the airplane to return to the original state of equilibrium after being disturbed.
Reference Flight Training Handbook, p. 275
FAA subject matter knowledge code H66

5231. Refer to Fig. 5. The horizontal dashed line from point C to point E represents the

A. ultimate load factor.

B. positive limit load factor.

C. airspeed range for normal operations.

5231. "B" is the correct answer. The horizontal dashed line represents the positive load limit. The horizontal scale represents speed and the vertical scale represents load factors (Gs). "A" is incorrect because 3.8 Gs is the maximum limit. "C" is incorrect because airspeed is represented by the vertical indicated airspeed mph lines.
Reference Flight Training Handbook, pp. 299–300
FAA subject matter knowledge code H66

5232. Refer to Fig. 5. The vertical line from point E to point F is represented on the airspeed indicator by the

A. upper limit of the yellow arc.

B. upper limit of the green arc.

C. blue radial line.

5232. "A" is the correct answer. The never exceed airspeed (V_{NE}) is marked by a red radial on the airspeed indicator. Prior to that is the yellow arc. Point E to point F represents the upper limit of the yellow arc.
Reference Flight Training Handbook, pp. 299–300
FAA subject matter knowledge code H66

5233. Refer to Fig. 5. The vertical line from point D to point G is represented on the airspeed indicator by the maximum speed limit of the

A. green arc.

B. yellow arc.

C. white arc.

5233. "A" is the correct answer. This vertical line represents the upper limit of the green arc and is the maximum structural cruising speed (V_{NO}).
Reference Flight Training Handbook, pp. 299–300
FAA subject matter knowledge code H66

5235. Propeller efficiency is the

A. ratio of thrust horsepower to brake horsepower.

B. actual distance a propeller advances in one revolution.

C. ratio of geometric pitch to effective pitch.

5235. "A" is the correct answer. The efficiency of any machine is the ratio of the useful power output to

the actual power input. Propeller efficiency is the ratio of thrust horsepower to brake horsepower.
Reference Flight Training Handbook, p. 290
FAA subject matter knowledge code H66

5236. A fixed-pitch propeller is designed for best efficiency only at a given combination of

A. altitude and rpm.

B. airspeed and rpm.

C. airspeed and altitude.

5236. "B" is the correct answer. Every fixed-pitch propeller must be a compromise because it can be efficient at only a given combination of airspeed and rpm.
Reference Flight Training Handbook, p. 289
FAA subject matter knowledge code H66

5237. The reason for variations in geometric pitch (twisting) along a propeller blade is that it

A. permits a relatively constant angle of incidence along its length when in cruising flight.

B. prevents the portion of the blade near the hub from stalling during cruising flight.

C. permits a relatively constant angle of attack along its length when in cruising flight.

5237. "C" is the correct answer. Twisting, or variations in the geometric pitch of the blades, permits the propeller to operate with a relatively constant angle of attack along its length when in cruising flight. To put it another way, propeller blades are twisted to change the blade angle in proportion to the differences in speed of rotation along the length of the propeller, thereby keeping thrust more nearly equalized along this length.
Reference Flight Training Handbook, p. 290
FAA subject matter knowledge code H66

5238. A propeller rotating clockwise as seen from the rear, creates a spiraling slipstream that tends to rotate the airplane to the

A. right around the vertical axis, and to the left around the longitudinal axis.

B. left around the vertical axis, and to the right around the longitudinal axis.

C. left around the vertical axis, and to the left around the longitudinal axis.

5238. "B" is the correct answer. Since an airplane's propeller rotates clockwise as viewed from the cockpit, the slipstream strikes the vertical tail surface on the left side (vertical axis), thus pushing the tail to

the right and yawing the nose of the airplane to the left (longitudinal axis).
Reference Flight Training Handbook, p. 34
FAA subject matter knowledge code H52

5239. When the angle of attack of a symmetrical airfoil is increased, the center of pressure

A. has very limited movement.

B. moves aft along the airfoil surface.

C. remains unaffected.

5239. "C" is the correct answer. When the angle of attack is increased to develop positive lift, the vectors remain opposite to each other and the center of pressure remains constant.
Reference Flight Training Handbook
FAA subject matter knowledge code H66

5240. Coning is caused by the combined forces of

A. drag, weight, and translational lift.

B. lift and centrifugal force.

C. flapping and centrifugal force.

5240. "B" is the correct answer. Coning is the upward bending of the blades caused by the combined forces of lift and centrifugal force.
Reference Basic Helicopter Handbook, p. 12
FAA subject matter knowledge code H71

5241. The forward speed of a rotorcraft is restricted primarily by

A. dissymmetry of lift.

B. transverse flow effect.

C. high-frequency vibrations.

5241. "A" is the correct answer. The stall of a rotor blade limits the high-airspeed potential of a helicopter. The airflow over the retreating blade of the helicopter slows down as the forward airspeed of the helicopter increases; the airflow over the advancing blade speeds up as forward airspeed increases. The retreating blade must, however, produce the same amount of lift as the advancing blade. Therefore, as the airflow over the retreating blade decreases with forward airspeed, the blade angle of attack must be increased to help equalize lift throughout the rotor disc area. As this increase in angle of attack is continued, the retreating blade will stall at some high forward airspeed.
Reference Basic Helicopter Handbook, p. 65
FAA subject matter knowledge code H78

5242. When hovering, a helicopter tends to move in the direction of tail rotor thrust. This statement is

A. true; the movement is called transverse tendency.

B. true; the movement is called translating tendency.

C. false; the movement is opposite the direction of tail rotor thrust, and is called translating tendency.

5242. "B" is the correct answer. The entire helicopter has a tendency to move in the direction of tail rotor thrust (to the right) when hovering. This movement is often referred to as translating tendency.
Reference Basic Helicopter Handbook, p. 15
FAA subject matter knowledge code H71.

5243. The purpose of lead-lag (drag) hinges in a three-bladed, fully articulated helicopter rotor system is to compensate for

A. Coriolis effect.

B. dissymmetry of lift.

C. blade flapping tendency.

5243. "A" is the correct answer. When a rotor blade of a three-bladed rotor system flaps upward, the center of mass of that blade moves closer to the axis of rotation and blade acceleration takes place. Conversely, when that blade flaps downward, its center of mass moves further from the axis of rotation and blade deceleration takes place. This is the Coriolis effect. The acceleration and deceleration actions (often referred to as leading, lagging, or hunting) of the rotor blades are absorbed by either dampers or the blade structure itself, depending on the design of the rotor system.
Reference Basic Helicopter Handbook, p. 14
FAA subject matter knowledge code H71

5244. What happens to the helicopter as it experiences translating tendency?

A. It tends to dip slightly to the right as the helicopter approaches approximately 15 knots in takeoff.

B. It gains increased rotor efficiency as air over the rotor system reaches approximately 15 knots.

C. It moves in the direction of tail rotor thrust.

5244. "C" is the correct answer. The entire helicopter has a tendency to move in the direction of tail rotor thrust (to the right) when hovering. This movement is often referred to as translating tendency.
Reference Basic Helicopter Handbook, p. 15
FAA subject matter knowledge code H71

5245. The unequal lift across the rotor disc that occurs in horizontal flight as a result of the difference in velocity of the air over the advancing half of the disc area and the air passing over the retreating half of the disc area is known as

A. coning.

B. disc loading.

C. dissymmetry of lift.

5245. "C" is the correct answer. Dissymmetry of lift is created by horizontal flight or by wind during hovering flight, and is the difference in lift that exists between the advancing blade half of the disc area and the retreating blade half.
Reference Basic Helicopter Handbook, p. 12
FAA subject matter knowledge code H71

5246. The lift differential that exists between the advancing blade and the retreating blade is known as

A. the Coriolis effect.

B. translational lift.

C. dissymmetry of lift.

5246. "C" is the correct answer. Dissymmetry of lift is created by horizontal flight or by wind during hovering flight, and is the difference in lift that exists between the advancing blade half of the disc area and the retreating blade half.
Reference Basic Helicopter Handbook, p. 12
FAA subject matter knowledge code H71

5247. Most helicopters by design tend to drift to the right when hovering in a no-wind condition. This statement is

A. false; helicopters have no tendency to drift, but will rotate in that direction.

B. true; the mast or cyclic pitch system of most helicopters is rigged forward. This with gyroscopic precession overcome this tendency.

C. true; the mast or cyclic pitch system of most helicopters is rigged to the left to overcome this tendency.

5247. "C" is the correct answer. The entire helicopter has a tendency to move in the direction of tail rotor thrust (to the right) when hovering. This movement is often referred to as translating tendency. To counteract this drift, the rotor mast in some helicopters is rigged slightly to the left side so that the tip-path plane has a built-in tilt to the left, thus producing a small sideward thrust. In other helicopters, drift is overcome by rigging the cyclic pitch system to give the required amount of tilt to the tip-path plane.

Reference Basic Helicopter Handbook, p. 15

FAA subject matter knowledge code H71

5248. When a rotorcraft transitions from straight-and-level flight into a 30° bank while maintaining a constant altitude, the total lift force must

A. increase and the load factor increases.

B. increase and the load factor decreases.

C. remain constant and the load factor decreases.

5248. "A" is the correct answer. The load factor is the actual load on the rotor blades at any time divided by the normal load or gross weight. The load factor is relatively small in banks up to 30°. For more than 30° of bank, the apparent increase in gross weight soars. If the weight of the helicopter is 1600 pounds, the weight supported by the rotor in a 30° bank at a constant altitude would be 1856 pounds.

Reference Basic Helicopter Handbook, pp. 20–21

FAA subject matter knowledge code H72

5249. Cyclic control pressure is applied during flight that results in a maximum increase in main rotor blade pitch angle at the "three o'clock" position. Which way will the rotor disc tilt?

A. Aft.

B. Left.

C. Right.

5249. "A" is the correct answer. The spinning main rotor of a helicopter acts like a gyroscope. Gyroscopic precession is the resultant action or deflection of a spinning object when a force is applied to this object. This action occurs approximately 90° in the direction of rotation from the point where the force is applied. The movement of the cyclic pitch control in a two-bladed rotor system increases the angle of attack of one rotor blade, with the result being that a greater lifting force is applied at this point in the plane of rotation. This same control movement simultaneously decreases the angle of attack of the other blade a like amount, thus decreasing the lifting force applied at this point in the plane of rotation. The blade with the increased angle of attack tends to rise; the blade with the decreased angle of attack tends to lower. However, because of the gyroscopic precession property, the blades do not rise or lower to maximum deflection until a point approximately 90° later in the plane of rotation.

Reference Basic Helicopter Handbook, p. 10

FAA subject matter knowledge code H71

5250. Cyclic control pressure is applied during flight that results in a maximum decrease in pitch angle of the rotor blades at the "12 o'clock" position. Which way will the rotor disc tilt?

A. Aft.

B. Left.

C. Forward.

5250. "B" is the correct answer. The spinning main rotor of a helicopter acts like a gyroscope. Gyroscopic precession is the resultant action or deflection of a spinning object when a force is applied to this object. This action occurs approximately 90° in the direction of rotation from the point where the force is applied. The movement of the cyclic pitch control in a two-bladed rotor system increases the angle of attack of one rotor blade, with the result being that a greater lifting force is applied at this point in the plane of rotation. This same control movement simultaneously decreases the angle of attack of the other blade a like amount, thus decreasing the lifting force applied at this point in the plane of rotation. The blade with the increased angle of attack tends to rise; the blade with the decreased angle of attack tends to lower. However, because of the gyroscopic precession property, the blades do not rise or lower to maximum deflection until a point approximately 90° later in the plane of rotation.

Reference Basic Helicopter Handbook, p. 10

FAA subject matter knowledge code H71

5251. The primary purpose of the tail rotor system is to

A. assist in making coordinated turns.

B. maintain heading during forward flight.

C. counteract the torque effect of the main rotor.

5251. "C" is the correct answer. The force that compensates for torque and keeps the fuselage from turning in the direction opposite to the main rotor is produced by means of an auxiliary rotor located on the end of the tail boom. This auxiliary rotor, generally referred to as a tail rotor, or antitorque rotor, produces thrust in the direction opposite to torque reaction developed by the main rotor.

Reference Basic Helicopter Handbook, p. 10

FAA subject matter knowledge code H71

5252. Can the tail rotor produce thrust to the left?

A. No; the right thrust can only be reduced, causing tail movement to the left.

B. Yes; primarily so that hovering turns can be accomplished to the right.

C. Yes; primarily to counteract the drag of the transmission during autorotation.

5252. "C" is the correct answer. The capability for tail rotors to produce thrust to the left (negative pitch angle) is necessary because, during autorotation, the drag of the transmission tends to yaw the nose to the left—in the same direction that the main rotor is turning.
Reference Basic Helicopter Handbook, p. 26
FAA subject matter knowledge code H73

5253. The main rotor blades of a fully articulated rotor system can

A. flap and feather collectively.

B. flap, drag, and feather independently.

C. feather independently, but cannot flap or drag.

5253. "B" is the correct answer. Fully articulated rotor systems generally consist of three or more rotor blades. In a fully articulated rotor system, each rotor blade is attached to the rotor hub by a horizontal hinge, called the flapping hinge, that permits the blades to flap up and down. Each rotor blade is also attached to the hub by a vertical hinge, called a drag or lag hinge, that permits each blade, independent of the others, to move back and forth in the plane of the rotor disc. This movement is called dragging, lead-lag, or hunting. The blades of a fully articulated rotor can also feather, that is, be rotated about their spanwise axis.
Reference Basic Helicopter Handbook, p. 32
FAA subject matter knowledge code H74

5254. A reciprocating engine in a helicopter is more likely to stop due to in-flight carburetor icing than the same type engine in an airplane.

A. This statement has no basis in fact. The same type engine runs equally well in either aircraft.

B. This statement is true. The freewheeling unit does not allow a windmilling (flywheel) effect to be exerted on a helicopter engine.

C. This statement is false. The clutch immediately releases the load from the helicopter engine under engine malfunctioning conditions.

5254. "B" is the correct answer. Carburetor icing is a frequent cause of engine failure. The vaporization of fuel, combined with the expansion of air as it passes through the carburetor, causes a sudden cooling of the mixture. Water vapor in the air is "squeezed out"

by this cooling, and if the temperature in the carburetor reaches 32°F or below, the moisture is deposited as frost or ice inside the carburetor passages. Even a slight accumulation of this deposit reduces power and may lead to complete engine failure, particularly when the throttle is partly or fully closed.
Reference Basic Helicopter Handbook, p. 73
FAA subject matter knowledge code H79

5255. What is the primary purpose of the clutch?

A. It allows the engine to be started without driving the main rotor system.

B. It provides disengagement of the engine from the rotor system for autorotation.

C. It transmits engine power to the main rotor, tail rotor, generator/alternator, and other accessories.

5255. "A" is the correct answer. Because of the much greater weight of a helicopter rotor in relation to the power of the engine than the weight of a propeller in relation to the power of the engine in an airplane, it is necessary to have the rotor disconnected from the engine to relieve the starter load. For this reason, it is necessary to have a clutch between the engine and rotor. The clutch allows the engine to be started and gradually assume the load of driving the heavy rotor system.
Reference Basic Helicopter Handbook, p. 29
FAA subject matter knowledge code H74

5256. What is the primary purpose of the freewheeling unit?

A. It allows the engine to be started without driving the main rotor system.

B. It provides speed reduction between the engine, main rotor system, and tail rotor system.

C. It provides disengagement of the engine from the rotor system for autorotation purposes.

5256. "C" is the correct answer. The freewheeling coupling provides for autorotative capabilities by automatically disconnecting the rotor system from the engine when the engine stops or slows below the equivalent of rotor rpm.
Reference Basic Helicopter Handbook, p. 30
FAA subject matter knowledge code H74

5257. The main rotor blades of a semirigid rotor system can

A. flap and feather as a unit.

B. flap, drag, and feather independently.

C. feather independently, but cannot flap or drag.

5257. "A" is the correct answer. In a semirigid rotor system, the rotor blades are rigidly interconnected to the hub, but the hub is free to tilt and rock with respect to the rotor shaft. The rotor flaps as a unit; that is, as one blade flaps up, the other blade flaps down an equal amount. Collective pitch control changes the pitch of each blade simultaneously and an equal amount, either increasing the pitch of both or decreasing the pitch of both. Summarizing, a semirigid rotor system can flap and feather as a unit.
Reference Basic Helicopter Handbook, p. 33
FAA subject matter knowledge code H74

5258. Rotorcraft climb performance is most adversely affected by

A. higher than standard temperature and low relative humidity.

B. lower than standard temperature and high relative humidity.

C. higher than standard temperature and high relative humidity.

5258. "C" is the correct answer. High elevations, high temperatures, and high moisture content, all of which contribute to a high-density altitude condition, lessen helicopter performance.
Reference Basic Helicopter Handbook, p. 55
FAA subject matter knowledge code H77

5259. The most unfavorable combination of conditions for rotorcraft performance is

A. low-density altitude, low gross weight, and calm wind.

B. high-density altitude, high gross weight, and calm wind.

C. high-density altitude, high gross weight, and strong wind.

5259. "B" is the correct answer. The performance of the helicopter is dependent on three major factors: density altitude (air density), gross weight, and wind velocity during takeoff, hovering, and landing. Helicopter performance is reduced because the thinner air at high-density altitudes reduces the amount of lift of the rotor blades. Also, the engine does not develop as much power because of the thinner air and the decreased atmospheric pressure. The heavier the gross weight, the greater the power required to hover and for flight in general, and the poorer the performance of the helicopter since less reserve power is available. No-wind conditions increase the amount of power necessary to hover, or require that

a lighter load be carried. Thus, no-wind conditions reduce helicopter performance.
Reference Basic Helicopter Handbook, pp. 51, 55, 60, 61
FAA subject matter knowledge code H77

5260. How does high-density altitude affect rotorcraft performance?

A. Engine and rotor efficiency is reduced.

B. Engine and rotor efficiency is increased.

C. It increases rotor drag, which requires more power for normal flight.

5260. "A" is the correct answer. Helicopter performance is reduced because the thinner air at high-density altitudes reduces the amount of lift of the rotor blades. Also, the engine does not develop as much power because of the thinner air and the decreased atmospheric pressure.
Reference Basic Helicopter Handbook, p. 55
FAA subject matter knowledge code H77

5261. A medium-frequency vibration that suddenly occurs during flight could be indicative of a defective

A. main rotor system.

B. tail rotor system.

C. transmission system.

5261. "B" is the correct answer. Abnormal vibrations in the helicopter generally fall into three ranges: low frequency—100 to 400 cycles per minute (cpm), medium frequency—1000 to 2000 cpm, and high frequency—2000 cpm or higher. In most helicopters, medium-frequency vibrations are a result of trouble with the tail rotor.
Reference Basic Helicopter Handbook, pp. 66–67
FAA subject matter knowledge code H78

5262. In most helicopters, medium-frequency vibrations indicate a defective

A. engine.

B. main rotor system.

C. tail rotor system.

5262. "C" is the correct answer. Abnormal vibrations in the helicopter generally fall into three ranges: low frequency—100 to 400 cycles per minute (cpm), medium frequency—1000 to 2000 cpm, and high frequency—2000 cpm or higher. In most helicopters, medium-frequency vibrations are a result of trouble with the tail rotor.
Reference Basic Helicopter Handbook, pp. 66–67
FAA subject matter knowledge code H78

5263. Abnormal helicopter vibrations in the low-frequency range are associated with which system or component?

A. Tail rotor.

B. Main rotor.

C. Transmission.

5263. "B" is the correct answer. Abnormal vibrations in this category are *always* associated with the main rotor.
Reference Basic Helicopter Handbook, p. 66
FAA subject matter knowledge code H78

5264. Helicopter low-frequency vibrations are always associated with the

A. main rotor.

B. tail rotor.

C. transmission.

5264. "A" is the correct answer. Abnormal vibrations in this category are *always* associated with the main rotor.
Reference Basic Helicopter Handbook, p. 66
FAA subject matter knowledge code H78

5265. A high-frequency vibration that suddenly occurs during flight could be an indication of a defective

A. transmission.

B. freewheeling unit.

C. main rotor system.

5265. "A" is the correct answer. In most helicopters, high-frequency vibrations are associated with the engine. However, any bearings in the engine, transmission, or tail rotor drive shaft that go bad result in vibrations with frequencies directly related to the speed of the engine.
Reference Basic Helicopter Handbook, p. 67
FAA subject matter knowledge code H78

5266. Ground resonance is more likely to occur with helicopters that are equipped with

A. rigid rotor systems.

B. semirigid rotor systems.

C. fully articulated rotor systems.

5266. "C" is the correct answer. Ground resonance may develop when a series of shocks cause the rotor head to become unbalanced. It occurs only in helicopters possessing three-bladed, fully articulated rotor systems and landing wheels.
Reference Basic Helicopter Handbook, p. 66
FAA subject matter knowledge code H78

5267. The proper action to initiate a quick stop is to apply

A. forward cyclic, while raising the collective and applying right antitorque pedal.

B. aft cyclic, while raising the collective and applying left antitorque pedal.

C. aft cyclic, while lowering the collective and applying right antitorque pedal.

5267. "C" is the correct answer. Begin the maneuver at a fast hover speed headed into the wind, at an altitude high enough to avoid danger to the tail rotor during the flare but low enough to stay out of the height velocity chart shaded area throughout the performance. The deceleration is initiated by applying aft cyclic to reduce forward speed. Simultaneously, the collective pitch should be lowered as necessary to counteract any climbing tendency. As collective pitch is lowered, right pedal should be increased to maintain heading and throttle should be adjusted to maintain rpm.
Reference Basic Helicopter Handbook, p. 97
FAA subject matter knowledge code H80

5268. What is an operational difference between the turn coordinator and the turn-and-slip indicator?

A. The turn coordinator is always electric; the turn-and-slip indicator is always vacuum-driven.

B. The turn coordinator indicates bank angle only; the turn-and-slip indicator indicates rate of turn and coordination.

C. The turn coordinator indicates roll rate, rate of turn, and coordination; the turn-and-slip indicator indicates rate of turn and coordination.

5268. "C" is the correct answer. A turn coordinator indicates the roll rate, the rate of turn, and coordination. The turn-and-slip indicator indicates the rate of turn and coordination.
Reference Instrument Flying Handbook, p. 38
FAA subject matter knowledge code H03

5269. What is an advantage of an electric turn coordinator if the airplane has a vacuum system for other gyroscopic instruments?

A. It is a backup in case of vacuum system failure.

B. It is more reliable than the vacuum-driven indicators.

C. It does not tumble as do vacuum-driven turn indicators.

5269. **"A" is the correct answer.** An electric turn coordinator provides an emergency backup in the event of a vacuum system failure.
Reference Instrument Flying Handbook, p. 38
FAA subject matter knowledge code I04

5270. If a standard rate turn is maintained, how long would it take to turn 360°?

A. 1 minute.

B. 2 minutes.

C. 3 minutes.

5270. **"B" is the correct answer.** A standard rate of turn is 3° per second: 360/3 = 120 seconds; 120 seconds = 2 minutes.
Reference Instrument Flying Handbook, p. 43
FAA subject matter knowledge code I04

5271. A detuning of engine crankshaft counterweights is a source of overstress that may be caused by

A. rapid opening and closing of the throttle.

B. carburetor ice forming on the throttle valve.

C. operating with an excessively rich fuel/air mixture.

5271. **"A" is the correct answer.** By rapidly opening and closing the throttle, a pilot may cause engine overstress that leads to a detuning of the engine crankshaft.
Reference Lycoming Service Manual
FAA subject matter knowledge code K20

5272. How can you determine if another aircraft is on a collision course with your aircraft?

A. The nose of each aircraft is pointed at the same point in space.

B. The other aircraft always appears to get larger and closer at a rapid rate.

C. There is no apparent relative motion between your aircraft and the other aircraft.

5272. **"C" is the correct answer.** If there is no apparent relative motion between your aircraft and another it is very probable that it is on a collision course with you.
Reference Aeronautical Information Manual, p. 8-8
FAA subject matter knowledge code J31

5273. Which is true regarding variometers?

A. Variometers do not utilize outside air static pressure lines.

B. A variometer is generally considered to be less sensitive and has a slower response time than a vertical-speed indicator.

C. A common problem in pellet variometers is stickiness of the piston because of dirt, moisture, or static electricity in the tapered tubes.

5273. **"C" is the correct answer.** One of the more common problems of pellet variometers is stickiness of the piston because of dirt, moisture, or static electricity in the tapered tubes.
Reference American Soaring Handbook, p. 7-12
FAA subject matter knowledge code N07

5274. Which is true regarding variometers?

A. An electric variometer does not utilize outside air static pressure lines.

B. A total energy variometer indicates actual thermal existence or nonexistence rather than indications of climb or descent due to stick thermals.

C. One of the advantages of the pellet variometer over the vane variometer is that dirt, moisture, and static electricity do not affect its operation.

5274. **"B" is the correct answer.** A total energy variometer indicates actual thermal existence or nonexistence rather than indications of climb or descent due to stick deflections.
Reference American Soaring Handbook, p. 7-17
FAA subject matter knowledge code N07

5275. Which is true concerning total energy compensators?

A. The instrument responds to up and down air currents only.

B. The instrument registers climbs that result from stick thermals.

C. The instrument reacts to climbs and descents like a conventional rate-of-climb indicator.

5275. **"A" is the correct answer.** A total energy compensation only responds to up and down air currents.
Reference American Soaring Handbook, p. 7-17
FAA subject matter knowledge code N07

5276. The primary purpose of wing spoilers is to decrease

A. the drag.

B. landing speed.

C. the lift of the wing.

5276. "C" is the correct answer. Wing spoilers decrease lift when extended, thus increasing drag.
Reference American Soaring Handbook, p. 1-9
FAA subject matter knowledge code N20

5277. That portion of the glider's total drag created by the production of lift is called

A. induced drag, and is not affected by changes in airspeed.

B. induced drag, and is greatly affected by changes in airspeed.

C. parasite drag, and is greatly affected by changes in airspeed.

5277. "B" is the correct answer. Induced drag is that portion of a glider's drag created by producing lift. Induced drag varies inversely with the square of the velocity.
Reference American Soaring Handbook, pp. 9-8, 9-15
FAA subject matter knowledge code N09

5278. The best L/D ratio of a glider occurs when parasite drag is

A. equal to induced drag.

B. less than induced drag.

C. greater than induced drag.

5278. "A" is the correct answer. L/D_{max} is that airspeed when parasite and induced drag are equal.
Reference Soaring Flight Manual, p. 1-6
FAA subject matter knowledge code N20

5279. A glider is designed for an L/D ratio of 22:1 at 50 mph in calm air. What would the approximate glide ratio be with a direct headwind of 25 mph?

A. 44:1.

B. 22:1.

C. 11:1.

5279. "C" is the correct answer. A headwind of 25 mph would reduce the glide ratio by half, thus answer "C" is correct.
Reference American Soaring Handbook, p. 6-21
FAA subject matter knowledge code N09

5280. Which is true regarding aerodynamic drag?

A. Induced drag is created entirely by air resistance.

B. All aerodynamic drag is created entirely by the production of lift.

C. Induced drag is a by-product of lift and is greatly affected by changes in airspeed.

5280. "C" is the correct answer. Induced drag is that portion of a glider's drag created by producing lift. Induced drag varies inversely with the square of the velocity.
Reference American Soaring Handbook, pp. 9-8, 9-15
FAA subject matter knowledge code N09

5281. At a given airspeed, what effect does an increase in air density have on the lift and drag of a glider?

A. Lift and drag decrease.

B. Lift increases but drag decreases.

C. Lift and drag increase.

5281. "C" is the correct answer. Lift and drag vary directly with the density of the air: as air density increases, lift and drag increase; as air density decreases, lift and drag decrease.
Reference PHOAK, p. 12
FAA subject matter knowledge code H66

5282. Both lift and drag would be increased when which of these devices are extended?

A. Flaps.

B. Spoilers.

C. Slats.

5282. "A" is the correct answer. Flaps increase both lift and drag.
Reference About Soaring, p. 4
FAA subject matter knowledge code N20

5283. If the airspeed of a glider is increased from 45 mph to 90 mph, the parasite drag will be

A. two times greater.

B. four times greater.

C. six times greater.

5283. "B" is the correct answer. Several factors affect parasite drag. If the speed is doubled, four times as much drag is produced.
Reference PHOAK, p. 8
FAA subject matter knowledge code H01

5284. If the indicated airspeed of a glider is decreased from 90 mph to 45 mph, the induced drag will be

A. four times less.

B. two times greater.

C. four times greater.

5284. "C" is the correct answer. Induced drag is the undesirable but unavoidable by-product of lift, and

it increases in direct proportion to increases in angle of attack. The greater the angle of attack up to the critical angle, the greater the amount of lift developed and the greater the induced drag. The induced drag varies inversely with the square of the velocity.
Reference PHOAK, p. 7
FAA subject matter knowledge N09

5285. Which is true regarding wing camber of a glider's airfoil?

A. The camber is the same on both the upper and lower wing surface.

B. The camber is less on the upper wing surface than it is on the lower wing surface.

C. The camber is greater on the upper wing surface than it is on the lower wing surface.

5285. "C" is the correct answer. Camber is the curvature of the airfoil from the leading edge to the trailing edge. Upper camber refers to the curvature of the upper surface; lower camber refers to the curvature of the lower surface; and mean camber refers to the mean line that is equidistant at all points between the upper and lower surfaces. In most gliders the upper surface has a greater camber.
Reference PHOAK, p. 2
FAA subject matter knowledge code N20

5286. If the glider's radius of turn is 175 ft at 40 mph, what would the radius of turn be if the TAS is increased to 80 mph while maintaining a constant angle of bank?

A. 350 ft.

B. 525 ft.

C. 700 ft.

5286. "C" is the correct answer. The radius of a turn increases in proportion to the square of the velocity. In this example the velocity is doubled, therefore the radius is quadrupled: $175 \times 4 = 700$ ft.
Reference PHOAK, p. 31
FAA subject matter knowledge code N09

5287. In regard to the location of the glider's CG and its effect on glider spin characteristics, which is true?

A. If the CG is too far aft, a flat spin may develop.

B. If the CG is too far forward, spin entry is impossible.

C. If the CG is too far aft, spins degenerate into CG high-speed spirals.

5287. "A" is the correct answer. If the CG is too far back, a flat spin develops and recovery may be impossible.
Reference Flight Training Handbook
FAA subject matter knowledge code H66

5288. The CG of most gliders is located

A. ahead of the aerodynamic center of the wing to increase lateral stability.

B. ahead of the aerodynamic center of the wing to increase longitudinal stability.

C. behind the aerodynamic center of the wing to increase longitudinal stability.

5288. "B" is the correct answer. Most gliders have the CG located ahead of the aerodynamic center of the wing to increase longitudinal stability.
Reference Soaring Flight Manual, p. 1-13
FAA subject matter knowledge code H52

5289. Loading a glider so that the CG exceeds the aft limits results in

A. excessive load factor in turns.

B. excessive upward force on the tail, causing the nose to pitch down.

C. loss of longitudinal stability, causing the nose to pitch up at slow speeds.

5289. "C" is the correct answer. Loading in a tail-heavy condition has a most serious effect on longitudinal stability and can reduce the airplane's capability to recover from stalls and spins. Another undesirable characteristic produced from tail-heavy loading is that it causes the nose to pitch up at a slow speed.
Reference PHOAK, p. 75
FAA subject matter knowledge code H04

5290. With regard to the effects of spoilers and wing flaps, which is true if the glider's pitch attitude is held constant when such devices are being operated? (Disregard negative flap angles above neutral position.)

A. Retracting flaps reduces the glider's stall speed.

B. Retracting flaps or extending spoilers increases the glider's rate of descent.

C. Retracting flaps or extending spoilers decreases the glider's rate of descent.

5290. "B" is the correct answer. Spoilers slow the glider and increase its rate of descent at the same time. Retracting the flaps causes an increase in the rate of descent.
Reference Soaring Flight Manual, p. 1-9
FAA subject matter knowledge code H20

5291. If the angle of attack is increased beyond the critical angle of attack, the wing no longer produces sufficient lift to support the weight of the glider

A. regardless of the airspeed or pitch attitude.

B. unless the airspeed is greater than the normal stall speed.

C. unless the pitch attitude is on or below the natural horizon.

5291. "A" is the correct answer. Just like a powered airplane, a glider can be stalled in any attitude and at any airspeed.
Reference Soaring Flight Manual, p. 14-5
FAA subject matter knowledge code N33

5292. What force causes the glider to turn in flight?

A. Vertical component of lift.

B. Horizontal component of lift.

C. Positive yawing movement of the rudder.

5292. "B" is the correct answer. The answer is quite simple. The airplane must be banked because the same force (lift) that sustains the airplane in flight is used to make the airplane turn. The airplane is banked and back elevator pressure is applied. This changes the direction of lift and increases the angle of attack on the wings, which increases the lift. The increased horizontal component of lift pulls the airplane around the turn.
Reference PHOAK, p. 31
FAA subject matter knowledge code N20

5293. Given:

Glider A:

Wingspan	51 ft
Average wing chord	4 ft

Glider B:

Wingspan	48 ft
Average wing chord	3.5 ft

Determine the correct aspect ratio and its effect on performance at low speeds.

A. Glider A has an aspect ratio of 13.7 and generates less lift with greater drag than glider B.

B. Glider B has an aspect ratio of 13.7 and generates greater lift with less drag than glider A.

C. Glider B has an aspect ratio of 12.7 and generates less lift with greater drag than glider A.

5293. "B" is the correct answer. To solve this problem divide the wingspan by the average wing chord to get the aspect ratio. A high aspect ratio correlates to a high glide ratio.
Reference Soaring Flight Manual, p. 1-7
FAA subject matter knowledge code N20

5294. Given:

Glider A:

Wingspan	48 ft
Average wing chord	4.5 ft

Glider B:

Wingspan	54 ft
Average wing chord	3.7 ft

Determine the correct aspect ratio and its effect on performance at low speeds.

A. Glider A has an aspect ratio of 10.6 and generates greater lift with less drag than glider B.

B. Glider B has an aspect ratio of 14.5 and generates greater lift with less drag than glider A.

C. Glider B has an aspect ratio of 10.6 and generates less lift with greater drag than glider A.

5294. "B" is the correct answer. To solve this problem divide the wingspan by the average wing chord to get the aspect ratio. A high aspect ratio correlates to a high glide ratio.
Reference Soaring Flight Manual, p. 1-7
FAA subject matter knowledge code N20

5295. The best L/D ratio for a glider is a value that

A. varies depending on the weight being carried.

B. remains constant regardless of airspeed changes.

C. remains constant and is independent of the weight being carried.

5295. "C" is the correct answer. The best L/D ratio for a glider is a value that remains constant and is independent of the weight being carried.
Reference About Soaring, p. 3
FAA subject matter knowledge code N09

5296. A glide ratio of 22:1 with respect to the air mass is

A. 11:1 in a tailwind and 44:1 in a headwind.

B. 22:1 regardless of wind direction and speed.

C. 11:1 in a headwind and 44:1 in a tailwind.

5296. "C" is the correct answer. A glide ratio of 22:1 with respect to the air mass is 11:1 in a headwind and 44:1 in a tailwind.
Reference American Soaring Handbook, p. 6-16
FAA subject matter knowledge code N06

5297. The advantage of total energy compensators is that this system

A. includes a speed ring around the rim of the variometer.

B. adds the effect of stick thermals to the total energy produced by thermals.

C. reduces climb and dive errors on variometer indications caused by airspeed changes.

5297. "C" is the correct answer. One of the main advantages of total energy compensators is that it responds only to changes in total energy. Stick deflection does not register as lift or sink, nor do changes in altitude or airspeed.
Reference American Soaring Handbook, p. 7-17
FAA subject matter knowledge code N07

5612. In the Northern Hemisphere, if a sailplane is accelerated or decelerated, the magnetic compass normally indicates

A. correctly, only when on a north or south heading.

B. a turn toward south while accelerating on a west heading.

C. a turn toward north while decelerating on an east heading.

5612. "A" is the correct answer. Remember, **ANDS**: **A**ccelerate—**N**orth, **D**ecelerate—**S**outh.

If the aircraft is accelerated on an east or west heading the compass indicates a turn to the north. If it is decelerated on an east or west heading the compass indicates a turn to the south.
Reference Instrument Flying Handbook, p. 48
FAA subject matter knowledge code H03

5613. When flying on a heading of west from one thermal to the next, the airspeed is increased to the speed-to-fly with the wings level. What does the conventional magnetic compass indicate while the airspeed is increasing?

A. A turn toward the south.

B. A turn toward the north.

C. Straight flight on a heading of 270°.

5613. "B" is the correct answer. Remember, **ANDS**: **A**ccelerate—**N**orth, **D**ecelerate—**S**outh.

If the aircraft is accelerated on an east or west heading the compass indicates a turn to the north. If it is decelerated on an east or west heading the compass indicates a turn to the south.
Reference Instrument Flying Handbook, p. 48
FAA subject matter knowledge code H03

5695. The antitorque system fails during cruising flight and a powered approach landing is commenced. If the helicopter yaws to the right just prior to touchdown, what could the pilot do to help swing the nose to the left?

A. Increase the throttle.

B. Decrease the throttle.

C. Increase collective pitch.

5695. "B" is the correct answer. Decrease the throttle to swing the nose to the left.
Reference Basic Helicopter Handbook, p. 69
FAA subject matter knowledge code H07

5696. If antitorque failure occurred during cruising flight, what could be done to help straighten out a left yaw prior to touchdown?

A. A normal running landing should be made.

B. Make a running landing using partial power and left cyclic.

C. Apply available throttle to help swing the nose to the right just prior to touchdown.

5696. "C" is the correct answer. Directional control should be maintained primarily with cyclic control and, secondarily, by gently applying throttle momentarily, with needles joined, to swing the nose to the right.
Reference Basic Helicopter Handbook, p. 69
FAA subject matter knowledge code H78

5697. Should a helicopter pilot ever be concerned about ground resonance during takeoff?

A. No; ground resonance occurs only during an autorotative touchdown.

B. Yes; although it is more likely to occur on landing, it can occur during takeoff.

C. Yes, but only during slope takeoffs.

5697. "B" is the correct answer. As the name implies, ground resonance occurs when the helicopter makes contact with the surface during landing or while in contact with the surface during an attempted takeoff.
Reference Basic Helicopter Handbook, p. 66
FAA subject matter knowledge code H78

5698. An excessively steep approach angle and abnormally slow closure rate should be avoided during an approach to a hover, primarily because

A. the airspeed indicator would be unreliable.

B. a go-around would be very difficult to accomplish.

C. settling with power could develop, particularly during the termination.

5698. "C" is the correct answer. The following condition is likely to cause settling with power, that is, a steep power approach in which airspeed is permitted to drop nearly to zero.
Reference Basic Helicopter Handbook, p. 66
FAA subject matter knowledge code H78

5699. During a near-vertical power approach into a confined area with the airspeed near zero, what hazardous condition may develop?

A. Ground resonance.

B. Settling with power.

C. Blade stall vibration.

5699. "B" is the correct answer. The following condition is likely to cause settling with power, that is, a steep power approach in which airspeed is permitted to drop nearly to zero.
Reference Basic Helicopter Handbook, p. 66
FAA subject matter knowledge code H78

5700. Which procedure results in recovery from settling with power?

A. Increase collective pitch and power.

B. Maintain constant collective pitch and increase throttle.

C. Increase forward speed and partially lower collective pitch.

5700. "C" is the correct answer. Recovery can be accomplished by increasing forward speed, and/or partially lowering collective pitch.
Reference Basic Helicopter Handbook, p. 66
FAA subject matter knowledge code H78

5701. The addition of power in a settling with power situation produces an

A. increase in airspeed.

B. even greater rate of descent.

C. increase in cyclic control effectiveness.

5701. "B" is the correct answer. The addition of more power produces an even greater rate of descent.
Reference Basic Helicopter Handbook, p. 66
FAA subject matter knowledge code H78

5702. Under which situation is accidental settling with power likely to occur?

A. A steep approach in which the airspeed is permitted to drop to nearly zero.

B. A shallow approach in which the airspeed is permitted to drop below 10 mph.

C. Hovering in ground effect during calm wind, high-density altitude conditions.

5702. "A" is the correct answer. The following condition is likely to cause settling with power, that is, a steep power approach in which airspeed is permitted to drop nearly to zero.
Reference Basic Helicopter Handbook, p. 66
FAA subject matter knowledge code H78

5703. Which is true with respect to recovering from an accidental settling with power situation?

A. Antitorque pedals should not be utilized during the recovery.

B. Recovery can be accomplished by increasing rotor rpm, reducing forward airspeed, and minimizing maneuvering.

C. Since the inboard portions of the main rotor blades are stalled, cyclic control effectiveness is reduced during the initial portion of the recovery.

5703. "C" is the correct answer. In recovering from a settling with power condition, the tendency on the part of the pilot to first try to stop the descent by increasing collective pitch results in increasing the stalled area of the rotor and increasing the rate of descent. Since inboard portions of the blades are stalled, cyclic control is reduced.
Reference Basic Helicopter Handbook, p. 66
FAA subject matter knowledge code H78

5704. When operating at high forward airspeed, retreating blade stall is more likely to occur under conditions of

A. low gross weight, high-density altitude, and smooth air.

B. high gross weight, low-density altitude, and smooth air.

C. high gross weight, high-density altitude, and turbulent air.

5704. "C" is the correct answer. When operating at high forward airspeed, retreating blade stall is more likely to occur under conditions of high gross weight, high-density altitude, and turbulent air.
Reference Basic Helicopter Handbook, p. 65
FAA subject matter knowledge code H81

5705. What are the major indications of an incipient retreating blade stall situation, in order of occurrence?

A. Low-frequency vibration, pitchup of the nose, and a tendency for the helicopter to roll.

B. Slow pitchup of the nose, high-frequency vibration, and a tendency for the helicopter to roll.

C. Slow pitchup of the nose, tendency for the helicopter to roll, followed by medium-frequency vibration.

5705. "A" is the correct answer. The major warnings of approaching retreating blade stall conditions in the order in which they generally are experienced are abnormal two-per-revolution vibration in two-bladed rotors or three-per-revolution vibration in three-bladed rotors, pitchup of the nose, and tendency for the helicopter to roll.
Reference Basic Helicopter Handbook, p. 65
FAA subject matter knowledge code H78

5706. How should a pilot react at the onset of retreating blade stall?

A. Reduce collective pitch, rotor rpm, and forward airspeed.

B. Reduce collective pitch, increase rotor rpm, and reduce forward airspeed.

C. Increase collective pitch, reduce rotor rpm, and reduce forward airspeed.

5706. B" is the correct answer. At the onset of blade stall the pilot should take the following corrective measures: reduce collective pitch, increase rotor rpm, reduce forward airspeed, and minimize maneuvering.
Reference Basic Helicopter Handbook, p. 65
FAA subject matter knowledge code H78

5709. To taxi on the surface in a safe and efficient manner, helicopter pilots should use the

A. cyclic pitch to control starting, taxi speed, and stopping.

B. collective pitch to control starting, taxi speed, and stopping.

C. antitorque pedals to correct for drift during crosswind conditions.

5709. "B" is the correct answer. To taxi on the surface in a safe and efficient manner, helicopter pilots should use the collective pitch to control starting, taxi speed, and stopping.
Reference Basic Helicopter Handbook, p. 79
FAA subject matter knowledge code H79

5710. During surface taxiing, the cyclic pitch stick is used to control

A. heading.

B. ground track.

C. forward movement.

5710. "B" is the correct answer. Use pedals to maintain heading and cyclic to maintain ground track.
Reference Basic Helicopter Handbook, p. 79
FAA subject matter knowledge code H80

5711. To taxi on the surface in a safe and efficient manner, one should use the cyclic pitch to

A. start and stop aircraft movement.

B. maintain heading during crosswind conditions.

C. correct for drift during crosswind conditions.

5711. "C" is the correct answer. During crosswind taxi, the cyclic should be held into the wind a sufficient amount to eliminate any drifting movement.
Reference Basic Helicopter Handbook, p. 79
FAA subject matter knowledge code H80

5713. Which statement is true about an autorotative descent?

A. Generally only the cyclic control is used to make turns.

B. The pilot should use the collective pitch control to control the rate of descent.

C. The rotor rpm tends to decrease if a tight turn is made with a heavily loaded helicopter.

5713. "A" is the correct answer. When making turns during an autorotative descent, generally use cyclic control only.
Reference Basic Helicopter Handbook, p. 93
FAA subject matter knowledge code H80

5714. Using right pedal to assist a right turn during an autorotative descent will probably result in what actions?

A. A decrease in rotor rpm, pitch up of the nose, a decrease in sink rate, and an increase in indicated airspeed.

B. An increase in rotor rpm, pitch up of the nose, a decrease in sink rate, and an increase in indicated airspeed.

C. An increase in rotor rpm, pitch down of the nose, an increase in sink rate, and a decrease in indicated airspeed.

5714. "C" is the correct answer. Use of antitorque pedals to assist or speed the turn causes loss of airspeed and downward pitching of the nose—especially when left pedal is used.
Reference Basic Helicopter Handbook, p. 93
FAA subject matter knowledge code H80

5715. Using left pedal to assist a left turn during an autorotative descent will probably cause the rotor rpm to

A. increase and the airspeed to decrease.

B. decrease and the aircraft nose to pitch down.

C. increase and the aircraft nose to pitch down.

5715. "B" is the correct answer. When making turns during an autorotative descent, generally use cyclic control only.
Reference Basic Helicopter Handbook, p. 93
FAA subject matter knowledge code H80

5717. When making a slope landing, the cyclic pitch control should be used to

A. lower the downslope skid to the ground.

B. hold the upslope skid against the slope.

C. place the rotor disc parallel to the slope.

5717. "B" is the correct answer. As the upslope skid touches the ground, apply cyclic stick in the direction of the slope. This holds the skid against the slope while the downslope skid is continuing to be let down with the collective pitch.
Reference Basic Helicopter Handbook, p. 98
FAA subject matter knowledge code H80

5722. If complete power failure should occur while cruising at altitude, the pilot should

A. partially lower the collective pitch, close the throttle, then completely lower the collective pitch.

B. lower the collective pitch as necessary to maintain proper rotor rpm, and apply right pedal to correct for yaw.

C. close the throttle, lower the collective pitch to the full-down position, apply left pedal to correct for yaw, and establish a normal power-off glide.

5722. "B" is the correct answer. The successful entry from powered flight to autorotation consists of the following transitions: changing of airflow from a downward flow to an upward flow; lowering collective pitch to maintain a tolerable angle of attack that would otherwise increase because of the descent; regaining rotor rpm and stabilizing rate of descent.
Reference Basic Helicopter Handbook, p. 67
FAA subject matter knowledge code H80

5723. When making an autorotation to touchdown, what action is most appropriate?

A. A slightly nose-high attitude at touchdown is the proper procedure.

B. The skids should be in a longitudinally level attitude at touchdown.

C. Aft cyclic application after touchdown is desirable to help decrease ground run.

5723. "B" is the correct answer. If a landing is to be made from the autorotative approach, the throttle should be rotated to the closed or override position at this time and held in this position as collective pitch is raised so that the rotor does not reengage. As the helicopter approaches normal hovering altitude, maintain a landing attitude with cyclic control, maintain heading with pedals, apply sufficient collective pitch to cushion the touchdown, and be sure the helicopter is landing parallel to its direction of motion upon contact with the surface.
Reference Basic Helicopter Handbook, p. 94
FAA subject matter knowledge code H80

5724. During the entry into a quick stop, how should the collective pitch control be used?

A. It should be lowered as necessary to prevent ballooning.

B. It should be raised as necessary to prevent a rotor overspeed.

C. It should be raised as necessary to prevent a loss of altitude.

5724. "A" is the correct answer. The deceleration is initiated by applying aft cyclic to reduce forward speed. Simultaneously, the collective pitch should be lowered as necessary to counteract any climbing tendency.
Reference Basic Helicopter Handbook, p. 97
FAA subject matter knowledge code H80

5725. During a normal approach to a hover, the collective pitch control is used primarily to

A. maintain rpm.

B. control the rate of closure.

C. control the angle of descent.

5725. "C" is the correct answer. A normal approach to a hover is basically a power glide made at an angle of descent of approximately 10°. This type of approach is used in the majority of cases. The angle of descent is primarily controlled by collect pitch, the airspeed is primarily controlled by the cyclic control, and heading on final approach is maintained with pedal control.

Reference Basic Helicopter Handbook, pp. 85, 86
FAA subject matter knowledge code H80

5726. During a normal approach to a hover, the cyclic pitch is used primarily to

A. maintain heading.

B. control rate of closure.

C. control angle of descent.

5726. "B" is the correct answer. A normal approach to a hover is basically a power glide made at an angle of descent of approximately 10°. This type of approach is used in the majority of cases. The angle of descent is primarily controlled by collect pitch, the airspeed is primarily controlled by the cyclic control, and heading on final approach is maintained with pedal control.

Reference Basic Helicopter Handbook, pp. 85, 86
FAA subject matter knowledge code H80

5727. Normal rpm should be maintained during a running landing primarily to ensure

A. adequate directional control until the helicopter stops.

B. that sufficient lift is available should an emergency develop.

C. longitudinal and lateral control, especially if the helicopter is heavily loaded or high-density altitude conditions exist.

5727. "A" is the correct answer. To ensure directional control, normal rotor rpm must be maintained until the helicopter stops.

Reference Basic Helicopter Handbook, p. 89
FAA subject matter knowledge code H80

5728. Which is true concerning a running takeoff?

A. If a helicopter cannot be lifted vertically, a running takeoff should be made.

B. One advantage of a running takeoff is that the additional airspeed can be converted quickly to altitude.

C. A running takeoff may be possible when gross weight or density altitude prevents a sustained hover at normal hovering altitude.

5728. "C" is the correct answer. A running takeoff is used when conditions of load and/or density altitude prevent a sustained hover at normal hovering altitude. It is often referred to as a high-altitude takeoff.

Reference Basic Helicopter Handbook, p. 89
FAA subject matter knowledge code H80

5729. When conducting a confined area-type operation, the primary purpose of the high reconnaissance is to determine the

A. type of approach to be made.

B. suitability of the area for landing.

C. height of the obstructions surrounding the area.

5729. "B" is the correct answer. The primary purpose of the high reconnaissance is to determine the suitability of an area for a landing.

Reference Basic Helicopter Handbook, p. 103
FAA subject matter knowledge code H81

5730. During a pinnacle approach to a rooftop heliport under conditions of high wind and turbulence, the pilot should make a

A. shallow approach, maintaining a constant line of descent with cyclic applications.

B. normal approach, maintaining a slower-than-normal rate of descent with cyclic applications.

C. steeper-than-normal approach, maintaining the desired angle of descent with collective applications.

5730. "C" is the correct answer. A steeper-than-normal approach may be used when barriers or excessive downdrafts exist.

Reference Basic Helicopter Handbook, p. 102
FAA subject matter knowledge code H81

5733. If ground resonance is experienced during rotor spin-up, what action should you take?

A. Taxi to a smooth area.

B. Make a normal takeoff immediately.

C. Close the throttle and slowly raise the spin-up lever.

5733. "B" is the correct answer. Corrective action could be an immediate takeoff if rpm is in proper range, or an immediate closing of the throttle and placing the blades in low pitch if rpm is low. This question appears to have two correct answers, but answer "B" pertains to helicopters only.

Reference Basic Helicopter Handbook, p. 66
FAA subject matter knowledge code H78

5734. The principal factor limiting the never-exceed speed (V_{NE}) of a gyroplane is

A. turbulence and altitude.

B. blade-tip speed, which must remain below the speed of sound.

C. lack of sufficient cyclic stick control to compensate for dissymmetry of lift or retreating blade stall, depending on which occurs first.

5734. "C" is the correct answer. Lack of sufficient cyclic stick control to compensate for dissymmetry of lift is the major factor limiting the gyroplane's never-exceed speed (V_{NE}).
Reference Air & Space 18A Maneuver Guide, p. 14
FAA subject matter knowledge code H78

5737. During the transition from prerotation to flight, all rotor blades change pitch

A. simultaneously, to the same angle of incidence.

B. simultaneously, but to different angles of incidence.

C. to the same degree at the same point in the cycle of rotation.

5737. "B" is the correct answer. During the transition from prerotation to flight, all rotor blades change pitch simultaneously, but to different angles of incidence.
Reference Air & Space 18A Flight Manual, p. 14
FAA subject matter knowledge code H71

5738. Select the true statement concerning gyroplane taxi procedures.

A. Avoid abrupt control movements when blades are turning.

B. The cyclic stick should be held in the neutral position at all times.

C. The cyclic stick should be held slightly aft of neutral at all times.

5738. "A" is the correct answer. The cyclic control should be neutralized during taxi. This avoids unwanted blade flapping.
Reference Air & Space 18A Flight Manual, p. 15
FAA subject matter knowledge code H80

5739. Frost covering the upper surface of an airplane wing usually causes

A. the airplane to stall at an angle of attack that is higher than normal.

B. the airplane to stall at an angle of attack that is lower than normal.

C. drag factors so large that sufficient speed cannot be obtained for takeoff.

5739. "B" is the correct answer. A heavy coat of hard frost causes a 5 to 10 percent increase in stall speed. Even a small amount of frost on airfoils may prevent an aircraft from becoming airborne at normal takeoff speed. Also possible is that, once airborne, an aircraft could have insufficient margin of airspeed above stall so that moderate gusts or turning flight could produce incipient or complete stalling.
Reference Aviation Weather, p. 102
FAA subject matter knowledge code H05

5752. Which procedure should you follow to avoid wake turbulence if a large jet crosses your course from left to right approximately 1 mile ahead and at your altitude?

A. Make sure you are slightly above the path of the jet.

B. Slow your airspeed to V_A and maintain altitude and course.

C. Make sure you are slightly below the path of the jet and perpendicular to the course.

5752. "A" is the correct answer. Pilots should fly at or above the preceding aircraft's flight path, altering course as necessary to avoid the area behind and below the generating aircraft.
Reference Aeronautical Information Manual, p. 626
FAA subject matter knowledge code J27

5753. To avoid possible wake turbulence from a large jet aircraft that has just landed prior to your takeoff, at which point on the runway should you plan to become airborne?

A. Past the point where the jet touched down.

B. At the point where the jet touched down, or just prior to this point.

C. Approximately 500 ft prior to the point where the jet touched down.

5753. "A" is the correct answer. If departing behind a landing aircraft, don't take off unless you can taxi onto the runway beyond the point at which his nose wheel touched down and have sufficient runway left for safe takeoff.
Reference Aeronautical Information Manual, p. 89
FAA subject matter knowledge code J27

5754. When landing behind a large aircraft, which procedure should be followed for vortex avoidance?

A. Stay above its final approach flight path all the way to touchdown.

B. Stay below and to one side of its final approach flight path.

C. Stay well below its final approach flight path and land at least 2000 ft behind.

5754. "A" is the correct answer. If landing behind another aircraft, keep your approach above his approach and keep your touchdown beyond the point where his nose wheel touched the runway.
Reference Aviation Weather, p. 89
FAA subject matter knowledge code J27

5755. With respect to vortex circulation, which is true?

A. Helicopters generate downwash turbulence, not vortex circulation.

B. The vortex strength is greatest when the generating aircraft is flying fast.

C. Vortex circulation generated by helicopters in forward flight trail behind in a manner similar to wingtip vortices generated by airplanes.

5755. "C" is the correct answer. In forward flight, departing or landing helicopters produce a pair of strong, high-speed trailing vortices similar to wingtip vortices of larger fixed wing aircraft.
Reference Aeronautical Information Manual, paragraph 7-56
FAA subject matter knowledge code J27

5756. Which is true with respect to vortex circulation?

A. Helicopters generate downwash turbulence only, not vortex circulation.

B. The vortex strength is greatest when the generating aircraft is heavy, clean, and slow.

C. When vortex circulation sinks into ground effect, it tends to dissipate rapidly and offer little danger.

5756. "B" is the correct answer. The strength of the vortex is governed by the weight, speed, and shape of the wing of the generating aircraft. The greatest vortex strength occurs when the generating aircraft is heavy, clean, and slow.
Reference Aeronautical Information Manual, paragraph 7-52
FAA subject matter knowledge code J27

5769. What corrective action should be taken during a landing if the glider pilot makes the roundout too soon while using spoilers?

A. Leave the spoilers extended and lower the nose slightly.

B. Retract the spoilers and leave them retracted until after touchdown.

C. Retract the spoilers until the glider begins to settle again, then extend the spoilers.

5769. "B" is the correct answer. If you begin your roundout too soon while using spoilers during a landing, you should retract the spoilers and leave them retracted until touchdown.
Reference Soaring Flight Manual, p. 14-14
FAA subject matter knowledge code N32

5770. What consideration should be given in the choice of a towplane for use in aerotows?

A. L/D ratio of the glider to be towed.

B. Gross weight of the glider to be towed.

C. Towplane's low wing loading and low power loading.

5770. "C" is the correct answer. The towplane wing loading and power loading should be considered when choosing a towplane.
Reference Soaring Flight Manual
FAA subject matter knowledge code N04

5771. Looseness in a glider's flight control linkage or attachments could result in

A. increased stalling speed.

B. loss of control during an aerotow in turbulence.

C. flutter while flying at near-maximum speed in turbulence.

5771."C" is the correct answer. Looseness in a glider's flight control linkage or attachments could result in flutter while flying at near-maximum speed in turbulence.
Reference Soaring Flight Manual
FAA subject matter knowledge code N20

5772. A left side slip is used to counteract a crosswind drift during the final approach for landing. An over-the-top spin would most likely occur if the controls were used in which of the following ways?

A. Holding the stick too far back and applying full right rudder.

B. Holding the stick in the neutral position and applying full right rudder.

C. Holding the stick too far to the left and applying full left rudder.

5772. "A" is the correct answer. An over-the-top spin would most likely occur if the stick was held too far back and applying full right rudder.
Reference About Soaring, pp. 39–41
FAA subject matter knowledge code N32

5788. The reason for retaining water ballast while thermals are strong is to

A. decrease forward speed.

B. decrease cruise performance.

C. increase cruise performance.

5788. "C" is the correct answer. In strong thermals, retain water ballast to increase your cruise performance.
Reference Soaring Flight Manual
FAA subject matter knowledge code N21

5789. When flying into a headwind, penetrating speed is the glider's

A. speed-to-fly.

B. minimum sink speed.

C. speed-to-fly plus one-half the estimated wind velocity.

5789."C" is the correct answer. When flying into a headwind on a cross-country, a good rule of thumb is to increase the speed-to-fly by one-half the estimated wind velocity.
Reference Soaring Flight Manual
FAA subject matter knowledge code N21

5815. A rule of thumb for flying a final approach is to maintain a speed that is

A. twice the glider's stall speed, regardless of windspeed.

B. twice the glider's stall speed plus one-half the estimated windspeed.

C. 50 percent above the glider's stall speed plus one-half the estimated windspeed.

5815. "B" is the correct answer. A rule of thumb for flying a final approach is to maintain a speed that is twice the glider's stall speed plus one-half the estimated windspeed.
Reference Soaring Flight Manual
FAA subject matter knowledge code N21

5829. Regarding lift as developed by a hot air balloon, which is true?

A. The higher the temperature of the ambient air, the greater the lift for any given envelope temperature.

B. The greater the difference between the temperature of the ambient air and the envelope air, the greater the lift.

C. The smaller the difference between the temperature of the ambient air and the envelope air, the greater the lift.

5829. "B" is the correct answer. Regarding lift as developed by a hot air balloon, the greater the difference between the temperature of the ambient air and the envelope air, the greater the lift.
Reference Soaring Flight Manual
FAA subject matter knowledge code O02

5830. What causes false lift that sometimes occurs during launch procedures?

A. Closing the maneuvering vent too rapidly.

B. Excessive temperature within the envelope.

C. Venturi effect of the wind on the envelope.

5830. "C" is the correct answer. The venturi effect of the wind on the envelope causes false lift that sometimes occurs during launch procedures.
Reference Soaring Flight Manual
FAA subject matter knowledge code O05

5831. The lifting forces that act on a hot air balloon are primarily the result of the interior air

A. pressure being greater than ambient pressure.

B. temperature being less than ambient temperature.

C. temperature being greater than ambient temperature.

5831. "C" is the correct answer. The lifting forces that act on a hot air balloon are primarily the result of the interior air temperature being greater than ambient temperature.
Reference Soaring Flight Manual
FAA subject matter knowledge code O02

5836. To perform a normal descent in a gas balloon, it is necessary to

A. valve air.

B. valve gas.

C. release ballast.

5836. "B" is the correct answer. To perform a normal descent in a gas balloon, it is necessary to valve gas.
Reference Soaring Flight Manual
FAA subject matter knowledge code P04

5837. What would cause a gas balloon to start a descent if a cold air mass is encountered and the envelope becomes cooled?

A. The expansion of the gas.

B. The contraction of the gas.

C. A barometric pressure differential.

5837. "B" is the correct answer. Contraction of the gas would cause a gas balloon to start a descent if a cold air mass is encountered and the envelope becomes cooled.
Reference Soaring Flight Manual
FAA subject matter knowledge code P04

5838. If a balloon inadvertently descends into stratus clouds and is shielded from the sun, and if no corrections are made, one can expect to descend

A. more slowly.

B. more rapidly.

C. at an unchanged rate.

5738. "B" is the correct answer. If a balloon inadvertently descends into stratus clouds and is shielded from the sun, and if no corrections are made, you can expect to descend more rapidly.
Reference Soaring Flight Manual
FAA subject matter knowledge code O03

5851. Why is a false lift dangerous?

A. Pilots are not aware of its effect until the burner sound changes.

B. To commence a descent, the venting of air will nearly collapse the envelope.

C. When the balloon's horizontal speed reaches the windspeed, the balloon could descend into obstructions downwind.

5851. "C" is the correct answer. A false lift is dangerous because when the balloon's horizontal speed reaches the windspeed, the balloon could descend into obstructions downwind.
Reference Soaring Flight Manual
FAA subject matter knowledge code O05

5854. False lift occurs whenever a balloon

A. ascends rapidly.

B. ascends due to solar assistance.

C. ascends into air moving faster than the air below.

5854. "C" is the correct answer. False lift occurs whenever a balloon ascends into air moving faster than the air below.
Reference Soaring Flight Manual
FAA subject matter knowledge code O05

5855. What is the relationship of false lift to the wind? False lift

A. exists only if the surface winds are calm.

B. increases if the vertical velocity of the balloon increases.

C. decreases as the wind accelerates the balloon to the same speed as the wind.

5855. "C" is the correct answer. False lift decreases as the wind accelerates the balloon to the same speed as the wind.
Reference Soaring Flight Manual
FAA subject matter knowledge code O05

12

Meteorology

STUDY GUIDE

Heat and Temperature

Heat is a form of energy. When a substance contains heat it exhibits the property we measure as temperature—the degree of "hotness" or "coldness." The earth receives energy from the sun in the form of solar radiation.

Temperature Variations

The amount of solar energy received by any region varies with time of day, season, and latitude. These differences in solar energy create temperature variations. Temperatures also vary with differences in topographical surface and with altitude. These temperature variations create forces that drive the atmosphere in its endless motions.

Variation with Altitude

Temperature normally decreases with increasing altitude throughout the troposphere. This decrease of temperature with altitude is defined as the *lapse rate*. The average decrease of temperature—average lapse rate—in the troposphere is 2°C per 1000 ft. An inversion often develops near the ground on clear, cool nights when the wind is light.

Sea Level Pressure

Standard sea level pressure is 1013.2 millibars (mb), 29.92 inches of mercury (in. Hg), 760 millimeters of mercury (mm Hg), or about 14.7 pounds per square inch (psi), at 15°C (59°F).

Pressure Gradient Force

Whenever a pressure difference develops over an area, the pressure gradient force begins moving the air directly across the isobars. The closer the spacing of isobars, the stronger the pressure gradient force. The stronger the pressure gradient force, the stronger the wind. Thus, closely spaced isobars mean strong winds; widely spaced isobars mean lighter winds.

Coriolis Force

The Coriolis force affects the paths of aircraft, missiles, flying birds, ocean currents, and most important to the study of weather, air currents. The force deflects air to the right in the Northern Hemisphere and to the left in the Southern Hemisphere.

The pressure gradient force drives the wind and is perpendicular to isobars. When a pressure gradient force is first established, wind begins to blow from higher to lower pressure directly across the isobars. However, the instant air begins moving, Coriolis force deflects it to the right. Soon the wind is deflected a full 90° and is then parallel to the isobars or contours. At this time, Coriolis force exactly balances pressure gradient force. With the forces in balance, the wind remains parallel to the isobars or contours.

The General Circulation

Pressure differences cause wind. As the air tries to blow outward from the high pressure, it is deflected to the right by the Coriolis force. Thus, the wind around a high blows clockwise. The high pressure with its associated wind system is an *anticyclone*. As winds try to blow inward toward the center of low pressure, they are deflected to the right. Thus, the wind around a low is counterclockwise. The low pressure and its wind system is a *cyclone*.

Wind, Pressure Systems, and Weather

Wind blows counterclockwise around a low and clockwise around a high. At the surface, when air converges into a low, it cannot go outward against the pressure gradient, nor can it go downward into the ground; it must go upward. Therefore, a low or trough is an area of rising air. Rising air is conducive to cloudiness and precipitation; thus we have the general association of low pressure with bad weather. Highs and ridges are areas of descending air.

Temperature–Dew Point Spread

The difference between air temperature and dew point temperature is popularly called the *spread*. As the spread becomes less, relative humidity increases, and it is 100 percent when temperature and dew point are the same. Some rain may reach the ground or it may evaporate as it falls into drier air. *Virga* is streamers of precipitation trailing beneath clouds but evaporating before reaching the ground.

Change of State

Evaporation, condensation, sublimation, freezing, and melting are changes of state. *Evaporation* is the changing of liquid water to water vapor. *Sublimation* is the changing of ice directly to water vapor, or water vapor to ice, bypassing the liquid state in each process.

Liquid, Freezing, and Frozen

Ice pellets always indicate freezing rain at higher altitude.

Stability and Instability

Stability runs the gamut from absolutely stable to absolutely unstable, and the atmosphere usually is in a delicate balance somewhere in between. A change in the ambient temperature lapse rate of an air mass can tip this balance.

Stratiform Clouds

Since stable air resists convection, clouds in stable air form in horizontal, sheetlike layers or *strata*. Thus, within a stable layer, clouds are *stratiform*. When stable air is forced upward, the air tends to retain horizontal flow, and any cloudiness is flat and stratified. When unstable air is forced upward, the disturbance grows, and any resulting cloudiness shows extensive vertical development.

You can estimate height of cumuliform cloud bases using the surface temperature–dew point spread. Unsaturated air in a convective current cools at about 5.4°F (3.0°C) per 1000 ft; dew point decreases at about 1°F (⅝°C) per 1000 ft. Thus, in a convective current, temperature and dew point converge at about 4.4°F (2.5°C) per 1000 ft. We can get a quick estimate of the height of a convective cloud base in thousands of feet by rounding these values and dividing into the spread or by multiplying the spread by their reciprocals. When using Fahrenheit, divide by 4 or multiply by 0.25; when using Celsius, divide by 2.2 or multiply by 0.45.

Clouds

Clouds give you an indication of air motion, stability, and moisture. Clouds formed by vertical currents in unstable air are *cumulus* meaning "accumulation" or "heap." Clouds formed by the cooling of a stable layer are *stratus*, meaning "stratified."

Standing lenticular altocumulus clouds are formed on the crests of waves created by barriers in the wind flow. The clouds show little movement, hence the name *standing*. Wind, however, can be quite strong blowing through such clouds. They are characterized by their smooth, polished edges. The presence of these clouds is a good indication of very strong turbulence, and they should be avoided.

Air Mass Modification

Just as an air mass takes on the properties of its source region, it tends to take on the properties of the underlying surface when it moves away from its source region, thus becoming modified. The ways air masses are modified include cool air moving over a warm surface is heated from below, generating instability and increasing the possibility of showers; or warm air moving over a cool surface is cooled from below, increasing stability. If air is cooled to its dew point, stratus and/or fog forms; evaporation from water surfaces and falling precipitation add water vapor to the air. When the water is warmer than the air, evaporation can raise the dew point sufficiently to saturate the air and form stratus or fog; and water vapor is removed by condensation and precipitation.

Stability

Stability of an air mass determines its typical weather characteristics. Characteristics typical of an unstable and a stable air mass are as follows: unstable air—cumuliform clouds, showery precipitation, rough air (turbulence), good visibility, except in blowing obstructions; stable air—stratiform clouds and fog, continuous precipitation, smooth air, and fair to poor visibility in haze and smoke. In the cold-front occlusion, the coldest air is under the cold front. When it overtakes the warm front, it lifts the warm front aloft, and cold air replaces cool air at the surface. Sufficient moisture must be available for clouds to form, or there will be no clouds. The degree of stability of the lifted air determines whether cloudiness will be predominately stratiform or cumuliform. If the air is unstable, cumuliform clouds develop. Precipitation from cumuliform clouds usually occurs as showers. An occluded front develops when a cold front overtakes a warm front.

Thunderstorms

For a thunderstorm to form, the air must have sufficient water vapor, an unstable lapse rate, and an initial upward boost (lifting) to start the storm process in motion.

COMPUTER-BASED QUESTIONS

5160. The need to slow an aircraft below V_A is brought about by the following weather phenomenon:

A. High-density altitude, which increases the indicated stall speed.

B. Turbulence, which causes an increase in stall speed.

C. Turbulence, which causes a decrease in stall speed.

5160. "B" is the correct answer. An airplane flying at a high speed with a low angle of attack suddenly encounters a vertical current of air moving upward. This increases the angle of attack on the wings. It has the same effect as applying a sharp back pressure on the elevator control. This increases load factors, which in turn increases stall speeds.
Reference PHOAK, p. 27
FAA subject matter knowledge code H01, H05

5301. Every physical process of weather is accompanied by or is the result of

A. a heat exchange.

B. the movement of air.

C. a pressure differential.

5301. "A" is the correct answer. Heat is a form of energy. When a substance contains heat it exhibits the property we measure as temperature—the degree of "hotness" or "coldness." The earth receives energy from the sun in the form of solar radiation. The amount of solar energy received by any region varies with time of day, season, and latitude. These differences in solar energy create temperature variations. Temperatures also vary with differences in topographical surface and with altitude. These temperature variations create forces that drive the atmosphere in its endless motions.
Reference Aviation Weather, pp. 6–7
FAA subject matter knowledge code I21

5302. What is the standard temperature at 10,000 ft?

A. –5°C.

B. –15°C.

C. +5°C.

5302. "A" is the correct answer. Temperature normally decreases with increasing altitude throughout the troposphere. This decrease of temperature with altitude is defined as the lapse rate. The average decrease of temperature—average lapse rate—in the troposphere is 2°C per 1000 ft.

–2°C × 10 = –20°C

+15°C = standard temperature

–20°C = temperature decrease

–5°C = standard temperature at 10,000 ft
Reference Aviation Weather, p. 9
FAA subject matter knowledge code I21

5303. What is the standard temperature at 20,000 ft?

A. –15°C.

B. –20°C.

C. –25°C.

5303. "C" is the correct answer. Temperature normally decreases with increasing altitude throughout the troposphere. This decrease of temperature with altitude is defined as the lapse rate. The average decrease of temperature—average lapse rate—in the troposphere is 2°C per 1000 ft.

–2°C × 20 = –40°C

+15°C = standard temperature

–40°C= temperature decrease

–25°C = standard temperature at 20,000 ft
Reference Aviation Weather, p. 9
FAA subject matter knowledge code I21

5304. Which conditions are favorable for the formation of a surface-based temperature inversion?

A. Clear, cool nights with calm or light wind.

B. Area of unstable air rapidly transferring heat from the surface.

C. Broad areas of cumulus clouds with smooth, level bases at the same altitude.

5304. "A" is the correct answer. An inversion often develops near the ground on clear, cool nights when wind is light.
Reference Aviation Weather, p. 9
FAA subject matter knowledge code I21

5305. What are the standard temperature and pressure values for sea level?

A. 15°C and 29.92 in. Hg.

B. 59°F and 1013.2 in. Hg.

C. 15°C and 29.92 mb.

5305. "A" is the correct answer. Standard sea level pressure is 1013.2 mb, 29.92 in. Hg, 760 mm Hg, or about 14.7 psi at 59°F (15°C).
Reference Aviation Weather, p. 13
FAA subject matter knowledge code I22

5306. Given:

Pressure altitude   12,000 ft
True air temperature   +50°F

From the conditions given, the approximate density altitude is

A. 11,900 ft.

B. 14,130 ft.

C. 18,150 ft.

5306. "B" is the correct answer. Use your E6B or electronic computer to determine the correct answer. Follow these steps:

1. Enter pressure altitude: 12,000 ft.

2. Enter the true air temperature: 50°F, or 10°C.

3. Read answer of 14,134 ft, which is closest to answer "B".

Reference Flight Training Handbook, p. 324
FAA subject matter knowledge code H06

5307. Given:

Pressure altitude   5000 ft
True air temperature   +30°C

From the conditions given, the approximate density altitude is

A. 7800 ft.

B. 8100 ft.

C. 8800 ft.

5307. "A" is the correct answer. Use your E6B or electronic computer to determine the correct answer. Follow these steps:

1. Enter pressure altitude: 5000 ft.

2. Enter the true air temperature: 30°C, or 86°F.

3. Read answer of 7801 ft, which is closest to answer "A".

Reference Flight Training Handbook, p. 324
FAA subject matter knowledge code H06

5308. Given:

Pressure altitude   6000 ft
True air temperature   +30°F

From the conditions given, the approximate density altitude is

A. 9000 ft.

B. 5500 ft.

C. 5000 ft.

5308. "B" is the correct answer. Use your E6B or electronic computer to determine the correct answer. Follow these steps:

1. Enter pressure altitude: 6000 ft

2. Enter the true air temperature: 30°F, or -1°C

3. Read answer of 5496 ft, which is closest to answer "B".

Reference Flight Training Handbook, p. 324
FAA subject matter knowledge code H06

5309. Given:

Pressure altitude   7000 ft
True air temperature   +15°C

From the conditions given, the approximate density altitude is

A. 5000 ft.

B. 8500 ft.

C. 9500 ft.

5309. "B" is the correct answer. Use your E6B or electronic computer to determine the correct answer. Follow these steps:

1. Enter pressure altitude: 7000 ft.

2. Enter the true air temperature: +15°C, or 59°F.

3. Read answer of 8595 ft, which is closest to answer "B".

Reference Flight Training Handbook, p. 324
FAA subject matter knowledge code H06

5310. What causes wind?

A. The earth's rotation.

B. Air mass modification.

C. Pressure differences.

5310. "C" is the correct answer. Pressure differences cause wind.
Reference Aviation Weather, p. 27
FAA subject matter knowledge code I23

5311. In the Northern Hemisphere, the wind is deflected to the

A. right by Coriolis force.

B. right by surface friction.

C. left by Coriolis force.

5311. "A" is the correct answer. The Coriolis force affects the path of aircraft, missiles, flying birds, ocean currents, and most important to the study of weather, air currents. The force deflects air to the right in the Northern Hemisphere and to the left in the Southern Hemisphere.
Reference Aviation Weather, p. 25
FAA subject matter knowledge code I23

5312. Why does the wind have a tendency to flow parallel to the isobars above the friction level?

A. Coriolis force tends to counterbalance the horizontal pressure gradient.

B. Coriolis force acts perpendicular to a line connecting the highs and lows.

C. Friction of the air with the earth deflects the air perpendicular to the pressure gradient.

5312. "A" is the correct answer. The pressure gradient force drives the wind and is perpendicular to the isobars. When a pressure gradient force is first established, wind begins to blow from higher to lower pressure directly across the isobars. However, the instant air begins moving, the Coriolis force deflects it to the right. Soon the wind is deflected a full 90° and is parallel to the isobars. At this time, the Coriolis force exactly balances the pressure gradient force. With the forces in balance, the wind remains parallel to the isobars.
Reference Aviation Weather, pp. 25–26
FAA subject matter knowledge code I23

5313. The wind system associated with a low-pressure area in the Northern Hemisphere is

A. an anticyclone and is caused by descending cold air.

B. a cyclone and is caused by the Coriolis force.

C. an anticyclone and is caused by the Coriolis force.

5313. "B" is the correct answer. As the air tries to blow outward from the high pressure it is deflected to the right by the Coriolis force. Thus, the wind around a high blows clockwise. The high pressure with its associated wind system is an anticyclone.
Reference Aviation Weather, p. 29
FAA subject matter knowledge code I23

5314. With regard to the windflow patterns shown on surface analysis charts; when the isobars are

A. close together, the pressure gradient force is slight and wind velocities are weaker.

B. not close together, the pressure gradient force is greater and wind velocities are stronger.

C. close together, the pressure gradient force is greater and wind velocities are stronger.

5314. "C" is the correct answer. Whenever a pressure difference develops over an area, the pressure gradient force begins moving the air directly across the isobars. The closer the spacing of the isobars, the stronger the pressure gradient force. The stronger the pressure gradient force, the stronger is the wind. Thus, closely spaced isobars mean strong winds; widely spaced isobars mean lighter wind.
Reference Aviation Weather, p. 24
FAA subject matter knowledge code I23

5315. What prevents air from flowing directly from high-pressure areas to low-pressure areas?

A. Coriolis force.

B. Surface friction.

C. Pressure gradient force.

5315. "A" is the correct answer. The Coriolis force prevents air from flowing from a high-pressure area to a low-pressure area.
Reference Aviation Weather, p. 25
FAA subject matter knowledge code I23

5316. While flying cross-country in the Northern Hemisphere, you experience a continuous left crosswind that is associated with a major wind system. This indicates that you

A. are flying toward an area of generally unfavorable weather conditions.

B. have flown from an area of unfavorable weather conditions.

C. cannot determine weather conditions without knowing pressure changes.

5316. "A" is the correct answer. Wind blows counterclockwise around a low and clockwise around a high. At the surface, when air converges into a low, it cannot go outward against the pressure gradient, nor can it go downward into the ground; it must go upward. Therefore, a low or trough is an area of rising air. Rising air is conducive to cloudiness and precipitation; thus, we have the general association of

low pressure and bad weather. Highs and ridges are areas of descending air.
Reference Aviation Weather, p. 35
FAA subject matter knowledge code I23

5317. Which is true with respect to a high- or low-pressure system?

A. A high-pressure area or ridge is an area of rising air.

B. A low-pressure area or trough is an area of descending air.

C. A high-pressure area or ridge is an area of descending air.

5317. "C" is the correct answer. A low or trough is an area of rising air. Highs and ridges are areas of descending air.
Reference Aviation Weather, p. 35
FAA subject matter knowledge code I24

5318. Which is true regarding high- or low-pressure systems?

A. A high-pressure area or ridge is an area of rising air.

B. A low-pressure area or trough is an area of rising air.

C. Both high- and low-pressure areas are characterized by descending air.

5318. "B" is the correct answer. Wind blows counterclockwise around a low and clockwise around a high. At the surface when air converges into a low, it cannot go outward against the pressure gradient, nor can it go downward into the ground; it must go upward. Therefore, a low or trough is an area of rising air. Rising air is conducive to cloudiness and precipitation; thus, we have the general association of low pressure and bad weather. Highs and ridges are areas of descending air.
Reference Aviation Weather, p. 35
FAA subject matter knowledge code I23

5319. When flying into a low-pressure area in the Northern Hemisphere, the wind direction and velocity will be from the

A. left and decreasing.

B. left and increasing.

C. right and decreasing.

5319. "B" is the correct answer. In the Northern Hemisphere, the wind around a low is counterclockwise; thus, the wind is from the left and increasing.
Reference Aviation Weather, p. 116
FAA subject matter knowledge code I23

5320. Which is true regarding actual air temperature and dew point temperature spread?

A. The temperature spread decreases as the relative humidity decreases.

B. The temperature spread decreases as the relative humidity increases.

C. The temperature spread increases as the relative humidity increases.

5320. "B" is the correct answer. The difference between air temperature and dew point temperature is popularly called the *spread*. As the spread becomes less, relative humidity increases. It is 100 percent when temperature and dew point are the same.
Reference Aviation Weather, p. 38
FAA subject matter knowledge code I24

5321. The general circulation of air associated with a high-pressure area in the Northern Hemisphere is

A. outward, downward, and clockwise.

B. outward, upward, and clockwise.

C. inward, downward, and clockwise.

5321. "A" is the correct answer. Wind blows counterclockwise around a low and clockwise around a high. At the surface, when air converges into a low, it cannot go outward against the pressure gradient, nor can it go downward into the ground; it must go upward. Therefore, a low or trough is an area of rising air. Rising air is conducive to cloudiness and precipitation; thus, we have the general association of low pressure and bad weather. Highs and ridges are areas of descending air.
Reference Aviation Weather, p. 35
FAA subject matter knowledge code I23

5322. Virga is best described as

A. streamers of precipitation trailing beneath clouds which evaporate before reaching the ground.

B. wall cloud torrents trailing beneath cumulonimbus clouds which dissipate before reaching the ground.

C. turbulent areas beneath cumulonimbus clouds.

5322. "A" is the correct answer. Virga is streamers of precipitation trailing beneath clouds which evaporate before reaching the ground.
Reference Aviation Weather, p. 39
FAA subject matter knowledge code I24

5323. Moisture is added to a parcel of air by

A. sublimation and condensation.

B. evaporation and condensation.

C. evaporation and sublimation.

5323. "C" is the correct answer. Evaporation, condensation, sublimation, freezing, and melting are changes of state. Evaporation is the changing of liquid water to water vapor. Sublimation is the changing of ice directly to water vapor, or water vapor to ice, bypassing the liquid state in each process.
Reference Aviation Weather, p. 39
FAA subject matter knowledge code I24

5324. Ice pellets encountered during flight normally are evidence that

A. a warm front has passed.

B. a warm front is about to pass.

C. there are thunderstorms in the area.

5324. "B" is the correct answer. As a warm front is about to pass, you may encounter ice pellets in flight.
Reference Aviation Weather, p. 43
FAA subject matter knowledge code I24

5325. What is indicated if ice pellets are encountered at 8000 ft?

A. Freezing rain at higher altitude.

B. You are approaching an area of thunderstorms.

C. You will encounter hail if you continue your flight.

5325. "A" is the correct answer. Ice pellets always indicate freezing rain at higher altitude.
Reference Aviation Weather, p. 43
FAA subject matter knowledge code I24

5326. Ice pellets encountered during flight are normally evidence that

A. a cold front has passed.

B. there are thunderstorms in the area.

C. freezing rain exists at higher altitudes.

5326. "C" is the correct answer. Ice pellets always indicate freezing rain at higher altitude.
Reference Aviation Weather, p. 43
FAA subject matter knowledge code I24

5327. When conditionally unstable air with high moisture content and very warm surface temperature is forecast, one can expect what type of weather?

A. Strong updrafts and stratonimbus clouds.

B. Restricted visibility near the surface over a large area.

C. Strong updrafts and cumulonimbus clouds.

5327. "C" is the correct answer. Characteristics typical of an unstable air mass are cumuliform clouds, showery precipitation, rough air (turbulence), and good visibility, except in blowing obstructions.
Reference Aviation Weather, p. 64
FAA subject matter knowledge code I25

5328. What is the approximate base of the cumulus clouds if the temperature at 2000 ft msl is 70°F and the dew point is 52°F?

A. 3000 ft msl.

B. 4000 ft msl.

C. 6000 ft msl.

5328. "C" is the correct answer. You can estimate the height of cumuliform cloud bases using surface temperature–dew point spread. Unsaturated air in a convective current cools at about 5.4°F (3.0°C) per 1000 ft; dew point decreases at about 1°F (⅝°C) per 1000 ft. Thus, in a convective current, temperature and dew point converge at about 4.4°F (2.5°C) per 1000 ft. We can get a quick estimate of the height of a convective cloud base in thousands of ft by rounding these values and dividing into the spread, or by multiplying the spread by their reciprocals. When using Fahrenheit, divide by 4 or multiply by 0.25; when using Celsius, divide by 2.2 or multiply by 0.45.
Reference Aviation Weather, p. 51
FAA subject matter knowledge code I25

5329. If clouds form as a result of very stable, moist air being forced to ascend a mountain slope, the clouds will be

A. cirrus type with no vertical development or turbulence.

B. cumulus type with considerable vertical development and turbulence.

C. stratus type with little vertical development and little or no turbulence.

5329. "C" is the correct answer. When stable air is forced upward, the air tends to retain horizontal flow, and any cloudiness is flat and stratified.
Reference Aviation Weather, p. 51
FAA subject matter knowledge code I25

5330. What determines the structure or type of clouds that form as a result of air being forced to ascend?

A. The method by which the air is lifted.

B. The stability of the air before lifting occurs.

C. The relative humidity of the air after lifting occurs.

5330. "B" is the correct answer. When stable air is forced upward, the air tends to retain horizontal flow, and any cloudiness is flat and stratified. When unstable air is forced upward, the disturbance grows, and any resulting cloudiness shows extensive vertical development.
Reference Aviation Weather, p. 51
FAA subject matter knowledge code I25

5331. Refer to the excerpt from a surface weather report:

ABC...194/89/45/2115/993...

At approximately what altitude agl should bases of convective-type cumuliform clouds be expected? (Use the most accurate method.)

A. 4400 ft.

B. 10,000 ft.

C. 17,600 ft.

5331. "B" is the correct answer. You can estimate the height of cumuliform cloud bases using surface temperature–dew point spread. Unsaturated air in a convective current cools at about 5.4°F (3.0°C) per 1000 ft; dew point decreases at about 1°F (5/9°C) per 1000 ft. Thus, in a convective current, temperature and dew point converge at about 4.4°F (2.5°C) per 1000 ft. We can get a quick estimate of the height of a convective cloud base in thousands of ft by rounding these values and dividing into the spread, or by multiplying the spread by their reciprocals. When using Fahrenheit, divide by 4 or multiply by 0.25; when using Celsius, divide by 2.2 or multiply by 0.45.
Reference Aviation Weather, p. 51
FAA subject matter knowledge code I25

5332. What are the characteristics of stable air?

A. Good visibility, steady precipitation, stratus clouds.

B. Poor visibility, steady precipitation, stratus clouds.

C. Poor visibility, intermittent precipitation, cumulus clouds.

5332. "B" is the correct answer. Characteristics typical of an unstable air mass are stratiform clouds and fog, continuous precipitation, smooth air, and fair to poor visibility in haze and smoke.
Reference Aviation Weather, p. 64
FAA subject matter knowledge code I24

5333. Which would decrease the stability of an air mass?

A. Warming from below.

B. Cooling from below.

C. A decrease in water vapor.

5333. "A" is the correct answer. Just as an air mass takes on the properties of its source region, it tends to take on the properties of the underlying surface when it moves away from its source region, thus becoming modified.
Reference Aviation Weather, p. 64
FAA subject matter knowledge code I27

5334. From which measurement of the atmosphere can stability be determined?

A. Atmospheric pressure.

B. The ambient lapse rate.

C. The dry adiabatic lapse rate.

5334. "B" is the correct answer. Stability runs the gamut from absolutely stable to absolutely unstable, and the atmosphere usually is in a delicate balance somewhere in between. A change in the ambient temperature lapse rate of an air mass can tip this balance.
Reference Aviation Weather, p. 49
FAA subject matter knowledge code I25

5335. What type of weather can one expect from moist, unstable air, and very warm surface temperatures?

A. Fog and low stratus clouds.

B. Continuous heavy precipitation.

C. Strong updrafts and cumulonimbus clouds.

5335. "C" is the correct answer. Unstable air favors convection. A cumulus cloud, meaning "heap," forms in a convective updraft and builds upward. Within an unstable layer, clouds are cumuliform, and the vertical extent of the cloud depends on the depth of the unstable layer.
Reference Aviation Weather, p. 50
FAA subject matter knowledge code I25

5336. Which would increase the stability of an air mass?

A. Warming from below.

B. Cooling from below.

C. Decrease in water vapor.

5336. "B" is the correct answer. Just as an air mass takes on the properties of its source region, it tends to take on the properties of the underlying surface when it moves away from its source region, thus becoming modified.
Reference Aviation Weather, p. 64
FAA subject matter knowledge code I25

5337. The conditions necessary for the formation of stratiform clouds are a lifting action and

A. unstable, dry air.

B. stable, moist air.

C. unstable, moist air.

5337. "B" is the correct answer. Since stable air resists convection, clouds in stable air form in horizontal, sheetlike layers or strata. Thus, within a stable layer, clouds are stratiform.
Reference Aviation Weather, p. 50
FAA subject matter knowledge code I26

5338. Which cloud types would indicate convective turbulence?

A. Cirrus clouds.

B. Nimbostratus clouds.

C. Towering cumulus clouds.

5338. "C" is the correct answer. When convection extends to greater heights, it develops larger cumulus clouds and cumulonimbus clouds with anvil-like tops. Cumulonimbus clouds gives visual warning of violent convective turbulence.
Reference Aviation Weather, p. 81
FAA subject matter knowledge code I25

5339. The presence of standing lenticular altocumulus clouds is a good indication of

A. lenticular ice formation in calm air.

B. very strong turbulence.

C. heavy icing conditions.

5339. "B" is the correct answer. Standing lenticular altocumulus clouds are formed on the crests of waves created by barriers in the wind flow. The clouds show little movement, hence the name "standing." Wind, however, can be quite strong blowing through such clouds. They are characterized by their smooth, polished edges. The presence of these clouds is a good indication of very strong turbulence, and they should be avoided.
Reference Aviation Weather, p. 58
FAA subject matter knowledge code I28

5340. The formation of either predominantly stratiform or predominantly cumuliform clouds is dependent on the

A. source of lift.

B. stability of the air being lifted.

C. temperature of the air being lifted.

5340. "B" is the correct answer. Clouds give you an indication of air motion, stability, and moisture. Clouds formed by vertical currents in unstable air are cumulus, meaning "accumulation." Clouds formed by the cooling of a stable layer are stratus, meaning "stratified."
Reference Aviation Weather, p. 53
FAA subject matter knowledge code I25

5341. Which combination of weather-producing variables would likely result in cumuliform-type clouds, good visibility, and showery rain?

A. Stable, moist air and orographic lifting.

B. Unstable, moist air and orographic lifting.

C. Unstable, moist air and no lifting mechanism.

5341. "B" is the correct answer. Sufficient moisture must be available for clouds to form, or there will be no clouds. The degree of stability of the lifted air determines whether cloudiness will be predominately stratiform or cumuliform. If the air is unstable, cumuliform clouds develop. Precipitation from cumuliform clouds is usually in the form of showers.
Reference Aviation Weather, p. 72
FAA subject matter knowledge code I27

5342. What is a characteristic of stable air?

A. Stratiform clouds.

B. Fair weather cumulus clouds.

C. Temperature decreases rapidly with altitude.

5342. "A" is the correct answer. Stability of an air mass determines its typical weather characteristics.
Reference Aviation Weather, p. 64
FAA subject matter knowledge code I27

5343. A moist, unstable air mass is characterized by

A. poor visibility and smooth air.

B. cumuliform clouds and showery precipitation.

C. stratiform clouds and continuous precipitation.

5343. "B" is the correct answer. Stability of an air mass determines its typical weather characteristics.
Reference Aviation Weather, p. 64
FAA subject matter knowledge code I27

5344. When an air mass is stable, which of these conditions are most likely to exist?

A. Numerous towering cumulus and cumulonimbus clouds.

B. Moderate to severe turbulence at the lower levels.

C. Smoke, dust, haze, etc., concentrated at the lower levels with resulting poor visibility.

5344. "C" is the correct answer. Stability of an air mass determines its typical weather characteristics.
Reference Aviation Weather, p. 64
FAA subject matter knowledge code I27

5345. Which is a characteristic of stable air?

A. Cumuliform clouds.

B. Excellent visibility.

C. Restricted visibility.

5345. "C" is the correct answer. Stability of an air mass determines its typical weather characteristics.
Reference Aviation Weather, p. 64
FAA subject matter knowledge code I27

5346. Which is a characteristic typical of a stable air mass?

A. Cumuliform clouds.

B. Showery precipitation.

C. Continuous precipitation.

5346. "C" is the correct answer. Stability of an air mass determines its typical weather characteristics.
Reference Aviation Weather, p. 64
FAA subject matter knowledge code I27

5347. Which is true regarding a cold-front occlusion?

A. The air ahead of the warm front is colder than the air behind the overtaking cold front.

B. The air ahead of the warm front is warmer than the air behind the overtaking cold front.

C. The air ahead of the warm front has the same temperature as the air behind the overtaking cold front.

5347. "B" is the correct answer. In the cold-front occlusion, the coldest air is under the cold front. When it overtakes the warm front, it lifts the warm front aloft, and cold air replaces cool air at the surface.
Reference Aviation Weather, p. 71
FAA subject matter knowledge code I27

5348. Which are the characteristics of a cold air mass moving over a warm surface?

A. Cumuliform clouds, turbulence, and poor visibility.

B. Cumuliform clouds, turbulence, and good visibility.

C. Stratiform clouds, smooth air, and poor visibility.

5348. "B" is the correct answer. Some typical characteristics of a cold air mass moving over a warm surface are cumuliform clouds, turbulence, and good visibility.
Reference Aviation Weather, p. 65
FAA subject matter knowledge code I27

5349. The conditions necessary for the formation of cumulonimbus clouds are a lifting action and

A. unstable, dry air.

B. stable, moist air.

C. unstable, moist air.

5349. "C" is the correct answer. For a thunderstorm to form, the air must have sufficient water vapor, an unstable lapse rate, and an initial upward boost (lifting) to start the storm process in motion.
Reference Aviation Weather, p. 111
FAA subject matter knowledge code I30

5350. Fog produced by frontal activity is a result of saturation due to

A. nocturnal cooling.

B. adiabatic cooling.

C. evaporation of precipitation.

5350. "C" is the correct answer. When relatively warm rain or drizzle falls through cool air, evaporation from the precipitation saturates the cool air and forms fog. Precipitation-induced fog can become quite dense and continue for an extended period of time. This fog may extend over large areas, completely suspending air operations. It is most commonly associated with warm fronts, but can occur with slow-moving cold fronts and with stationary fronts.
Reference Aviation Weather p. 128
FAA subject matter knowledge code I31

5351. What is an important characteristic of wind shear?

A. It is present at only lower levels and exists in a horizontal direction.

B. It is present at any level and exists in only a vertical direction.

C. It can be present at any level and can exist in both a horizontal and vertical direction.

5351. "C" is the correct answer. Wind shear generates eddies between two wind currents of differing velocities. The differences may be in wind speed, wind direction, or both. Wind shear may be associated with either a wind shift or a wind speed gradient at any level in the atmosphere.
Reference Aviation Weather, p. 86
FAA subject matter knowledge code I28

5352. Hazardous wind shear is commonly encountered

A. near warm or stationary frontal activity.

B. when the wind velocity is stronger than 35 knots.

C. in areas of temperature inversion and near thunderstorms.

5352. "C" is the correct answer. A temperature inversion forms near the surface on a clear night with calm or light surface wind. Wind just above the inversion may be relatively strong. A wind shear zone develops between the calm and the stronger winds above. Eddies in the shear zone cause airspeed fluctuations as an aircraft climbs or descends through the inversion. The fluctuation in airspeed can induce a stall precariously close to the ground. Hazardous turbulence is present in all thunderstorms. The strongest turbulence within the cloud occurs with shear between updrafts and downdrafts. Outside the cloud, shear turbulence has been encountered several thousand ft above and 20 miles laterally from a severe storm. The first gust causes a rapid and sometimes drastic change in surface wind ahead of an approaching storm.
Reference Aviation Weather, pp. 88, 114–115
FAA subject matter knowledge code I28

5353. Low-level wind shear may occur when

A. surface winds are light and variable.

B. there is a low-level temperature inversion with strong winds above the inversion.

C. surface winds are above 15 knots and there is no change in wind direction and wind speed with height.

5353. "B" is the correct answer. A temperature inversion forms near the surface on a clear night with calm or light surface wind. Wind just above the inversion may be relatively strong. A wind shear zone develops between the calm and the stronger winds above. Eddies in the shear zone cause airspeed fluctuations as an aircraft climbs or descends through the inversion. The fluctuation in airspeed can induce a stall precariously close to the ground.
Reference Aviation Weather, p. 88
FAA subject matter knowledge code I28

5354. If a temperature inversion is encountered immediately after takeoff or during an approach to a landing, a potential hazard exists due to

A. wind shear.

B. strong surface winds.

C. strong convective currents.

5354. "A" is the correct answer. A temperature inversion forms near the surface on a clear night with calm or light surface wind. Wind just above the inversion may be relatively strong. A wind shear zone develops between the calm and the stronger winds above. Eddies in the shear zone cause airspeed fluctuations as an aircraft climbs or descends through the inversion. The fluctuation in airspeed can induce a stall precariously close to the ground.
Reference Aviation Weather, p. 88
FAA subject matter knowledge code I28

5355. Given:

Winds at 3000 ft agl	30 knots
Surface winds	Calm

While approaching for landing under clear skies a few hours after sunrise, one should

A. allow a margin of approach airspeed above normal to avoid stalling.

B. keep the approach airspeed at or slightly below normal to compensate for floating.

C. not alter your approach airspeed because these conditions are nearly ideal.

5355. "A" is the correct answer. When taking off or landing in calm wind under clear skies within a few hours before or after sunrise, be prepared for a temperature inversion near the ground. You can be relatively certain of a shear zone in the inversion if you know the wind at 2000 to 4000 ft is 25 knots or more. Allow a margin of airspeed above normal climb or approach speed to alleviate the danger of a stall in the event of turbulence or sudden change in wind velocity.
Reference Aviation Weather, p. 88
FAA subject matter knowledge code I28

5356. Convective currents are most active on warm summer afternoons when winds are

A. light.

B. moderate.

C. strong.

5356. "A" is the correct answer. Convective currents are a common cause of turbulence, especially at low altitudes. These currents are localized vertical air movements, both ascending and descending. For every rising current there is a compensating downward current. The downward currents frequently occur over broader areas than do the upward currents, and therefore, they have a slower vertical speed than do the rising currents. Convective currents are most active on warm summer afternoons when winds are light.

Reference Aviation Weather, pp. 80–81

FAA subject matter knowledge code I28

5357. When flying low over hilly terrain, ridges, or mountain ranges, the greatest potential danger from turbulent air currents is usually encountered on the

A. leeward side when flying with a tailwind.

B. leeward side when flying into the wind.

C. windward side when flying into the wind.

5357. "B" is the correct answer. Dangerous downdrafts may be encountered on the leeward side when flying into the wind.

Reference Aviation Weather, p. 84

FAA subject matter knowledge code I28

5358. During an approach, the most important and most easily recognized means of being alerted to possible wind shear is monitoring the

A. amount of trim required to relieve control pressures.

B. heading changes necessary to remain on the runway centerline.

C. power and vertical velocity required to remain on the proper glidepath.

5358. "C" is the correct answer. When the rate of descent on an ILS approach differs from the usual values for the aircraft, the pilot should beware of a potential wind shear situation. Since rate of descent on the glide slope is directly related to ground speed, a high descent rate would indicate a strong tailwind. Conversely, a low descent rate denotes a strong shear wind. The power needed to hold the glide slope is different from typical, no-shear conditions. Less power than normal is needed to maintain the glide slope when a tailwind is present, and more power is needed for a strong headwind.

Reference Pilot Windshear Guide

FAA subject matter knowledge code K04

5359. During departure, under conditions of suspected low-level wind shear, a sudden decrease in headwind causes

A. a loss in airspeed equal to the decrease in wind velocity.

B. a gain in airspeed equal to the decrease in wind velocity.

C. no change in airspeed, but ground speed will decrease.

5359. "A" is the correct answer. The worst situation on departure occurs when the aircraft encounters a rapidly increasing tailwind, decreasing headwind, and/or downdraft. Taking off under these circumstances leads to a decreased performance condition. An increasing tailwind or decreasing headwind, when encountered, causes a decrease in indicated airspeed.

Reference Pilot Windshear Guide

FAA subject matter knowledge code K04

5360. Which situation would most likely result in freezing precipitation?

A. Rain falling from air that has a temperature of 32°F or less into air having a temperature of more than 32°F.

B. Rain falling from air that has a temperature of 0°C or less into air having a temperature of 0°C or more.

C. Rain falling from air that has a temperature of more than 32°F into air having a temperature of 32°F or less.

5360. "C" is the correct answer. Precipitation can change its state as the temperature of its environment changes.

Reference Aviation Weather, p. 43

FAA subject matter knowledge code I24

5361. Which statement is true concerning the hazards of hail?

A. Hail damage in horizontal flight is minimal due to the vertical movement of hail in the clouds.

B. Rain at the surface is a reliable indication of no hail aloft.

C. Hailstones may be encountered in clear air several miles from a thunderstorm.

5361. "C" is the correct answer. Large hail occurs with severe thunderstorms that are built to great heights. Eventually the hailstones fall, possibly some distance from the storm core. Hail has been observed in clear air several miles from the parent thunderstorm.

Reference Aviation Weather, p. 115

FAA subject matter knowledge code I30

5362. Hail is most likely to be associated with

A. cumulus clouds.

B. cumulonimbus clouds.

C. stratocumulus clouds.

5362. "B" is the correct answer. Hail competes with turbulence as the greatest thunderstorm hazard to aircraft.
Reference Aviation Weather, p. 115
FAA subject matter knowledge code I30

5363. The most severe weather conditions, such as destructive winds, heavy hail, and tornadoes, are generally associated with

A. slow-moving warm fronts that slope above the tropopause.

B. squall lines.

C. fast-moving occluded fronts.

5363. "B" is the correct answer. A squall line is a nonfrontal, narrow band of active thunderstorms. Tornadoes occur with isolated thunderstorms at times, but much more frequently they form with steady-state thunderstorms associated with cold fronts or squall lines.
Reference Aviation Weather, pp. 113, 114
FAA subject matter knowledge code I30

5364. Of the following, which is accurate regarding turbulence associated with thunderstorms?

A. Outside the cloud, shear turbulence can be encountered 50 miles laterally from a severe storm.

B. Shear turbulence is encountered only inside cumulonimbus clouds or within a 5-mile radius of them.

C. Outside the cloud, shear turbulence can be encountered 20 miles laterally from a severe storm.

5364. "C" is the correct answer. Hazardous turbulence is present in all thunderstorms. The strongest turbulence within the cloud occurs with shear between updrafts and downdrafts. Outside the cloud, shear turbulence has been encountered several thousand ft above and 20 miles laterally from a severe storm.
Reference Aviation Weather, pp. 114–115
FAA subject matter knowledge code I30

5365. If airborne radar is indicating an extremely intense thunderstorm echo, this thunderstorm should be avoided by a distance of at least

A. 20 miles.

B. 10 miles.

C. 5 miles.

5365. "A" is the correct answer. The most intense echoes are severe thunderstorms. Avoid the most intense echoes by at least 20 miles; that is, echoes should be separated by at least 40 miles before you fly between them.
Reference Aviation Weather, p. 121
FAA subject matter knowledge code I31

5366. Which statement is true regarding squall lines?

A. They are always associated with cold fronts.

B. They are slow in forming, but rapid in movement.

C. They are nonfrontal and often contain severe, steady-state thunderstorms.

5366. "C" is the correct answer. A squall line is a nonfrontal, narrow band of active thunderstorms. It often contains severe steady-state thunderstorms and presents the single most intense weather hazard to aircraft.
Reference Aviation Weather, p. 114
FAA subject matter knowledge code I30

5367. Which statement is true concerning squall lines?

A. They form slowly, but move rapidly.

B. They are associated with frontal systems only.

C. They offer the most intense weather hazards to aircraft.

5367. "C" is the correct answer. A squall line is a nonfrontal, narrow band of active thunderstorms. It often contains severe steady-state thunderstorms and presents the single most intense weather hazard to aircraft.
Reference Aviation Weather, p. 114
FAA subject matter knowledge code I30

5368. Select the true statement pertaining to the life cycle of a thunderstorm.

A. Updrafts continue to develop throughout the dissipating stage of a thunderstorm.

B. The beginning of rain at the earth's surface indicates the mature stage of the thunderstorm.

C. The beginning of rain at the earth's surface indicates the dissipating stage of the thunderstorm.

5368. "B" is the correct answer. Precipitation beginning to fall from the cloud base is your signal that a downdraft has developed and a cell has entered the mature stage.
Reference Aviation Weather, p. 111
FAA subject matter knowledge code I30

5369. What visible signs indicate extreme turbulence in thunderstorms?

A. The base of the clouds near the surface, heavy rain, and hail.

B. A low ceiling and visibility, hail, and precipitation static.

C. Cumulonimbus clouds, very frequent lightning, and roll clouds.

5369. "C" is the correct answer. Hazardous turbulence is present in all thunderstorms. The strongest turbulence within the cloud occurs with shear between updrafts and downdrafts. Outside the cloud, shear turbulence has been encountered several thousand ft above and 20 miles laterally from a severe storm. Often a "roll cloud" on the leading edge of a storm marks the eddies in this shear. The roll cloud is most prevalent with cold-front or squall line thunderstorms and signifies an extremely turbulent zone. The more frequent the lightning, the more severe the thunderstorm.
Reference Aviation Weather, pp. 114–115, 116
FAA subject matter knowledge code I30

5370. Which weather phenomenon signals the beginning of the mature stage of a thunderstorm?

A. The start of rain.

B. The appearance of an anvil top.

C. The growth rate of the cloud is maximum.

5370. "A" is the correct answer. Precipitation beginning to fall from the cloud base is your signal that a downdraft has developed and a cell has entered the mature stage.
Reference Aviation Weather, p. 111
FAA subject matter knowledge code I30

5371. What feature is normally associated with the cumulus stage of a thunderstorm?

A. Roll cloud.

B. Continuous updraft.

C. Beginning of rain at the surface.

5371. "B" is the correct answer. Although most cumulus clouds do not grow into thunderstorms, every thunderstorm begins as a cumulus. The key feature of the cumulus stage is an updraft. The updraft varies in strength and extends from very near the surface to the cloud top. The growth rate of the cloud may exceed 3000 ft per minute, so it is inadvisable to attempt to climb over rapidly building cumulus clouds.
Reference Aviation Weather, p. 111
FAA subject matter knowledge code I30

5372. During the life cycle of a thunderstorm, which stage is characterized predominantly by downdrafts?

A. Mature.

B. Developing.

C. Dissipating.

5372. "C" is the correct answer. Downdrafts characterize the dissipating stage of the thunderstorm, and the storm dies rapidly.
Reference Aviation Weather, p. 111
FAA subject matter knowledge code I30

5373. What minimum distance should exist between intense radar echoes before any attempt is made to fly between these thunderstorms?

A. 20 miles.

B. 30 miles.

C. 40 miles.

5373. "C" is the correct answer. The most intense echoes are severe thunderstorms. Avoid the most intense echoes by at least 20 miles; that is, echoes should be separated by at least 40 miles before you fly between them.
Reference Aviation Weather, p. 121
FAA subject matter knowledge code I30

5374. Which inflight hazard is most commonly associated with warm fronts?

A. Advection fog.

B. Radiation fog.

C. Precipitation-induced fog.

5374. "C" is the correct answer. When relatively warm rain or drizzle falls through cool air, evaporation from the precipitation saturates the cool air and forms fog. Precipitation-induced fog can become quite dense and continue for an extended period of time. This fog may extend over large areas, completely suspending air operations. It is most commonly associated with warm fronts, but can occur with slow-moving cold fronts and with stationary fronts.
Reference Aviation Weather, p. 128
FAA subject matter knowledge code I27

5375. Which is true regarding the use of airborne weather-avoidance radar for the recognition of certain weather conditions?

A. The radarscope provides no assurance of avoiding instrument weather conditions.

B. The avoidance of hail is assured when flying between and just clear of the most intense echoes.

C. The clear area between intense echoes indicates that visual sighting of storms can be maintained when flying between the echoes.

5375. "A" is the correct answer. Weather radar detects only precipitation drops; it does not detect minute cloud droplets. Therefore, the radarscope provides no assurance of avoiding instrument weather in clouds and fog.
Reference Aviation Weather, p. 121
FAA subject matter knowledge code I30

5376. A situation most conducive to the formation of advection fog is

A. a light breeze moving colder air over a water surface.

B. an air mass moving inland from the coastline during the winter.

C. a warm, moist air mass settling over a cool surface under no-wind conditions.

5376. "B" is the correct answer. Advection fog forms when moist air moves over colder ground or water. It is most common along coastal areas. This fog frequently forms offshore as a result of cold water and is carried inland by the wind.
Reference Aviation Weather, p. 127
FAA subject matter knowledge code I31

5377. Advection fog has drifted over a coastal airport during the day. What may tend to dissipate or lift this fog into low stratus clouds?

A. Nighttime cooling.

B. Surface radiation.

C. Wind of 15 knots or stronger.

5377. "C" is the correct answer. Advection fog deepens as wind speed increases up to about 15 knots. Wind much stronger than 15 knots lifts the fog into a layer of low stratus or stratocumulus.
Reference Aviation Weather, p. 127
FAA subject matter knowledge code I31

5378. What lifts advection fog into low stratus clouds?

A. Nighttime cooling.

B. Dryness of the underlying land mass.

C. Surface winds of approximately 15 knots or stronger.

5378. "C" is the correct answer. Advection fog deepens as wind speed increases up to about 15 knots. Wind much stronger than 15 knots lifts the fog into a layer of low stratus or stratocumulus.
Reference Aviation Weather, p. 127
FAA subject matter knowledge code I31

5379. In what ways do advection fog, radiation fog, and steam fog differ in their formation or location?

A. Radiation fog is restricted to land areas; advection fog is most common along coastal areas; steam fog forms over a water surface.

B. Advection fog deepens as wind speed increases up to 20 knots; steam fog requires calm or very light wind; radiation fog forms when the ground or water cools the air by radiation.

C. Steam fog forms from moist air moving over a colder surface; advection fog requires cold air over a warmer surface; radiation fog is produced by radiational cooling of the ground.

5379. "A" is the correct answer. Radiation fog is relatively shallow fog. Radiation fog is restricted to land. Advection fog forms when moist air moves over colder ground or water. It is most common along coastal areas. Steam fog, often called "sea smoke," forms in winter when cold, dry air passes from land areas over comparatively warm ocean waters.
Reference Aviation Weather, pp. 126–127
FAA subject matter knowledge code I31

5380. With respect to advection fog, which statement is true?

A. It is slow to develop, and dissipates quite rapidly.

B. It forms almost exclusively at night or near daybreak.

C. It can appear suddenly during day or night, and it is more persistent than radiation fog.

5380. "C" is the correct answer. Advection fog is usually more extensive and much more persistent than radiation fog. Advection fog can move in rapidly regardless of the time of day or night.
Reference Aviation Weather, p. 127
FAA subject matter knowledge code I31

5381. Which feature is associated with the tropopause?

A. Constant height above the earth.

B. Abrupt change in temperature lapse rate.

C. Absolute upper limit of cloud formation.

5381. "B" is the correct answer. Tropopause is the transition zone between the troposphere and stratosphere, usually characterized by an abrupt change of lapse rate.
Reference Aviation Weather, p. 212
FAA subject matter knowledge code I31

5382. A common location of clear air turbulence is

A. in an upper trough on the polar side of a jet stream.

B. near a ridge aloft on the equatorial side of a high-pressure flow.

C. south of an east-west oriented high-pressure ridge in its dissipating stage.

5382. "A" is the correct answer. A preferred location of clear air turbulence is in an upper trough on the cold (polar) side of the jet stream.
Reference Aviation Weather, p. 142
FAA subject matter knowledge code I32

5383. The jet stream and its associated clear air turbulence can sometimes be visually identified in flight by

A. dust or haze at flight level.

B. long streaks of cirrus clouds.

C. a constant outside air temperature.

5383. "B" is the correct answer. Long streaks of cirrus clouds can sometimes provide a pilot with a visual clue to the location of the jet stream and its associated clear air turbulence.
Reference Aviation Weather, p. 139
FAA subject matter knowledge code I32

5384. During the winter months in the middle latitudes, the jet stream shifts toward the

A. north and speed decreases.

B. south and speed increases.

C. north and speed increases.

5384. "B" is the correct answer. In midaltitude, wind speed in the jet stream averages considerably stronger in winter than in summer. Also, the jet shifts farther south in winter than in summer.
Reference Aviation Weather, p. 137
FAA subject matter knowledge code I32

5385. The strength and location of the jet stream is normally

A. weaker and farther north in the summer.

B. stronger and farther north in the winter.

C. stronger and farther north in the summer.

5385. "A" is the correct answer. In midaltitude, wind speed in the jet stream averages considerably stronger in winter than in summer. Also, the jet shifts farther south in winter than in summer.
Reference Aviation Weather, p. 137
FAA subject matter knowledge I32

5386. Select the true statement concerning thermals.

A. Thermals are unaffected by wind aloft.

B. Strong thermals have proportionately increased sink in the air between them.

C. A thermal invariably remains directly above the surface area from which it developed.

5386. "B" is the correct answer. Thermals are localized vertical air movements that both ascend and descend. For every rising current there is a compensating downward current. The downward currents frequently occur over broader areas than do the upward currents, and therefore they have a slower vertical speed than do the rising currents.
Reference Aviation Weather, p. 80
FAA subject matter knowledge code I28

5387. A thermal column is rising from an asphalt parking lot and the wind is from the south at 12 knots. Which statement would be true?

A. As altitude is gained, the best lift is found directly above the parking lot.

B. As altitude is gained, the center of the thermal is found farther north of the parking lot.

C. The slowest rate of sink would be close to the thermal and the fastest rate of sink farther from it.

5387. "B" is the correct answer. Wind causes a thermal to lean with altitude. When seeking the thermal you must make allowance for the wind. The thermal at lower levels usually is upwind from the visual cue.
Reference Aviation Weather, p. 175
FAA subject matter knowledge code I35

5388. Which is true regarding the development of convective circulation?

A. Cool air must sink to force the warm air upward.

B. Warm air is less dense and rises on its own accord.

C. Warmer air covers a larger surface area than cool air; therefore, the warmer air is less dense and rises.

5388. "A" is the correct answer. Thermals depend on sinking cold air forcing warm air upward.
Reference Aviation Weather, p. 186
FAA subject matter knowledge code I23

5389. Which is generally true when comparing the rate of vertical motion of updrafts with that of downdrafts associated with thermals?

A. Updrafts and downdrafts move vertically at the same rate.

B. Downdrafts have a slower rate of vertical motion than do updrafts.

C. Updrafts have a slower rate of vertical motion than do downdrafts.

5389. "B" is the correct answer. For every rising current there is a compensating downward current. The downward currents frequently occur over broader areas than do the upward currents, and therefore they have a slower vertical speed than do the rising currents. Convective currents are most active on warm summer afternoons when winds are light.
Reference Aviation Weather, p. 81
FAA subject matter knowledge code I27

5390. Which thermal index would predict the best probability of good soaring conditions?

A. –10.

B. –5.

C. +20.

5390. "A" is the correct answer. Strength of thermals is proportional to the magnitude of the negative value of the thermal index. A thermal index of –8 or –10 predicts very good lift and a long soaring day. Thermals with this high a negative value are strong enough to hold together even on a windy day.
Reference Aviation Weather, p. 186
FAA subject matter knowledge code I35

5391. Which is true regarding the effect of fronts on soaring conditions?

A. A slow moving front provides the strongest lift.

B. Good soaring conditions usually exist after passage of a warm front.

C. Frequently the air behind a cold front provides excellent soaring days.

5391. "C" is the correct answer. A front can, on occasion, provide excellent lift for a short period. In the central and eastern United States, the most favorable weather for cross-country soaring occurs behind a cold front.
Reference Aviation Weather, pp. 190–191
FAA subject matter knowledge code I35

5392. Convective circulation patterns associated with sea breezes are caused by

A. water absorbing and radiating heat faster than the land.

B. land absorbing and radiating heat faster than the water.

C. cool and less dense air moving inland from over the water, causing it to rise.

5392. "B" is the correct answer. In many coastal areas during the warm seasons, a pleasant breeze from the sea occurs almost daily. Caused by the heating of land on warm, sunny days, the sea breeze usually begins during early forenoon, reaches a maximum during the afternoon, and subsides around dusk after the land has cooled. The leading edge of the cool sea breeze forces warmer air inland to rise. Rising air from over land returns seaward at a higher altitude to complete the convective cell.
Reference Aviation Weather, p. 191
FAA subject matter knowledge code I35

5393. The conditions most favorable to wave formation over mountainous areas are a layer of

A. stable air at mountaintop altitude and a wind of at least 20 knots blowing across the ridge.

B. unstable air at mountaintop altitude and a wind of at least 20 knots blowing across the ridge.

C. moist, unstable air at mountaintop altitude and wind of less than 5 knots blowing across the ridge.

5393. "A" is the correct answer. The great attraction of soaring in the mountain waves stems from the continuous lift to great heights. A strong mountain wave requires marked stability in the airstream disturbed by the mountains. Wind speed at the level of the summit should exceed a minimum that varies from 15 to 25 knots depending on the height of the range, and the wind direction should be within 30° normal to the range.
Reference Aviation Weather, p. 198
FAA subject matter knowledge code I35

5394. When soaring in the vicinity of mountain ranges, the greatest potential danger from vertical and rotor-type currents is usually encountered on the

A. leeward side when flying with a tailwind.

B. leeward side when flying into the wind.

C. windward side when flying into the wind.

5394. "B" is the correct answer. Dangerous downdrafts may be encountered on the leeward side when flying into the wind.
Reference Aviation Weather, p. 84
FAA subject matter knowledge code I35

5395. Which is true regarding ridge soaring with the wind direction perpendicular to the ridge?

A. When flying between peaks along a ridge, the pilot can expect a significant decrease in wind and lift.

B. When very close to the surface of the ridge, the glider's speed should be reduced to the minimum sink speed.

C. If the glider drifts downwind from the ridge and sinks slightly lower than the crest of the ridge, the glider should be turned away from the ridge and a high speed attained.

5395. "C" is the correct answer. You want to leave the area of sink. To do this turn away from the ridge and increase speed.
Reference Soaring Handbook
FAA subject matter knowledge code N06

5396. Refer to Fig. 6. With regard to the soundings taken at 1400 hours, between what altitudes could optimum thermaling be expected at the time of the sounding?

A. From 2500 to 6000 ft.

B. From 6000 to 10,000 ft.

C. From 13,000 to 15,000 ft.

5396. "A" is the correct answer. The line representing the lapse rate must slope parallel to, or slope more than, the dry adiabats. The 1400 GMT sounding slopes more than the adiabats from 2500 to 6000 ft.
Reference Aviation Weather, p. 185
FAA subject matter knowledge code I35

5397. Refer to Fig. 6. With regard to the soundings taken at 0900 hours, from 2500 ft to 15,000 ft, as shown on the adiabatic chart, what minimum surface temperature is required for instability to occur and for good thermals to develop from the surface to 15,000 ft msl?

A. 58°F.

B. 68°F.

C. 80°F.

5397. "C" is the correct answer. Find the intersection of 0900 GMT sounding and 15,000 ft. Follow a parallel line to the diagonals back to the surface at 2500 ft msl. The surface temperature must exceed about 80°F.
Reference Aviation Weather, p. 185
FAA subject matter knowledge code I35

5398. During preflight preparation, weather report forecasts that are not routinely available at the local service outlet (FSS or WSFO) can best be obtained by means of the

A. request/reply service.

B. air route traffic control center.

C. pilot's automatic telephone answering service.

5398. "A" is the correct answer. The request/reply service is available at all FSSs, WSOs, and WSFOs. You may request through the service any reports or forecasts not routinely available at your service outlet.
Reference Aviation Weather Services, p. 1–17
FAA subject matter knowledge code I40

5399. The most current en route and destination weather information for an instrument flight should be obtained from

A. the FSS or WSO.

B. the ATIS broadcast.

C. NOTAMs (Class II).

5399. "A" is the correct answer. Flight service stations (FSSs) are air traffic facilities that provide pilot briefings, en route communications, and VFR search and rescue services, assist lost aircraft and aircraft in emergency situations, relay ATC clearances, originate Notices to Airmen, broadcast aviation weather and National Airspace System (NAS) information, receive and process IFR flight plans, and monitor navaids. In addition, at selected locations FSSs provide en route flight advisory service (Flight Watch), take weather observations, issue airport advisories, and advise Customs and Immigration of transborder flight.
Reference Aeronautical Informational Manual, paragraph 4-3
FAA subject matter knowledge code J11

5400. FSSs in the conterminous 48 United States having voice capability on VORs or radio beacons (NDBs) broadcast

A. AIRMETs and SIGMETs at 15 minutes past the hour and each 15 minutes thereafter as long as they are in effect.

B. AIRMETs and nonconvective SIGMETs at 15 minutes and 45 minutes past the hour for the first hour after issuance.

C. hourly weather reports at 15 and 45 minutes past each hour for those reporting stations within approximately 150 nautical miles of the broadcast stations.

5400. "B" is the correct answer. Weather advisory broadcasts—FAA FSSs broadcast severe weather forecast alerts (AWW), convective SIGMETs, SIGMETs, CWAs, and AIRMETs during their valid period when they pertain to the area within 150 nautical miles of the FSS or a broadcast facility controlled by the FSS as follows: SIGMETs, CWAs, and AIRMETs—upon receipt and at 30 minute intervals at H + 15 and H – 45 for the first hour after issuance.

Reference Aeronautical Informational Manual, paragraph 4-3
FAA subject matter knowledge code J25

5401. Transcribed weather broadcasts (TWEBs) may be monitored by tuning the appropriate radio receiver to certain

A. NDB but not VOR frequencies.

B. VOR and NDB frequencies.

C. VOR but not NDB frequencies.

5401. "B" is the correct answer. Equipment is provided at selected FSSs by which meteorological and aeronautical data are recorded on tapes and broadcast continuously over selected low-frequency (190–535 kHz) navigational aids (L/MF ranges of H facilities) and/or VORs. Generally, the broadcast contains route-oriented data with specially prepared NWS forecasts, inflight advisories, and winds aloft plus preselected current information, such as weather reports, NOTAMs, and special notices.

Reference Aeronautical Information Manual, paragraph 7-8
FAA subject matter knowledge code J25

5402. The remarks section of the hourly aviation weather report contains the following coded information:

RADAT 87045

What is the meaning of this information?

A. Radar echoes with tops at 45,000 ft were observed on the 087 radial of the VORTAC.

B. A pilot reported thunderstorms 87 DME miles distance on the 045 radial of the VORTAC.

C. Relative humidity was 87 percent and the freezing level (0°C) was at 4500 ft msl.

5402. "C" is the correct answer. Upper air observation stations append in remarks freezing level data. Code for the remark is as follows:

RADAT—a contraction identifying the remark as "freezing level data."

RADAT 87045—Relative humidity 87%, only crossing of 0°C isotherm was 4500 ft msl.

Reference Aviation Weather Services, pp. 2-11, 2-15
FAA subject matter knowledge code I41

5403. What is meant by the entry in the remarks section of this surface aviation weather report for BOI?

BOI SP 1854 -X M7 OVC 1 1/2R+F 990/63/61/3205/980/RF2 RB12

A. Rain and fog obscuring two-tenths of the sky; rain began at 1912.

B. Rain and fog obscuring two-tenths of the sky; rain began at 1812.

C. Runway fog, visibility 2 miles; base of the rain clouds 1200 ft.

5403. "B" is the correct answer. Remarks, if any, follow altimeter setting separated from it by a slash. Often some of the most important information in an observation may be the remarks portion. Bases and tops of clouds or obscuring phenomena may be reported.

Obscuring phenomena

Coded elements	Coded remarks
D5	Dust obscuring ⁵⁄₁₀ of the sky
S7	Snow obscuring ⁷⁄₁₀ of the sky
BS3	Blowing snow obscuring ³⁄₁₀ of the sky
RF	Rain and fog obscuring ²⁄₁₀ of the sky

Weather and obstruction to vision

Coded elements	Coded remarks
R12	Rain began 12 minutes after the hour.

Reference Aviation Weather Services, pp. 2-8–2-11
FAA subject matter knowledge code I41

5404. The station originating the following weather report has a field elevation of 3500 ft msl. If the sky cover is one continuous layer, what is its thickness?

M5 OVC 1/2HK 173/73/72/0000/002/OVC 75

A. 2500 ft.

B. 3500 ft.

C. 4000 ft.

5404. "B" is the correct answer. Take the field elevation of 3500 ft msl and add the 500 ft overcast ceiling (M5). This gives you a cloud base at 4000 ft msl. Subtracting (OVC75) 7500 ft from 4000 ft leaves 3500 ft.

Reference Aviation Weather Services, p. 2-10
FAA subject matter knowledge code I41

5405. What wind conditions would you anticipate when squalls are reported at your destination?

A. Rapid variations in wind speed of 15 knots or more between peaks and lulls.

B. Peak gusts of at least 35 knots combined with a change in wind direction of 30° or more.

C. Sudden increases in wind speed of at least 15 knots to a sustained speed of 20 knots or more for at least 1 minute.

5405. "C" is the correct answer. A squall is a sudden increase in speed of at least 15 knots to a sustained speed of 20 knots or more lasting for at least one minute.
Reference Aviation Weather Services, p. 2-8
FAA subject matter knowledge code I41

5406. What significant cloud coverage is reported by a pilot in this SA?

MOB...M9 OVC 2LF 131/44/43/3212/991/UA/OV 15NW MOB 1355/SK OVC 025/045 OVC 090

A. Three separate overcast layers exist with bases at 2500, 7500, and 13,500 ft.

B. The top of lower overcast layer is 2500 ft; base and top of second overcast layer is 4500 and 9000 ft, respectively.

C. The base of second overcast layer is 2500 ft; top of second overcast layer is 7500 ft; base of third overcast layer is 13,500 ft.

5406. "B" is the correct answer. UA means it's a pilot. Report SK OVC is the top of the lower overcast (2500 ft msl); the second number (045) is the base of the next layer of clouds (4500 ft msl); and the last number (090) is the top of the overcast (9000 ft msl).
Reference Aviation Weather Services, p. 2–10
FAA subject matter knowledge code I41

5407. To best determine observed weather conditions between weather reporting stations, the pilot should refer to

A. pilot reports.

B. area forecasts.

C. prognostic charts.

5407. "A" is the correct answer. No observation is more timely than the one you make from your cockpit. Pilot reports help fill the gaps between stations.
Reference Aviation Weather Services, p. 3-1
FAA subject matter knowledge code I42

5408. Which is true concerning this radar weather report for OKC?

OKC 1934 LN STRW+/+ 86/40 164/60 199/115 15W2425 MT 570 AT 159/65 2 INCH HAIL RPRTED THIS ECHO

A. There are three cells with tops at 11,500, 40,000, and 60,000 ft.

B. The line of cells is moving 080 with winds reported up to 40 knots.

C. The maximum top of the cells is 57,000 ft located 65 nautical miles south-southeast of the station.

5408. "C" is the correct answer. Thunderstorms and a general area of precipitation can be observed by radar. The report includes the location of the precipitation along with the type, intensity, and intensity trend. Maximum top and location (57,000 ft msl on radial 159° at 65 nautical miles in this example).
Reference Aviation Weather Services, p. 3-2
FAA subject matter knowledge code I42

5409. What is the meaning of the term MVFR, as used in the categorical outlook portion of terminal and area forecasts?

A. A ceiling less than 1000 ft, and/or visibility less than 3 miles.

B. A ceiling of 1000 to 3000 ft, and/or visibility of 3 to 5 miles.

C. A ceiling of 3000 to 5000 ft, and visibility of 5 to 7 miles.

5409. "B" is the correct answer. MVFR—marginal VFR ceiling 1000 to 3000 ft and/or visibility 3 to 5 miles inclusive.
Reference Aviation Weather Services, p. 4-2
FAA subject matter knowledge code I43

5410. The contraction WND in the 6-hour categorical outlook in the terminal forecast means that the wind during that period is forecast to be

A. 15 to 20 knots.

B. less than 25 knots.

C. 25 knots or stronger.

5410. "C" is the correct answer. The term "WND" is not included if winds (sustained or gusts) are forecast to be less than 25 knots.
Reference Aviation Weather Services, p. 4-2
FAA subject matter knowledge code I43

5411. Which statement pertaining to a terminal forecast is true?

A. The term WND in the categorical outlook implies surface winds are forecast to be 10 knots or greater.

B. The term CHC TRW VCNTY in the remarks section pertains to an area within a 5-mile radius of the airport.

C. The term VFR CIGS ABV 100 in the categorical outlook implies ceilings above 10,000 ft and visibility more than 5 miles.

5411. "C" is the correct answer. VFR CIG ABV 100—ceiling greater than 10,000 ft and visibility greater than 5 miles.
Reference Aviation Weather Services, p. 4-2
FAA subject matter knowledge code I43

5412. The absence of a visibility entry in a terminal forecast specifically implies that the surface visibility is expected to be more than

A. 3 miles.

B. 6 miles.

C. 10 miles.

5412. "B" is the correct answer. Absence of a visibility entry specifically implies visibility more than 6 statute miles.
Reference Aviation Weather Services, p. 4-1
FAA subject matter knowledge code I43

5413. Terminal forecasts are issued how many times a day and cover what period to time?

A. Three times daily and are valid for 24 hours including a 6-hour categorical outlook.

B. Four times daily and are valid for 18 hours including a 4-hour categorical outlook.

C. Six times daily and are valid for 12 hours with an additional 6-hour categorical outlook.

5413. "A" is the correct answer. Scheduled forecasts are issued for their respective areas three times daily and are valid for 24 hours. The last 6 hours of the forecast is a categorical outlook.
Reference Aviation Weather Services, pp. 4-1, 4-2
FAA subject matter knowledge code I43

5414. Which information is contained in the HAZARDS section of the area forecast?

A. A summary of general weather conditions for the entire region covered in the area forecast.

B. A brief list of weather phenomena that meet AIRMET and/or SIGMET criteria and the location of each.

C. A brief summary of significant weather and clouds that do not meet AIRMET, but meet SIGMET criteria.

5414. "B" is the correct answer. A 12-hour forecast that identifies and locates aviation weather hazards that meet inflight advisory criteria and thunderstorms that are forecast to be at least scattered in area coverage. These hazards include IFR conditions, icing (ICG), turbulence (TURBC), mountain obstructions (MTN OBSCN), and thunderstorms (TSTMS).
Reference Aviation Weather Service, p. 4-10
FAA subject matter knowledge code I43

5415. The section of the area forecast entitled SGFNT CLOUD AND WX contains a summary of

A. forecast sky cover, cloud tops, visibility, and obstructions to vision along specific routes.

B. only those weather systems producing liquid or frozen precipitation, fog, thunderstorms, or IFR ceilings.

C. sky condition, cloud heights, visibility, weather and/or obstructions to visibility, and surface winds of 30 knots or more.

5415. "C" is the correct answer. Surface visibility and obstructions to vision are included when forecast visibility is 5 miles or less. Precipitation, thunderstorms, and sustained winds of 30 knots or greater are always included when forecast.
Reference Aviation Weather Services, p. 4-11
FAA subject matter knowledge code I43

5416. In the HAZARDS AND FLIGHT PRECAUTIONS section of an area forecast, what is indicated by the forecast term FLT PRCTNS...IFR...TX AR LA MS TN AL AND CSTL WTRS?

A. IFR conditions that meet inflight advisory criteria are forecast for the states listed.

B. Each state and geographic area listed is reporting ceilings and visibilities below VFR minimums.

C. IFR conditions, turbulence, and icing are all forecast within the valid period for the listed states.

5416. "A" is the correct answer. IFR conditions are forecast within a 12-hour period for the listed states within the designated FA boundary.
Reference Aviation Weather Services, p. 4-10
FAA subject matter knowledge code I43

5417. In the area forecast (FA), what method is used to describe the location of each icing phenomenon?

A. VOR points outline the affected area(s) within the designated FA boundary, but not beyond the FA boundary.

B. State names and portions of states, such as northwest and south central, are used to outline each affected area.

C. VOR points are used to outline the area of icing, including VOR points outside the designated FA boundary, if necessary.

5417. "C" is the correct answer. The area forecast includes a forecast of non-thunderstorm-related icing of light or greater intensity for up to 12 hours. The location of each icing phenomenon is specified in a separate paragraph containing (1) the affected states or areas within the designated FA boundary, (2) the VOR points outlining the entire area of icing, and (3) the type, intensity, and heights of the icing.
Reference Aviation Weather Services, p. 4-11
FAA subject matter knowledge code I43

5418. What single reference contains information regarding expected frontal movement, turbulence, and icing conditions for a specific area?

A. Area forecast.

B. Surface analysis chart.

C. Weather depiction chart.

5418. "A" is the correct answer. An area forecast is a forecast of general weather conditions over an area the size of several states. It includes sections on icing, turbulence, and frontal movements.
Reference Aviation Weather Services, p. 4-10
FAA subject matter knowledge code I43

5419. The National Aviation Weather Advisory Unit prepares FAs for the contiguous United States

A. twice each day.

B. three times each day.

C. every 6 hours unless significant changes in weather require it more often.

5419. "B" is the correct answer. An area forecast is a forecast of general weather conditions over an area the size of several states. FAs are issued three times a day by the National Aviation Weather Advisory Unit.
Reference Aviation Weather Services, pp. 4-9–4-10
FAA subject matter knowledge code I43

5420. Which forecast provides specific information concerning expected sky cover, cloud tops, visibility, weather, and obstructions to vision in a route format?

A. Area forecast.

B. Terminal forecast.

C. Transcribed weather broadcast.

5420. "C" is the correct answer. The TWEB route forecast is similar to the area forecast except information is contained in a route format. Forecast sky cover (height and amount of cloud bases), cloud tops, visibility (including vertical visibility), weather, and obstructions to vision are described for a corridor 25 miles either side of the route.
Reference Aviation Weather Services, p. 4-13
FAA subject matter knowledge code I43

5421. To obtain a continuous transcribed weather briefing including winds aloft and route forecasts for a cross-country flight, a pilot could monitor

A. a TWEB on a low-frequency radio receiver.

B. the regularly scheduled weather broadcast on a VOR frequency.

C. a high-frequency radio receiver turned to en route flight advisory service.

5421. "A" is the correct answer. The TWEB is a continuous broadcast on low/medium frequencies (200 to 415 kHz) and selected VORs (108.0 to 117.95 MHz).
Reference Aviation Weather Services, p. 1-8
FAA subject matter knowledge code J25

5422. SIGMETs are issued as a warning of weather conditions that are hazardous

A. to all aircraft.

B. particularly to heavy aircraft.

C. particularly to light airplanes.

5422. "A" is the correct answer. A SIGMET advises of weather potentially hazardous to all aircraft other than convective activity. In the conterminous United States, items covered include severe icing, severe or extreme turbulence, and dust storms, sandstorms, or volcanic ash lowering visibilities to less than 3 miles.
Reference Aviation Weather Service, p. 4-17
FAA subject matter knowledge code I43

5423. Which correctly describes the purpose of convective SIGMETs (WST)?

A. They consist of an hourly observation of tornadoes, significant thunderstorm activity, and large hailstone activity.

B. They contain both an observation and a forecast of all thunderstorm and hailstone activity. The forecast is valid for 1 hour only.

C. They consist of either an observation and a forecast or just a forecast for tornadoes, significant thunderstorm activity, or hail greater than or equal to ¾ inch in diameter.

5423. "C" is the correct answer. Convective SIGMETs are issued in the conterminous United States for severe thunderstorms, hail at the surface greater than or equal to ¾ inches in diameter, or tornadoes.
Reference Aviation Weather Services, p. 4-14
FAA subject matter knowledge code I43

5424. What values are used for winds aloft forecasts?

A. True direction and mph.

B. True direction and knots.

C. Magnetic direction and knots.

5424. "B" is the correct answer. On the winds aloft forecasts wind speed is always given in knots and wind direction is in relation to north. "A" is incorrect because the wind speed is always in knots, and "C" is incorrect because wind direction is referenced to true north.
Reference Aviation Weather Services, p. 4-18
FAA subject matter knowledge code I43

5425. On a surface analysis chart, the solid lines that depict sea level pressure patterns are called

A. isobars.

B. isogons.

C. millibars.

5425. "A" is the correct answer. A surface analysis is commonly referred to as a surface weather chart. Isobars are solid lines depicting the sea level pressure pattern. They are usually spaced at 4 millibar intervals.
Reference Aviation Weather Services, p. 5-1
FAA subject matter knowledge code I44

5426. Dashed lines on a surface analysis chart, if depicted, indicate that the pressure gradient is

A. weak.

B. strong.

C. unstable.

5426. "A" is the correct answer. When the pressure gradient is weak, dashed isobars are sometimes inserted at 2 millibar intervals to more clearly define the pressure pattern.
Reference Aviation Weather Services, p. 5-1
FAA subject matter knowledge code I44

5427. Which chart provides a ready means of locating observed frontal positions and pressure centers?

A. Surface analysis chart.

B. Constant pressure analysis chart.

C. Weather depiction chart.

5427. "A" is the correct answer. The surface analysis provides you with a ready means of locating pressure systems and fronts.
Reference Aviation Weather Services, p. 5-4
FAA subject matter knowledge code I44

5428. On a surface analysis chart, close spacing of the isobars indicates a

A. weak pressure gradient.

B. strong pressure gradient.

C. strong temperature gradient.

5428. "B" is the correct answer. Close spacing of the isobars indicates a strong pressure gradient.
Reference Aviation Weather Service, p. 5-1
FAA subject matter knowledge code I44

5429. The surface analysis chart depicts

A. frontal locations and expected movement, pressure centers, cloud coverage, and obstructions to vision at the time of chart transmission.

B. actual frontal positions, pressure patterns, temperature, dew point, wind, weather, and obstructions to vision at the valid time of the chart.

C. actual pressure distribution, frontal systems, cloud heights and coverage, temperature, dew point, and wind at the time shown on the chart.

5429. "B" is the correct answer. The surface analysis also gives you an overview of winds, temperatures, and dew point temperatures as of chart time.
Reference Aviation Weather Services, p. 5-4
FAA subject matter knowledge code I44

5430. Which provides a graphic display of both VFR and IFR weather?

A. Surface weather map.

B. Radar summary chart.

C. Weather depiction chart.

5430. "C" is the correct answer. The weather depiction chart is a choice place to begin your weather briefing and flight planning. From it you can determine general weather conditions more readily than any other source. The chart shows observed ceiling

and visibility by categories as follows: IFR, MVFR, and VFR.
Reference Aviation Weather Services, pp. 6-1, 6-3
FAA subject matter knowledge code I45

5431. When total sky cover is few or scattered, the height shown on the weather depiction chart is the

A. top of the lowest layer.

B. base of the lowest layer.

C. base of the highest layer.

5431. "B" is the correct answer. Cloud height, above ground level, is entered under the station circle in hundreds of ft, the same as coded in an SA report. If total sky cover is few or scattered, the cloud height entered is the base of the lowest layer.
Reference Aviation Weather Services, p. 6-1
FAA subject matter knowledge code I45

5432. What information is provided by the radar summary chart that is not shown on other weather charts?

A. Lines and cells of hazardous thunderstorms.

B. Ceilings and precipitation between reporting stations.

C. Areas of cloud cover and icing levels within the clouds.

5432. "A" is the correct answer. The radar summary chart aids in preflight planning by identifying general areas and movement of precipitation and/or thunderstorms.
Reference Aviation Weather Services, p. 7-5
FAA subject matter knowledge code I46

5433. Which weather chart depicts conditions forecast to exist at a specific time in the future?

A. Freezing level chart.

B. Weather depiction chart.

C. 12-hour significant weather prognostication chart.

5433. "C" is the correct answer. Significant weather prognostication charts, also called "progs," portray forecast weather that might influence flight planning. The charts show conditions as they are forecast to be at the time of the chart.
Reference Aviation Weather Services, p. 8-1
FAA subject matter knowledge code I47

5434. What weather phenomenon is implied within an area enclosed by small scalloped lines on a U.S. high-level significant weather prognostication chart?

A. Cirriform clouds, light to moderate turbulence, and icing.

B. Cumulonimbus clouds, icing, and moderate or greater turbulence.

C. Cumuliform or standing lenticular clouds, moderate to severe turbulence, and icing.

5434. "B" is the correct answer. Small-scalloped lines enclose areas of expected cumulonimbus development. Cumulonimbus clouds imply moderate or greater turbulence and icing.
Reference Aviation Weather Services, p. 8-7
FAA subject matter knowledge code I47

5435. The U.S. high-level significant weather prognostication chart forecasts significant weather for what airspace?

A. 18,000 to 45,000 ft.

B. 24,000 to 45,000 ft.

C. 24,000 to 63,000 ft.

5435. "C" is the correct answer. The U.S. high-level significant weather prog encompasses airspace from 24,000 to 63,000 ft pressure altitude.
Reference Aviation Weather Services, p. 8-7
FAA subject matter knowledge code I47

5436. What is the upper limit of the low-level significant weather prognostication chart?

A. 30,000 ft.

B. 24,000 ft.

C. 18,000 ft.

5436. "B" is the correct answer. The U.S. high-level significant weather prog, encompasses airspace from 24,000 to 63,000-ft pressure altitude.
Reference Aviation Weather Services, p. 8-7
FAA subject matter knowledge code I47

5437. Refer to Fig. 7. According to the lifted index and K-index shown on the stability chart, which area of the United States would have the least satisfactory conditions for thermal soaring on the day of the soundings?

A. Southeastern.

B. North central.

C. Western seaboard.

5437. "B" is the correct answer. As the air is "lifted" it cools by expansion. The temperature the parcel would have at 500 millibars is then subtracted from the environmental 500-millibar temperature. The difference is the lifted index, which may be positive, zero, or negative. The north-central area has the largest positive or stable K-index.

Reference Aviation Weather Services, p. 10-2

FAA subject matter knowledge code I49

5438. A freezing level panel of the composite moisture stability chart is an analysis of

A. forecast freezing level data from surface observations.

B. forecast freezing level data from upper air observations.

C. observed freezing level data from upper air observations.

5438. "C" is the correct answer. The freezing level panel is an analysis of observed freezing level data from upper air observations.

Reference Aviation Weather Services, p. 10-4

FAA subject matter knowledge code I49

5439. The difference found by subtracting the temperature of a parcel of air theoretically lifted from the surface to 500 millibars and the existing temperature at 500 millibars is called the

A. lifted index.

B. negative index.

C. positive index.

5439. "A" is the correct answer. The lifted index is computed as if a parcel of air near the surface were lifted to 500 millibars. As the air is "lifted" it cools by expansion. The temperature the parcel would have at 500 millibars is then subtracted from the environmental 500-millibar temperature. The difference is the lifted index, which may be positive, zero, or negative.

Reference Aviation Weather Services, p. 10-2

FAA subject matter knowledge code I49

5440. Hatching on a constant pressure analysis chart indicates

A. a hurricane eye.

B. wind speeds of 70 to 110 knots.

C. wind speeds of 110 to 150 knots.

5440. "B" is the correct answer. To aid identifying areas of strong winds, hatching denotes wind speeds of 70 to 110 knots.

Reference Aviation Weather Services, p. 12-3

FAA subject matter knowledge code I51

5441. What flight planning information can a pilot derive from constant pressure analysis charts?

A. Winds and temperatures aloft.

B. Clear air turbulence and icing conditions.

C. Frontal systems and obstructions to vision aloft.

5441. "A" is the correct answer. From the charts you can approximate the observed temperature, wind, and temperature/dew point spread along your proposed route.

Reference Aviation Weather Services, p. 12-10

FAA subject matter knowledge code I51

5442. From which of the following can the observed temperature, wind, and temperature/dew point spread be determined at a specified altitude?

A. Stability charts.

B. Winds aloft forecasts.

C. Constant pressure analysis charts.

5442. "C" is the correct answer. From the charts you can approximate the observed temperature, wind, and temperature/dew point spread along your proposed route.

Reference Aviation Weather Services, p. 12-10

FAA subject matter knowledge code I51

5443. The minimum vertical wind shear value critical for probable moderate or greater turbulence is

A. 4 knots per 1000 ft.

B. 6 knots per 1000 ft.

C. 8 knots per 1000 ft.

5443. "B" is the correct answer. The vertical shear critical for probable turbulence is 6 knots per 1000 ft.

Reference Aviation Weather Services, p. 13-6

FAA subject matter knowledge code I52

5444. A pilot reporting turbulence that momentarily causes slight, erratic changes in altitude and/or attitude should report it as

A. light chop.

B. light turbulence.

C. moderate turbulence.

5444. "B" is the correct answer. Turbulence that momentarily causes slight, erratic changes in altitude and/or attitude (pitch, roll, yaw) should be reported as light turbulence.

Reference Aviation Weather Services, p. 14-2

FAA subject matter knowledge code I53

5445. When turbulence causes changes in altitude and/or attitude, but aircraft control remains positive, that should be reported as

A. light turbulence.

B. severe turbulence.

C. moderate turbulence.

5445. "C" is the correct answer. Turbulence that causes changes in altitude and/or attitude and variations in indicated airspeed, but the aircraft remains in positive control, should be reported as moderate turbulence.
Reference Aviation Weather Services, p. 14-2
FAA subject matter knowledge code I53

5446. Turbulence that is encountered above 15,000 ft agl and not associated with cumuliform cloudiness, including thunderstorms, should be reported as

A. severe turbulence.

B. clear air turbulence.

C. convective turbulence.

5446. "B" is the correct answer. High-level turbulence (normally above 15,000 ft agl) not associated with cumuliform cloudiness, including thunderstorms, should be reported as clear air turbulence, preceded by the appropriate intensity, or as light or moderate chop.
Reference Aviation Weather Services, p. 14-2
FAA subject matter knowledge code I53

5447. Which type of jet stream can be expected to cause the greater turbulence?

A. A straight jet stream associated with a low-pressure trough.

B. A curving jet stream associated with a deep low-pressure trough.

C. A jet stream occurring during the summer at the lower latitudes.

5447. "B" is the correct answer. A curving jet stream associated with a deep low-pressure trough usually creates greater turbulence than a straight jet stream.
Reference Aviation Weather, pp. 136–138
FAA subject matter knowledge code I32

5448. A strong wind shear can be expected

A. in the jet stream front above a core having a speed of 60 to 90 knots.

B. if the 5°C isotherms are spaced between 7° to 10° of latitude.

C. on the low-pressure side of a jet stream core where the speed at the core is stronger than 110 knots.

5448. "C" is the correct answer. A strong wind shear can be expected on the low-pressure side of a jet stream core where the speed at the core is stronger than 110 knots.
Reference Aviation Weather, pp. 136–138
FAA subject matter knowledge code I32

5449. Low-level wind shear is best described as a

A. violently rotating column of air extending from a cumulonimbus cloud.

B. change in wind direction and/or speed within a very short distance in the atmosphere.

C. downward motion of the air associated with continuous winds blowing with an easterly component due to the rotation of the earth.

5449. "B" is the correct answer. Wind shear is best described as a change in wind direction and/or speed within a very short distance in the atmosphere.
Reference PHOAK, pp. 113–114
FAA subject matter knowledge code H05

5450. One of the most dangerous features of mountain waves is the turbulent areas in and

A. below rotor clouds.

B. above rotor clouds.

C. below lenticular clouds.

5450. "A" is the correct answer. A dangerous feature of mountain waves is the turbulent area in and below rotor clouds.
Reference Aviation Weather, p. 200
FAA subject matter knowledge code I35

5669. A pilot is entering an area where significant clear air turbulence has been reported. Which action is appropriate upon encountering the first ripple?

A. Maintain altitude and airspeed.

B. Adjust airspeed to that recommended for rough air.

C. Enter a shallow climb or descent at maneuvering speed.

5669. "B" is the correct answer. In an area where significant clear air turbulence has been reported or is forecast, it is suggested that the pilot adjust his speed to fly at the recommended rough airspeed on encountering the first ripple, because the intensity of such turbulence may rapidly build. In areas where moderate or severe clear air turbulence is expected, it is desirable to adjust your airspeed prior to the turbulence encounter.
Reference AC-00-30, Clear Air Turbulence
FAA subject matter knowledge code K02

5670. If severe turbulence is encountered during flight, the pilot should reduce airspeed to

A. minimum control speed.

B. design-maneuvering speed.

C. maximum structural cruising speed.

5670. "B" is the correct answer. Design maneuvering speed (V_A) is the maximum speed at which the maximum load limit can be imposed (either by gust or full deflection of the control surfaces) without causing structural damage.
Reference Flight Training Handbook, p. 325
FAA subject matter knowledge code H66

5731. What type of approach should be made to a rooftop heliport under conditions of relatively high wind and turbulence?

A. A normal approach.

B. A steeper-than-normal approach.

C. A shallower-than-normal approach.

5731. "B" is the correct answer. A steeper-than-normal approach may be used when barriers or excessive downdrafts exist.
Reference Basic Helicopter Handbook, p. 102
FAA subject matter knowledge code H81

5732. If turbulence and downdrafts are expected during a pinnacle approach to a rooftop heliport, plan to make a

A. steeper-than-normal approach.

B. normal approach, maintaining a lower-than-normal airspeed.

C. shallow approach, maintaining a higher-than normal airspeed.

5732. "A" is the correct answer. When you make an approach to a pinnacle in turbulent conditions, plan a steeper-than-normal approach.
Reference Basic Helicopter Handbook, p. 103
FAA subject matter knowledge code H81

5740. To determine pressure altitude prior to takeoff, the altimeter should be set to

A. the current altimeter setting.

B. 29.92 in. Hg and the altimeter indication noted.

C. the field elevation, and the pressure reading in the altimeter setting window noted.

5740. "B" is the correct answer. Set the altimeter to 29.92 in. Hg and read the altitude on the scale.
Reference Instrument Flying Handbook, p. 28
FAA subject matter knowledge code I04

5742. Refer to Fig. 47. At the 0900 hours sounding and the line plotted from the surface to 10,000 ft, what temperature must exist at the surface for instability to take place between these altitudes? Any temperature

A. less than 68°F.

B. more than 68°F.

C. less than 43°F.

5742. "B" is the correct answer. Find the intersection of the 0900 GMT sounding and the 10,000-ft altitude. Follow a line parallel to the diagonals and downward to the right to intercept the line representing the surface 2500 ft msl. Draw a line vertically downward and read the temperature, 68°F. Any temperature greater than this results in instability.
Reference Aviation Weather, p. 184
FAA subject matter knowledge code I35

5743. Refer to Fig. 47. At the sounding taken at 0900 hours from 2500 ft to 15,000 ft, what minimum surface temperature is required for instability to occur and for good thermals to develop from the surface to 15,000 ft msl?

A. 58°F.

B. 68°F.

C. 80°F.

5743. "C" is the correct answer. Find the intersection of the 0900 GMT sounding and the 15,000-foot altitude. Follow a line parallel to the diagonals and downward to the right to intercept the line representing the surface 2500 ft msl. Draw a line vertically downward and read the temperature, 80°F. Temperatures greater than this result in instability.
Reference Aviation Weather, p. 184
FAA subject matter knowledge code I35

5744. Refer to Fig. 47. At the soundings taken at 1400 hours, is the atmosphere stable or unstable and at what altitudes?

A. Stable from 6000 to 10,000 ft.

B. Stable from 10,000 to 13,000 ft.

C. Unstable from 10,000 to 13,000 ft.

5744. "B" is the correct answer. If the sounding line is parallel to or has less slope than the diagonals, the air is stable.
Reference Aviation Weather, p. 184.
FAA subject matter knowledge code I35

5745. Which thermal index would predict the best probability of good soaring conditions?

A. +5.

B. –5.

C. –10.

5745. "C" is the correct answer. Strength of thermals is proportional to the magnitude of the negative value of the thermal index. A thermal index of –8 or –10 predicts very good lift and a long soaring day. Thermals with this high a negative value are strong enough to hold together even on a windy day.
Reference Aviation Weather, p. 186.

FAA subject matter knowledge code I35

5746. Which is true regarding the effect of fronts on soaring conditions?

A. Good soaring conditions usually exist after passage of a warm front.

B. Excellent soaring conditions usually exist in the cold air ahead of a warm front.

C. Frequently the air behind a cold front provides excellent soaring for several days.

5746. "C" is the correct answer. The most favorable weather for soaring occurs behind a cold front.
Reference Aviation Weather, p. 190

FAA subject matter knowledge code I04

5747. Which is true regarding ridge soaring with the wind direction perpendicular to the ridge?

A. When very close to the surface of the ridge, the glider's speed should be reduced to the minimum sink speed.

B. When the wind and lift are very strong on the windward side of the ridge, a weak sink condition exists on the leeward side.

C. If the glider drifts downwind from the ridge and sinks slightly lower than the crest of the ridge, the glider should be turned away from the ridge and a high speed attained.

5747. "C" is the correct answer. If you sink below the crest of the ridge you are working, turn away from the ridge as rapidly as possible and renew your attempt to climb farther from the hill.
Reference Aviation Weather, p. 197

FAA subject matter knowledge code I35

5806. When preparing for an autotow with a strong crosswind, where should the glider and tow rope be placed?

A. Straight behind the tow car.

B. Obliquely to the line of takeoff on the upwind side of the tow car.

C. Obliquely to the line of takeoff on the downwind side of the tow car.

5806. "C" is the correct answer. The glider and tow rope should be placed obliquely to the line of takeoff on the downwind side of the tow car. This precludes overrunning the tow rope.
Reference Soaring Flight Manual

FAA subject matter knowledge code N31

13

Performance

Many accidents have occurred because pilots have failed to understand the effect of varying conditions on airplane performance. In addition to the effects of weight and balance previously discussed, other factors such as density altitude, humidity, winds, runway gradient, and runway surface conditions all have a profound effect in changing airplane performance.

Density Altitude

Air density is perhaps the single most important factor affecting airplane performance. It has a direct bearing on the power output of the engine, the efficiency of the propeller, and the lift generated by the wings. When the air temperature increases, the density of the air decreases. Also, as altitude increases, the density of the air decreases.

Density altitude is determined by first finding pressure altitude and correcting this altitude for nonstandard temperature variations. It is important to remember that as air density decreases (higher density altitude) airplane performance decreases, and as air density increases (lower density altitude) airplane performance increases.

Humidity

Because of evaporation, the atmosphere always contains some moisture in the form of water vapor. Usually during the operation of small airplanes the effect of humidity is not considered when determining density altitude, but keep in mind that high humidity decreases airplane performance which results in, among other things, longer takeoff distances and decreased angle of climb.

Density Altitude Effect on Engine Power and Propeller Efficiency

An increase in air temperature or humidity, or a decrease in air pressure, resulting in a higher density altitude, significantly decreases power output and propeller efficiency. The engine produces power in proportion to the weight or density of the air. Therefore, as air density decreases, the power output of the engine decreases. The propeller produces thrust in proportion to the mass of air being accelerated through the rotating blades. If the air is less dense, propeller efficiency is decreased.

Effect of Wind on Airplane Performance

Surface winds during takeoffs and landings have, in a sense, an opposite effect on airplane performance to winds aloft during flight. During takeoff, a headwind shortens the takeoff run and increases the angle of climb. During takeoff, a tailwind increases the takeoff run and decreases the angle of climb. During landing, a headwind steepens the approach angle and shortens the landing roll, while a tailwind decreases the approach angle and increases the landing roll. Downwind operations should be considered very carefully by the pilot before being attempted.

Runway Surface Condition and Gradient

The takeoff distance is affected by the surface condition of the runway. If the runway is muddy, wet, soft, rough, or covered with tall grass, these conditions act as a retarding force and increase the takeoff distance.

Ground Effect

When an airplane is flown at approximately one wingspan or less above the surface, the vertical component of airflow is restricted and modified, and changes occur in the normal pattern of the airflow around the wing and from the wingtips. This change alters the direction of the relative wind in a manner that produces a smaller angle of attack. This means that a wing operating in ground effect with a given angle of attack generates less induced drag than a wing out of ground effect. Therefore, it is more efficient.

Use of Performance Charts

Two commonly used methods of depicting performance data are (1) tables, which are compact arrangements of conditions and performance values placed in an orderly sequence—usually arranged in rows and columns, and (2) graphs, which are pictorial presentations consisting of straight lines, curves, broken lines, or a series of bars representing the successive changes in the value of a variable quantity or quantities. Because all values are not listed on the tables or graphs, interpolation is often required to determine intermediate values for a particular flight condition or performance situation.

Standard atmospheric conditions [temperature 59°F (15°C), zero relative humidity, and a pressure of 29.92 in. Hg at sea level] are used in the development of performance charts.

Isosceles Triangle Method

Time/distance to station can also be found by application of the isosceles triangle principle (that is, if two angles of a triangle are equal, two of the sides are also equal), as follows:

1. With the aircraft established on a radial inbound, rotate the OSB 10 degrees to the left.
2. Turn 10 degrees to the right and note the time.
3. Maintain constant heading until the CDI centers, and note the elapsed time.
4. Time to station is the same as the time taken to complete the 10-degree change of bearing.

Converting Minutes to Equivalent Hours

Because speed is sometimes expressed in miles per hour, it frequently is necessary to convert minutes into equivalent hours when solving speed, time, and distance problems. To convert minutes to hours, divide by 60 (60 minutes = 1 hour); thus, 30 minutes equals 30 ÷ 60 = 0.5 hour. To convert hours to minutes, multiply by 60; thus, 0.75 hour equals 0.75 × 60 = 45 minutes.

Time

To find the time (T) in flight, divide the distance (D) by the groundspeed (GS); T = D ÷ GS. The time it takes to fly 210 miles at a groundspeed of 140 mph is 210 ÷ 140 = 1.5 hours, or 1 hour, 30 minutes (0.5 hour × 60 minutes = 30 minutes).

Distance

To find the distance flown in a given time, multiply groundspeed by time; D = GS × T. The distance flown in 1 hour, 45 minutes at a groundspeed of 120 mph is 120 × 1.75 = 210 miles.

Groundspeed

To find the groundspeed, divide the distance flown by the time; GS = D ÷ T. If an airplane flies 270 miles in 3 hours, the groundspeed is 270 ÷ 3 = 90 mph.

COMPUTER-BASED QUESTIONS

5208. At higher elevation airports the pilot should know that indicated airspeed

A. will be unchanged, but groundspeed will be faster.

B. will be higher, but groundspeed will be unchanged.

C. should be increased to compensate for the thinner air.

5208. "A" is the correct answer. Pilots should be aware that at higher elevation airports the indicated airspeed will be unchanged, but groundspeed will be faster.
Reference Flight Training Handbook, p. 315
FAA subject matter knowledge code H66

5234. The performance tables of an aircraft for take-off and climb are based on

A. pressure/density altitude.

B. cabin altitude.

C. true altitude.

5234. "A" is the correct answer. Pressure and density altitudes are the factors used in the performance tables of the aircraft for takeoff and climb.
Reference Flight Training Handbook, p. 314
FAA subject matter knowledge code H66

5451. Refer to Fig. 8. Given:

Fuel quantity	47 gallons
Power-cruise (lean)	55 percent

Approximately how much flight time would be available with a night VFR fuel reserve remaining?

A. 3 hours, 8 minutes.

B. 3 hours, 22 minutes.

C. 3 hours, 43 minutes.

5451. "B" is the correct answer. Enter the chart (Fig. 8) at the cruise (lean) curve. At the intersection of 55 percent maximum continuous power vertical line and the cruise (lean) curve, move horizontally to the fuel flow gallons per hour axis. Read approximately 11.4 gph fuel flow. Divide 47 gallons by 11.4 gph to get 4 hours, 7 minutes. Since you must have 45 minutes of reserve fuel at night, you must now subtract 45 minutes from the 4 hours, 7 minutes. This leaves 3 hours, 22 minutes.
Reference PHOAK, p. 93
FAA subject matter knowledge code H06

5452. Refer to Fig. 8. Given:

Fuel quantity	65 gallons
Best power (level flight)	55 percent

Approximately how much flight time would be available with a day VFR fuel reserve remaining?

A. 4 hours, 17 minutes.

B. 4 hours, 30 minutes.

C. 5 hours, 4 minutes.

5452. "B" is the correct answer. Enter the chart (Fig. 8) at the best power level flight curve. At the intersection of the 55 percent maximum continuous power vertical line and the best power level flight curve, move horizontally to the fuel flow gallons per hour axis. Read approximately 13 gph fuel flow. Divide 65 gallons by 13 gph to get 5 hours. Since you must have 30 minutes of reserve fuel during the day, you must subtract 30 minutes from the 5 hours. This leaves 4 hours, 30 minutes.

Reference PHOAK, p. 93

FAA subject matter knowledge code H06

5453. Refer to Fig. 8. Approximately how much fuel would be consumed when climbing at 75 percent power for 7 minutes?

A. 1.82 gallons.

B. 1.97 gallons.

C. 2.15 gallons.

5453. "C" is the correct answer. Enter the chart (Fig. 8) at the takeoff and climb curve. At the intersection of the 75 percent maximum continuous power vertical line and the takeoff and climb curve, move horizontally to the fuel flow gallons per hour axis. Read approximately 18.4 gph fuel flow. Divide the 18.4 gph by 60 minutes to get a fuel flow per minute of 0.30 gallon. Multiply that by 7 minutes to get 2.15 gallons.

Reference PHOAK, p. 93

FAA subject matter knowledge code H06

5454. Refer to Fig. 8. Determine the amount of fuel consumed during takeoff and climb at 70 percent power for 10 minutes.

A. 2.66 gallons.

B. 2.88 gallons.

C. 3.2 gallons.

5454. "B" is the correct answer. Enter the chart (Fig. 8) at the takeoff and climb curve. Interpolate a vertical line between the 65 percent and 75 percent maximum continuous power lines. At the intersection of this 70 percent vertical line and the takeoff and climb curve, move horizontally to the fuel flow gallons per hour axis. Read approximately 17.3 gph fuel flow. Divide the 17.3 gallons by 60 to get a fuel flow per minute of 0.288 gallon. Multiply this by 10 to get 2.88 gallons per hour.

Reference PHOAK, p. 93

FAA subject matter knowledge code H06

5455. Refer to Fig. 8. With 38 gallons of fuel aboard at cruise power (55 percent), how much flight time is available with night VFR fuel reserve still remaining?

A. 2 hours, 34 minutes.

B. 2 hours, 49 minutes.

C. 3 hours, 18 minutes.

5455. "A" is the correct answer. Enter the chart (Fig. 8) at the cruise (lean) curve at the intersection of the 55 percent maximum continuous power vertical line and the cruise (lean) curve, and move horizontally to the fuel flow gallons per hour axis. Read approximately 11.4 gph fuel flow. Divide 38 gallons by 11.4 to get 3 hours, 20 minutes. Since you must have 45 minutes of reserve fuel at night, you must subtract 45 minutes from the 3 hours, 20 minutes. This leaves 2 hours, 35 minutes. "A" is the closest answer.

Reference PHOAK, p. 93

FAA subject matter knowledge code H06

5456. Refer to Fig. 9. Using a normal climb, how much fuel would be used from engine start to 12,000-ft pressure altitude:

Aircraft weight	3800 pounds
Airport pressure altitude	4000 ft
Temperature	26°C

A. 46 pounds.

B. 51 pounds.

C. 58 pounds.

5456. "C" is the correct answer. Enter the chart (Fig. 9) at the 3800 pounds aircraft weight section. Read across the 4000-ft line to get 12 pounds of fuel used. Next, read across from the 12,000-ft level to get 51 pounds of fuel used. Subtract the 12 pounds of fuel from the 51 pounds, leaving 39 pounds. Now find the standard temperature at 4000 ft (4000 ft × 2°C/1000 ft = 8°C). Take a standard day of 15°C and subtract 8°C, leaving 7°C. The given temperature is 26°C: 26°C − 7°C = 19°C. You now add 19 percent to the fuel used (0.19 × 39 lb of fuel = 7.41 lb; 7.41 lb + 39 lb = 46.41 lb). Next, add the 12 pounds of fuel for start, taxi, and takeoff to get the final answer of 58.41 pounds.

Reference PHOAK, pp. 87–97

FAA subject matter knowledge code H04

5457. Refer to Fig. 9. Using a normal climb, how much fuel would be used from engine start to 10,000-ft pressure altitude?

Aircraft weight	3500 pounds
Airport pressure altitude	4000 ft
Temperature	21°C

A. 23 pounds.

B. 31 pounds.

C. 35 pounds.

5457. "C" is the correct answer. Enter the chart (Fig. 9) at the 3500 pounds aircraft weight section. Read across the 4000-ft line to get 11 pounds of fuel used. Next, read across from the 10,000-ft level to get 31 pounds of fuel used. Subtract the 11 pounds of fuel from the 31 pounds, leaving 20 pounds. Now find the standard temperature at 4000 ft (4000 ft × 2°C/1000 ft = 8°C). Take a standard day of 15°C and subtract 8°C, leaving 7°C. The given temperature is 21°C: 21°C – 7°C = 14°C. You now add 14 percent to the fuel used (0.14 × 20 lb of fuel = 2.8 lb; 2.8 lb + 20 lb = 22.8 lb). Next, add the 12 pounds of fuel for start, taxi, and takeoff to get the final answer of 34.8 pounds.

Reference PHOAK, pp. 87–97

FAA subject matter knowledge code H04

5458. Refer to Fig. 10. Using a maximum rate of climb, how much fuel would be used from engine start to 6000-ft pressure altitude?

Aircraft weight	3200 pounds
Airport pressure altitude	2000 ft
Temperature	27°C

5458. "C" is the correct answer. Enter the chart (Fig. 10) at the 3200 pounds aircraft weight section. Read across the 2000-ft line to get 4 pounds of fuel used. Next, read across from the 6000-ft level to get 14 pounds of fuel used. Subtract the 4 pounds of fuel used from the 14 pounds of fuel used to get 10 pounds. Standard temperature at 2000 ft is 11°C (15°C – 2°C/1000 ft = 11°C). The actual temperature is 27°C. This is 16°C above standard. You now calculate 16 percent of the fuel used (10 lb × 0.16 = 1.6 lb). Add the 1.6 pounds to the 10 pounds to get 11.6 pounds. Now, add the 12 pounds for start, taxi, and takeoff to the 11.6 to get 23.6 pounds. "C" is the closest answer.

Reference PHOAK, pp. 87–97

FAA subject matter knowledge code H04

5459. Refer to Fig. 10. Using a maximum rate of climb, how much fuel would be used from engine start to 10,000-ft pressure altitude?

Aircraft weight	3800 pounds
Airport pressure altitude	4000 ft
Temperature	30°C

A. 28 pounds.

B. 35 pounds.

C. 40 pounds.

5459. "C" is the correct answer. Enter the chart (Fig. 10) at the 3800 pounds aircraft weight section. Read across the 4000-ft line to 12 pounds of fuel used. Next, read across from the 10,000-ft level to get 35 pounds of fuel used: 35 lb – 12 lb = 23 lb of fuel used. Now find the standard temperature at 4000 ft (C/1000 ft = 8°C): 15°C – 8°C = 7°C. The actual temperature is 30°C (30°C – 7°C = 23°C). You now add 23 percent to the fuel used (23 lb × 0.23 = 5.29 lb): 5.29 lb + 23 lb = 28.29 lb. Now add the 12 pounds for start, taxi, and takeoff to the 28.29 pounds to get 40.29 pounds.

Reference PHOAK, pp. 87–97

FAA subject matter knowledge code H04

5460. Refer to Fig. 11. If the cruise altitude is 7500 ft, using 64 percent power at 2500 rpm, what would be the range with 48 gallons of usable fuel?

A. 635 miles.

B. 645 miles.

C. 810 miles.

5460. "C" is the correct answer. Enter the chart (Fig. 11) at the 7500-ft altitude column. Next, find the 2500 rpm and 64 percent power line (Note: This is the same line). Now move across to the far right under the 48-gallon (no reserve) column. The maximum range is 810 miles.

Reference PHOAK, p. 93

FAA subject matter knowledge code H04

5461. Refer to Fig. 11. What would be the endurance at an altitude of 7500 ft using 52 percent power? Note: With 48 gallons fuel—no reserve.

A. 6.1 hours.

B. 7.7 hours.

C. 8.0 hours

5461. "B" is the correct answer. Enter the chart (Fig. 11) at the 7500-ft altitude column. Find 52 percent power and move across to the 48-gallon (no reserve) column. Under ENDR hours read 7.7 hours.

Reference PHOAK, p. 93

FAA subject matter knowledge code H04

5462. Refer to Fig. 11. What would be the approximate true airspeed and fuel consumption per hour at an altitude of 7500 ft using 52 percent power?

A. 103 mph TAS, 7.7 gph.

B. 105 mph TAS, 6.1 gph.

C. 105 mph TAS, 6.2 gph.

5462. "C" is the correct answer. Enter the chart (Fig. 11) at the 7500-ft altitude column. Find 52 percent power and move across to the TAS mph column. Read 105 mph. Next, move to the gallons per hour column and read 6.2 gph.

Reference PHOAK, p. 93

FAA subject matter knowledge code H04

5463. Refer to Fig. 12. Given:

Pressure altitude	18,000 ft
Temperature	–21°C
Power	2400 rpm at 28 MP
Recommended lean mixture usable fuel	425 pounds

What is the approximate flight time available under the given conditions? (Allow for VFR day fuel reserve.)

A. 3 hours, 46 minutes.

B. 4 hours, 1 minute.

C. 4 hours, 31 minutes.

5463. "B" is the correct answer. Enter the chart (Fig. 12) at 2400 rpm. Find 28 MP and move to the right along the line until you reach the –21°C column. Read the fuel flow of 94 lb/hr. Divide this fuel flow into the usable fuel to get the total time (425 lb ÷ 94 lb/hr = 4 hours, 31 minutes). Subtract the 30 minutes VFR day reserve from the 4 hours, 31 minutes to get 4 hours, 1 minute.

Reference PHOAK, pp. 92–94

FAA subject matter knowledge code H04

5464. Refer to Fig. 12. Given:

Pressure altitude	18,000 ft
Temperature	–41°C
Power	2500 rpm at 26 MP
Recommended lean mixture usable fuel	318 pounds

What is the approximate flight time available under the given conditions? (Allow for VFR night fuel reserve.)

A. 2 hours, 27 minutes.

B. 3 hours, 12 minutes.

C. 3 hours, 42 minutes.

5464. "A" is the correct answer. Enter the chart (Fig. 12) at 2500 rpm. Find 26 MP and move to the right along the line until you reach the –41°C column. Read the fuel flow of 99 lb/hr. Divide this fuel flow into the usable fuel to get the total time (318 lb ÷ 99 lb/hr = 3 hours, 13 minutes). Subtract the 45 minutes

VFR night reserve from the 3 hours, 13 minutes to get 2 hours, 28 minutes.

Reference PHOAK, pp. 92–94

FAA subject matter knowledge code H04

5465. Refer to Fig. 12. Given:

Pressure altitude	18,000 ft
Temperature	–1°C
Power	2200 rpm at 20 MP
Best fuel economy usable fuel	344 pounds

What is the approximate flight time available under the given conditions? (Allow for VFR day fuel reserve.)

A. 4 hours, 50 minutes.

B. 5 hours, 20 minutes.

C. 5 hours, 59 minutes.

5465. "C" is the correct answer. Enter the chart (Fig. 12) at 2200 rpm. Find 22 MP and move to the right along the line until you reach the –1°C column. Read the fuel flow of 59 lb/hr. To get best economy subtract 6 lb/hr to get 53 lb/hr. Divide this fuel flow into the usable fuel to get the total time (344 lb ÷ 53 lb/hr = 6 hours, 29 minutes). Subtract the 30 minutes VFR day reserve from the 6 hours, 29 minutes to get 5 hours, 59 minutes.

Reference PHOAK, pp. 92–94

FAA subject matter knowledge code H04

5466. An airplane descends to an airport under the following conditions:

Cruising altitude	6500 ft
Airport elevation	700 ft
Descends to	800 ft agl
Rate of descent	500 fpm
Average true airspeed	110 knots
True course	335°
Average wind velocity	060° at 15 knots
Variation	3°W
Deviation	+2°
Average fuel consumption	8.5 gph

Determine the approximate time, compass heading, distance, and fuel consumed during the descent.

A. 10 minutes, 348°, 18 nautical miles, 1.4 gallons.

B. 10 minutes, 355°, 17 nautical miles, 2.4 gallons.

C. 12 minutes, 346°, 18 nautical miles, 1.6 gallons.

5466. "A" is the correct answer. Complete the following steps:

1. Determine the descent.

6500 ft – 700 ft (airport elevation) – 800 ft (pattern altitude) = 5000 ft

2. Determine time to descent.

5000 ft ÷ 500 fpm = 10 minutes

3. Determine fuel used.

8.5 gph × 10 min = 1.4 gph

4. Use the wind side of your flight computer to determine the wind correction angle and groundspeed.

WCA = 8°
GS = 108 knots

5. Determine the true heading by taking the true course and adding the wind correction angle (TH = TC + WCA).

335° true course + 8° right wind correction angle = 343° true heading

6. Determine the compass heading by adding variation and deviation.

343° true heading plus + 3° variation + 2° deviation = 348° compass heading

7. Determine the distance flown.

108 knots × 10 minutes = 18 nautical miles
Reference PHOAK, pp. 92–94
FAA subject matter knowledge code H04

5467. An airplane descends to an airport under the following conditions:

Cruising altitude	7500 ft
Airport elevation	1300 ft
Descends to	800 ft agl
Rate of descent	300 fpm
Average true airspeed	120 knots
True course	165°
Average wind velocity	240° at 20 knots
Variation	4°E
Deviation	–2°
Average fuel consumption	9.6 gph

Determine the approximate time, compass heading, distance, and fuel consumed during the descent.

A. 16 minutes, 168°, 30 nautical miles, 2.9 gallons.

B. 18 minutes, 164°, 34 nautical miles, 3.2 gallons.

C. 18 minutes, 168°, 34 nautical miles, 2.9 gallons.

5467. "C" is the correct answer. Complete the following steps:

1. Determine the descent.

7500 ft – 1300 ft (airport elevation) – 800 ft (pattern altitude) = 5400 ft

2. Determine time to descent.

5400 ft ÷ 300 fpm = 18 minutes

3. Determine fuel used.

9.6 gph × 18 min = 2.9 gph

4. Use the wind side of your flight computer to determine the wind correction angle and groundspeed.

WCA = 9°
GS = 113 knots

5. Determine the true heading by taking the true course and adding the wind correction angle.

165° true course + 9° right wind correction angle = 174° true heading

6. Determine the compass heading by adding variation and deviation.

174° true heading –4° variation – 2° deviation = 168° compass heading

7. Determine the distance flown.

113 knots × 18 minutes = 34 nautical miles
Reference PHOAK, pp. 87–95
FAA subject matter knowledge code H04

5468. An airplane descends to an airport under the following conditions:

Cruising altitude	10,500 ft
Airport elevation	1700 ft
Descends to	1000 ft agl
Rate of descent	600 fpm
Average true airspeed	135 knots
True course	263°
Average wind velocity	330° at 30 knots
Variation	7°E
Deviation	+3°
Average fuel consumption	11.5 gph

Determine the approximate time, compass heading, distance, and fuel consumed during the descent.

A. 9 minutes, 274°, 26 nautical miles, 2.8 gallons.

B. 13 minutes, 274°, 28 nautical miles, 2.5 gallons.

C. 13 minutes, 271°, 26 nautical miles, 2.5 gallons.

5468. "C" is the correct answer. Complete the following steps:

1. Determine the altitude you must descend.

10,500 ft – 1700 ft (airport elevation) – 1000 ft (pattern altitude) = 7800 ft

2. Determine time to descend.

7800 ft ÷ 600 fpm = 13 minutes

3. Determine fuel used.

11.5 gph × 13 min = 2.5 gph

4. Use the wind side of your flight computer to determine the wind correction angle and groundspeed.

WCA = 12°R
GS = 120 knots

5. Determine the true heading.

263° true course + 12° right wind correction angle = 275° true heading

6. Determine the compass heading.

275° true heading plus –7° variation + 3° deviation = 271° compass heading

7. Determine the distance flown.

120 knots × 13 minutes = 26 nautical miles

Reference PHOAK, pp. 87–95
FAA subject matter knowledge code H04

5469. If fuel consumption is 80 pounds per hour and groundspeed is 180 knots, how much fuel is required for an airplane to travel 460 nautical miles?

A. 205 pounds.

B. 212 pounds.

C. 460 pounds.

5469. "A" is the correct answer. Use the following steps:

1. 460 nm ÷ 180 kt = 2.56 hr

2. 2.56 hr × 80 lb = 204.8 lb

Answer "A" is the closest.
Reference PHOAK, pp. 161–163
FAA subject matter knowledge code H06

5470. If an airplane is consuming 95 pounds of fuel per hour at a cruising altitude of 6500 ft and the groundspeed is 173 knots, how much fuel is required to travel 450 nautical miles?

A. 248 pounds.

B. 265 pounds

C. 284 pounds.

5470. "A" is the correct answer. Use the following steps:

1. 450 nm ÷ 173 kt = 2.6 hr

2. 95 lb/hr × 2.6 hr = 247 lb

Answer "A" is the closest.
Reference PHOAK, pp. 161–163
FAA subject matter knowledge code H06

5471. If an airplane is consuming 12.5 gallons of fuel per hour at a cruising altitude of 8500 ft and the groundspeed is 145 knots, how much fuel is required to travel 435 nautical miles?

A. 27 gallons.

B. 34 gallons.

C. 38 gallons.

5471. "C" is the correct answer. Use the following steps:

1. 453 nm ÷ 145 kt = 3 hr

2. 12.5 gph × 3 hr = 37.5 gal

Answer "C" is the closest.
Reference PHOAK, pp. 161–163
FAA subject matter knowledge code H06

5472. If an airplane is consuming 9.5 gallons of fuel per hour at a cruising altitude of 6000 ft and the groundspeed is 135 knots, how much fuel is required to travel 490 nautical miles?

A. 27 gallons.

B. 30 gallons.

C. 35 gallons.

5472. "A" is the correct answer. Use the following steps:

1. 490 nm ÷ 135 kt = 3.63 hr

2. 9.5 gph × 3.63 hr = 34.5 gal

Answer "C" is the closest.
Reference PHOAK, pp. 161–163
FAA subject matter knowledge code H06

5473. If an airplane is consuming 14.8 gallons of fuel per hour at a cruising altitude of 7500 ft and the groundspeed is 167 knots, how much fuel is required to travel 560 nautical miles?

A. 50 gallons.

B. 53 gallons.

C. 57 gallons.

5473. "A" is the correct answer. Use the following steps:

1. 560 nm ÷ 167 kt = 3.35 hr

2. 14.8 gph × 3.35 hr = 49.6 gal

Answer "A" is the closest.
Reference PHOAK, pp. 161–163
FAA subject matter knowledge code H06

5474. If fuel consumption is 14.7 gallons per hour and groundspeed is 157 knots, how much fuel is required for an airplane to travel 612 nautical miles?

A. 58 gallons.

B. 60 gallons.

C. 64 gallons.

5474. "A" is the correct answer. Use the following steps:

1. 612 nm ÷ 157 kt = 3.9 hr

2. 14.7 gph × 3.9 hr = 57.33 gal

Answer "A" is the closest.
Reference PHOAK, pp. 161–163
FAA subject matter knowledge code H06

5475. Given:

True course	105°
True heading	085°
True airspeed	95 knots
Groundspeed	87 knots

Determine the wind direction and speed.

A. 020° and 32 knots.

B. 030° and 38 knots.

C. 200° and 32 knots.

5475. "A" is the correct answer. To solve a wind flight problem you need to follow these steps on your E6B wind side:

1. Turn the compass azimuth so the true course/magnetic course is positioned at the true index. In this problem it's 105°.

2. Put 87 knots under the groundspeed grommet.

3. Note the wind correction angle by comparing course to heading—20°L.

4. Put in the wind correction at the TAS arc—95 knots.

5. Rotate the compass azimuth so the 95-knot point is on the centerline of the disc.

6. Read the wind direction under the true index—020°—and the wind speed between the grommet and the 95-knot point—32 knots.
Reference G6-B Booklet
FAA subject matter knowledge code H06

5476. Given:

True course	345°
True heading	355°
True airspeed	85 knots
Groundspeed	95 knots

Determine the wind direction and speed.

A. 095° and 19 knots.

B. 113° and 19 knots.

C. 238° and 18 knots.

5476. "B" is the correct answer. To solve a wind flight problem you need to follow these steps on your E6B wind side:

1. Turn the compass azimuth so the true course/magnetic course is positioned at the true index. In this problem it's 345°.

2. Put 95 knots under the groundspeed grommet.

3. Note the wind correction angle by comparing course to heading—10°R.

4. Put in the wind correction at the TAS arc—85 knots.

5. Rotate the compass azimuth so the 85-knot point is on the centerline of the disc.

6. Read the wind direction under the true index—113°—and the wind speed between the grommet and the 85-knot point—19 knots.
Reference G6-B Booklet
FAA subject matter knowledge code H06

5477. You have flown 52 miles, are 6 miles off course, and have 118 miles yet to fly. To converge on your destination, the total correction angle would be

A. 095°.

B. 6°.

C. 10°.

5477. "C" is the correct answer. To determine the required correction, use the formula

$$\frac{\text{miles off course} \times 60}{\text{number of miles flown}}$$

= correction to parallel course

Thus, $\frac{6 \times 60}{52} = 6.92$.

The next step is to determine the correction to intercept the course. Use this formula to solve the remainder of the problem:

$$\frac{\text{miles off course} \times 60}{\text{number of miles to go}}$$

= intercept correction

$$\frac{6 \times 60}{118} = 3.05°$$

3.05 + 6.92 = 9.97° to intercept
Reference Instrument Flying Handbook, pp. 136–139
FAA subject matter knowledge code H07

5478. Given:

Distance off course	9 miles
Distance flown	95 miles
Distance to fly	125 miles

To converge at the destination, the total correction angle would be

A. 4°.

B. 6°.

C. 10°.

5478. "C" is the correct answer. Use the formula

$$\frac{\text{miles off course} \times 60}{\text{number of miles flown}}$$

= correction to parallel course

to determine the correction required.

Thus, $\frac{9 \times 60}{95} = 5.68°$ to parallel.

The next step is to determine the correction to intercept the course. Use this formula:

$$\frac{\text{miles off course} \times 60}{125} = 4.32°$$

5.68 + 4.32 = 10.0°
Reference Instrument Flying Handbook, pp. 136–139
FAA subject matter knowledge code H07

5479. True course measurements on a sectional aeronautical chart should be made at a meridian near the midpoint of the course because the

A. values of isogonic lines change from point to point.

B. angles formed by isogonic lines and lines of latitude vary from point to point.

C. angles formed by lines of longitude and the course line vary from point to point.

5479. "C" is the correct answer. Because meridians converge toward the poles, course measurement should be taken at a meridian near the midpoint of the course rather than at the point of departure.
Reference PHOAK, p. 169
FAA subject matter knowledge code H07

5480. Refer to Fig. 52, point A. Given:

Departure point	Georgetown Airport (Q61)
Departure time	0637
Winds aloft forecast (FD) at your altitude	1008

At 0755, the balloon should be

A. over Auburn Airport (AUN).

B. over the town of Auburn.

C. slightly west of the town of Garden Valley.

5480. "A" is the correct answer.

Time = 0735 − 0637 = 1 hr, 18 min = 1.3 hr
Distance = 1.3 × 8 kt = 10.4 nm

The balloon will be just over AUN.
Reference PHOAK, pp. 168–175
FAA subject matter knowledge code H07

5481. Given:

Wind	175° at 20 knots
Distance	135 nautical miles
True course	075°
True airspeed	80 knots
Fuel consumption	105 lb/hr

Determine the time en route and fuel consumption.

A. 1 hour, 28 minutes and 73.2 pounds.

B. 1 hour, 38 minutes and 158 pounds.

C. 1 hour, 40 minutes and 175 pounds.

5481. "C" is the correct answer. Find the groundspeed by using the wind side of your E6B. The groundspeed is 81 knots. Divide 135 nautical miles by 81 knots to get 1.67 hours (1 hour, 40 minutes). The fuel burn is computed as 105 lb/hr × 1.67 hr = 175 lb.
Reference PHOAK, pp. 161–163
FAA subject matter knowledge code H06

5482. Refer to Fig. 13. Given:

Aircraft weight	3400 pounds
Airport pressure altitude	6000 ft
Temperature at 6000 ft	10°C

Using a maximum rate of climb under the given conditions, how much fuel would be used from engine start to a pressure altitude of 16,000 ft?

A. 43 pounds.

B. 45 pounds.

C. 49 pounds.

5482. "A" is the correct answer. Use the following procedure:

1. Enter the chart (Fig. 13) at 3400 pounds. Figure the fuel required to climb from sea level to the airport's pressure altitude of 6000 ft (interpolate between 4000 ft and 8000 ft):

$$\frac{9 + 19}{2} = 14 \text{ lb.}$$

2. Next, find on the chart the fuel required to climb from sea level to a pressure altitude of 16,000 ft. This is 39 pounds.

3. Subtract 14 pounds of fuel from the 39 pounds of fuel to get 25 pounds.

4. Correct for nonstandard temperature. Standard temperature at 6000 ft would be 3°C: 10°C – 3°C = 7°C above standard; 1.07 × 25 lb = 26.75 lb.

5. Add 16 pounds for start, taxi, and takeoff to get the answer 42.75 pounds.

Reference PHOAK, pp. 161–163

FAA subject matter knowledge code H06

5483. Refer to Fig. 13. Given:

Aircraft weight	4000 pounds
Airport pressure altitude	2000 ft
Temperature at 2000 ft	32°C

Using a maximum rate of climb under the given conditions, how much time would be required to climb to a pressure altitude of 8000 ft?

A. 7 minutes.

B. 8.4 minutes.

C. 11.2 minutes.

5483. "B" is the correct answer. Use the following procedure:

1. Enter the chart (Fig. 13) at 4000 pounds. Figure the time required to climb from sea level to the airport's pressure altitude of 2000 ft. (Interpolate between sea level and 4000 ft):

$$\frac{0 + 4}{2} = 2 \text{ min.}$$

2. Next, find on the chart the time required to climb from sea level to a pressure altitude of 8000 ft. This is 9 minutes.

3. Subtract 2 minutes from 9 minutes to get a 7-minute time to climb.

4. Correct for nonstandard temperature. Standard temperature at 2000 ft would be 11°C: 32°C – 11°C = 21°C above standard; 0.21 × 7 min = 1.47; 1.47 + 7 = 8.47 min.

Reference PHOAK, pp. 161–163

FAA subject matter knowledge code H06

5484. Refer to Fig. 14. Given:

Aircraft weight	3700 pounds
Airport pressure altitude	4000 ft
Temperature at 4000 ft	21°

Using a normal climb under the given conditions, how much fuel would be used from engine start to a pressure altitude of 12,000 ft?

A. 30 pounds.

B. 37 pounds.

C. 46 pounds.

5484. "C" is the correct answer. Use the following procedure:

1. Enter the chart (Fig. 14) at 3700 pounds. Figure the fuel required to climb from sea level to the airport's pressure altitude of 4000 ft. This is 12 pounds.

2. Next, find on the chart the fuel required to climb from sea level to a pressure altitude of 12,000 ft. This is 37 pounds.

3. Subtract 12 pounds of fuel from the 37 pounds of fuel to get 25 pounds.

4. Correct for nonstandard temperature. Standard temperature at 4000 ft would be 7°C: 21°C – 7°C = 14°C above standard; 1.20 × 25 lb = 30 lb.

5. Add 16 pounds for start, taxi, and takeoff to get 46 pounds.

Reference PHOAK, pp. 161–163

FAA subject matter knowledge code H06

5485. Refer to Fig. 14. Given:

Weight	3400 pounds
Airport pressure altitude	4000 ft
Temperature at 4000 ft	14°C

Using a normal climb under the given conditions, how much time would be required to climb to a pressure altitude of 8000 ft?

A. 4.8 minutes.

B. 5 minutes.

C. 5.5 minutes.

5485. "C" is the correct answer. Use the following procedure:

1. Enter the chart (Fig. 14) at 3400 pounds. Find the time required to climb from sea level to the airport's pressure altitude of 4000 ft. This is 5 minutes.

2. Next, find on the chart the time required to climb from sea level to a pressure altitude of 8000 ft. This is 10 minutes.

3. Subtract 5 minutes from 10 minutes to get a 5-minute time to climb.

4. Correct for nonstandard temperature. Standard temperature at 4000 ft would be 7°C: 14°C – 7°C = 7°C above standard; 1.1 × 5 min = 5.5 min.

Reference PHOAK, pp. 161–163

FAA subject matter knowledge code H06

5486. Refer to Fig. 15. Given:

Airport pressure altitude	4000 ft
Airport temperature	12°C
Cruise pressure altitude	9000 ft
Cruise temperature	–4°C

What is the distance required to climb to cruise altitude under the given conditions?

A. 6 miles.

B. 8.5 miles.

C. 11 miles.

5486. "B" is the correct answer. Use the following procedure:

1. Enter the chart (Fig. 15) at 4°C. Move straight up until you reach the 9000-ft pressure altitude line. Now move horizontally to the right until you intersect the distance nautical miles curve. From that point, move straight down and read the distance. This is 14.5 nautical miles.

2. Enter the chart at 12°C and move straight up until you reach the 4000-ft pressure altitude line. Now move horizontally to the right until you intersect the distance nautical miles curve. From that point, move straight down and read the distance. This is 6 nautical miles. Subtract 6 nautical miles from 14.5 nautical miles to get the answer 8.5 nautical miles.

Reference PHOAK pp. 161–163

FAA subject matter knowledge code H04

5487. Refer to Fig. 15. Given:

Airport pressure altitude	2000 ft
Airport temperature	20°C
Cruise pressure altitude	10,000 ft
Cruise temperature	0°C

What are the fuel, time, and distance required to climb to cruise altitude under the given conditions?

A. 5 gallons, 9 minutes, 13 nautical miles.

B. 6 gallons, 11 minutes, 16 nautical miles.

C. 7 gallons, 12 minutes, 18 nautical miles.

5487. "A" is the correct answer. By using Fig. 15 you can determine the necessary information to solve this problem. The climb from sea level to 10,000 ft will consume 6.5 gallons of fuel, and will take 11 minutes and 16 nautical miles. Now, subtract the following figures for climbing from sea level to the airport elevation (2000 ft): 1.5 gallons of fuel used, 2 minutes time to climb, and 3.0 nautical miles.

Fuel: 6.5 – 1.5 = 5.0
Time: 11 – 2 = 9
Distance: 16 – 3 = 13

Reference PHOAK pp. 161–163

FAA subject matter knowledge code H04

5488. An airplane departs an airport under the following conditions:

Airport elevation	1000 ft
Cruise altitude	9500 ft
Rate of climb	500 fpm
Average true airspeed	135 knots
True course	215°
Average wind velocity	290° at 20 knots
Variation	3°W
Deviation	–2°
Average fuel consumption	13 gph

Determine the approximate time, compass heading, distance, and fuel consumed during the climb.

A. 14 minutes, 235°, 26 nautical miles, 3.9 gallons.

B. 17 minutes, 224°, 36 nautical miles, 3.7 gallons.

C. 17 minutes, 242°, 31 nautical miles, 3.5 gallons.

5488. "B" is the correct answer. Use the following procedure:

1. Determine the time to climb.

9500 ft – 1000 ft = 8500 ft
Time = 8500 ÷ 500 fpm = 17 min or 0.283 hr

2. Determine the fuel required.

13 gph × 0.283 hr = 3.679 gal

3. Using the wind triangle compute the wind correction angle and groundspeed.

WCA = 8°R
GS = 128 knots

4. Determine the true heading.

TC + WCA = TH
215° + 8°R = 223°

5. Determine the compass heading.

TH + VAR + DEV = CH
223° + 3° + −2° = 224°

6. Determine the distance flown.

128 kt × 0.283 hr = 36.2 nm
Reference PHOAK, pp. 161–163
FAA subject matter knowledge code H06

5489. An airplane departs an airport under the following conditions:

Airport elevation	1500 ft
Cruise altitude	9500 ft
Rate of climb	500 fpm
Average true airspeed	160 knots
True course	145°
Average wind velocity	080° at 15 knots
Variation	5°E
Deviation	−3°
Average fuel consumption	14 gph

Determine the approximate time, compass heading, distance, and fuel consumed during the climb.

A. 14 minutes, 128°, 35 nautical miles, 3.2 gallons.

B. 16 minutes, 132°, 41 nautical miles, 3.7 gallons.

C. 16 minutes, 128°, 32 nautical miles, 3.8 gallons.

5489. "B" is the correct answer. Use the following procedure:

1. Determine the time to climb.

9500 ft − 1500 ft = 8000 ft
Time = 8000 ft ÷ 500 fpm = 16 min (0.27 hr)

2. Determine the fuel required.

14 gph × 0.27 hr = 3.78 gal

3. Using the wind triangle compute the wind correction angle and groundspeed.

WCA = 5°L
GS = 154 knots

4. Determine the true heading.

TC + WCA = TH
145° − 5°L = 140°

5. Determine the compass heading.

TH + VAR + DEV = CH
140° + −5°E + −3° = 132°

6. Determine the distance flown.

154 kt × 16 min = 42 nm
Reference PHOAK, pp. 161–163
FAA subject matter knowledge code H06

5601. During a night operation, the pilot of aircraft 1 sees only the green light of aircraft 2. If the aircraft are converging, which pilot has the right-of-way?

A. The pilot of aircraft 2; aircraft 2 is to the right of aircraft 1.

B. The pilot of aircraft 1; aircraft 1 is to the right of aircraft 2.

C. The pilot of aircraft 2; aircraft 2 is to the left of aircraft 1.

5601. "B" is the correct answer. The green wingtip light on aircraft 2 would be its right wing, therefore, aircraft 1 is to the right of aircraft 2 and has the right of way.
Reference FAR 91.113
FAA subject matter knowledge code B08

5602. A pilot flying a single-engine airplane observes a multiengine airplane approaching on a collision course from the left. Which pilot should give way?

A. Each pilot should alter course to the right.

B. The pilot of the single-engine airplane should give way; the other airplane is to the left.

C. The pilot of the multiengine airplane should give way; the single-engine airplane is to its right.

5602. "C" is the correct answer. When aircraft of the same category are converging at approximately the same altitude (except head-on, or nearly so), the aircraft to the other's right has the right-of-way.
Reference FAR 91.113(d)
FAA subject matter knowledge code B08

5614. What effect does an uphill runway slope have on takeoff performance?

A. Increases takeoff speed.

B. Increases takeoff distance.

C. Decreases takeoff distance.

5614. "B" is the correct answer. An uphill runway slope increases the takeoff distance required.
Reference PHOAK, p. 83
FAA subject matter knowledge code H04

5615. Refer to Fig. 31. Runway 30 is being used for landing. Which surface wind would exceed the airplane's crosswind capability of 0.2 V_{SO}, if V_{SO} is 60 knots?

A. 260° at 20 knots.

B. 275° at 25 knots.

C. 315° at 35 knots.

5615. "A" is the correct answer. First you have to determine the airplane's crosswind capability.

$60 \times 0.2 = 12$ knots maximum crosswind

Next, compute the angle between the wind and the runway.

Runway		Wind		Wind angle
300°	–	260°	=	40°
300°	–	275°	=	25°
300°	–	315°	=	15°

Using the crosswind component chart, determine the crosswind for each wind angle. Only answer "A" exceeds the 12-knot crosswind component of the airplane.

Reference Flight Training Handbook, p. 109
FAA subject matter knowledge code H04

5616. Refer to Fig. 31. If the tower-reported surface wind is 010° at 18 knots, what is the crosswind component for a Runway 08 landing?

A. 7 knots.

B. 15 knots.

C. 17 knots.

5616. "C" is the correct answer. Follow these steps:

1. Determine the angle between the wind and the runway.

080° (runway) – 010° (wind) = 70° wind angle

2. Use the chart to find 17 knots.

Reference Flight Training Handbook, p. 109
FAA subject matter knowledge code H04

5617. Refer to Fig. 31. The surface wind is 180° at 25 knots. What is the crosswind component for a Runway 13 landing?

A. 19 knots.

B. 21 knots.

C. 23 knots.

5617. "A" is the correct answer. Follow these steps:

1. Determine the angle between the wind and the runway.

180° (wind) – 130° (runway) = 50° wind angle.

2. Use the chart to find 19 knots.

Reference Flight Training Handbook, p. 109
FAA subject matter knowledge code H04

5618. Refer to Fig. 31. What is the headwind component for a Runway 13 takeoff if the surface wind is 190° at 15 knots?

A. 7 knots.

B. 13 knots.

C. 15 knots.

5618. "A" is the correct answer.

1. Determine the angle between the wind and the runway.

190°(wind direction) – 130° (runway) = 60° wind angle.

2. Use the chart to find 7 knots.

Reference Flight Training Handbook, p. 109
FAA subject matter knowledge code H04

5619. Refer to Fig. 32. Given:

Temperature	75°F
Pressure altitude	6000 ft
Weight	2900 pounds
Headwind	20 knots

To safely take off over a 50-ft obstacle in 1000 ft, what weight reduction is necessary?

A. 50 pounds.

B. 100 pounds.

C. 300 pounds.

5619. "C" is the correct answer. You can solve this problem by working through the chart backwards. Start at the right side of the chart. At the 1000-ft point, move horizontally until you intercept the 20-knot headwind point. Follow the sloping lines until you reach the reference line. Next, continue horizontally until you intersect the other vertical reference line. You should have a straight line through the weight section. Move to the bottom left side of the chart and find the 75°F point and move up to intersect the 6000-ft pressure altitude line. Follow the slope to the right until you intersect the reference line. Follow the sloping line until you intersect the line you drew across the weight section. Where these lines intersect, draw a line straight down to read the maximum weight of the airplane to clear a 50-ft obstacle. The weight is 2600 pounds.

Subtract the maximum weight (2600 pounds) from the weight of the airplane (2900) to get the necessary weight reduction.

$$2900 \text{ lb} - 2600 \text{ lb} = 300 \text{ lb}$$

Reference PHOAK, p. 77–97
FAA subject matter knowledge code H04

5620. Refer to Fig. 32. Given:

Temperature   50°F
Pressure altitude   Sea level
Weight   2700 pounds
Wind   Calm

What is the total takeoff distance over a 50-ft obstacle?

A. 550 ft.

B. 650 ft.

C. 750 ft.

5620. "B" is the correct answer. Use the following procedure:

1. Enter the chart at 50°F. Move up to the sea level pressure altitude line.

2. Move horizontally to the weight reference line. Follow this line until you intercept the aircraft weight of 2700 pounds.

3. Move horizontally until you intercept the wind reference line.

4. With calm winds move horizontally to read total takeoff distance over a 50-ft obstacle, or 650 ft.

Reference PHOAK, p. 97

FAA subject matter knowledge code H04

5621. Refer to Fig. 32. Given:

Temperature   100°F
Pressure altitude   4000 ft
Weight   3200 pounds
Wind   Calm

What is the ground roll required for takeoff over a 50-ft obstacle?

A. 1180 ft.

B. 1350 ft.

C. 1850 ft.

5621. "B" is the correct answer. Use the following procedure:

1. Enter the chart at 100°F. Proceed up until you intercept the 4000-ft pressure altitude line.

2. Move horizontally to the weight reference line. Follow this line until you intercept the aircraft weight of 3200 pounds.

3. Move horizontally to intercept the headwind reference line.

4. With calm winds move horizontally to read a total takeoff distance of 1850 ft.

5. Note that the ground roll is approximately 73 percent of total takeoff distance over a 50-ft obstacle; 1850 ft × 0.73 = 1350 ft of ground roll.

Reference PHOAK, p. 97

FAA subject matter knowledge code H04

5622. Refer to Fig. 32. Given:

Temperature   30°F
Pressure altitude   6000 ft
Weight   3300 pounds
Headwind   20 knots

What is the total takeoff distance over a 50-ft obstacle?

A. 1100 ft.

B. 1300 ft.

C. 1500 ft.

5622. "C" is the correct answer. Use the following procedure:

1. Enter the chart at 30°F. Move up to the 6000-ft pressure altitude line.

2. Move horizontally to the weight reference line.

3. Intercept the 3300 pounds aircraft weight curve.

4. Move horizontally to the wind reference line. Maintain a proportional line down and to the right until you reach the 20-knot headwind line. Proceed from there to the right and read 1500 ft.

Reference PHOAK, p. 97

FAA subject matter knowledge code H04

5623. Refer to Fig. 33. Given:

Weight   4000 pounds
Pressure altitude   5000 ft
Temperature   30°F

What is the maximum rate of climb under the given conditions?

A. 655 ft/min.

B. 702 ft/min.

C. 774 ft/min.

5623. "B" is the correct answer. Interpolate:

For 4000 ft: $\dfrac{800 + 655}{2} = 727.5$ fpm

For 8000 ft: $\dfrac{695 + 555}{2} = 625$ fpm.

727.5 fpm − 625 fpm = 102.5 fpm
102.5 fpm ÷ 4 (4000 ft) = 25.6 fpm
727.5 fpm − 25.6 fpm = 701.9 fpm

Reference PHOAK, p. 94

FAA subject matter knowledge code H04

5624. Refer to Fig. 33. Given:

Weight	3700 pounds
Pressure altitude	22,000 ft
Temperature	−10°C

What is the maximum rate of climb under the given conditions?

A. 305 ft/min.

B. 320 ft/min.

C. 384 ft/min.

5624. "C" is the correct answer. Interpolate:

$$\text{For 20,000 ft: } \frac{600 + 470}{2} = 535 \text{ fpm}$$

$$\text{For 24,000 ft: } \frac{295 + 170}{2} = 232.5 \text{ fpm}$$

535 fpm + 232.5 fpm = 767.5; 767.5 ÷ 2 = 383.7 fpm
Reference PHOAK, p. 94
FAA subject matter knowledge code H04

5625. Refer to Fig. 34. Given:

Pressure altitude	6000 ft
Temperature	+3°C
Power	2200 rpm at −22 MP
Usable fuel available	465 pounds

What is the maximum available flight time under the conditions stated?

A. 6 hours, 27 minutes.

B. 6 hours, 39 minutes.

C. 6 hours, 56 minutes.

5625. "B" is the correct answer. Enter the chart at 2200 rpm. Move to the right and find 22 MP. Follow that to the right to intersect the 3°C column and read 70 PPH.

Time = 465 lb ÷ 70 PPH = 6.6 hr

Convert 0.6 to minutes: 0.6 × 60 = 36. Thus, the closest answer is 6 hours, 39 minutes.
Reference PHOAK, p. 94
FAA subject matter knowledge code H04

5626. Refer to Fig. 34. Given:

Pressure altitude	6000 ft
Temperature	−17°C
Power	2300 rpm − 23 MP
Usable fuel available	370 pounds

What is the maximum available flight time under the conditions stated?

A. 4 hours, 20 minutes.

B. 4 hours, 30 minutes.

C. 4 hours, 50 minutes.

5626. "B" is the correct answer. Enter the chart at 2300 rpm. Move to the right and find 23 MP. Follow that to the right to intersect the 17°C column and read 82 PPH.

370 lb ÷ 82 PPH = 4.5

Convert 0.5 to minutes: 0.5 × 60 = 30 minutes. Thus, the closest answer is 4 hours, 31 minutes.
Reference PHOAK, p. 94
FAA subject matter knowledge code H04

5627. Refer to Fig. 34. Given:

Pressure altitude	6000 ft
Temperature	+13°C
Power	2500 rpm at 23 MP
Usable fuel available	460 pounds

What is the maximum available flight time under the conditions stated?

A. 4 hours, 58 minutes.

B. 5 hours, 7 minutes.

C. 5 hours, 12 minutes.

5627. "C" is the correct answer. Enter the chart at 2500 rpm. Move to the right and find 23 MP. Follow that to the right to intersect the 3°C column and read 90 PPH. Repeat the same procedure and determine the fuel flow using the 23°C row. This is 87 PPH. Interpolate:

$$\frac{90 + 87}{2} = 88.5 \text{ PPH}$$

460 lb ÷ 88.5 PPH = 5.2 hr
0.2 × 60 = 12 min

Thus, the answer is 5 hours, 12 minutes.
Reference PHOAK, p. 94
FAA subject matter knowledge code H04

5628. Refer to Fig. 35. Given:

Temperature	70°F
Pressure altitude	Sea level
Weight	3400 pounds
Headwind	16 knots

Determine the approximate ground roll.

A. 689 ft.

B. 716 ft.

C. 1275 ft.

5628. "A" is the correct answer. Enter the chart at 70°F and proceed up to intersect the sea level pressure altitude line. From there proceed horizontally until reaching the weight line representing 3400 pounds. Then, intercept the headwind reference line. Proceed down and to the right to intercept a vertical 16 knot headwind line. Read 1275 ft at the total distance over a 50-ft obstacle. Apply the notes: 1275 ft × 0.53 = 676 ft of ground roll.

Reference PHOAK, p. 97

FAA subject matter knowledge code H04

5629. Refer to Fig. 35. Given:

Temperature	85°F
Pressure altitude	6000 ft
Weight	2800 pounds
Headwind	14 knots

Determine the approximate ground roll.

A. 742 ft.

B. 1280 ft.

C. 1480 ft.

5629. "A" is the correct answer. Enter the chart at 85°F and move up to intercept the 6000-ft pressure altitude line. Proceed to the right to intercept the weight reference line at 2800 pounds. Continue to the right to intercept the headwind line. Proceed down and to the right to intercept the 14-knot headwind line. Read 1400 ft as the total takeoff distance over a 50-ft obstacle. Apply the notes: 1400 ft × 0.53 = 742 ft of ground roll.

Reference PHOAK, p. 97

FAA subject matter knowledge code H04

5630. Refer to Fig. 35. Given:

Temperature	50°F
Pressure altitude	Sea level
Weight	3000 pounds
Headwind	10 knots

Determine the approximate ground roll.

A. 425 ft.

B. 636 ft.

C. 836 ft.

5630. "B" is the correct answer. Enter the chart at 50°F and proceed up to intercept the sea level pressure altitude line. Move to the right to intercept the weight reference line at 3000 pounds. Continue to the right to intercept the headwind reference line. Proceed down and to the right to intercept the 10-knot headwind line. Read 1200 ft as the total takeoff distance over a 50-ft obstacle. Apply the notes: 1200 ft × 0.53 = 636 ft of ground roll.

Reference PHOAK, p. 99

FAA subject matter knowledge code H04

5631. Refer to Fig. 35. Given:

Temperature	80°F
Pressure altitude	4000 ft
Weight	2800 pounds
Headwind	24 knots

What is the total landing distance over a 50-ft obstacle?

A. 1125 ft.

B. 1250 ft.

C. 1325 ft.

5631. "A" is the correct answer. Enter the chart at 80°F and move up to intercept the 4000-ft pressure altitude line. Move to the right to intercept the weight reference line at 2800 pounds. Continue to the right to intercept the headwind line. Proceed down and to the right to intercept the 24-knot headwind line. Read 1125 ft as the total takeoff distance over a 50-ft obstacle.

Reference PHOAK, p. 97

FAA subject matter knowledge code H04

5655. When taxiing during strong quartering tailwinds, which aileron positions should be used?

A. Neutral.

B. Aileron up on the side from which the wind is blowing.

C. Aileron down on the side from which the wind is blowing.

5655. "C" is the correct answer. Caution is required when taxiing airplanes of the high-wing type in strong quartering tailwinds. When taxiing with a strong quartering tailwind, the elevator should be held in the down position (elevator control forward) and the aileron on the upwind side should be held in the down position (aileron control in the direction opposite to the direction from which the wind is blowing).

Reference Flight Training Handbook, p. 56

FAA subject matter knowledge code H55

5656. While taxiing a light, high-wing airplane during strong quartering tailwinds, the aileron control should be positioned

A. neutral at all times.

B. toward the direction from which the wind is blowing.

C. opposite the direction from which the wind is blowing.

5656. "C" is the correct answer. Caution is required when taxiing airplanes of the high-wing type in strong quartering tailwinds. When taxiing with a strong quartering tailwind, the elevator should be held in the down position (elevator control forward) and the aileron on the upwind side should be held in the down position (aileron control in the direction opposite to the direction from which the wind is blowing).
Reference Flight Training Handbook, p. 56
FAA subject matter knowledge code H55

5657. Refer to Fig. 51. The pilot generally calls ground control after landing when the aircraft is completely clear of the runway. This is when you

A. pass the red symbol shown at the top of the figure.

B. are on the dashed-line side of the middle symbol.

C. are on the solid-line side of the middle symbol.

5657. "C" is the correct answer. For runways these markings indicate where an aircraft is supposed to stop. They consist of four yellow lines two solid and two dashed, spaced 6 inches apart and extending across the width of the taxiway or runway. The solid lines are always on the side where the aircraft is to hold.
Reference Aeronautical Information Manual, paragraph 2-34
FAA subject matter knowledge code J05

5658. Refer to Fig. 51. The red symbol at the top would most likely be found

A. upon exiting all runways prior to calling ground control.

B. where a roadway may be mistaken as a taxiway.

C. near the approach end of ILS runways.

5658. "B" is the correct answer. Typically this sign would be located on a taxiway intended to be used in only one direction or at the intersection of vehicle roadways with runways, taxiways, or aprons where the roadway may be mistaken for a taxiway or other aircraft movement surface.
Reference Aeronautical Information Manual, paragraph 2-37
FAA subject matter knowledge code J05

5659. Refer to Fig. 51. While clearing an active runway you are most likely clear of the ILS critical area when you pass which symbol?

A. Top red.

B. Middle yellow.

C. Bottom yellow.

5659. "C" is the correct answer. This sign has a yellow background with a black inscription with a graphic depicting the ILS pavement holding position. This sign is located adjacent to the ILS holding position marking on the pavement and can be seen by pilots leaving the critical area.
Reference Aeronautical Information Manual, paragraph 2-38
FAA subject matter knowledge code J05

5660. Refer to Fig. 51. Which symbol does not directly address runway incursion with other aircraft?

A. Top red.

B. Middle yellow.

C. Bottom yellow.

5660. "A" is the correct answer. Typically this sign would be located on a taxiway intended to be used in only one direction or at the intersection of vehicle roadways with runways, taxiways, or aprons where the roadway may be mistaken for a taxiway or other aircraft movement surface.
Reference Aeronautical Information Manual, paragraph 2-37
FAA subject matter knowledge code J05

5661. With regard to the technique required for a crosswind correction on takeoff, a pilot should use

A. aileron pressure into the wind and initiate the liftoff at a normal airspeed in both tailwheel and nosewheel type airplanes.

B. right rudder pressure, aileron pressure into the wind, and higher than normal liftoff airspeed in both tricycle and conventional gear airplanes.

C. rudder as required to maintain directional control, aileron pressure into the wind, and higher than normal liftoff airspeed in both conventional and nosewheel type airplanes.

5661. "C" is the correct answer. If a significant crosswind exists, the main wheels should be held on the ground slightly longer than in a normal takeoff so that a smooth but very definite liftoff can be made. It is important to establish and maintain the proper amount of crosswind correction prior to liftoff; aileron pressure toward the wind to keep the upwind wing from rising and rudder pressure as needed to prevent weathervaning.
Reference Flight Training Handbook, p. 91
FAA subject matter knowledge code H57

5662. When turbulence is encountered during the approach to a landing, what action is recommended and for what primary reason?

A. Increase the airspeed slightly above normal approach speed to attain more positive control.

B. Decrease the airspeed slightly below normal approach speed to avoid overstressing the airplane.

C. Increase the airspeed slightly above normal approach speed to penetrate the turbulence as quickly as possible.

5662. "A" is the correct answer. Power-on approaches at an airspeed slightly above the normal approach speed should be used for landing in significantly turbulent air. This provides for more positive control of the airplane when strong horizontal wind gusts or up- and downdrafts are experienced.
Reference Flight Training Handbook, p. 109
FAA subject matter knowledge code H58

5663. A pilot's most immediate and vital concern in the event of complete engine failure after becoming airborne on takeoff is

A. maintaining a safe airspeed.

B. landing directly into the wind.

C. turning back to the takeoff field.

5663. "A" is the correct answer. If an engine failure should occur immediately after takeoff and before a safe maneuvering altitude is attained, it is usually inadvisable to attempt to turn back to the field from which the takeoff was made. Instead, it is generally safer to immediately establish the proper glide attitude and select a field directly ahead or slightly to either side of the takeoff path.
Reference Flight Training Handbook, p. 115
FAA subject matter knowledge code H58

5664. Which type of approach and landing is recommended during gusty wind conditions?

A. A power-on approach and power-on landing.

B. A power-off approach and power-on landing.

C. A power-on approach and power-off landing.

5664. "A" is the correct answer. An adequate amount of power should be used to maintain the proper airspeed throughout the approach and the throttle retarded to idling position only after the main wheels contact the landing surface.
Reference Flight Training Handbook, p. 110
FAA subject matter knowledge code H58

5665. A proper crosswind landing on a runway requires that, at the moment of touchdown, the

A. direction of motion of the airplane and its lateral axis be perpendicular to the runway.

B. direction of motion of the airplane and its longitudinal axis be parallel to the runway.

C. downwind wing be lowered sufficiently to eliminate the tendency for the airplane to drift.

5665. "B" is the correct answer. The primary objective is to land the airplane without subjecting it to any side loads that result from touching down while drifting. To do this, align the airplane's longitudinal axis with its direction of movement.
Reference Flight Training Handbook, p. 108
FAA subject matter knowledge code H58

5666. What is the general direction of movement of the other aircraft if during a night flight you observe a steady white light and a rotating red light ahead and at your altitude? The other aircraft is

A. headed away from you.

B. crossing to your left.

C. approaching you head-on.

5666. "A" is the correct answer. Airplane position lights are arranged similar to those of boats and ships. A red light is positioned on the left wingtip, a green light on the right wingtip, and a white light on the tail. This arrangement provides a means by which pilots can determine the general direction of movement of other airplanes in flight.
Reference Flight Training Handbook, p. 196
FAA subject matter knowledge code H58

5683. Refer to Fig. 41. Given:

Helicopter gross weight   1225 pounds
Ambient temperature   77°F

Determine the in-ground-effect hover ceiling.

A. 6750 ft.

B. 7250 ft.

C. 8000 ft.

5683. "A" is the correct answer. Follow these steps:

1. Enter the in-ground-effect chart at 1225 pounds and proceed upward to 25°C.

2. From that intersection proceed horizontally and read the hovering ceiling. This is 6750 ft.
Reference Test Book, p. 89
FAA subject matter knowledge code H77

5684. Refer to Fig. 41. Given:

Helicopter gross weight   1175 pounds
Ambient temperature   95°F

Determine the out-of-ground effect hover ceiling.

A. 5000 ft.

B. 5250 ft.

C. 6250 ft.

5684. "B" is the correct answer. Follow these steps:

1. Enter the out-of-ground effect chart at 1175 pounds and proceed upward to 35°C.

2. From that intersection proceed horizontally and read the hovering ceiling. This is 5250 ft.
Reference Test Book, p. 89
FAA subject matter knowledge code H77

5685. Refer to Fig. 41. Given:

Helicopter gross weight   1275 pounds
Ambient temperature   9°F

Determine the in-ground-effect hover ceiling.

A. 6600 ft.

B. 7900 ft.

C. 8750 ft.

5685. "B" is the correct answer. Follow these steps:

1. Enter the in-ground-effect chart at 1275 pounds and proceed upward to –12.8°C.

2. From that intersection proceed horizontally and read the hovering ceiling. This is 7900 ft.
Reference Test Book, p. 90
FAA subject matter knowledge code H77

5686. As altitude increases, the V_{NE} of a helicopter

A. increases.

B. decreases.

C. remains the same.

5686. "B" is the correct answer. As the altitude increases, the never-exceed airspeed for most helicopters decreases.
Reference Basic Helicopter Handbook, p. 37
FAA subject matter knowledge code H75

5687. Refer to Fig. 42. Departure is planned from a heliport that has a reported pressure altitude of 4100 ft. What rate of climb could be expected in this helicopter if the ambient temperature is 90°F?

A. 210 ft/min.

B. 250 ft/min.

C. 390 ft/min.

5687. "B" is the correct answer. Draw a line midway between and parallel to the 80°F and 100°F lines. Enter the chart at 4100-ft pressure altitude and intersect the 90°F line. Proceed downward to the rate of climb axis and read 250 ft/min.
Reference Basic Helicopter Handbook, p. 57
FAA subject matter knowledge code H77

5688. Refer to Fig. 41. Departure is planned for a flight from a heliport with a pressure altitude of 3800 ft. What rate of climb could be expected in this helicopter during departure if the ambient temperature is 70°F?

A. 330 ft/min.

B. 360 ft/min.

C. 400 ft/min.

5688. "A" is the correct answer. Draw a line midway between and parallel to the 60°F and 80°F lines. Enter the chart at 4100-ft pressure altitude and intersect the 70°F line. Proceed downward to the rate of climb axis and read 315 ft/min. The closest answer is A: 330 ft/min.
Reference PHOAK, p. 57
FAA subject matter knowledge code H77

5689. Refer to Fig. 43. Given:

Ambient temperature   60°F
Pressure altitude   2000 ft

What is the rate of climb?

A. 480 ft/min.

B. 515 ft/min.

C. 540 ft/min.

5689. "B" is the correct answer. Enter the chart at 2000-ft pressure altitude and move horizontally until you intersect the 60°F line. Proceed downward to the scale and read the rate of climb: 515 ft/min.
Reference PHOAK, p. 57
FAA subject matter knowledge code H77

5690. Refer to Fig. 43. Given:

Ambient temperature   80°F
Pressure altitude   2500 ft

What is the rate of climb?

A. 350 ft/min.

B. 395 ft/min.

C. 420 ft/min.

5690. "B" is the correct answer. Enter the chart at 2500-ft pressure altitude and move horizontally un-

til you intersect the 80°F line. Proceed downward to the scale and read the rate of climb: 395 ft/min.
Reference PHOAK, p. 57
FAA subject matter knowledge code H77

5691. Refer to Fig. 44. Given:

Ambient temperature   40°F
Pressure altitude   1000 ft

What is the rate of climb?

A. 810 ft/min.

B. 830 ft/min.

C. 860 ft/min.

5691. "C" is the correct answer. Enter the chart at 1000-ft pressure altitude point and move horizontally until you intersect the 40°F line. Proceed downward to the scale and read the rate of climb: 860 ft/min.
Reference PHOAK, p. 57
FAA subject matter knowledge code H77

5692. Refer to Fig. 44. Given:

Ambient temperature   60°F
Pressure altitude   2000 ft

What is the rate of climb?

A. 705 ft/min.

B. 630 ft/min.

C. 755 ft/min.

5692. "A" is the correct answer. Enter the chart at 2000-ft pressure altitude and move horizontally until you intersect the 60°F line. Proceed downward to the scale and read the rate of climb: 705 ft/min.
Reference PHOAK, p. 57
FAA subject matter knowledge code H77

5693. Refer to Figs. 45 and 46. Given:

Pressure altitude   4000 ft
Ambient temperature   80°F

To clear a 50-ft obstacle, a jump takeoff would require

A. more distance than a running takeoff.

B. less distance than a running takeoff.

C. the same distance as a running takeoff.

5693. "A" is the correct answer. Enter the chart at 4000 pressure altitude and move horizontally to intersect the 80°F line. Move down to the scale and read the total takeoff distance to clear a 50-ft obstacle. This is 1230 ft. Repeat the procedure to deter-

mine the jump takeoff distance to clear a 50-ft obstacle. This is 1440 ft. The jump takeoff distance exceeds the running takeoff distance by 210 ft.
Reference PHOAK, p. 55
FAA subject matter knowledge code H77

5694. Refer to Figs. 45 and 46. Given:

Pressure altitude   4000 ft
Ambient temperature   80°F

The takeoff distance to clear a 50-ft obstacle is

A. 1225 ft for a jump takeoff.

B. 1440 ft for a running takeoff.

C. less for a running takeoff than for a jump takeoff.

5694. "C" is the correct answer. Enter the chart at 4000 pressure altitude and move horizontally to intersect the 80°F line. Move down to the scale and read the total takeoff distance to clear a 50-ft obstacle. This is 1230 ft. Repeat the procedure to determine the jump takeoff distance to clear a 50-ft obstacle. This is 1440 ft. The jump takeoff distance exceeds the running takeoff distance by 210 ft.
Reference PHOAK, p. 55
FAA subject matter knowledge code H77

5707. The most power is required to hover over which surface?

A. High grass.

B. Concrete ramp.

C. Rough/uneven ground.

5707. "A" is the correct answer. Tall grass tends to disperse or absorb the ground effect. More power is required to hover, and takeoff may be very difficult.
Reference Basic Helicopter Handbook, p. 72
FAA subject matter knowledge code H79

5708. Which flight technique is recommended for use during hot weather?

A. During takeoff accelerate quickly into forward flight.

B. During takeoff accelerate slowly into forward flight.

C. Use minimum allowable rpm and maximum allowable manifold pressure during all phases of flight.

5708. "B" is the correct answer. In hot weather it is recommended that you accelerate very slowly into forward flight.
Reference Basic Helicopter Handbook, p. 72
FAA subject matter knowledge code H79

5712. A pilot is hovering during calm wind conditions. The greatest amount of engine power is required when

A. ground effect exists.

B. making a left-pedal turn.

C. making a right-pedal turn.

5712. "B" is the correct answer. During a hovering turn to the left, the rpm decreases if throttle is not added; in a hovering turn to the right, rpm increases if throttle is not reduced slightly. This is caused by the amount of engine power that is being absorbed by the tail rotor, which is dependent on the pitch angle at which the tail rotor blades are operating.
Reference Basic Helicopter Handbook, p. 77
FAA subject matter knowledge code H80

5716. When planning slope operations, only slopes of 5 degrees gradient or less should be considered, primarily because

A. ground effect is lost on slopes of steeper gradient.

B. downwash turbulence is more severe on slopes of steeper gradient.

C. most helicopters are not designed for operations on slopes of steeper gradient.

5716. "C" is the correct answer. The slope must be shallow enough to allow the pilot to hold the helicopter against it with the cyclic stick during the entire landing. A slope of 5 degrees is considered maximum for normal operation of most helicopters.
Reference Basic Helicopter Handbook, p. 98
FAA subject matter knowledge code H80

5718. Takeoff from a slope is normally accomplished by

A. making a downslope running takeoff if the surface is smooth.

B. simultaneously applying collective pitch and downslope cyclic control.

C. bringing the helicopter to a level attitude before completely leaving the ground.

5718. "C" is the correct answer. As the downslope skid is rising and the helicopter approaches a level attitude, move the cyclic stick back to the neutral position, keeping the rotor disc parallel to the true horizon. Continue to apply up-collective pitch, and take the helicopter straight up to a hover before moving away from the slope.
Reference Basic Helicopter Handbook, p. 98
FAA subject matter knowledge code H80

5719. What is the procedure for a slope landing?

A. Use maximum rpm and maximum manifold pressure.

B. If the slope is 10 degrees or less, the landing should be made perpendicular to the slope.

C. When parallel to the slope, slowly lower the upslope skid to the ground prior to lowering the downslope skid.

5719. "B" is the correct answer. When the slope is 10 degrees or less, you should land perpendicular to the slope.
Reference Basic Helicopter Handbook, p. 98
FAA subject matter knowledge code H80

5720. You are hovering during calm wind conditions and decide to make a right-pedal turn. In most helicopters equipped with reciprocating engines, the engine rpm tends to

A. increase.

B. decrease.

C. remain unaffected.

5720. "A" is the correct answer. During a hovering turn to the left, the rpm decreases if throttle is not added; in a hovering turn to the right, rpm increases if throttle is not reduced slightly. This is caused by the amount of engine power that is being absorbed by the tail rotor, which is dependent on the pitch angle at which the tail rotor blades are operating.
Reference Basic Helicopter Handbook, p. 77
FAA subject matter knowledge code H80

5721. During calm wind conditions, in most helicopters, which of these flight operations would require the most power?

A. A left-pedal turn.

B. A right-pedal turn.

C. Hovering in ground effect.

5721. "A" is the correct answer. During a hovering turn to the left, the rpm decreases if throttle is not added; in a hovering turn to the right, rpm increases if throttle is not reduced slightly. This is caused by the amount of engine power that is being absorbed by the tail rotor, which is dependent on the pitch angle at which the tail rotor blades are operating.
Reference Basic Helicopter Handbook, p. 77
FAA subject matter knowledge code H80

5735. Why should gyroplane operations within the cross-hatched portion of a height vs. velocity chart be avoided?

A. The rotor rpm may build excessively high if it is necessary to flare at such low altitudes.

B. Sufficient airspeed may not be available to ensure a safe landing in case of an engine failure.

C. Turbulence near the surface can dephase the blade dampers causing geometric unbalanced conditions on the rotor system.

5735. "B" is the correct answer. This type of chart is often referred to as the "height-velocity curve diagram" or "dead man's curve." Such charts are prepared by the manufacturer and, as required by regulations, are published in the gyroplane flight manual generally under the performance section. From it you can determine what altitudes and airspeeds are required to safely make an autorotative landing in case of an engine failure. To restate it in another way, the chart can be used to determine those altitude-airspeed combinations from which it would be nearly impossible to successfully complete an autorotative landing.
Reference Basic Helicopter Handbook, p. 68
FAA subject matter knowledge code H78

5736. The principal reason the shaded area of a height vs. velocity chart should be avoided is

A. rotor rpm may decay before ground contact is made if an engine failure should occur.

B. rotor rpm may build excessively high if it is necessary to flare at such low altitudes.

C. insufficient airspeed would be available to ensure a safe landing in case of an engine failure.

5736. "C" is the correct answer. This type of chart is often referred to as the "height-velocity curve diagram" or "dead man's curve." Such charts are prepared by the manufacturer and, as required by regulations, are published in the gyroplane flight manual generally under the performance section. From it you can determine what altitudes and airspeeds are required to safely make an autorotative landing in case of an engine failure. To restate it in another way, the chart can be used to determine those altitude-airspeed combinations from which it would be nearly impossible to successfully complete an autorotative landing.
Reference Basic Helicopter Handbook, p. 68
FAA subject matter knowledge code H78

5749. When in the vicinity of a VOR that is being used for navigation on VFR flights, it is important to

A. make 90 degree left and right turns to scan for other traffic.

B. exercise sustained vigilance to avoid aircraft that may be converging on the VOR from other directions.

C. pass the VOR on the right side of the radial to allow room for aircraft flying in the opposite direction on the same radial.

5749. "B" is the correct answer. All operators should emphasize the need for sustained vigilance in the vicinity of VORs and airway intersections due to the convergence of traffic.
Reference PHOAK, p. 252
FAA subject matter knowledge code J31

5750. Choose the correct statement regarding wake turbulence.

A. Vortex generation begins with the initiation of the takeoff roll.

B. The primary hazard is loss of control because of induced roll.

C. The greatest vortex strength is produced when the generating airplane is heavy, clean, and fast.

5750. "B" is the correct answer. In rare instances a wake encounter could cause inflight structural damage of catastrophic proportions. However, the usual hazard is associated with induced rolling moments that can exceed the roll-control authority of the encountering aircraft.
Reference Aeronautical Information Manual, paragraph 7-52
FAA subject matter knowledge code J27

5751. During a takeoff made behind a departing large jet airplane, the pilot can minimize the hazard of wingtip vortices by

A. being airborne prior to reaching the jet's flight path until able to turn clear of its wake.

B. maintaining extra speed on takeoff and climbout.

C. extending the takeoff roll and not rotating until well beyond the jet's rotation point.

5751. "A" is the correct answer. The following vortex avoidance procedures are recommended when departing behind a larger aircraft: note the larger aircraft's rotation point, rotate prior to the larger aircraft's rotation point, and continue to climb above the larger aircraft's climb path until turning clear of its wake.
Reference Aeronautical Information Manual, paragraph 7-55
FAA subject matter knowledge code J27

5773. Refer to Fig. 48. If a dual glider weighs 1040 pounds and an indicated airspeed of 55 mph is maintained, how much altitude is lost while traveling 1 mile?

A. 120 ft.

B. 240 ft.

C. 310 ft.

5773. "B" is the correct answer. Enter the chart at 55 mph and proceed vertically to intercept the L/D dual curve. Proceed horizontally to the left and read the L/D of 22. Calculate the altitude loss using the relation: L/D = glide ratio = horizontal distance traveled divided by vertical distance traveled.
Reference Soaring Flight Manual, p. 2–7
FAA subject matter knowledge code N21

5774. Refer to Fig. 48. If a dual glider weighs 1040 pounds, what is the minimum sink speed and rate of sink?

A. 38 mph and 2.6 ft/sec.

B. 42 mph and 3.1 ft/sec.

C. 38 mph and 3.6 ft/sec.

5774. "B" is the correct answer. The glider's gross weight is 1040 pounds. Use the dual glider sink speed. Find 42 mph at 3.1 ft per second sink.
Reference Soaring Flight Manual
FAA subject matter knowledge code N21

5775. Refer to Fig. 48. If the airspeed of a glider is increased from 54 mph to 650 mph, the L/D ratio would

A. decrease and the rate of sink would increase.

B. increase and the rate of sink would decrease.

C. decrease and the rate of sink would decrease.

5775. "A" is the correct answer. Use the following procedure:

1. Enter the chart at 54 mph.

2. Draw a vertical line to intercept the L/D curve.

3. At this point draw two horizontal lines to find the L/D values.

4. Repeat steps 1–3 to find the L/D values for 60 mph.

5. Figure the changes in L/D for single and dual operations. Single operation L/D decreases to 18.4; dual operation L/D is 20.8
Reference Soaring Flight Manual
FAA subject matter knowledge code N21

5776. Minimum sink speed is the airspeed that results in the

A. least loss of altitude in a given time.

B. least loss of altitude in a given distance.

C. shallowest glide angle in any convective situation.

5776. "A" is the correct answer. Minimum sink is the airspeed that results in the minimum loss of altitude in a given time period.
Reference Soaring Flight Manual
FAA subject matter knowledge code N21

5777. Refer to Fig. 49. If the airspeed is 70 mph and the sink rate is 5.5 ft/sec, what is the effective L/D ratio with respect to the ground?

A. 19:1.

B. 20:1.

C. 21:1.

5777. "A" is the correct answer. Enter the chart at 70 mph and move vertically to intercept the L/D curve. Now move horizontally and read an L/D ratio of 19:1.
Reference Soaring Flight Manual
FAA subject matter knowledge code N20

5778. Refer to Fig. 49. If the airspeed is 50 mph and the sink rate is 3.2 ft/sec, what is the effective L/D ratio with respect to the ground?

A. 20:1

B. 21:1

C. 23:1

5778. "C" is the correct answer. Enter the chart at 50 mph and move vertically to intercept the L/D curve. Now move horizontally and read an L/D ratio of 23:1.
Reference Soaring Flight Manual
FAA subject matter knowledge code N20

5779. The glider has a normal L/D ratio of 23:1 at an airspeed of 50 mph. What would be the effective L/D ratio with respect to the ground with a 10-mph tailwind?

A. 23:1.

B. 25:1.

C. 27.6:1.

5779. "C" is the correct answer. To determine the glide ratio, divide the horizontal distance traveled by the vertical distance traveled. A tailwind increases the horizontal distance traveled but does not increase the sink rate.

$$23 \times (50 \text{ mph} + 10 \text{ mph}) \div 50 = 27.6 \text{ L/D}$$

Reference Soaring Flight Manual
FAA subject matter knowledge code N34

5780. If the glider has drifted a considerable distance from the airport while soaring, the best speed to use to reach the airport when flying into a headwind is the

A. best glide speed.

B. minimum sink speed.

C. speed-to-fly plus half the estimated windspeed at the glider's altitude.

5780. "C" is the correct answer. Use the speed-to-fly plus half the wind velocity at the glider's altitude.
Reference Soaring Flight Manual
FAA subject matter knowledge code N34

5781. The maximum airspeed at which abrupt and full deflection of the controls would not cause structural damage to a glider is called the

A. speed-to-fly.

B. maneuvering speed.

C. never-exceed speed.

5781. "B" is the correct answer. The calibrated design maneuvering airspeed is the maximum speed at which the limit load can be imposed (either by gusts or full deflection of the control surfaces) without causing structural damage.
Reference Flight Training Handbook, p. 325
FAA subject matter knowledge code N21

5782. Which is true regarding minimum control airspeed while thermaling?

A. Minimum control airspeed may coincide with minimum sink airspeed.

B. Minimum control airspeed is greater than minimum sink airspeed.

C. Minimum control airspeed never coincides with minimum sink airspeed.

5782. "A" is the correct answer. The steep angles of bank often necessary to remain within a thermal radius may cause minimum control airspeed to coincide with minimum sink speed.
Reference Soaring Flight Manual, p. 2–9
FAA subject matter knowledge code N21

5783. Refer to Fig. 50. Which is true when the glider is operated in the high-performance category and the dive brakes/spoilers are in the closed position?

A. The design dive speed is 150 mph.

B. The never-exceed speed is 150 mph.

C. The design maneuvering speed is 76 mph.

5783. "B" is the correct answer. Follow these steps:

1. Using the key, locate the high performance category line.

2. Use the no brake V_{NE} line.

3. Read the V_{NE} of 150 mph.
Reference Soaring Flight Manual
FAA subject matter knowledge code N21

5784. Refer to Fig. 50. If the glider's airspeed is 70 mph and a vertical gust of 30 ft/sec is encountered, which would most likely occur?

A. The glider would momentarily stall.

B. The maximum load factor would be exceeded.

C. The glider would gain 1800 ft in 1 minute.

5784. "A" is the correct answer. Follow these steps:

1. Enter the chart at 70 mph.

2. Move vertically to the 30 FPS gust. Note that this position is out of the envelope, therefore, the glider would momentarily stall.
Reference Soaring Flight Manual
FAA subject matter knowledge code N21

5785. Regarding the effect of loading on glider performance, a heavily loaded glider would

A. have a lower glide ratio than when lightly loaded.

B. have slower forward speed than when lightly loaded.

C. make better flight time on a cross-country flight between thermals than when lightly loaded.

5785. "C" is the correct answer. A heavy glider has a higher airspeed at which the best glide ratio is obtained than a lighter glider. The maximum glide ratio is unaffected by weight.
Reference Soaring Flight Manual
FAA subject matter knowledge code N21

5786. When flying into a strong headwind on a long final glide or a long glide back to the airport, the recommended speed to use is the

A. best glide speed.

B. minimum sink speed.

C. speed-to-fly plus half the estimated windspeed at the glider's flight altitude.

5786. "C" is the correct answer. Use the speed-to-fly plus half the wind velocity at the glider's altitude.
Reference Soaring Flight Manual
FAA subject matter knowledge code N34

5787. Which procedure can be used to increase forward speed on a cross-country flight?

A. Maintain minimum sink speed plus or minus one-half the estimated wind velocity.

B. Use water ballast while thermals are strong and dump the water when thermals are weak.

C. Use water ballast while thermals are weak and dump the water when thermals are strong.

5787. "B" is the correct answer. A heavy glider has a higher airspeed at which the best glide ratio is obtained than a lighter glider. The maximum glide ratio is unaffected by weight.
Reference Soaring Flight Manual
FAA subject matter knowledge code N21

5790. Which is true regarding the effect on a glider's performance by the addition of ballast or weight?

A. The glide ratio at a given airspeed will increase.

B. The heavier the glider is loaded, the less the glide ratio will be at all airspeeds.

C. A higher airspeed is required to obtain the same glide ratio as when lightly loaded.

5790. "C" is the correct answer. A heavy glider has a higher airspeed at which the best glide ratio is obtained than a lighter glider. The maximum glide ratio is unaffected by weight.
Reference Soaring Flight Manual
FAA subject matter knowledge code N21

5791. When flying on a heading of east from one thermal to the next, the airspeed is increased to the speed-to-fly with wings level. What will the conventional magnetic compass indicate while the airspeed is increasing?

A. A turn toward the south.

B. A turn toward the north.

C. Straight flight on a heading of 090°.

5791. "B" is the correct answer. Remember:

ANDS: Accelerate—North, Decelerate—South
Reference PHOAK, p. 71
FAA subject matter knowledge code N04

5797. During an aerotow, moving from the inside to the outside of the towplane's flight path during a turn causes the

A. towline to slacken.

B. glider's airspeed to increase, resulting in a tendency to climb.

C. glider's airspeed to decrease, resulting in a tendency to descend.

5797. "B" is the correct answer. Moving to the outside of the towplane's turn increases the airspeed and cause the glider to climb.
Reference Soaring Flight Manual
FAA subject matter knowledge code N30

5798. During an aerotow, is it good operating practice to release from a low-tow position?

A. No. The tow ring may strike and damage the glider after release.

B. No. The towline may snap forward and strike the towplane after release.

C. Yes. Low-tow position is the correct position for releasing from the towplane.

5798. "A" is the correct answer. By releasing from a low-tow position, you risk having the tow ring strike the glider.
Reference Soaring Flight Manual
FAA subject matter knowledge code N04

5799. During an aerotow, if slack develops in the towline, the glider pilot should correct this situation by

A. making a shallow-banked coordinated turn to either side.

B. increasing the glider's pitch attitude until the towline becomes taut.

C. yawing the glider's nose to one side with rudder while keeping the wings level with the ailerons.

5799. "C" is the correct answer. During aerotows, you can correct slack in the towline by yawing the glider's nose while keeping the wings level.
Reference Soaring Flight Manual
FAA subject matter knowledge code N31

5800. During aerotow takeoffs in crosswind conditions, the glider starts drifting downwind after becoming airborne and before the towplane lifts off. The glider pilot should

A. not correct for a crosswind during this part of the takeoff.

B. crab into the wind to remain in the flight path of the towplane.

C. hold upwind rudder in order to crab into the wind and remain in the flight path of the towplane.

5800. "B" is the correct answer. If you begin to drift in a crosswind, you should crab the glider to remain in position.
Reference Soaring Flight Manual
FAA subject matter knowledge code N30

5801. When should the wing runner raise the glider's wing to the level position in preparation for takeoff?

A. When the towplane pilot fans the towplane's rudder.

B. When the glider pilot is seated and has fastened the safety belt.

C. After the glider pilot gives a thumbs-up signal to take up towline slack.

5801. "C" is the correct answer. The wing runner should only raise the wing when the pilot is ready for takeoff.
Reference Soaring Flight Manual
FAA subject matter knowledge code N31

5802. During an aerotow, the sailplane moves to one side of the towplane's flight path. This was most likely caused by

A. variations in the heading of the towplane.

B. entering wingtip vortices created by the towplane.

C. flying the sailplane in a wing-low attitude or holding unnecessary rudder pressure.

5802. "C" is the correct answer. This was most likely caused by flying the sailplane in a wing-low attitude or holding unnecessary rudder pressure.
Reference Soaring Flight Manual
FAA subject matter knowledge code N30

5803. In which manner should the sailplane be flown while turning during an aerotow?

A. By flying inside the towplane's flight path.

B. By flying outside the towplane's flight path.

C. By banking at the same point in space where the towplane banked and using the same degree of bank and rate of roll.

5803. "C" is the correct answer. You should bank at the same angle and roll rate as the towplane.
Reference Soaring Flight Manual
FAA subject matter knowledge code N30

5804. What corrective action should the sailplane pilot take during takeoff if the towplane is still on the ground and the sailplane is airborne and drifting to the left?

A. Crab into the wind to maintain a position directly behind the towplane.

B. Establish a right wing-low drift correction to remain in the flight path of the towplane.

C. Wait until the towplane becomes airborne before attempting to establish a drift correction.

5804. "A" is the correct answer. If you begin to drift in a crosswind, you should crab the glider to remain in position.
Reference Soaring Flight Manual
FAA subject matter knowledge code N30

5805. At what point during an autotow should the glider pilot establish the maximum pitch attitude for the climb?

A. Immediately after takeoff.

B. 100 ft above the ground.

C. 200 ft above the ground.

5805. "C" is the correct answer. At 200 ft agl you should establish the maximum pitch attitude to climb.
Reference Soaring Flight Manual
FAA subject matter knowledge code N31

5808. Given:

Glider's max auto/winch tow speed   66 mph
Surface wind (direct headwind)   5 mph
Wind gradient   4 mph

When the glider reaches an altitude of 200 ft the auto/winch speed should be

A. 42 mph.

B. 46 mph.

C. 56 mph.

5808. "A" is the correct answer. Figure aerotows as follows:

1. Subtract wind: 66 mph − 5 mph = 61 mph.

2. Subtract a safety margin of 5 mph: 61 mph − 5 mph = 56 mph.

3. Between 100 and 200 ft, tow speed should be reduced by 10 mph: 56 mph − 10 mph = 46 mph.

4. Subtract the wind gradient: 46 mph − 4 mph = 42 mph.
Reference Soaring Flight Manual
FAA subject matter knowledge code N31

5809. The towrope breaks when at the steepest segment of the climb during a winch launch. To recover to a normal gliding attitude, the pilot should

A. relax the back stick pressure to avoid excessive loss of altitude.

B. apply forward pressure until the buffeting sound and vibration disappear.

C. move the stick fully forward immediately and hold it there until the nose crosses the horizon.

5809. "C" is the correct answer. If the towrope breaks during the climb, the pilot should move the stick fully forward immediately and hold it there until the nose crosses the horizon.
Reference Soaring Flight Manual
FAA subject matter knowledge code N31

5810. Which would cause pitch oscillations or porpoising during a winch launch?

A. Excessive winch speed.

B. Insufficient winch speed.

C. Excessive slack in the towline.

5810. "C" is the correct answer. Too much slack in the towline may cause pitch oscillations during launch.
Reference Soaring Flight Manual
FAA subject matter knowledge code N31

5811. During an auto launch, the pitch angle of the glider should not exceed

A. 10° at 50 ft, 20° at 100 ft, and 45° at 200 ft.

B. 15° at 50 ft, 30° at 100 ft, and 45° at 200 ft.

C. 15° at 50 ft, 20° at 100 ft, and 40° at 200 ft.

5811. "B" is the correct answer. The pitch angle should not exceed 15 degrees at 50 ft, 30 degrees at 100 ft, and 45 degrees at 200 ft.
Reference Soaring Flight Manual
FAA subject matter knowledge code N31

5812. To stop pitch oscillation during a winch launch, the pilot should

A. increase the back pressure on the control stick and steepen the angle of climb.

B. relax the back pressure on the control stick and shallow the angle of climb.

C. extend and retreat the spoilers several times until the oscillations subside.

5812. "B" is the correct answer. Release back pressure to reduce the deck angle until the oscillations subside.
Reference Soaring Flight Manual
FAA subject matter knowledge code N09

5813. What should be expected when making a downwind landing?

A. The likelihood of undershooting the intended landing spot and a faster airspeed at touchdown.

B. The likelihood of overshooting the intended landing spot and a faster groundspeed at touchdown.

C. The likelihood of undershooting the intended landing spot and a faster groundspeed at touchdown.

5813. "B" is the correct answer. The increase in groundspeed during a tailwind landing tends to make you overshoot your touchdown point.
Reference Soaring Flight Manual
FAA subject matter knowledge code N32

5814. What corrective action should be taken if, while thermaling at minimum sink speed in turbulent air, the left wing drops while turning to the left?

A. Apply right rudder pressure to slow the rate of turn.

B. Lower the nose before applying right aileron pressure.

C. Apply right aileron pressure to counteract the overbanking tendency.

5814. "B" is the correct answer. Lower the nose to obtain flying speed.
Reference Soaring Flight Manual
FAA subject matter knowledge code N32

5816. To stop a ground loop to the left after landing a glider, it would be best to lower the

A. right wing in order to shift the CG.

B. left wing to compensate for crosswind.

C. nose skid to the ground and apply wheel brake.

5816. "C" is the correct answer. Lower the nose to the ground and apply the wheel brake if a ground loop is beginning to develop.
Reference Soaring Flight Manual
FAA subject matter knowledge code N32

5817. In which situation is a hazardous stall more likely to occur if inadequate airspeed allowance is made for wind velocity gradient?

A. During the approach to a landing.

B. While thermaling at high altitudes.

C. During takeoff and climb while on aerotow.

5817. "A" is the correct answer. Stalls are most likely to occur during the approach to a landing.
Reference Soaring Flight Manual
FAA subject matter knowledge code N21

5818. With regard to two or more gliders flying in the same thermal, which is true?

A. All turns should be to the right.

B. Turns should be in the same direction as the highest glider.

C. Turns should be made in the same direction as the first glider to enter the thermal.

5818. "C" is the correct answer. Turns should be made in the same direction as the first glider to enter the thermal.
Reference Soaring Flight Manual
FAA subject matter knowledge code N33

5819. Which is true regarding the direction in which turns should be made during slope soaring?

A. All reversing turns should be made to the left.

B. All reversing turns should be made into the wind away from the slope.

C. The upwind turn should be made to the left; the downwind turn should be made to the right.

5819. "B" is the correct answer. Always turn away from the slope and into the wind when turning during slope soaring.
Reference Soaring Flight Manual
FAA subject matter knowledge code N33

5820. Which airspeed should be used when circling within a thermal?

A. Best L/D speed.

B. Maneuvering speed.

C. Minimum sink speed for the angle of bank.

5820. "C" is the correct answer. When circling in a thermal use the minimum sink speed for the angle of bank.
Reference Soaring Flight Manual
FAA subject matter knowledge code N33

5821. Which is a recommended procedure for an off-field landing?

A. A recommended landing site would be a pasture.

B. Always land into the wind even if you have to land downhill on a sloping field.

C. If the field slopes, it is usually best to land uphill, even with a tailwind.

5821. "C" is the correct answer. If the field slopes, it is usually best to land uphill, even with a tailwind.
Reference Soaring Flight Manual
FAA subject matter knowledge code N34

5822. What would be a proper action or procedure to use if you are getting too low on a cross-country flight in a sailplane?

A. Fly directly into the wind and make a straight-in approach at the end of the glide.

B. Have a suitable landing area selected upon reaching 2000 ft agl, and a specific field chosen upon reaching 1500 ft agl.

C. Continue on course until descending to 500 ft, then select a field and confine the search for lift to an area within gliding range of a downwind leg for the field you have chosen.

5822. "B" is the correct answer. At 2000 ft agl, pick a suitable landing site; at 1500 ft agl, pick a specific field.
Reference Soaring Flight Manual
FAA subject matter knowledge code N34

5823. What is the proper speed to fly when passing through lift with no intention to work the lift?

A. Best L/D speed.

B. Maximum safe speed.

C. Minimum sink speed.

5823. "C" is the correct answer. The proper speed to fly is minimum sink speed.
Reference Soaring Flight Manual
FAA subject matter knowledge code N21

5824. What is the proper airspeed to use when flying between thermals on a cross-country flight against a headwind?

A. The best L/D speed increased by one-half the estimated wind velocity.

B. The best L/D speed decreased by one-half the estimated wind velocity.

C. The minimum sink speed increased by one-half the estimated wind velocity.

5824. "A" is the correct answer. Use the best L/D speed and increase it by one-half the wind speed when flying between thermals on a cross-country flight.
Reference Soaring Flight Manual
FAA subject matter knowledge code N33

5828. It may be possible to make changes in the direction of flight in a hot air balloon by

A. using the maneuvering vent.

B. operating at different flight altitudes.

C. flying a constant atmospheric pressure gradient.

5828. "B" is the correct answer. It may be possible to make changes in the direction of flight in a hot air balloon by operating at different flight altitudes.
Reference Balloon Flight Manual
FAA subject matter knowledge code O05

5833. If ample fuel is available, within which temperature range will propane fuel vaporize sufficiently to provide enough fuel pressure for burner operation during flight?

A. 0°F to 30°F.

B. 10°F to 30°F.

C. 30°F to 90°F.

5833. "C" is the correct answer. If ample fuel is available, propane fuel will vaporize sufficiently from 30°F to 90°F to provide enough fuel pressure for burner operation during flight.
Reference Balloon Flight Manual
FAA subject matter knowledge code O02

5842. What effect, if any, does ambient temperature have on propane tank pressure?

A. It has no effect.

B. As temperature decreases, propane tank pressure decreases.

C. As temperature decreases, propane tank pressure increases.

5842. "B" is the correct answer. As ambient temperature decreases, propane tank pressure decreases.
Reference Balloon Flight Manual
FAA subject matter knowledge code O02

5852. If you are over a heavily wooded area with no open fields in the vicinity and have only about 10 minutes of fuel remaining, you should

A. stay low and keep flying in the hope that you will find an open field.

B. climb as high as possible to see where the nearest landing field is.

C. land in the trees while you have sufficient fuel for a controlled landing.

5852. "C" is the correct answer. If you are over a heavily wooded area with no open fields in the vicinity and have only about 10 minutes of fuel remaining, you should land in the trees while you have sufficient fuel for a controlled landing.
Reference Balloon Flight Manual
FAA subject matter knowledge code O05

5853. Which precaution should be exercised if confronted with the necessity of having to land when the air is turbulent?

A. Land in the center of the largest available field.

B. Throw propane equipment overboard immediately prior to touchdown.

C. Land in the trees to absorb shock forces, thus cushioning the landing.

5853. "A" is the correct answer. If confronted with the necessity of having to land when the air is turbulent, you should land in the center of the largest available field.
Reference Balloon Flight Manual
FAA subject matter knowledge code O05

5856. The weigh-off procedure is useful because the

A. pilot can adjust the altimeter to the correct setting.

B. ground crew can assure that downwind obstacles are cleared.

C. pilot will learn what the equilibrium conditions are prior to being committed to fly.

5856. "C" is the correct answer. The weight-off procedure is useful because the pilot will learn what the equilibrium conditions are prior to being committed to fly.
Reference Balloon Flight Manual
FAA subject matter knowledge code O03

5861. If powerlines become a factor during a balloon flight, a pilot should know that

A. it is safer to contact the lines than to chance ripping.

B. contact with powerlines creates no great hazard for a balloon.

C. it is better to chance ripping at 25 ft above the ground than contacting the lines.

5861. "C" is the correct answer. If powerlines become a factor during a balloon flight, it is better to chance ripping at 25 ft above the ground than contacting the lines.
Reference Balloon Flight Manual
FAA subject matter knowledge code O30

5862. The windspeed is such that it is necessary to deflate the envelope as rapidly as possible during a landing. When should the deflation port (rip panel) be opened?

A. Prior to ground contact.

B. The instant the gondola contacts the surface.

C. As the balloon skips off the surface the first time and the last of the ballast has been discharged.

5862. "A" is the correct answer. When the wind-speed is such that it is necessary to deflate the envelope as rapidly as possible during a landing the deflation port should be opened prior to ground contact.

Reference Balloon Flight Manual

FAA subject matter knowledge code O05

5863. The term "to weigh off" as used in ballooning means to determine the

A. standard weight and balance of the balloon.

B. static equilibrium of the balloon as loaded for flight.

C. amount of gas required for an ascent to a prese-lected altitude.

5863. "B" is the correct answer. "To weigh off" means to determine the static equilibrium of the balloon as loaded for flight.

Reference Balloon Flight Manual

FAA subject matter knowledge code P01

14

Flight and Navigation Instruments

STUDY GUIDE

In the broad sense of the term, radio navigation includes any method by which a pilot follows a predetermined flight path over the earth's surface by utilizing the properties of radio waves.

The VOR, or omnirange, is the primary navigation facility for civil aviation in the National Airspace System. The VOR generates directional information and transmits it by ground equipment to the aircraft, providing 360 magnetic courses to or from the VOR station. These courses are called radials and are oriented from the station.

VOR facilities operate within the 108.0–117.95 MHz frequency band. H-VORs and L-VORs have a normal usable distance of 40 nautical miles below 18,000 ft. T-VORs are short-range facilities that have a power output of approximately 50 watts and a usable distance of 25 nautical miles at 12,000 ft and below.

Distance Measuring Equipment

Used in conjunction with the nationwide VOR system, distance measuring equipment (DME) has made it possible for you to immediately know the exact geographic position of your aircraft by observation of your VOR and DME indicating equipment.

Area Navigation

Area navigation (RNAV) allows a pilot to fly a selected course to a predetermined point without the need to overfly ground-based navigation facilities.

Principles of ADF Receiver Operation

The automatic direction finder (ADF) used with the nondirectional homing beacon is a radio receiver that determines the bearing from the aircraft to the transmitting station.

Instrument Landing System

An instrument landing system consists of a localizer radio course, a glideslope radio course, two VHF marker beacons, and approach lights.

SDF and LDA

These navaids are similar to a standard ILS localizer and are used for nonprecision instrument approaches.

Time and Distance

Time and distance from the station is determined from the following formulas:

$$\text{Time to station} = \frac{60 \times \text{minutes flown between bearing change}}{\text{degrees of bearing change}}$$

$$\text{Distance to station} = \frac{\text{TAS} \times \text{minutes flown}}{\text{degrees of bearing change}}$$

COMPUTER-BASED QUESTIONS

5490. Which is true about homing when using ADF during crosswind conditions?

A. Homing to a radio station results in a curved path that leads to the station.

B. Homing is a practical navigation method for flying both to and from a radio station.

C. Homing to a radio station requires that the ADF have an automatically or manually rotatable azimuth.

5490. "A" is the correct answer. Homing to the station is a common procedure, but results in drifting downwind, resulting in a curved flight path to the station.
Reference PHOAK, p. 188
FAA subject matter knowledge code H07

5491. Which is true regarding tracking on a desired bearing when using ADF during crosswind conditions?

A. To track outbound, heading corrections should be made away from the ADF pointer.

B. When on the desired track outbound, with the proper drift correction established, the ADF pointer is deflected to the windward side of the tail position.

C. When on the desired track inbound, with the proper drift correction established, the ADF pointer is deflected to the windward side of the nose position.

5491. "B" is the correct answer. When the wind drift correction is established, the ADF needle indicates the amount of correction to the right or left for a crosswind.
Reference PHOAK, p. 188
FAA subject matter knowledge code H07

5492. An aircraft is maintaining a magnetic heading of 265° and the ADF shows a relative bearing of 065°. This indicates that the aircraft is crossing the

A. 065° magnetic bearing FROM the radio beacon.

B. 150° magnetic bearing FROM the radio beacon.

C. 330° magnetic bearing FROM the radio beacon.

5492. "B" is the correct answer. Magnetic bearing to the station is the angle formed by a line drawn from the aircraft to magnetic north. The magnetic bearing to the station can be determined by adding the relative bearing to the magnetic heading of the aircraft: 65° + 265° = 330°. To determine the magnetic bearing from the station, 180° is added to or subtracted from the magnetic bearing to the station. This is the reciprocal bearing and is used when plotting position fixes: 330° − 180° = 150°.
Reference PHOAK, pp. 187–188
FAA subject matter knowledge code H07

5493. The magnetic heading is 315° and the ADF shows a relative bearing of 140°. The magnetic bearing FROM the radio beacon would be

A. 095°.

B. 175°.

C. 275°.

5493. "C" is the correct answer. Magnetic bearing to the station is the angle formed by a line drawn from the aircraft to magnetic north. The magnetic bearing to the station can be determined by adding the relative bearing to the magnetic heading of the aircraft: 140° + 315° = 455°. To determine the magnetic bearing from the station, 180° is added to or subtracted from the magnetic bearing to the station. This is the reciprocal bearing and is used when plotting position fixes: 455° − 180° = 275°.
Reference PHOAK, pp. 187–188
FAA subject matter knowledge code H07

5494. The magnetic heading is 350° and the relative bearing to a radio beacon is 240°. What would be the magnetic bearing TO the radio beacon?

A. 050°.

B. 230°.

C. 295°.

5494. "B" is the correct answer. Magnetic bearing to the station is the angle formed by a line drawn from the aircraft to magnetic north. The magnetic bearing to the station can be determined by adding the relative bearing to the magnetic heading of the aircraft: 240° + 350° = 590°; 590° − 360° = 230°.

Reference PHOAK, p. 187

FAA subject matter knowledge code H07

5495. The ADF is tuned to a radio beacon. If the magnetic heading is 040° and the relative bearing is 290°, the magnetic bearing TO the radio beacon would be

A. 150°.

B. 285°.

C. 330°.

5495. "C" is the correct answer. Magnetic bearing to the station is the angle formed by a line drawn from the aircraft to magnetic north. The magnetic bearing to the station can be determined by adding the relative bearing to the magnetic heading of the aircraft: 040° + 290° = 330°.

Reference PHOAK, p. 187

FAA subject matter knowledge code H07

5496. If the relative bearing to a nondirectional radio beacon is 045° and the magnetic heading is 355°, the magnetic bearing TO the radio beacon would be

A. 040°.

B. 065°.

C. 220°.

5496. "A" is the correct answer. Magnetic bearing to the station is the angle formed by a line drawn from the aircraft to magnetic north. The magnetic bearing to the station can be determined by adding the relative bearing to the magnetic heading of the aircraft: 045° + 355° = 400°; 400° − 360° = 040°.

Reference PHOAK, p. 187

FAA subject matter knowledge code H07

5497. Refer to Fig. 16. If the aircraft continues its present heading as shown in instrument group 3, what will be the relative bearing when the aircraft reaches the magnetic bearing of 030° FROM the NDB?

A. 030°.

B. 060°.

C. 240°.

5497. "C" is the correct answer. When using a fixed card ADF instrument, you need the following formula (MH) magnetic heading + RB (relative bearing) = MB (magnetic bearing TO the station). To get the bearing FROM the station, you add 180° to the magnetic bearing.

$$330° + ? = 30° + 180° = 210°$$
$$330° + 240° (−360°) = 210°$$

Remember that any time the sum of the heading exceeds 360°, subtract 360° to get the correct answer. The answer is 240°.

Reference Instrument Flying Handbook, p. 145

FAA subject matter knowledge code H07

5498. Refer to Fig. 16. At the position indicated by instrument group 1, what would be the relative bearing if the aircraft were turned to a magnetic heading of 090°?

A. 150°.

B. 190°.

C. 250°.

5498. "C" is the correct answer. Remember, magnetic bearing = magnetic heading + relative bearing: 300° + 40° = 340°. If the aircraft's position in relation to the station does not change and it turns to a heading of 090° then you would be on the 250° relative bearing: 340° − 090° = 250°.

Reference Instrument Flying Handbook

FAA subject matter knowledge code I08

5499. Refer to Fig. 16. At the position indicated by instrument group 1, to intercept the 330° magnetic bearing to the NDB at a 30° angle, the aircraft should be turned

A. left to a heading of 270°.

B. right to a heading of 330°.

C. right to a heading of 360°.

5499. "C" is the correct answer. Only two headings could intercept the 330° bearing at a 30° angle: 300° or at 360°. Only a 360° heading will intercept the 330° bearing to the station.

Reference Instrument Flying Handbook, p. 145

FAA subject matter knowledge code I08

5500. Which situation would result in reverse sensing of a VOR receiver?

A. Flying a heading that is reciprocal to the bearing selected on the OBS.

B. Setting the OBS to a bearing that is 90° from the bearing on which the aircraft is located.

C. Failing to change the OBS from the selected inbound course to the outbound course after passing the station.

5500. "A" is the correct answer. When flying TO a station, always fly the selected course with a TO indication. When flying FROM a station, always fly the selected course with a FROM indication. If this is not done, the action of the course deviation needle will be reversed. To further explain this reverse action, if the aircraft is flown toward a station with a FROM indication or away from a station with a TO indication, the course deviation needle will indicate in an opposite direction to that which it should.
Reference PHOAK, p. 186
FAA subject matter knowledge code I08

5501. To track outbound on the 180 radial of a VOR station, the recommended procedure is to set the OBS to

A. 360° and make heading corrections toward the CDI needle.

B. 180° and make heading corrections away from the CDI needle.

C. 180° and make heading corrections toward the CDI needle.

5501. "C" is the correct answer. When navigating from a station, determine the outbound radial and use this radial. If the aircraft drifts, do not reset the course selector, but correct for drift and fly toward the CDI needle.
Reference PHOAK, p. 186
FAA subject matter knowledge code I08

5502. To track inbound on the 215 radial of a VOR station, the recommended procedure is to set the OBS to

A. 215° and make heading corrections toward the CDI needle.

B. 215° and make heading corrections away from the CDI needle.

C. 035° and make heading corrections toward the CDI needle.

5502. "C" is the correct answer. When navigating to a station, determine the inbound radial and use this radial. If the aircraft drifts, do not reset the course se-

lector, but correct for drift and fly a heading that compensates for wind drift.
Reference PHOAK, p. 186
FAA subject matter knowledge code I08

5503. When diverting to an alternate airport because of an emergency, pilots should

A. rely on radio as the primary method of navigation.

B. climb to a higher altitude because it will be easier to identify checkpoints.

C. apply rule-of-thumb computations, estimates, and other appropriate shortcuts to divert to the new course as soon as possible.

5503. "C" is the correct answer. In the event the diversion to an alternate airport results from an emergency, it is important for the pilot to divert to the new course as early as possible. Because of the limitations in cockpit space and available equipment, however, and because the pilot's attention must be divided between solving the problem and operating the airplane, advantage must be taken of all possible shortcuts and rule-of-thumb computations.
Reference Flight Training Handbook, p. 179
FAA subject matter knowledge code H61

5504. To use VHF/DF facilities for assistance is locating your position, you must have an operative VHF

A. transmitter and receiver.

B. transmitter and receiver, and an operative ADF receiver.

C. transmitter and receiver, and an operative VOR receiver.

5504. "A" is the correct answer. VHF direction finding ground equipment is used directly with ASR radar to locate and direct lost aircraft. The bearing information is presented both by a pointer and by a bright straight line on the radar display, starting from the location of the DF antenna and passing through the radar target representing the transmitting aircraft. Other than a VHF transmitter, no additional airborne equipment is needed to actuate the ground equipment.
Reference Instrument Flying Handbook, p. 126
FAA subject matter knowledge code H08

5505. Which maximum range factor decreases as weight decreases?

A. Altitude.

B. Airspeed.

C. Angle of attack.

5505. "B" is the correct answer. As the weight decreases the airspeed for best L/D also decreases.
Reference Flight Training Handbook, p. 310
FAA subject matter knowledge code H66

5506. Refer to Fig. 17. Which illustration indicates that the airplane will intercept the 360° radial at a 60° angle inbound, if the present heading is maintained?

A. 3.

B. 4.

C. 5.

5506. "A" is the correct answer. In order to intercept the 360 radial at a 60° angle inbound, the HSI course indicator must be pointing to 180°. The airplane course must be either 120° or 240°. These are the only two headings that intercept at a 60° heading. Instrument 3 is the closest answer even though the course selection in the window is not the same as indicated by the course arrow.
Reference Instrument Flying Handbook, p. 53
FAA subject matter knowledge code I04

5507. Refer to Fig. 17. Which statement is true regarding illustration 2, if the present heading is maintained?

A. The airplane will cross the 180 radial at a 45° angle outbound.

B. The airplane will intercept the 225 radial at a 45° angle.

C. The airplane will intercept the 360 radial at a 45° angle inbound.

5507. "C" is the correct answer. The bearing pointer shows the VOR is approximately 10° to the right of the airplane. The airplane's present heading will cross the 360 radial at a 45° angle: 225° − 180° = 45°.
Reference Instrument Flying Handbook, p. 53
FAA subject matter knowledge code I04

5508. Refer to Fig. 17. Which illustration indicates that the airplane will intercept the 060 radial at a 75° angle outbound, if the present heading is maintained?

A. 4.

B. 5.

C. 6.

5508. "B" is the correct answer. Only two headings can intercept the 060 radial at a 75° angle outbound—345° and 135°: 60° + 75° = 135°, and 60° − 75° = 345°. Only "B" shows a 345° heading.
Reference Instrument Flying Handbook, p. 53
FAA subject matter knowledge code I04

5509. Refer to Fig. 17. Which illustration indicates that the airplane should be turned 150° left to intercept the 360 radial at a 60° angle inbound?

A. 1.

B. 2.

C. 3.

5509. "A" is the correct answer. The only two headings that can intercept the 360 radial inbound at a 60° angle are 120° and 240°. Only instrument #1 could turn left 150° and fly one of those headings.
Reference Instrument Flying Handbook, p. 53
FAA subject matter knowledge code I04

5510. Refer to Fig. 17. Which is true regarding illustration 4, if the present heading is maintained?

A. The airplane will cross the 060 radial at a 15° angle.

B. The airplane will intercept the 240 radial at a 30° angle.

C. The airplane will cross the 180 radial at a 75° angle.

5510."C" is the correct answer. The bearing pointer indicates that you are on the 095 radial from the station. If you continue to fly 255 you will cross the 180 radial at a 75° angle: 225° − 180° = 75°.
Reference Instrument Flying Handbook, p. 53
FAA subject matter knowledge code I04

5511. Refer to Fig. 18. To intercept a magnetic bearing of 240° FROM a 030° angle (while outbound), the airplane should be turned

A. left 065°.

B. left 125°.

C. right 270°.

5511. "B" is the correct answer. The tail of the needle indicates that you are presently on the 165° magnetic bearing from the station: 130° + 35° = 165°. The only two headings that will intercept the 240° magnetic bearing from the station at a 30° angle are a 210° heading or a 270° heading. To solve this problem, add the intercept angle to the 240° bearing to get the answer of 270°. Finding the number of degrees of left turn required is simple. Just count the number of degrees left from your present heading of 035° to a new heading of 270°. You need to turn left 125°.
Reference Instrument Flying Handbook, pp. 145–154
FAA subject matter knowledge code H07

5512. Refer to Fig. 18. If the airplane continues to fly on the heading as shown, what magnetic bearing

FROM the station would be intercepted at a 35° angle outbound?

A. 035°.

B. 070°.

C. 215°.

5512. "B" is the correct answer. You are flying a 165° bearing from the station (130° + 35° = 165°). In order to find the intercept bearing, add the angle of intercept to the heading you're flying: 35° + 35° = 70°.

Reference Instrument Flying Handbook, pp. 145–154

FAA subject matter knowledge code H07

5513. Refer to Fig. 19. If the airplane continues to fly on the magnetic heading as illustrated, what magnetic bearing FROM the station would be intercepted at a 35° angle?

A. 090°.

B. 270°.

C. 305°.

5513. "C" is the correct answer. You are flying a 270° bearing from the station. In order to find the intercept bearing, subtract the intercept angle from the heading you are flying: 340° − 35° = 305°.

Reference Instrument Flying Handbook, pp. 145–154

FAA subject matter knowledge code H07

5514. Refer to Fig. 19. If the airplane continues to fly on the magnetic heading as illustrated, what magnetic bearing FROM the station would be intercepted at a 030° angle?

A. 090°.

B. 270°.

C. 310°.

5514. "C" is the correct answer. To solve this problem, take the magnetic bearing you are flying (340°) and subtract 30°: 340° − 30° = 310°.

Reference Instrument Flying Handbook, pp. 245–254

FAA subject matter knowledge code H07

5515. The relative bearing on an ADF changes from 265° to 260° in 2 minutes of elapsed time. If the groundspeed is 145 knots, the distance to that station would be

A. 26 nautical miles.

B. 37 nautical miles.

C. 58 nautical miles.

5515. "C" is the correct answer. Distance is determined by the formula: Distance to station = TAS × minutes flown ÷ degrees of bearing change.

$$\text{Distance} = \frac{145\,\text{kt} \times 2\,\text{min}}{5°} = 58\,\text{nm}$$

Reference Instrument Flying Handbook, pp. 136–138

FAA subject matter knowledge code I08

5516. The ADF indicates a wingtip bearing change of 10° in 2 minutes of elapsed time, and the TAS is 160 knots. What is the distance to the station?

A. 15 nautical miles.

B. 32 nautical miles.

C. 36 nautical miles.

5516. "B" is the correct answer. Distance is determined by the formula: Distance to station = TAS × minutes flown ÷ degrees of bearing change.

$$\text{Distance} = \frac{160\,\text{kt} \times 2\,\text{min}}{10°} = 32\,\text{nm}$$

Reference Instrument Flying Handbook, p. 138

FAA subject matter knowledge code I08

5517. With a TAS of 115 knots, the relative bearing on an ADF changes from 090° to 095° in 1.5 minutes of elapsed time. The distance to the station would be

A. 12.5 nautical miles.

B. 24.5 nautical miles.

C. 34.5 nautical miles.

5517. "C" is the correct answer. Distance is determined by the formula: Distance to station = TAS × minutes flown ÷ degrees of bearing change.

$$\text{Distance} = \frac{115\,\text{kt} \times 1.5\,\text{min}}{5°} = 34.5\,\text{nm}$$

Reference Instrument Flying Handbook, p. 138

FAA subject matter knowledge code I08

5518. Given:

Wingtip bearing change	5°
Time elapsed between bearing change	5 minutes
True airspeed	115 knots

The distance to the station is

A. 36 nautical miles.

B. 57.5 nautical miles.

C. 115 nautical miles.

5518. "C" is the correct answer. Distance is determined by the formula: Distance to station = TAS × minutes flown ÷ degrees of bearing change.

$$\text{Distance} = \frac{115 \text{ kt} \times 5 \text{ min}}{5°} = 115 \text{ nm}$$

Reference Instrument Flying Handbook, p. 138
FAA subject matter knowledge code I08

5519. The ADF is tuned to a nondirectional radio beacon and the relative bearing changes from 095° to 100° in 1.5 minutes of elapsed time. The time en route to that station would be

A. 18 minutes.

B. 24 minutes.

C. 30 minutes.

5519. "A" is the correct answer. Time is determined by the formula: Time to station = 60 × minutes flown between bearing change ÷ degrees of bearing change.

$$\text{Time} = \frac{60 \times 1.5 \text{ min}}{5°} = 18 \text{ min}$$

Reference Instrument Flying Handbook, p. 138
FAA subject matter knowledge code I08.

5520. The ADF is tuned to a nondirectional radio beacon and the relative bearing changes from 270° to 265° in 2.5 minutes of elapsed time. The time en route to that beacon would be

A. 9 minutes.

B. 18 minutes.

C. 30 minutes.

5520. "C" is the correct answer. Time is determined by the formula: Time to station = 60 × minutes flown between bearing change ÷ degrees of bearing change.

$$\text{Time} = \frac{60 \times 2.5 \text{ min}}{5°} = 30 \text{ min}$$

Reference Instrument Flying Handbook, p. 138
FAA subject matter knowledge code I08

5521. The ADF is tuned to a nondirectional radio beacon and the relative bearing changes from 085° to 090° in 2 minutes of elapsed time. The time en route to the station would be

A. 15 minutes.

B. 18 minutes.

C. 24 minutes.

5521. "C" is the correct answer. Time is determined by the formula: Time to station = 60 × minutes flown between bearing change ÷ degrees of bearing change.

$$\text{Time} = \frac{60 \times 2 \text{ min}}{5°} = 24 \text{ min}$$

Reference Instrument Flying Handbook, p. 138
FAA subject matter knowledge code I08

5522. If the relative bearing changes from 090° to 100° in 2.5 minutes of elapsed time, the time en route to the station would be

A. 12 minutes.

B. 15 minutes.

C. 18 minutes.

5522. "B" is the correct answer. Time is determined by the formula: Time to station = 60 × minutes flown between bearing change ÷ degrees of bearing change.

$$\text{Time} = \frac{60 \times 2.5 \text{ min}}{10°} = 15 \text{ min}$$

Reference Instrument Flying Handbook, p. 138
FAA subject matter knowledge code I08

5523. The ADF is tuned to a nondirectional radio beacon and the relative bearing changes from 090° to 100° in 2.5 minutes of elapsed time. If the true airspeed is 90 knots, the distance and time en route to that radio beacon would be

A. 15 miles and 22.5 minutes.

B. 22.5 miles and 15 minutes.

C. 32 miles and 18 minutes.

5523. "B" is the correct answer. Time and distance are determined by the following formulas:

Time to station = 60 × minutes flown between bearing change ÷ degrees of bearing change.

$$\text{Time} = \frac{60 \times 2.5 \text{ min}}{10°} = 15 \text{ min}$$

Distance to station = TAS × minutes flown ÷ degrees of bearing change.

$$\text{Distance} = \frac{90 \text{ kt} \times 2.5 \text{ min}}{10°} = 22.5 \text{ nm}$$

Reference Instrument Flying Handbook, p. 138
FAA subject matter knowledge code I08

5524. Given:

Wingtip bearing change   10°
Elapsed time between bearing change   4 minutes
Rate of fuel consumption   11 gph

Calculate the fuel required to fly to the station.

A. 4.4 gallons.

B. 8.4 gallons.

C. 12 gallons.

5524. "A" is the correct answer. Determine the time to station using the formula:

Time to station = 60 × minutes flown between bearing change ÷ degrees of bearing change.

$$\text{Time} = \frac{60 \times 4 \text{ min}}{10°} = 24 \text{ min}$$

Then determine the fuel used: 11 gph × 24 min ÷ 60 min = 4.4 gal.

Reference Instrument Flying Handbook, p. 138
FAA subject matter knowledge code I08

5525. Given:

Wingtip bearing change	5°
Elapsed time between bearing change	6 minutes
Rate of fuel consumption	12 gph

The fuel required to fly to the station is

A. 8.2 gallons.

B. 14.4 gallons.

C. 18.7 gallons.

5525. "B" is the correct answer. Determine the time to station using the formula:

Time to station = 60 × minutes flown between bearing change ÷ degrees of bearing change.

$$\text{Time} = \frac{60 \times 6 \text{ min}}{5°} = 72 \text{ min}$$

Then determine the fuel used: 12 gph × 72 min ÷ 60 min = 14.4 gal.

Reference Instrument Flying Handbook, p. 138
FAA subject matter knowledge code I08

5526. Given:

Wingtip bearing change	15°
Elapsed time between bearing change	6 minutes
Rate of fuel consumption	8.5 gph

Calculate the approximate fuel required to fly to the station.

A. 3.4 gallons.

B. 6.8 gallons.

C. 17.8 gallons.

5526. "A" is the correct answer. Determine the time to station using the formula:

Time to station = 60 × minutes flown between bearing change ÷ degrees of bearing change.

$$\text{Time} = \frac{60 \times 6 \text{ min}}{15°} = 24 \text{ min}$$

Then, determine the fuel used: 8.5 gph × 24 min ÷ 60 min = 3.4 gal.

Reference Instrument Flying Handbook, p. 138
FAA subject matter knowledge code I08

5527. Given:

Wingtip bearing change	15°
Elapsed time between bearing change	7.5 minutes
True airspeed	85 knots
Rate of fuel consumption	9.6 gph

The time, distance, and fuel required to fly to the station is

A. 30 minutes, 42.5 miles, 4.8 gallons.

B. 32 minutes, 48 miles, 5.5 gallons.

C. 48 minutes, 48 miles, 4.5 gallons.

5527. "A" is the correct answer. Time and distance are determined by the following formulas:

Time to station = 60 × minutes flown between bearing change ÷ degrees of bearing change.

$$\text{Time} = \frac{60 \times 7.5 \text{ min}}{15°} = 30 \text{ min}$$

Distance to station = TAS × minutes flown ÷ degrees of bearing change.

$$\text{Distance} = \frac{85 \text{ kt} \times 7.5 \text{ min}}{15°} = 42.5 \text{ nm}$$

Then, determine the fuel used: 9.6 gph × 30 min ÷ 60 min = 4.8 gal.

Reference Instrument Flying Handbook, p. 138
FAA subject matter knowledge code I08

5528. While maintaining a constant heading, a relative bearing of 15° doubles in 6 minutes. The time to the station is

A. 3 minutes.

B. 6 minutes.

C. 12 minutes.

5528. "B" is the correct answer. The time to the station equals the time for the relative bearing to double; in this case 6 minutes.

Reference Instrument Flying Handbook, p. 138
FAA subject matter knowledge code I08

5529. While maintaining a constant heading, the ADF needle increases from a relative bearing of 045° to 090° in 5 minutes. The time to the station being used is

A. 5 minutes.

B. 10 minutes.

C. 15 minutes.

5529. "A" is the correct answer. The time to the station equals the time for the relative bearing to double; in this case 5 minutes.

Reference Instrument Flying Handbook, p. 138

FAA subject matter knowledge code I08

5530. While cruising at 135 knots and on a constant heading, the ADF needle decreases from a relative bearing of 315° to 270° in 7 minutes. The approximate time and distance to the station being used is

A. 7 minutes and 16 miles.

B. 14 minutes and 28 miles.

C. 19 minutes and 38 miles.

5530. "A" is the correct answer. The time to the station equals the time for the relative bearing to double; in this case 7 minutes.

$$\text{Distance} = 7 \text{ min} \times 135 \text{ kt} = 15.75 \text{ miles.}$$

Reference Instrument Flying Handbook, p. 138

FAA subject matter knowledge code I08

5531. While maintaining a constant heading, a relative bearing of 10° doubles in 5 minutes. If the true airspeed is 105 knots, the time and distance to the station being used is approximately

A. 5 minutes and 8.7 miles.

B. 10 minutes and 17 miles.

C. 15 minutes and 31.2 miles.

5531. "A" is the correct answer. The time to the station equals the time for the relative bearing to double; in this case 5 minutes.

$$\text{Distance} = 5 \text{ min} \times 105 \text{ kt} = 8.75 \text{ miles.}$$

Reference Instrument Flying Handbook, p. 138

FAA subject matter knowledge code I08

5532. When checking the course sensitivity of a VOR receiver, how many degrees should the OBS be rotated to move the CDI from the center to the last dot on either side?

A. 5° to 10°.

B. 10° to 12°.

C. 18° to 20°.

5532. "B" is the correct answer. Course sensitivity may be checked by noting the number of degrees of change in course selection as you rotate the OBS to move the CDI from center to the last dot on either side. This should be between 10° and 12°.

Reference Instrument Flying Handbook, pp. 136–140

FAA subject matter knowledge code I08

5533. An aircraft 60 miles from a VOR station has a CDI indication of one-fifth deflection; this represents a course centerline deviation of approximately

A. 6 miles.

B. 2 miles.

C. 1 mile.

5533. "B" is the correct answer. One-fifth deflection is approximately one dot.

Reference Instrument Flying Handbook, p. 137

FAA subject matter knowledge code I08

5534. Refer to Fig. 20. Using instrument group 3, if the aircraft makes a 180° turn to the left and continues straight ahead, it will intercept which radial?

A. 135 radial.

B. 270 radial.

C. 360 radial.

5534. "A" is the correct answer. You currently are on a 300° heading and on the 135 radial. A left 180° turn will put you on a heading of 120°. That puts you in a position to intercept the 135 radial outboard.

Reference Instrument Flying Handbook, p. 52.

FAA subject matter knowledge code I04

5535. Refer to Fig. 20. Which instrument shows the aircraft in a position where a 180° turn would result in the aircraft intercepting the 150 radial at a 30° angle?

A. 2.

B. 3.

C. 4.

5535. "C" is the correct answer. After making the turn to intercept the 150 radial at a 30° angle, you would have to be on a heading of 180° or 120°. RMI 4 shows you heading south toward the 150° radial.

Reference Instrument Flying Handbook, p. 52

FAA subject matter knowledge code I04

5536. Refer to Fig. 20. Which instrument shows the aircraft in a position where a straight course after a 90° left turn would result in intercepting the 180 radial?

A. 2.

B. 3.

C. 4.

5536. "B" is the correct answer. After the 90° left turn, RMI 3 would indicate that you are southeast of the station. Flying a heading of 210° will be toward the 180 radial.

Reference Instrument Flying Handbook, p. 52
FAA subject matter knowledge code I04

5537. Refer to Fig. 20. Which instrument shows the aircraft to be northwest of the VORTAC?

A. 1.

B. 2.

C. 3.

5537. "B" is the correct answer. The tail of the VOR indicator on the RMI 2 indicates that you are on the 310 radial. This is northwest of the VORTAC.

Reference Instrument Flying Handbook, p. 52
FAA subject matter knowledge code I04

5538. Refer to Fig. 20. Which instrument(s) show(s) that the aircraft is getting further from the selected VORTAC?

A. 4.

B. 1 and 4.

C. 2 and 3.

5538. "A" is the correct answer. RMI 4 is the only indicator showing that you are heading away from the VORTAC.

Reference Instrument Flying Handbook, p. 52
FAA subject matter knowledge code I04

5539. While maintaining a magnetic heading of 270° and a true airspeed of 120 knots, the 360 radial of a VOR is crossed at 1237 and the 350 radial is crossed at 1244. The approximate time and distance to this station are

A. 42 minutes and 84 nautical miles.

B. 42 minutes and 91 nautical miles.

C. 44 minutes and 96 nautical miles.

5539. "A" is the correct answer. To get the estimated time en route, take the time in seconds and divide it by the degrees of bearing change: 420 sec ÷ 10° = 42 min. You can solve this problem by using the formula: TAS × minutes to fly ÷ degrees of bearing change. Thus,

$$\frac{120\,\text{kt} \times 7\,\text{min}}{10°} = 84\,\text{nm}.$$

Reference Instrument Flying Handbook, p. 138
FAA subject matter knowledge code I08

5540. Refer to Fig. 21. If the time flown between aircraft positions 2 and 3 is 13 minutes, what is the estimated time to the station?

A. 13 minutes.

B. 17 minutes.

C. 26 minutes.

5540. "A" is the correct answer. Time to the station equals the time required to complete the bearing change.

Reference Instrument Flying Handbook, p. 139
FAA subject matter knowledge code I08

5541. Refer to Fig. 22. If the time flown between aircraft positions 2 and 3 is 8 minutes, what is the estimated time to the station?

A. 8 minutes.

B. 16 minutes.

C. 48 minutes.

5541. "A" is the correct answer. Time to the station equals the time required to complete the bearing change.

Reference Instrument Flying Handbook, p. 139
FAA subject matter knowledge code I08

5542. Refer to Fig. 23. If the time flown between aircraft positions 2 and 3 is 13 minutes, what is the estimated time to the station?

A. 7.8 minutes.

B. 13 minutes.

C. 26 minutes.

5542. "B" is the correct answer. Time to the station equals the time required to complete the bearing change.

Reference Instrument Flying Handbook, p. 139
FAA subject matter knowledge code I08

5543. Refer to Fig. 24. If the time flown between aircraft positions 2 and 3 is 15 minutes, what is the estimated time to the station?

A. 15 minutes.

B. 30 minutes.

C. 60 minutes.

5543. "A" is the correct answer. Time to the station equals the time required to complete the bearing change.

Reference Instrument Flying Handbook, p. 139
FAA subject matter knowledge code I08

5544. Inbound on the 040 radial, a pilot selects the 055° radial, turns 15 to the left, and notes the time. While maintaining a constant heading, the pilot notes the time for the CDI to center is 15 minutes. Based on this information, the ETE to the station is

A. 8 minutes.

B. 15 minutes.

C. 30 minutes.

5544. "B" is the correct answer. Time to the station equals the time required to complete the bearing change.
Reference Instrument Flying Handbook, p. 139
FAA subject matter knowledge code I08

5545. Inbound on the 090 radial, a pilot rotates the OBS 010° to the left, turns 010° to the right, and notes the time. While maintaining a constant heading the pilot determines that the elapsed time for the CDI to center is 8 minutes. Based on this information, the ETE to the station is

A. 8 minutes.

B. 16 minutes.

C. 24 minutes.

5545. "A" is the correct answer. Time to the station equals the time required to complete the bearing change.
Reference Instrument Flying Handbook, p. 139
FAA subject matter knowledge code I08

5546. Inbound on the 315 radial, a pilot selects the 320 radial, turns 5° to the left, and notes the time. While maintaining a constant heading, the pilot notes the time for the CDI to center is 12 minutes. The ETE to the station is

A. 10 minutes.

B. 12 minutes.

C. 24 minutes.

5546. "B" is the correct answer. Time to the station equals the time required to complete the bearing change.
Reference Instrument Flying Handbook, p. 139
FAA subject matter knowledge code I08

5547. Inbound on the 190 radial, a pilot selects the 195 radial, turns 5° to the left, and notes the time. While maintaining a constant heading, the pilot notes the time for the CDI to center is 10 minutes. The ETE to the station is

A. 10 minutes.

B. 15 minutes.

C. 20 minutes.

5547. "A" is the correct answer. Time to the station equals the time required to complete the bearing change.
Reference Instrument Flying Handbook, p. 139
FAA subject matter knowledge code I08

5548. Refer to Figs. 25 and 25A. During the ILS RWY 13L procedure at DSM, what altitude minimum applies if the glideslope becomes inoperative?

A. 1420 ft.

B. 1360 ft.

C. 1121 ft.

5548. "B" is the correct answer. If the glideslope becomes inoperative, use the S-LOC minimums; in this case 1360 ft.
Reference Instrument Approach Plate Legend
FAA subject matter knowledge code J42

5549. What does the absence of the procedure turn barb on the plan view on an approach chart indicate?

A. A procedure turn is not authorized.

B. Teardrop-type procedure turn is authorized.

C. Racetrack-type procedure turn is authorized.

5549. "A" is the correct answer. The absence of the procedure turn barb on the plan view of an approach chart indicates that a procedure turn is not authorized.
Reference Instrument Flying Handbook, p. 184
FAA subject matter knowledge code I10

5550. When making an instrument approach at the selected alternate airport, what landing minimums apply?

A. Standard alternate minimums.

B. The IFR alternate minimums listed for that airport.

C. The landing minimums published for the type of procedure selected.

5550. "C" is the correct answer. If the pilot elects to proceed to the selected alternate airport, the alternate ceiling and visibility minimums are disregarded and the published landing minimum is applicable for the new destination utilizing facilities as appropriate to the procedure. In other words, the alternate airport becomes a new destination, and the pilot uses the landing minimum appropriate to the type of procedure selected.
Reference Instrument Flying Handbook, p. 189
FAA subject matter knowledge code I10

5551. How should the pilot make a VOR receiver check when the aircraft is located on the designated checkpoint on the airport surface?

A. Set the OBS on 180° plus or minus 4°; the CDI should center with a FROM indication.

B. Set the OBS on the designated radial. The CDI must center within plus or minus 4° of that radial with a FROM indication.

C. With the aircraft headed directly toward the VOR and the OBS set to 000°, the CDI should center within plus or minus 4° of that radial with a TO indication.

5551. "B" is the correct answer. Airborne and ground check points consist of certified radials that should be received at specific points on the airport surface or over specific landmarks while airborne in the immediate vicinity of the airport. Should an error in excess of plus or minus 4° be indicated through use of a ground check, or plus or minus 6° using the airborne check, IFR flight shall not be attempted without first correcting the source of the error.
Reference Aeronautical Information Manual, paragraph 1-4(f)
FAA subject matter knowledge code B10

5552. When using VOT to make a VOR receiver check, the CDI should be centered and the OBS should indicate that the aircraft is on the

A. 090 radial.

B. 180 radial.

C. 360 radial.

5552. "C" is the correct answer. To use the VOT service, tune in the VOT frequency on your VOR receiver. With the course deviation indicator (CDI) centered, the omnibearing selector should read 0° with the to/from indication showing FROM or the omnibearing selector should read 180° with the to/from indication showing TO.
Reference Aeronautical Information Manual, paragraph 1-4(b)
FAA subject matter knowledge code J01

5553. When the CDI needle is centered during an airborne VOR check, the omnibearing selector and the to/from indicator should read

A. within 4° of the selected radial.

B. within 6° of the selected radial.

C. 0° TO, only if you are due south of the VOR.

5553. "B" is the correct answer. Airborne and ground check points consist of certified radials that should be received at specific points on the airport surface or over specific landmarks while airborne in the immediate vicinity of the airport. Should an error in excess of plus or minus 4° be indicated through use of a ground check, or plus or minus 6° using the airborne check, IFR flight shall not be attempted without first correcting the source of the error.
Reference Aeronautical Information Manual, paragraph 1-4(f)
FAA subject matter knowledge code B10

5554. Refer to Fig. 52, point B. Given:

Sacramento (SAC) tower reports

Wind	290° at 8 knots
Highest flight altitude	1400 ft msl

If you depart for a 2-hour balloon flight, which situation best describes what ATC might require of you?

A. Your flight path will require no communication with Sacramento Approach Control.

B. You must communicate with Sacramento Approach Control because you will enter the Alert Area.

C. You will not have to contact Sacramento Approach Control.

5554. "C" is the correct answer. Class B airspace is from 1600 ft msl to 4100 ft msl. Since you will not enter the Class B airspace, no communication is required.
Reference Sectional Chart
FAA subject matter knowledge code J37

5555. For airship IFR operations off established airways, route of flight portion of an IFR flight plan should list VOR navigational aids that are no more than

A. 40 miles apart.

B. 70 miles apart.

C. 80 miles apart.

5555. "C" is the correct answer. To facilitate use of VOR, VORTAC, or TACAN aids, operate off established airways below 18,000 ft msl. Use aids not more than 80 nautical miles apart. These aids are depicted on en route low altitude charts.
Reference Aeronautical Information Manual, paragraph 5-7(c)
FAA subject matter knowledge code J15

5556. Which is true regarding the use of a standard instrument departure (SID) chart?

A. At airfields where SIDs have been established, SID usage is mandatory for IFR departures.

B. To use a SID, the pilot must possess at least the textual description of the approved standard departure.

C. To use a SID, the pilot must possess both the textual and graphic form of the approved standard departure.

5556. "B" is the correct answer. Pilots of civil aircraft operating from locations where SID procedures are effective may expect ATC clearance containing a SID. Use of a SID requires pilot possession of at least the textual description of the SID procedures.
Reference Aeronautical Information Manual, paragraph 5-26
FAA subject matter knowledge code J16

5557. Which is true regarding STARs?

A. STARs are used to separate IFR and VFR traffic.

B. STARs are established to simplify clearance delivery procedures.

C. STARs are used at certain airports to decrease traffic congestion.

5557. "B" is the correct answer. A STAR is an ATC coded departure procedure that has been established at certain airports to simplify clearance delivery procedures.
Reference Aeronautical Information Manual, paragraph 5-36
FAA subject matter knowledge code J18

5558. While being radar vectored, an approach clearance is received. The last assigned altitude should be maintained until

A. reaching the FAF.

B. advised to begin descent.

C. established on a segment of a published route or instrument approach procedure.

5558. "C" is the correct answer. While being radar vectored, the pilot, when an approach clearance is received, shall, in addition to complying with the minimum altitudes for IFR operations (§91.77), maintain his last assigned altitude unless a different altitude is assigned by ATC, or until the aircraft is established on a segment of a published route of IAP.
Reference Aeronautical Information Manual, paragraph 5-47
FAA subject matter knowledge code J18

5559. Flight service stations in the conterminous 48 United States having voice capability on VORs or radio beacons (NDBs) broadcast

A. AIRMETs and SIGMETs at 15 minutes past the hour and each 15 minutes thereafter as long as they are in effect.

B. AIRMETs and nonconvective SIGMETs upon receipt and at 15 minutes and 45 minutes past the hour for the first hour after issuance.

C. hourly weather reports at 15 and 45 minutes past each hour for those reporting stations within approximately 150 nautical miles of the broadcast station.

5559. "B" is the correct answer. Weather advisory broadcasts—FAA FSSs broadcast severe weather forecast alerts (AWW), convective SIGMETs, SIGMETs, CWAs, and AIRMETs during their valid period when they pertain to the area within 150 nautical miles of the FSS or a broadcast facility controlled by the FSS as follows: SIGMETs, CWAs, and AIRMETs are broadcast upon receipt and at 30 minute intervals at H + 15 and H + 45 for the first hour after issuance.
Reference Aeronautical Information Manual, paragraph 7-9
FAA subject matter knowledge code J25

5560. To obtain a continuous transcribed weather briefing including winds aloft and route forecasts for a cross-country flight, a pilot could monitor

A. a TWEB on a low-frequency radio receiver.

B. the regularly scheduled weather broadcast on a VOR frequency.

C. a high-frequency radio receiver tuned to en route flight advisory service.

5560. "A" is the correct answer. Transcribed weather broadcast (TWEB) equipment is provided at selected FSSs by which meteorological and aeronautical data are recorded on tape and are broadcast continuously over selected low-frequency (190–535 kHz) navigational aids (L/MF), H facilities, and/or VORs. Generally the broadcast contains route-oriented data with specially prepared NWS forecasts, inflight advisories, and winds aloft, plus preselected current information such as weather reports, NOTAMs, and special notices.
Reference Aeronautical Information Manual, paragraph 7-8
FAA subject matter knowledge code J25

5561. Refer to Figs. 26 and 26A. The final approach fix for the precision approach is located at

A. DENAY intersection.

B. Glideslope intercept.

C. ROMEN intersection/locator outer marker.

5561. "B" is the correct answer. The lightning flash symbol is used to depict the final approach on a precision approach. This is at the glideslope intercept altitude.

Reference Instrument Approach Plate Legend

FAA subject matter knowledge code J42

5562. When operating an airship under IFR with a VFR-on-top clearance, what altitude should be maintained?

A. The last IFR altitude assigned by ATC.

B. An IFR cruising altitude appropriate to the magnetic course being flown.

C. A VFR cruising altitude appropriate to the magnetic course being flown and as restricted by ATC.

5562. "C" is the correct answer. Each person operating an aircraft under IFR in level cruising flight in controlled airspace shall maintain the altitude or flight level assigned that aircraft by ATC. However, if the ATC clearance assigns "VFR conditions on-top," that person shall maintain an altitude or flight level as prescribed by § 91.159. On a magnetic course of 0° through 170°, this is any odd thousand-ft msl latitude + 500 ft (such as 3500, 5500, or 7500); or on a magnetic course of 180° through 359°, this is any even thousand-ft msl altitude + 500 ft (such as 4500, 6500, or 8500).

Reference FAR 91.179, 91.159

FAA subject matter knowledge code B10

15

Sectional Charts

STUDY GUIDE

The National Ocean Survey (NOS) publishes and sells aeronautical charts of the United States and of foreign areas. The scale of the sectional charts is 1:500,000 (1 inch = 6.86 nautical miles), and the scale of VFR terminal area charts is 1:250,000 (1 inch = 3.43 nautical miles). The aeronautical information on sectional charts includes visual and radio aids to navigation, airports, controlled airspace, restricted areas, obstructions, and related data.

Sectional Aeronautical Charts

The pilot should have little difficulty in reading these aeronautical charts. In many respects they are similar to automobile road maps. The chart name or title appears on each chart. The chart legend lists various aeronautical symbols, as well as information concerning terrain and contour elevations. By referring to the legend, aeronautical, topographical, and obstruction symbols (such as radio and television towers) can be identified. Many landmarks that can be easily recognized from the air, such as stadiums, racetracks, pumping stations, and refineries, are identified by brief descriptions, water tanks and oil tanks are shown by small black circles and are labeled accordingly. Many items are exaggerated on the chart in order to be more readily seen. Remember, however, that some information on aeronautical charts may be obsolete, depending on the date the chart was published. Check the information concerning the scheduled date of the next edition of the chart to determine that the latest edition is being used.

Relief

The elevation of land surface—relief—is shown on aeronautical charts by brown contour lines drawn at 250-ft intervals. These areas are emphasized by various tints, as indicated in the color code appearing on each chart.

Aeronautical Data

The aeronautical information on sectional charts is, for the most part, self-explanatory. Information concerning very high frequency (VHF) radio facilities, such as tower frequencies, omnidirectional radio ranges (VOR), and other VHF communications frequencies, is shown in blue. Low frequency/medium frequency (LF/MF) radio facilities are shown in magenta (purplish shade of red).

Airport and Air Navigation Lighting and Marking Aids

On sectional charts, lighting aids are shown by a blue star or dot along with certain other symbols and coded information.

COMPUTER-BASED QUESTIONS

5564. Which is true relating to the blue and magenta colors used to depict airports on sectional aeronautical charts?

A. Class E airports are shown in blue; Class C and D are magenta.

B. Class B airports are shown in blue; Class D and E are magenta.

C. Class E airports are shown in magenta; Class B, C, and D are blue.

5564. "C" is the correct answer. Airports and information pertaining to airports having an operating control tower (Class B, C, and D airspace), are shown in blue. All other airports and information pertaining to these airports are shown in magenta adjacent to the airport symbol, which is also in magenta (Class E airspace).
Reference PHOAK, p. 167
FAA subject matter knowledge code H07

5565. Refer to Fig. 52, point A. The floor of the Class E airspace above Georgetown Airport (Q61) is at

A. the surface.

B. 3788 ft msl.

C. 700 ft agl.

5565. "B" is the correct answer. The airspace areas shown as Class E extend upward from 700 ft agl when in conjunction with an airport for which an approved instrument approach procedure has been prescribed (encircled by a magenta band on sectional charts), or from 1200 ft agl unless otherwise specified. In this case the answer requires msl altitudes: 1200 ft + 2585 ft = 3788 ft msl.
Reference FAR 71.71
FAA subject matter knowledge code A64

5566. Refer to Fig. 52, point G. The floor of Class E airspace over the town of Woodland is

A. 700 ft agl over part of the town and no floor over the remainder.

B. 1200 ft agl over part of the town and no floor over the remainder.

C. both 700 ft and 1200 ft agl.

5566. "C" is the correct answer. The airspace areas shown as Class E extend upward from 700 ft agl when in conjunction with an airport for which an approved instrument approach procedure has been prescribed (encircled by a magenta band on sectional charts), or from 1200 ft agl unless otherwise specified. In this case it is both 700 ft and 1200 ft agl.
Reference FAR 71.71
FAA subject matter knowledge code J08

5567. Refer to Fig. 52, point E. The floor of the Class E airspace over University Airport (0O5) is

A. the surface.

B. 700 ft agl.

C. 1200 ft agl.

5567. "B" is the correct answer. The airspace areas shown as Class E extend upward from 700 ft agl when in conjunction with an airport for which an approved instrument approach procedure has been prescribed (encircled by a magenta band on sectional charts), or from 1200 ft agl unless otherwise specified. In this case it is 700 ft agl.
Reference FAR 71.71
FAA subject matter knowledge code J08

5568. Refer to Fig. 52, point H. The floor of the Class E airspace over the town of Auburn is

A. 1200 ft msl.

B. 700 ft agl.

C. 1200 ft agl.

5568. "C" is the correct answer. The airspace areas shown as Class E extend upward from 700 ft agl when in conjunction with an airport for which an approved instrument approach procedure has been prescribed (encircled by a magenta band on sectional charts), or from 1200 ft agl unless otherwise specified. In this case Class E airspace begins at 1200 ft agl in the unshaded areas.
Reference FAR 71.71
FAA subject matter knowledge code J08

5569. Refer to Fig. 53, point A. The thin black shaded line is most likely

A. an arrival route.

B. a military training route.

C. a state boundary line.

5569. "B" is the correct answer. A thin black shaded line is most likely a military training route.
Reference PHOAK, p. 167
FAA subject matter knowledge code H07

5570. Refer to Fig. 53, point B. The 16 indicates

A. an antenna top at 1600 ft agl.

B. the maximum elevation figure for that quadrangle.

C. the minimum safe sector altitude for that quadrangle.

5570. "B" is the correct answer. Larger boldface blue numbers denote maximum elevation figures (MEF). These figures are shown in quadrangles bounded by ticked lines of latitude and longitude, and are represented in thousands and hundreds of ft above mean sea level. The MEF is based on information available concerning the highest known feature in each quadrangle, including terrain and obstructions.
Reference PHOAK, p. 167
FAA subject matter knowledge code H07

5571. Refer to Fig. 53, point C. If at 1000 ft msl and drifting at 10 knots toward Firebaugh Airport (Q49), at what approximate distance from the airport should you begin a 100 ft/min ascent to arrive at the center of the airport at 3000 ft?

A. 3.5 nautical miles.

B. 5 nautical miles.

C. 8 nautical miles.

5571. "A" is the correct answer. Use the following steps:

$$\frac{3000 \text{ ft} - 1000 \text{ ft}}{} = 20 \text{ min}$$

$$\frac{10 \text{ kt}}{} = 0.17 \text{ mph}$$

$$0.17 \text{ mph} \times 20 \text{ minutes} = 3.4$$

Reference PHOAK, pp. 168–179
FAA subject matter knowledge code H07

5572. Refer to Fig. 54, point A. What minimum altitude is required to avoid the Livermore Airport (LVK) Class D airspace?

A. 2503 ft msl.

B. 2901 ft msl.

C. 3297 ft msl.

5572. "B" is the correct answer. Class D airspace extends up to and including 2900 ft msl. This is shown by the [29] on the chart.
Reference Sectional Chart Legend
FAA subject matter knowledge code J06

5573. Refer to Fig. 54, point E. A balloon drifts over the town of Brentwood on a magnetic course of 185° at 10 knots. If wind conditions remain the same, after 1 hour, 30 minutes the pilot

A. with no radio aboard, must be above 2900 ft msl and must have an operating transponder aboard.

B. must remain above 600 ft msl for national security reasons.

C. with no radio aboard, must be above 2900 ft msl.

5573. "C" is the correct answer. Class D airspace requires communications be established while operating in Class D airspace, so "C" is correct.
Reference FAR 91.129
FAA subject matter knowledge code J37

5574. Refer to Fig. 54, point A. Flight over Livermore Airport (LVK) at 300 ft msl

A. requires a transponder, but ATC communication is not necessary.

B. does not require a transponder or ATC communication.

C. cannot be accomplished without meeting all Class B airspace requirements.

5574. "A" is the correct answer. Although this question has no correct answer, be sure to mark an answer to receive credit.
Reference Aeronautical Information Manual
FAA subject matter knowledge code J37

5575. Refer to Fig. 52, point I. The rectangular box depicted is airspace within which

A. there is a high volume of pilot training activities or an unusual type of aerial activity, neither of which is hazardous to aircraft.

B. the flight of aircraft is prohibited.

C. the flight of aircraft, while not prohibited, is subject to restriction.

5575. "A" is the correct answer. Alert areas are depicted on aeronautical charts to inform nonparticipating pilots of areas that may contain a high volume of pilot training or an unusual type of aerial activity. Pilots should be particularly alert when flying in these areas.
Reference Aeronautical Information Manual, paragraph 3-46
FAA subject matter knowledge code J37

5576. Refer to Fig. 54, point D. The thinner outer circle depicted around San Francisco International Airport is

A. the outer segment of Class B airspace.

B. an area within which an appropriate transponder must be used from outside of the Class B airspace from the surface to 10,000 ft msl.

C. a Mode C veil boundary where a balloon may penetrate without a transponder provided it remains below 8000 ft.

5576. "B" is the correct answer. A thin blue line marks the areas where a transponder must be used from outside of the Class B airspace from the surface to 10,000 ft msl.
Reference FAR 91.215
FAA subject matter knowledge code B11

5577. When fixed-wing special visual flight rules (SVFR) operation is prohibited at an airport, the sectional aeronautical chart

A. depicts "TTTT" symbols in a circular fashion around that airport.

B. states "NO SVFR" near the airport symbol.

C. does not depict this information.

5577. "B" is the correct answer. Remember, the "TTTT" symbol is no longer being used. The chart now indicates "NO SVFR" at airports where special VFR is prohibited.
Reference Aeronautical Information Manual, paragraph 4-85
FAA subject matter knowledge code J14

5578. Refer to Fig. 53, point D. A balloon departs Mendota Airport (Q84) and drifts for a period of 1 hour and 30 minutes in a wind of 230° at 10 knots. What maximum elevation figure would assure obstruction clearance during the next 1½ hours of flight?

A. 1600 ft msl.

B. 3200 ft msl.

C. 9400 ft msl.

5578. "C" is the correct answer. The larger boldface blue numbers denote maximum elevation figures (MEF). These figures are shown in quadrangles bounded by ticked lines of latitude and longitude, and are represented in thousands and hundreds of ft above mean sea level. The MEF is based on information available concerning the highest known feature in each quadrangle, including terrain and obstructions.
Reference PHOAK, p. 167
FAA subject matter knowledge code H07

5579. Refer to Fig. 52, point C. If Sutter County Airport (O52) is departed at 0630 and at 0737 the town of Olivehurst is reached, the wind direction and speed would be approximately

A. 098° at 6 knots.

B. 098° at 17 knots.

C. 278° at 8 knots.

5579. "C" is the correct answer. Since a flight from O52 to the town of Olivehurst is west to east only "C" is correct.
Reference PHOAK, pp. 161–179
FAA subject matter knowledge code J37

5580. Refer to Fig. 52, point D. If you depart Lincoln Airport (O51) and track a true course of 075° with a groundspeed of 12 knots, your position after 1 hour and 20 minutes of flight would be over the town of

A. Foresthill.

B. Clipper Gap.

C. Weimar.

5580. "B" is the correct answer. 12 kt × 1.33 hr = 16 nm. Tracking a course of 075° would put you over Clipper Gap.
Reference PHOAK, pp. 161–179
FAA subject matter knowledge code J37

5581. Refer to Fig. 52, point D. The highest obstruction with high-intensity lighting within 10 nautical miles of Lincoln Airport (O51) is how high above the ground?

A. 1254 ft.

B. 662 ft.

C. 299 ft.

5581. "C" is the correct answer. High-intensity lighting is shown on sectional charts by a chevron with small arrows emitting from the top.
Reference Sectional Chart Legend
FAA subject matter knowledge code H61

5582. Refer to Fig. 53, point D. While drifting above the Mendota Airport (Q84) with a northwesterly wind of 8 knots, you

A. are required to contact ATC on frequency 122.9 MHz.

B. should remain higher than 2000 ft agl until you are at least 8 nautical miles southeast of the airport.

C. will be over Firebaugh Airport (Q49) in approximately 1 hour.

5582. "B" is the correct answer. Since you are drifting to the southeast, you should cross the Mendota State Wildlife Area at 2000 ft agl or higher.
Reference Sectional Chart Legend
FAA subject matter knowledge code H61

5583. Refer to Fig. 52, point F. Mosier Airport is

A. an airport restricted to use by private and recreational pilots.

B. a restricted military staging field within restricted airspace.

C. a nonpublic use airport.

5583. "C" is the correct answer. Mosier Airport is depicted as a private or nonpublic use airport.
Reference Sectional Chart Legend
FAA subject matter knowledge code J37

5584. Refer to Fig. 54, point B. After launching from Rio Vista Airport (O88) with a southerly wind, you discover flight visibility to be approximately 2½ miles, you must

A. contact Travis AFB on remote frequency 122.8 MHz to advise of your intentions.

B. stay below 1200 ft to remain in Class G.

C. stay below 700 ft to remain in Class G.

5584. "C" is the correct answer. You must descend to stay below 700 ft to remain in Class G airspace.
Reference Aeronautical Information Manual, paragraph 5-34
FAA subject matter knowledge code J37

5585. Refer to Fig. 52, point D. The terrain at the obstruction approximately 8 nautical miles east-southeast of the Lincoln Airport is approximately how much higher than the airport elevation?

A. 376 ft.

B. 835 ft.

C. 1135 ft.

5585. "B" is the correct answer.

1254 ft msl – 300 ft agl = 954 ft msl terrain height at the obstruction

954 ft msl – 119 ft msl (airport elevation) = 835 ft higher than airport elevation.
Reference PHOAK, p. 167
FAA subject matter knowledge code B08

5586. Refer to Fig. 54, point C. Given:

Departure point	Meadowlark Airport
Departure time	0710
Wind	180° at 8 knots

At 0917 the balloon should be

A. east of VINCO intersection.

B. over the town of Brentwood.

C. 3 miles south of the town of Brentwood.

5586. "A" is the correct answer. The balloon is traveling north at approximately 8 nautical miles per hour. If you took off at 0710 and the time is now 0917, you have been aloft 2 hours, 7 minutes (2.12 hours):

2.12 hr × 8 nm/hr = 17 nm. Answer "A" is correct.
Reference PHOAK, pp. 168–179
FAA subject matter knowledge code J37

5587. Refer to Fig. 54, point F. The Class C airspace at Metropolitan Oakland International (OAK) that extends from the surface upward has a ceiling of

A. both 2300 ft and 3000 ft msl.

B. 8000 ft msl.

C. 2100 ft agl.

5587. "A" is the correct answer. The T indicates that the ceiling of Class C airspace extends up to but does not include the base of the overlying Class B airspace. The bases at point F are indicated by the 21 and 30 numbers indicating 2100 ft msl and 3000 ft msl, respectively.
Reference Sectional Chart Legend
FAA subject matter knowledge code J37

5588. Refer to Fig. 53. Given:

Altitude	1000 ft agl
Position	7 nautical miles north of point E
Time	1500 local
Flight visibility	1 statute mile

You are VFR approaching Madera Airport (point E) for a landing from the north.

A. You are in violation of the FARs; you need 3 miles of visibility under VFR.

B. You are required to descend to below 700 ft agl before entering Class E airspace and may continue for landing.

C. You may descend to 800 ft agl (pattern altitude) after entering Class E airspace and continue to the airport.

5588. "B" is the correct answer. In order to avoid Class E airspace you must descend to below 700 ft agl to continue for landing.
Reference FAR 71.71
FAA subject matter knowledge code B09

5589. Refer to Fig. 52, point E. A balloon is launched at University Airport (O05) and drifts south-south-westerly toward the depicted obstruction. If the altimeter was set to 0 ft upon launch, what should it indicate if the balloon is to clear the obstruction by 500 ft above its top?

A. 520 ft.

B. 813 ft.

C. 881 ft.

5589. "B" is the correct answer. If you set the altimeter to zero at launch and want to clear the obstruction by 500 ft, subtract the elevation of the airport (68 ft) from the height of the obstacle (381 ft): 381 ft − 68 ft = 313 ft; 313 ft + 500 ft = 813 ft.
Reference PHOAK, p. 62
FAA subject matter knowledge code H03

5590. A free balloon flight through a restricted area is

A. never permitted.

B. permitted anytime, but caution should be exercised because of high-speed military aircraft.

C. permitted at certain times, but only with prior permission by the appropriate authority.

5590. "C" is the correct answer. No person may operate an aircraft within a restricted area (designated in part 73) contrary to the restrictions imposed, or within a prohibited area, unless that person has the permission of the using or controlling agency, as appropriate.
Reference FAR 91.133
FAA subject matter knowledge code B02

5591. Refer to Figs. 55 and 55A. En route on V112 from BTG VORTAC to LTJ VORTAC, the minimum altitude crossing GYMME intersection is

A. 6400 ft.

B. 6500 ft.

C. 7000 ft.

5591. "C" is the correct answer. Since you are flying from BTG VORTAC to LTJ VORTAC, you must use an altitude of 7000 ft. (Note the direction of the arrow just prior to GYMME intersection.)
Reference Low Altitude Chart Legend
FAA subject matter knowledge code J35

5592. Refer to Figs. 55 and 55A. En route on V448 from YKM VORTAC to BTG VORTAC, what minimum navigation equipment is required to identify ANGOO intersection?

A. One VOR receiver.

B. One VOR receiver and DME.

C. Two VOR receivers.

5592. "A" is the correct answer. One VOR receiver, used correctly and operating properly, will provide positive and accurate course guidance between most airports on or off Federal airways. Dual VOR receivers reduce your en route workload considerably. VOR in combination with DME provides the navigational information that, without these aids, requires constant division of attention between basic aircraft control, computation, navigation, and coordination with air traffic control.
Reference Instrument Flying Handbook, p. 133
FAA subject matter knowledge code I08

5593. Refer to Figs. 55 and 55A. En route on V468 from BTG VORTAC to YKM VORTAC, the minimum en route altitude at TROTS intersection is

A. 7100 ft.

B. 10,000 ft.

C. 11,500 ft.

5593. "C" is the correct answer. The minimum en route altitude is printed just above or near the depicted airway.
Reference Low Altitude Chart Legend
FAA subject matter knowledge code J35

5594. Refer to Figs. 27 and 27A. In the DEN ILS RWY 34R procedure, the FAF intercept altitude is

A. 7488 ft msl.

B. 7500 ft msl.

C. 9000 ft msl.

5594. "B" is the correct answer. The lightning flash symbol is used to depict the final approach on a precision approach. This is at the glideslope intercept altitude.
Reference Instrument Approach Plate Legend
FAA subject matter knowledge code J33

5595. Refer to Figs. 27 and 27A. The symbol [8100] in the MSA circle of the ILS RWY 35R procedure at DEN represents a minimum safe sector altitude within 25 nautical miles of

A. Denver VORTAC.

B. Gandi outer marker.

C. 3000 ft msl.

5595. "A" is the correct answer. Minimum safe altitudes (MSA) are published for emergency use on in-

strument approach procedure (IAP) charts except RNAV IAPs. The MSA is defined using NDB- or VOR-type facilities within 25 (normally) or 30 nautical miles (maximum) of the airport.
Reference Aeronautical Information Manual, paragraph 5-45
FAA subject matter knowledge code J18

5596. Refer to Figs. 28 and 28A. During the ILS RWY 31R procedure at DSM, the minimum altitude for glideslope interception is

A. 2365 ft msl.

B. 2500 ft msl.

C. 3000 ft msl.

5596. "A" is the correct answer. Although this question has no correct answer, be sure to mark an answer to receive credit.
Reference Approach Chart Legend
FAA subject matter knowledge code J37

5597. Refer to Figs. 28 and 28A. If the glideslope becomes inoperative during the ILS RWY 31 R procedure at DSM, what MDA applies?

A. 1157 ft.

B. 1320 ft.

C. 1360 ft.

5597. "B" is the correct answer. If the glideslope becomes inoperative, use the S-LOC minimums; in this case 1320 ft.
Reference Instrument Approach Plate Legend
FAA subject matter knowledge code J42

5598. Refer to Figs. 29 and 29A. When approaching the ATL ILS RWY 8L, how far from the FAF is the missed approach point?

A. 4.8 nautical miles.

B. 5.2 nautical miles.

C. 12.0 nautical miles.

5598. "B" is the correct answer. The speed/time portion of the approach plate (lower right corner) states "FAF to MAP 5.2 NM."
Reference Instrument Approach Plate Legend
FAA subject matter knowledge code J42

5599. Refer to Figs. 30 and 30A. When approaching the VOR/DME-A, the symbol [2800] in the MSA circle represents a minimum safe sector altitude within 25 nautical miles of

A. DEANI intersection.

B. White Cloud VORTAC.

C. Baldwin Municipal Airport.

5599. "B" is the correct answer. Minimum safe altitudes (MSA) are published for emergency use on instrument approach procedure (IAP) charts except RNAV IAPs. The MSA is defined using NDB- or VOR-type facilities within 25 (normally) or 30 nautical miles (maximum) of the airport.
Reference Aeronautical Information Manual, paragraph 5-45
FAA subject matter knowledge code J18

5600. Refer to Figs. 30 and 30A. What minimum navigation equipment is required to complete the VOR/DME-A procedure?

A. One VOR receiver.

B. One VOR receiver and DME.

C. Two VOR receivers and DME.

5600. "B" is the correct answer. One VOR must be used to track the 345° radial. DME is required to identify DEANI, HOPPR, the missed approach point, and the fix for the missed approach holding pattern.
Reference Instrument Approach Plate Legend
FAA subject matter knowledge code J42

16

Medical Facts for Pilots

STUDY GUIDE

Alcohol

Extensive research has provided a number of facts about the hazards of alcohol consumption and flying. As little as 1 ounce of liquor, one bottle of beer, or 4 ounces of wine can impair flying skills, with the alcohol consumed in these drinks being detectable in the breath and blood for at least 3 hours.

Hypoxia

Hypoxia is a state of oxygen deficiency in the body sufficient to impair functions of the brain and other organs.

Hyperventilation in Flight

Hyperventilation, or an abnormal increase in the volume of air breathed in and out of the lungs, can occur subconsciously when a stressful situation is encountered in flight. As hyperventilation "blows off" excessive carbon dioxide from the body, a pilot can experience symptoms of light-headedness, suffocation drowsiness, tingling in the extremities, and coolness and may react to them with even greater hyperventilation.

   The symptoms of hyperventilation subside within a few minutes after the rate and depth of breathing are consciously brought back under control. Early symptoms of hyperventilation and hypoxia are similar. Moreover, hyperventilation and hypoxia can occur at the same time.

Carbon Monoxide Poisoning in Flight

Carbon monoxide is a colorless, odorless, and tasteless gas contained in exhaust fumes. When breathed even in minute quantities over a period of time, it can significantly reduce the ability of the blood to carry oxygen. Consequently, effects of hypoxia occur.

Illusions Leading to Spatial Disorientation

Various complex motions and forces, and certain visual scenes encountered in flight, can create illusions of motion and position. Spatial disorientation from these illusions can be prevented only by visual reference to reliable, fixed points on the ground or to flight instruments.

Scanning for Other Aircraft

Effective scanning is accomplished with a series of short, regularly spaced eye movements that bring successive areas of the sky into the central visual field. Each movement should not exceed 10°, and each area should be observed for at least 1 second to enable detection.

COMPUTER-BASED QUESTIONS

5757. As hyperventilation progresses a pilot can experience

A. decreased breathing rate and depth.

B. heightened awareness and feeling of well-being.

C. symptoms of suffocation and drowsiness.

5757. "C" is the correct answer. Hyperventilation, or an abnormal increase in the volume of air breathed in and out of the lungs, can occur subconsciously when a stressful situation is encountered in flight. As hyperventilation "blows off" excessive carbon dioxide from the body, a pilot can experience symptoms of light-headedness, suffocation drowsiness, tingling in the extremities, and coolness and may react to them with even greater hyperventilation.
Reference PHOAK, p. 249
FAA subject matter knowledge code H50

5758. To scan properly for traffic a pilot should

A. continuously sweep the vision field.

B. concentrate on any peripheral movement detected.

C. systematically focus on different segments of the vision field for short intervals.

5758. "C" is the correct answer. Effective scanning is accomplished with a series of short, regularly spaced eye movements that bring successive areas of the sky into the central visual field. Each movement should not exceed 10°, and each area should be observed for at least 1 second to enable detection.
Reference PHOAK, p. 251
FAA subject matter knowledge code J31

5759. Which is a common symptom of hyperventilation?

A. Drowsiness.

B. Decreased breathing rate.

C. Euphoria—a sense of well-being.

5759. "A" is the correct answer. Hyperventilation, or an abnormal increase in the volume of air breathed in and out of the lungs, can occur subconsciously when a stressful situation is encountered in flight. As hyperventilation "blows off" excessive carbon dioxide from the body, a pilot can experience symptoms of light-headedness, suffocation drowsiness, tingling in the extremities, and coolness, and may react to them with even greater hyperventilation.
Reference PHOAK, p. 249
FAA subject matter knowledge code H50

5760. Which would most likely result in hyperventilation?

A. Insufficient oxygen.

B. Excessive carbon monoxide.

C. Insufficient carbon dioxide.

5760. "C" is the correct answer. Hyperventilation, or an abnormal increase in the volume of air breathed in and out of the lungs, can occur subconsciously when a stressful situation is encountered in flight. As hyperventilation "blows off" excessive carbon dioxide from the body, a pilot can experience symptoms of light-headedness, suffocation drowsiness, tingling in the extremities, and coolness, and may react to them with even greater hyperventilation.
Reference PHOAK, p. 249
FAA subject matter knowledge code J31

5761. Hypoxia is the result of which of these conditions?

A. Excessive oxygen in the bloodstream.

B. Insufficient oxygen reaching the brain.

C. Excessive carbon dioxide in the bloodstream.

5761. "B" is the correct answer. Hypoxia is a state of oxygen deficiency in the body sufficient to impair functions of the brain and other organs.
Reference PHOAK, p. 247
FAA subject matter knowledge code H50

5762. To overcome the symptoms of hyperventilation, a pilot should

A. swallow or yawn.

B. slow the breathing rate.

C. increase the breathing rate.

5762. "B" is the correct answer. The symptoms of hyperventilation subside within a few minutes after the rate and depth of breathing are consciously brought back under control.

Reference PHOAK, p. 249

FAA subject matter knowledge code H50

5763. Which is true regarding the presence of alcohol in the human body?

A. A small amount of alcohol increases vision acuity.

B. An increase in altitude decreases the adverse effect of alcohol.

C. Judgment and decision-making abilities can be adversely affected by even small amounts of alcohol.

5763. "C" is the correct answer. Extensive research has provided a number of facts about the hazards of alcohol consumption and flying. As little as 1 ounce of liquor, one bottle of beer, or 4 ounces of wine can impair flying skills, with the alcohol consumed in these drinks being detectable in the breath and blood for at least 3 hours.

Reference PHOAK, p. 247

FAA subject matter knowledge code J31

5764. Hypoxia susceptibility due to inhalation of carbon monoxide increases as

A. humidity decreases.

B. altitude increases.

C. oxygen demand increases.

5764. "B" is the correct answer. Carbon monoxide is a colorless, odorless, and tasteless gas contained in exhaust fumes. When breathed even in minute quantities over a period of time, it can significantly reduce the ability of the blood to carry oxygen. Consequently, effects of hypoxia occur.

Reference PHOAK, p. 249

FAA subject matter knowledge code J31

5765. To best overcome the effects of spatial disorientation, a pilot should

A. rely on body sensations.

B. increase the breathing rate.

C. rely on aircraft instrument indications.

5765. "C" is the correct answer. Various complex motions and forces and certain visual scenes encountered in flight can create illusions of motion and position. Spatial disorientation from these illusions can be prevented only by visual reference to reliable, fixed points on the ground or to flight instruments.

Reference PHOAK, p. 249

FAA subject matter knowledge code J31

5792. Select the true statement concerning oxygen systems that are often installed in sailplanes.

A. Most civilian aircraft oxygen systems use low-pressure cylinders for oxygen storage.

B. When aviation breathing oxygen is not available, hospital or welder's oxygen serves as a good substitute.

C. In case of a malfunction of the main oxygen system, a bailout bottle may serve as an emergency oxygen supply.

5792. "C" is the correct answer. If the main oxygen system fails, the bailout bottle may be used as a backup oxygen source.

Reference The Soaring Flight Manual

FAA subject matter knowledge code N24

Part II

Oral Test Questions

NTSB 830

1. *Is a gear-up landing in a retractable-gear airplane considered an accident?*

If no injuries occurred, it's not an accident. According to the regulation, damage limited to bent fairings or cowlings, dented skin, and damage to the landing gear, wheels, tires, flaps, brakes, or wingtips are not considered substantial damage; thus, no accident occurred.
Reference NTSB 830

2. *What is a serious injury?*

Any injury resulting from an aircraft accident that requires 48 hours or more of hospitalization.
Reference NTSB 830

3. *How long after an accident or incident must the pilot in command file a report to the NTSB?*

10 days.
Reference NTSB 830

4. *Does an inflight fire require a report?*

Yes, the operator must immediately notify the NTSB.
Reference NTSB 830

5. *Does a crewmember have to submit a report about an accident or incident?*

Yes, each crewmember must submit a report if physically able.
Reference NTSB 830

6. *Assume you taxi into an unlighted fence post during a night flight and scrape a wingtip. Must this be reported to the NTSB?*

No, since no substantial damage occurred.
Reference NTSB 830

FAR Part 1

1. *Define the following abbreviations:*

V_A
V_F
V_{FE}
V_{LE}
V_{LO}
V_{MC}
V_{NE}
V_R
V_S
V_{SO}
V_{S1}
V_X
V_Y

V_A means design maneuvering speed.

V_F means design flap speed.

V_{FE} means maximum flap extended speed.

V_{LE} means maximum landing gear extended speed.

V_{LO} means maximum landing gear operating speed.

V_{MC} means minimum control speed with the critical engine inoperative.

V_{NE} means never-exceed speed.

V_R means rotation speed.

V_S means the stalling speed or the minimum steady flight speed at which the airplane is controllable.

V_{SO} means the stalling speed or the minimum steady flight speed in the landing configuration.

V_{S1} means the stalling speed or the minimum steady flight speed obtained in a specific configuration.

V_X means speed for best angle of climb.

V_Y means speed for best rate of climb.
Reference AIM, p. 9

2. *Define interstate air commerce.*

Interstate air commerce means the carriage by aircraft of persons or property for compensation or hire, or the carriage of mail by aircraft, or the operation or navigation of aircraft in the conduct or furtherance of a business or vocation, in commerce between a place in any state of the United States, or the District of Columbia, and a place in any other state of the United States, or the District of Columbia; or between places in the same state of the United States through the airspace over any place outside thereof; or between places in the same territory or possession of the United States, or the District of Columbia.
Reference AIM, p. 4

3. *What is considered a major alteration?*

Major alteration means an alteration not listed in the aircraft, aircraft engine, or propeller specifications

that might appreciably affect weight, balance, structural strength, performance, powerplant operation, flight characteristics, or other qualities affecting airworthiness; or that is not done according to accepted practices or cannot be done by elementary operations.
Reference AIM, p. 5

4. *Define class as it pertains to aircraft.*

Class, as used with respect to the certification of aircraft, means a broad grouping of aircraft having similar characteristics of propulsion, flight, or landing. Examples include airplane, rotorcraft, glider, balloon, landplane, or seaplane.
Reference AIM, p. 2

5. *What is the difference between VFR and VMC?*

VFR refers to visual flight rules. VMC refers to visual meteorological conditions.

FAR Part 61

1. *Discuss offenses involving alcohol or drugs.*

If you are convicted of an offense involving drugs or alcohol, you could lose your pilot certificate or ratings. You must also send a written report of any motor vehicle offense involving alcohol within 60 days of the incident.
Reference FAR 61.15

2. *What area of regulations does FAR Part 61 cover?*

FAR Part 61 describes the requirements for the issuance of pilot and flight instruction certificates and ratings.
Reference FAR 61.1

3. *A temporary pilot certificate is valid for how long?*

It is good for a period of not more than 120 days.
Reference FAR 61.17

4. *Do you have to carry your pilot license with you when you fly?*

You must have a valid current pilot certificate in your personal possession when you act as pilot in command. Additionally, you must have a current and appropriate medical certificate with you.
Reference FAR 61.3

5. *What is the duration of a pilot or flight instructor certificate?*

A pilot certificate has no specific expiration date. However, an instructor rating or student pilot license expires at the end of the 24th month after the month in which it was issued.
Reference FAR 61.19

6. *What is the duration of medical certificates?*

A first-class medical certificate expires on the last day, six months after the month of the examination.

A second-class medical certificate expires on the last day, 12 months after the month of the examination.

A third-class medical certificate expires on the last day, 24 months after the month of the examination.

However, a first-class medical certificate may be used as a second class during months 7 to 12 and as a third class during months 13 to 24. A second-class medical certificate may be used as a third class during months 13 to 24.
Reference FAR 61.23

7. *How long after you change your name must you notify the FAA?*

30 days.
Reference FAR 61.25

8. *Explain how to replace a lost or destroyed pilot certificate.*

By mailing a request and $2.00 to the FAA in Oklahoma City, Oklahoma.
Reference FAR 61.29

9. *When do you need a type rating?*

To act as pilot in command in aircraft that weighs more than 12,500 pounds or is turbojet powered, you must have a valid type rating.
Reference FAR 61.31

10. *When do you need a high-performance sign-off?*

To act as pilot in command in a high-performance aircraft with more than 200 horsepower or retractable landing gear, flaps, and a controllable propeller, you must have received flight instruction and have your logbook signed off showing competency.
Reference FAR 61.31

11. *Is a single-engine land certificate all that is required to fly a tailwheel airplane?*

A tailwheel sign-off is required to act as pilot in command of a tailwheel airplane.
Reference FAR 61.31

12. *What requirement must be met to fly above 25,000 ft as pilot in command?*

High altitude training, both flight and ground, must be received if you plan on flying above 25,000 ft.
Reference FAR 61.31

13. *How long is a commercial written test valid?*

2 years.
Reference FAR 61.35

14. *What is the penalty if you are caught copying, removing, or helping another person on an FAA written test?*

Cheating is the basis for suspending or revoking any certificate or rating held. Plus, you cannot take any written test for a period of 1 year.
Reference FAR 61.37

15. *How long will you have to wait to retake a failed written test?*

For the first failure, all you need is a written statement from a CFI that you have received additional ground instruction. If you fail the second time, you have to wait 30 days.
Reference FAR 61.49

16. *Does a pilot have to log all his flight time?*

No, only that time that is necessary to meet currency requirements. However, he must log time to show he meets the flight requirement for any ratings or certificates.
Reference FAR 61.51

17. *Discuss the flight review.*

Each pilot must complete 1 hour of ground instruction and 1 hour of flight instruction and successfully complete a flight review every 24 months. The review is given by a qualified CFI.
Reference FAR 61.56

18. *Discuss the recency of flight experience requirements to act as pilot in command.*

In order to act as pilot in command you must have made three takeoffs and landings within 90 days to carry passengers or students. The takeoffs and landings must be in the same category and class to be used and they must be to a full stop if you are using a tailwheel airplane or flying at night.
Reference FAR 61.57

19. *How long do you have to notify the FAA if you change your address?*

30 days.
Reference FAR 61.60

20. *What are the eligibility requirements for a commercial pilot?*

To be eligible for a commercial pilot license, a person must be 18 years old, read, speak, and understand English, hold a current second-class medical certificate, and pass written, oral, and flight tests.
Reference FAR 61.123

21. *What are the experience requirements for a commercial pilot?*

A commercial pilot must have 250 hours of flight time and at least 50 hours of cross-country experience. Additionally he must have 10 hours of dual instruction in a complex airplane plus 10 hours in preparation for the commercial checkride. Most students do these hours concurrently.
Reference FAR 61.123

Airspace

1. *Discuss Class B airspace.*

Generally it is the airspace from the surface up to 10,000 ft msl surrounding some of the country's busiest airports, such as Atlanta, Chicago, Miami, etc. It looks like an upside-down wedding cake. All aircraft must have an ATC clearance to operate in Class B airspace.
Reference AIM, paragraph 3-12

2. *Where does Class A airspace begin?*

Class A airspace starts at 18,000 ft msl up to and including 60,000 ft or flight level 600.
Reference AIM, paragraph 3-11

3. *What type of operation must you use above 18,000 ft msl?*

You must be on an IFR flight plan.
Reference AIM, paragraph 3-11

4. *What is Class C airspace?*

Class C is the airspace from the surface to 4000 ft above the airport elevation surrounding those airports with an operating control tower and a radar approach control. The normal radius is 20 nautical miles.
Reference AIM, paragraph 3-13

5. What is the maximum speed limit in Class B airspace?

250 knots below 10,000 ft.
Reference AIM, paragraph 3-12

6. What is the definition of Class D airspace?

It's the airspace surrounding an airport with a control tower from the surface up to 2500 ft.
Reference AIM, paragraph 3-14

7. What is Class E airspace?

Basically it is all the airspace that is not Class A, B, C, or D.
Reference AIM, paragraph 3-15

FAR Part 91

1. Explain pilot-in-command authority.

The pilot in command is directly responsible for and is the final authority in the operation of that aircraft. In an emergency you can deviate from any FAR necessary to meet that emergency. A written report on the emergency must be sent to the FAA, if they request it.
Reference FAR 91.3

2. Where can an airplane's operating limitations be located?

You can find the limitations in several places: the aircraft flight manual, the pilot's handbook, markings on placards, or any combination of these.
Reference FAR 91.9

3. Explain the regulations concerning the use of alcohol or drugs.

No person may act as a crewmember if he has consumed alcohol within the preceding 8 hours or if his blood alcohol content is 0.04 percent or greater. Additionally, as pilot in command you cannot carry any passenger who appears to be under the influence of alcohol or drugs unless that person is a medical patient under a doctor's care.
Reference FAR 91.17

4. When must you use seat belts and shoulder harness?

Crewmembers (i.e., students and instructors) must keep their seat belt fastened at all times while at the controls, and must use the shoulder harness during takeoffs and landings. Additionally, the pilot in command must ensure that each passenger over the age of 2 years is briefed on the use of seat belts and shoulder harnesses. He must also notify each passenger to fasten their seat belts and shoulder harnesses prior to takeoff and landing. Each passenger must use a seat belt and shoulder harness during takeoff and landing.
Reference FAR 91.105

5. Explain the regulation concerning operating near other aircraft.

Basically, you cannot operate so close to another aircraft that you create a hazard. If you want to fly in formation, you must make arrangements with each pilot in command of each aircraft in the formation. You cannot operate an airplane carrying passengers for hire in formation flight.
Reference FAR 91.111

6. If two aircraft are approaching head on, who has the right of way?

Regardless of category, both pilots should alter course to their right. If two airplanes (same category) are converging at the same altitude but not head on, the airplane to the other's right has the right-of-way. During an approach for landing, the aircraft at the lower altitude has the right-of-way. You can't use this rule to cut in front of another pilot. Of course, any aircraft in distress has the right-of-way over others.
Reference FAR 91.113

7. What is the minimum altitude you may fly?

Legally, over congested areas, you must maintain 1000 ft above the highest obstacle and remain 2000 ft laterally away from it. If you are over an area that is "other than congested," you must maintain 500 ft agl. Over open water or sparsely populated areas you must maintain 500 ft away from any person, vessel, structure, or vehicle. This altitude must also allow for a safe emergency landing without undue hazards to persons or property at all times.
Reference FAR 91.119

8. What documents are required by FAR 91 to be on board an aircraft?

A—Valid **A**irworthiness certificate

R—FAA **R**egistration certificate

R—FCC **R**adio station license, if a radio is installed

O—**O**perating limitations

W—**W**eight and balance
Reference FAR 91

9. *Do any limitations apply to a temporary registration certificate?*

You cannot operate outside the 48 contiguous states.
Reference FAR 91

10. *In what form may the required operating limitations and weight and balance be provided?*

Placards, instrument markings, and/or an approved airplane flight manual.
Reference FAR 91

11. *As a commercial pilot, can you carry a passenger while flying in formation with another aircraft?*

No. No person may operate aircraft in formation while carrying passengers for hire.
Reference FAR 91.319

12. *What is an SFAR?*

A special Federal aviation regulation. It is usually a regulation that is not permanent in nature, but is included in another regulation. An example would be SFAR 65, Prohibition Against Certain Flight between the U.S. and Libya.
Reference SFAR 65

13. *Explain how a non-turbine-powered, small airplane may be operated with inoperative equipment or instruments.*

If the inoperative equipment or instrument is not required by an AD or § 91.33 or required for the type of flight to be conducted, the equipment may be either

1. placarded and disconnected with an entry in the aircraft logbook by pilot or mechanic that the safety of flight is not affected, or

2. removed from the aircraft with the cockpit control switch placarded, weight and balance recomputed, and an entry in the aircraft logbook by the pilot or mechanic that the safety of flight is not affected.

Reference FAR 91.33

14. *What is necessary to operate an aircraft with inoperative equipment or instruments not permitted to be inoperative by an MEL or § 91.337?*

A special flight permit or ferry permit.
Reference FAR 91.33

15. *When do your navigation lights have to be turned on?*

From sunset to sunrise.
Reference FAR 91

16. *When may a pilot log takeoffs and landings for night currency?*

From 1 hour after sunset to 1 hour before sunrise.
Reference FAR 91

17. *What color are runway lights?*

Runway lights are white.
Reference FAR 91

18. *What color are taxiway lights?*

Taxiway lights are blue.
Reference FAR 91

19. *How much fuel is required for a night VFR flight?*

Enough fuel for the flight plus 45 minutes reserve.
Reference FAR 91

20. *How should you scan for other airplanes?*

Scan the horizon in 10-degree segments making sure you look around any blind spots.
Reference FAR 91

21. *What aircraft has the right-of-way over all other aircraft?*

An aircraft in distress.
Reference FAR 91

FAR Part 125

1. *What kind of operation would be governed by FAR 125?*

FAR 125 applies to operations of aircraft that seat 20 or more passengers or have a maximum payload capacity of 6000 pounds or more. It covers operations that are not subject to FAR 121 or 135.
Reference FAR 125.1

2. *What is the definition of holding out?*

Holding out is the solicitation of passengers or cargo for hire.
Reference AC 120-12A

3. *What is the definition of common carriage?*

A common carriage is an operation that advertises a willingness to transport people or cargo from place to place for compensation.
Reference AC 120-12A

4. *Give an example of a FAR 125 operation.*

A good example would be a company utilizing a large (20 or more seats and/or 6000 pounds cargo capacity) aircraft to transport its employees from one location to another.
Reference AC 120-12A

5. Does a FAR 125 operator still have to comply with FAR 91 rules and regulations?

Yes, any FAR 125, 135, or 121 operator must still comply with FAR 91.
Reference FAR 125.23

6. What requirements must be met to act as second in command in a FAR 125 operation?

You must have at least a commercial certificate with appropriate category and class ratings and an instrument rating.
Reference FAR 125.283

7. What requirements must be met to act as pilot in command in a FAR 125 operation?

A commercial license with appropriate category, class, and type ratings, an instrument rating, and 1200 hours as a pilot, 500 hours cross-country, 100 hours at night, 75 hours instrument time, 50 of which were in actual IFR.
Reference FAR 125.281

FAR Part 135

1. FAR 135 concerns what type of operations?

The carriage in air commerce of persons or property for compensation or hire as a commercial operator (not an air carrier) in aircraft having a maximum seating capacity of less than 20 passengers or a maximum payload capacity of less than 6000 pounds, or the carriage in air commerce of persons or property in common carriage operations solely between points entirely within any state of the United States in aircraft having a maximum seating capacity of 30 seats or less or a maximum payload capacity of 7500 pounds or less.
Reference AIM, p. 200

2. As a commercial pilot, what type of operations can you do without having to meet the requirements of FAR 135?

FAR 135 does not apply to

1. Student instruction;
2. Nonstop sightseeing flights that begin and end at the same airport, and are conducted within a 25 statute mile radius of that airport;

3. Aerial work operations, including crop dusting, seeding, spraying, and bird chasing;
4. Powerline or pipeline patrol, or similar types or patrol approved by the Administrator;
5. Nonstop flights conducted within a 25 statute mile radius of the airport of takeoff carrying persons for the purpose of intentional parachute jumps;
6. The number of flights does not exceed a total of six in any calendar year.

Reference AIM, p. 201

3. What minimum flight experience requirements must you meet to be a FAR 135 pilot in VFR conditions?

As pilot in command of an aircraft under VFR unless that person:

1. Holds at least a commercial pilot certificate with appropriate category and class ratings and if required, an appropriate type rating for that aircraft, and
2. Has had at least 500 hours as a pilot, including at least 100 hours of cross-country flight time, at least 25 hours of which were at night.

Reference AIM, p. 238

4. Do you need any special license or certificate to fly under FAR 135?

No person may operate an aircraft under this part without an air taxi/commercial operator (ATCO) operating certificate and appropriate operations specifications issued under this part.
Reference AIM, p. 202

5. What is an ATCO certificate?

An air taxi commercial operator (ATCO) certificate is issued by the FAA to an individual or corporation meeting certain strict requirements including

1. An operation manual detailing how the operation will be conducted;
2. The airplane(s) to be used in the operation;
3. The names and qualifications of management personnel.

Reference FAR 135

6. How long is an ATCO certificate effective?

An ATCO certificate is effective until surrendered, suspended, or revoked.
Reference FAR 135.9(a); AIM, p. 203

7. *In what instances, and to what extent, may an ATCO certificate holder deviate from the rules of that certificate?*

In an emergency involving the safety of persons or property, the certificate holder may deviate from the rules of FAR 135 relating to aircraft and equipment and weather minimums to the extent required to meet that emergency.
Reference AIM, p. 205

8. *How long must load manifests be kept?*

The certificate holder shall keep copies of completed load manifests for at least 30 days at its principal operations base.
Reference AIM, p. 210

9. *Discuss aircraft maintenance logs and their use under FAR 135.*

Each certificate holder shall provide an aircraft maintenance log to be carried on board each aircraft for recording or deferring mechanical irregularities and their correction. The pilot in command shall enter or have entered in the aircraft maintenance log each mechanical irregularity that comes to the pilot's attention during flight time. Before each flight, the pilot in command shall determine the status of each irregularity entered in the maintenance log at the end of the preceding flight. Each person who takes corrective action concerning a reported or observed failure or malfunction of an airframe, powerplant, propeller, rotor, or appliance shall record the action taken in the aircraft maintenance log.
Reference AIM, p. 210

10. *What inflight reports must be made to ATC without specific request?*

In addition to those reports required for VFR or IFR flight, whenever a pilot operating under FAR 135 encounters a potentially hazardous meteorological condition or an irregularity in a ground communications or navigational facility in flight, the knowledge of which the pilot considers essential to the safety of other flights, the pilot shall notify an appropriate ground radio station as soon as practicable.
Reference AIM, p. 210

11. *What minimum flight experience must you meet to act as pilot in command on a FAR 135 certificate conduction during IFR operations?*

You must have a minimum of 1200 hours flight time as a pilot with 500 hours of cross-country, 100 hours of nighttime, and 75 hours of instrument time, 50 of which must have been in actual flight.
Reference FAR 135.243

12. *Discuss the contents of H.M.R. 175.*

H.M.R. 175 is the regulation concerning the carriage of hazardous material.
Reference FAR 135

13. *Explain the oxygen requirements for FAR 135 operations in unpressurized aircraft.*

The pilots must use oxygen for flights above 10,000 ft through 12,000 ft if they stay there for more than 30 minutes.
Reference FAR 135.89

Loads and Load Factors

1. *What is a good rule of thumb for determining maneuvering speed?*

An approximate maneuvering speed can be determined by multiplying the stalling speed by 1.7.
Reference PHOAK, p. 25

2. *What bank angle would you use in a steep power turn?*

50 degrees to 5 degrees is acceptable.
Reference Commercial Practical Test Standards

3. *Explain the effect of load factors during a spin.*

Since the airplane is in a stalled condition, the load factor is very small. It is usually 1 G or slightly higher.
Reference Flight Training Handbook

4. *What happens to the airplane controllability as the CG is moved aft?*

Generally speaking, the airplane becomes less controllable, especially at slow flight speeds.
Reference Flight Training Handbook

5. *What is the load factor in a 60-degree bank?*

The load factor is 2.
Reference PHOAK, p. 24

6. *What is the maximum speed at which an airplane can safely be stalled?*

V_A or designed maneuvering speed.
Reference PHOAK, p. 24

7. *What is the maximum load limit for normal, utility, and acrobatic airplanes?*

Normal load limit is 3.8. Utility load limit is 4.4.
Acrobatic load limit is 6.0.
Reference PHOAK, p. 24

8. Load limits increase dramatically after the airplane reaches approximately what bank angle?

50 degrees of bank.
Reference PHOAK, p. 24

Weight and Balance

1. Define the following terms:
1. ARM (moment ARM)
2. Center of gravity (CG)
3. Center of gravity limits
4. Datum
5. Moment
6. Mean aerodynamic chord (MAC)

1. ARM is the horizontal distance in inches from the datum line to the center of gravity of an item.
2. Center of gravity is the point about which an airplane would balance if it were suspended at that point.
3. Center of gravity limits are specific forward and aft points within which the CG must be located during flight.
4. Datum is an imaginary vertical line from which all ARM measurements are taken.
5. Moment is the product of the weight of an object multiplied by its ARM.
6. Mean aerodynamic chord is the average distance from the leading edge to the trailing edge of the wing.
Reference PHOAK, pp. 75–76

2. Define empty weight.

Empty weight is the weight of the airframe, engines, all the fixed permanent equipment, and the unused fuel and oil. You should point out that some manufacturers include *all* the oil in their empty weight.
Reference PHOAK, p. 76

3. What is tare?

Tare is the weight of the equipment used to weigh the airplane.
Reference PHOAK, p. 76

4. What does a moment, expressed in negative inches, refer to?

It indicates a component or object that is located forward of the datum line.
Reference PHOAK, p. 77

5. Assume you have an airplane with two radios. If you remove one for repair, is the airplane still legal for flight?

No, the airplane would not be in compliance with its weight and balance forms. A new weight and balance would have to be calculated minus the radio.
Reference CFI Exam Handbook, pp. 73–74

6. Compare the center of pressure with the center of gravity.

The CP is aft of the CG to create a natural tendency to nose down from a stall.

7. Compare the flight characteristics of an airplane with an aft CG to a forward CG.

Higher true airspeed due to decreased tail-down force, lower stall speed due to decreased angle of attack, less stable, less controllable.

8. What is FAA form 337?

Form 337 is used to indicate a change in aircraft weight and/or to show major alterations and repairs.
Reference FAA Form 337

9. What is zero fuel weight?

It's the maximum weight an aircraft can weigh without fuel.
Reference FAR 1

10. Work several weight and balance problems for the aircraft you are planning to use during your checkride. Remember, it's much better to work out any problems now, rather than when you are seated across from the examiner during your checkride!
Reference the approved aircraft flight manual or your pilots' handbook

Advanced Aircraft Systems

The following questions are based on the systems of a general airplane. Where appropriate, I've utilized fill-in-the-blank spaces so you can write in the correct answer referencing your aircraft's pilot operating handbook.

1. Discuss the elevators.

The elevators control the airplane's movements about its lateral axis. In essence, the elevators are an

angle of attack control. Some airplanes have a "stabilator," which serves the same purpose as the horizontal stabilizer and elevator combined.
Reference Flight Training Handbook

2. *Discuss ailerons.*

Ailerons control the airplane around its longitudinal axis. In a left turn, the right aileron deflects downward and the left aileron deflects upward. The downward deflected aileron changes the camber of that wing, increasing the angle of attack and increasing lift. At the same time, the left aileron moves upward resulting in a decreased angle of attack and a decrease in lift. This causes the airplane to roll and bank to the left. This bank causes the horizontal component of lift to pull the airplane in the desired direction of turn.
Reference Flight Training Handbook

3. *Discuss the different types of ailerons.*

There are two basic types: the differential type and the Frise type. The differential type aileron raises an aileron a greater distance than the other aileron is lowered. Since the raised aileron has more surface area exposed to the airflow (increased drag) than to the lowered aileron, adverse yaw is reduced. Frise type ailerons project the leading edge of the aileron down into the airflow, creating drag. This equalizes the drag created by the lowered aileron on the opposite wing and helps reduce adverse yaw.
Reference Flight Training Handbook

3. *Discuss the rudder.*

The rudder controls the airplane around its vertical axis. This motion is referred to as yaw. The rudder does NOT turn the airplane. Its primary purpose is to counteract the effect of adverse yaw and help to provide directional control.
Reference Flight Training Handbook

4. *Discuss the trim devices.*

Trim tabs, balance tabs, or servo tabs are secondary flight controls. They are used to reduce the force required to operate the primary flight controls.

Trim tabs are a small adjustable surface attached to the trailing edge of the aileron, rudder, or elevator. They can be adjusted in several ways, manually or by cockpit controls. The tab is deflected in the opposite direction from the primary flight control. The airflow striking the tab causes the main control surface to be deflected to a position that will correct the unbalanced condition of the airplane.

Balance tabs are basically the same as trim tabs except that they are connected to the control surface by a rod and automatically move in the opposite direction.

Servo tabs are usually found on larger airplanes. When the controls are moved, only the servo moves and the force of the airflow on the servo tab moves the primary control surface.
Reference Flight Training Handbook

5. *Discuss the purpose and use of wing flaps.*

Wing flaps enable a pilot to make a steeper approach to a landing without increasing airspeed. They also provide increased lift under certain conditions. Additionally they allow a slower approach speed, which results in a shorter landing roll. There are three basic types of flaps:

1. Plain flaps—a portion of the trailing edge of the wing that is hinged, allowing it to move downward.
2. Split flaps—hinged at the bottom of the trailing edge of the wing.
3. Fowler—extends down and back on tracks behind the trailing edge of the wing.

Reference PHOAK

6. *What instruments utilize the pitot static system?*

The altimeter, vertical speed indicator (VSI), and airspeed indicator.
Reference Flight Training Handbook

7. *Discuss how an altimeter works.*

The case houses an aneroid wafer that expands and contracts with pressure differences. The wafer is mechanically linked to the gears that drive the pointers on the dial.
Reference Instrument Flying Handbook

8. *What instruments operate off of the vacuum system?*

The directional gyro, the attitude indicator, and the turn coordinator.
Reference Instrument Flying Handbook

9. *Why is the turn coordinator electric?*

To act as a backup to the vacuum-driven instruments.
Reference Instrument Flying Handbook

10. *Explain compass errors.*

The compass is subject to numerous errors including oscillation error, which is erratic movement of the compass card by turbulence, etc.; variation error, which is due to the difference between true north and magnetic north; and deviation error, which is caused by electrical and magnetic fields in the aircraft. It also has accelerator errors: Accelerate-North, Decelerate-South. Finally, it has a turning error. This means in turns to the south, the compass will lead, while in turns to the north the compass will lag.
Reference Instrument Flying Handbook

11. *Explain the operation of a four-stroke, five-event cycle engine.*

On the intake stroke, the piston moves downward, the intake valve is open, the exhaust valve is closed, and the fuel/air mixture is taken in.

On the compression stroke; the piston moves upward, both valves are closed, and the fuel/air mixture is compressed and ignited just before top dead center.

On the power stroke, the mixture burns, the temperature and pressure rises, and the expansion forces the piston downward to power the crankshaft. Both valves are still closed.

On the exhaust stroke, the piston is moving upward, the exhaust valve opens, and burned gases are ejected.

12. *Explain the purpose of a mixture control?*

It prevents the mixture from becoming too rich at high altitudes due to the decreasing density of the air.
Reference Instrument Flying Handbook

13. *What is the result of flying with a too-rich mixture?*

You may experience spark plug fouling and loss of power.
Reference Instrument Flying Handbook

14. *What is the result of flying with a too-lean mixture?*

You may experience overheating, engine roughness, and a loss of power.
Reference Instrument Flying Handbook

15. *At what altitude should you lean the mixture?*

At any altitude, providing the mixture is enriched before increasing power above 75 percent.
Reference Instrument Flying Handbook

16. *Explain the operation of a magneto-type ignition system.*

The aircraft battery operates a starter, which rotates the engine crankshaft. This causes the magneto to rotate and produce electrical current to the spark plugs.
Reference Instrument Flying Handbook

17. *What is the purpose of a dual ignition system?*

Primarily for safety. It acts as a backup in case of the failure of one system. It also promotes complete and even combustion of the mixture.
Reference Instrument Flying Handbook

18. *Explain detonation.*

The fuel/air mixture explodes instead of burning evenly due to excessively high temperatures and pressures within the cylinder, causing a loss of power, engine overheating, preignition, and physical damage. It is extremely difficult to detect above other aircraft noises. It may be accompanied by whitish-orange exhaust flames and black puffs of smoke.
Reference Instrument Flying Handbook

19. *What causes detonation?*

The use of fuel with an octane lower than recommended by the manufacturer, running excessively lean mixtures, or excessively high manifold pressure and cylinder head temperatures.
Reference Instrument Flying Handbook

20. *Explain preignition.*

That is the ignition of the fuel/air mixture prior to the spark from the spark plugs.
Reference Instrument Flying Handbook

21. *What is one difference between detonation and preignition?*

If the conditions for detonation exist in one cylinder, all cylinders may be affected. Preignition usually affects only one or two cylinders.
Reference Instrument Flying Handbook

22. *What are the advantages of a fuel-injected engine over a carburetor type engine?*

Fuel injection engines offer better fuel economy, easier starts, a more even fuel distribution, and no carburetor icing.
Reference Instrument Flying Handbook

23. *What are the disadvantages of a fuel injected system?*

Some disadvantages are hot start problems and vapor lock.
Reference Instrument Flying Handbook

24. *Name three causes of vapor lock.*

Low fuel pressure, high fuel temperature, and excessive fuel turbulence.
Reference Instrument Flying Handbook

25. *Why is an engine stopped by shutting off fuel instead of turning off the ignition?*

To complete the burning of any fuel in the cylinders.
Reference Instrument Flying Handbook

26. *What is a P lead?*

The magneto grounding wire. Failure of this wire may lead to a "hot" pump.
Reference Instrument Flying Handbook

27. *Explain the difference between a fixed-pitch propeller and a constant-speed propeller.*

The blade angle of a fixed-pitch propeller cannot be changed in flight by the pilot. A constant-speed propeller automatically changes blade angle to maintain a constant rpm as set by the pilot.
Reference Instrument Flying Handbook

28. *What is meant by a 35-ampere battery?*

It can provide 35 amperes for 1 hour, or 1 amp for 35 hours.
Reference Instrument Flying Handbook

29. *How can a pilot decrease cylinder head temperatures?*

By decreasing manifold pressure, enriching the mixture, opening cowl flaps, or decreasing the angle of attack.
Reference Instrument Flying Handbook

30. *What is the purpose of a magneto ground check before shutting down engines?*

To ensure that the magnetos are grounded and the prop is not "hot."
Reference Instrument Flying Handbook

31. *Explain pressurized airplane characteristics.*

Pressurization in most light airplanes is taken from the turbocharger's compressor or from an engine-driven pneumatic pump. The flow of air into the cabin is controlled by an outflow valve, which maintains a constant pressure (or cabin altitude) by dumping excess pressure overboard.
Reference AC 61-107

32. *Explain oxygen systems in nonpressurized aircraft.*

Most high-altitude airplanes come equipped with a built-in oxygen system. Another option is the portable system, which normally contains a tank, regulator, masks, outlets, and a pressure gauge.
Reference AC 61-107

The following questions require that you use the pilot's operating handbook for the particular airplane you plan on using during your checkride.

Limitations

1. *What is the maximum demonstrated crosswind component?*

2. *What is*

V_{NE}?   _____ knots/mph

V_A?   _____ knots/mph

V_{FE}?   _____ knots/mph

V_F?   _____ knots/mph

V_{LE}?   _____ knots/mph

V_{LO}?   _____ knots/mph

V_{S1}?   _____ knots/mph

V_{SO}?   _____ knots/mph

3. *What is the fuel capacity?*
Usable?

4. *What type fuel does it use?*

5. *How many fuel pumps does your airplane have?*

6. *How much oil does the sump hold?*

Engines

7. *What type of engine or engines are installed?*

8. *What is the horsepower?*

Propeller

9. *What type of propeller is installed on this airplane?*

10. *How is it controlled?*

Electrical System

11. *Explain the electrical system.*

12. *Where is the battery located?*

13. *Explain an external power start.*

Environmental Systems

14. *Explain the heating system.*

15. *Does the aircraft have an oxygen system?*

16. *Explain any deicing or anti-icing system on your airplane.*

Aerodynamics

1. *What is the purpose of the elevator?*

The elevator controls movement about the lateral axis (pitch).
Reference Flight Training Handbook

2. *What is the purpose of the ailerons?*

The ailerons control movement about the longitudinal axis (roll).
Reference Flight Training Handbook

3. *Explain adverse yaw.*

The downward moving aileron in a turn produces more lift, which increases the drag.
Reference Flight Training Handbook

4. *What are some airplane designs that minimize adverse yaw?*

Frise type (differential ailerons).
Reference Flight Training Handbook

5. *What is the purpose of the rudder?*

The rudder controls movement about the vertical axis (yaw).
Reference Flight Training Handbook

6. *Explain the purpose of the horizontal and vertical stabilizers.*

They provide stability in the pitch and yaw axis.
Reference Flight Training Handbook

7. *What are spoilers?*

Spoilers are movable surfaces on the upper surface of a wing to disrupt airflow and reduce lift, allowing an increased rate of descent without increasing airspeed.
Reference Flight Training Handbook

8. *Explain the center of pressure in relation to angle of attack.*

The center of pressure moves forward as the angle of attack increases.
Reference Flight Training Handbook

9. *Explain the flight characteristics on the back side of the power curve.*

As you increase power, it produces a slower airspeed in level flight.
Reference Flight Training Handbook

10. *What are the advantages of having flaps on an airplane?*

They allow for a lower landing speed, which decreases landing distance. They also allow a steeper angle of descent without an increase in the speed, permitting short-field takeoffs and landings over obstructions.
Reference Flight Training Handbook

11. *How many different ways can flaps be controlled?*

The three basic ways are manually, electrically, and hydraulically.
Reference Flight Training Handbook

12. *What type of flaps are used on general aviation aircraft?*

There are four major types of flaps: plain, split, slotted, and fowler.
Reference Flight Training Handbook

13. *Compare lift and drag associated with various flap settings.*

By lowering the flaps you increase lift and drag. First lift is increased, then drag increases.
Reference Flight Training Handbook

14. *Name the three types of trim devices.*

Trim tabs, balance tabs, and servo tabs.
Reference Flight Training Handbook

15. *What is the purpose of trim tabs?*

To relieve the pilot of maintaining continuous control pressure.
Reference Flight Training Handbook

16. *Explain the proper method of trimming an airplane.*

Use control pressure to place the airplane in the desired attitude. Use trim to reduce control pressure.
Reference Flight Training Handbook

17. *What is a trim tab?*

A small adjustable hinged surface, located on the trailing edge of the aileron, rudder, or elevator. It is used to maintain balance in straight and level flight and during other prolonged flight conditions without the pilot having to hold pressure on the controls. This is accomplished by deflecting the tab in the direction opposite to that in which the primary control surface must be held.
Reference Flight Training Handbook

18. *What is a balance tab?*

Balancing tabs look like trim tabs and are hinged in approximately the same places as trim tabs would be. The essential difference between the two is that the balancing tab is coupled to the control surface by a rod so that when the primary control surface is moved in any direction the tab is automatically moved in the opposite direction.
Reference Flight Training Handbook

19. *What is a servo tab?*

Servo tabs are very similar in operation and appearance to trim tabs. Servo tabs are used primarily on the large airplanes. They aid the pilot in moving the control surface and in holding it in the desired position. Only the servo tab moves in response to movement of the pilot's flight control, and the force of the airflow on the servo tab then moves the primary control surface.
Reference Flight Training Handbook

20. *Does an airplane climb because of excess lift?*

No, it is a fallacy to think an airplane climbs because of excess lift. An airplane climbs because the power available is greater than the power required for flight.
Reference Flight Training Handbook

21. *Explain incidence.*

Incidence is the angle of the wing relative to the longitudinal axis of the airplane.
Reference Flight Training Handbook

22. *What is the angle of attack?*

The angle of attack is most frequently defined as the angle between the chord line of the wing and the relative wind. Generally it is sufficient to say that the angle of attack is simply the angular difference between where the wing is headed and where it is actually going.
Reference Flight Training Handbook

23. *Explain the critical angle of attack.*

When the angle of attack increases to approximately 18 to 20 degrees the air can no longer flow smoothly over the top wing surface. Because the airflow cannot make such a great change in direction so quickly, it becomes impossible for the air to follow the contour of the wing. This is the stalling or critical angle of attack.
Reference Flight Training Handbook

24. *What is aspect ratio?*

The aspect ratio is the ratio of wingspan to wing chord.
Reference Flight Training Handbook

25. *What is taper ratio?*

The taper ratio can be in planform or thickness, or both. In its simplest terms, it is a decrease from wingroot to wingtip in wing chord or wing thickness.
Reference Flight Training Handbook

26. *What is sweepback?*

Sweepback is the rearward slant of a wing, horizontal tail, or other airfoil surface.
Reference Flight Training Handbook

27. *Can a seaplane experience ground effect?*

Yes. Ground effect is due to the interference of the ground (or water) surface with the airflow patterns about the airplane in flight.
Reference Flight Training Handbook

28. *Discuss dynamic stability.*

Dynamic stability is the overall tendency that the airplane displays after its equilibrium is disturbed.
Reference Flight Training Handbook

29. *Discuss longitudinal stability.*

Longitudinal stability is the quality that makes an airplane stable about its lateral axis. It involves the pitching motion as the airplane's nose moves up and down in flight. A longitudinally unstable airplane has a tendency to dive or climb, or even to stall.
Reference Flight Training Handbook

30. *Define a stall.*

A stall results from a loss of lift on an airfoil because its critical angle of attack has been exceeded.
Reference Flight Training Handbook

31. *How do you recover from a stall?*

You must decrease the angle of attack.
Reference Flight Training Handbook

32. *Define a spin.*

A spin is an aggravated stall, resulting in autorotation.
Reference Flight Training Handbook

33. *What is required before an airplane can spin?*

The airplane must first be stalled prior to spinning.

34. *What maintenance can you perform as an owner-pilot?*

As an owner-pilot, FAR Part 43 allows you to perform certain types of inspections and maintenance on your airplane. Here is a partial list of what you can do:

1. Repair or change tires and tubes.
2. Clean, grease, or replace landing-gear wheel bearings.
3. Add air or oil to landing-gear shock struts.
4. Replace defective safety wire and cotter keys.
5. Lubricate items not requiring disassembly (other than removal of nonstructural items, such as cover plates, cowling, or fairings).
6. Replenish hydraulic fluid.
7. Refinish the exterior or interior of the aircraft (excluding balanced control surfaces when removal or disassembly of any primary structure or operating system is not required).
8. Replace side windows and safety belts.
9. Replace seats or seat parts with approved replacement parts.
10. Replace bulbs, reflectors, and lenses of position and landing lights

11. Replace cowling if removal of the propeller is not required.
12. Replace, clean, or set spark plug clearances.
13. Replace hose connections, except hydraulic connections.
14. Replace prefabricated fuel lines.
15. Replace the battery and check fluid level and specific gravity.

Although this work is allowed by FAA, each individual should make a self-analysis to determine his or her ability to perform the work satisfactorily.
Reference FAR 43

35. *If you do work on your airplane, what records must you keep?*

If any of the work discussed in the previous question is performed, an entry must be made in the appropriate logbook. The entry should contain:

1. Date the work was accomplished
2. Description of work
3. Number of hours on the aircraft
4. Certificate number of the pilot performing the work
5. Signature

Reference FAR 43

Meteorology

Briefings

1. *What is the primary source for obtaining preflight briefings and inflight weather information?*

Flight service stations (FSSs) are the primary sources for obtaining weather information.
Reference AIM, paragraph 7-3

2. *What is included in a standard weather briefing?*

A standard weather briefing includes information on adverse conditions, whether VFR flight is not recommended, a weather synopsis, the current conditions, and en route forecasts, as well as the destination forecast, winds aloft, and any pertinent NOTAMS and/or ATC delays.
Reference AIM, paragraph 7-3

3. *What is an abbreviated briefing?*

The briefer provides you with only the information you request. He assumes that you received a prior briefing or received information from another source.
Reference AIM, paragraph 7-3

4. *Can a briefer give you information on military training routes?*

Yes. He can advise you on military activity within the flight plan area.
Reference AIM, paragraph 7-3

5. *What are some other sources for obtaining weather briefings?*

1. AM weather on some PBS television stations (at the time of publishing this service was in jeopardy of being canceled).
2. DUATS—direct user access systems.
3. TWEB—transcribed weather broadcast.
4. ATIS—automatic terminal information service.
5. Private weather reporting companies.
6. Some weather service offices.

Reference AIM, paragraph 7-3

6. *Where can you find a list of flight service stations and their telephone numbers?*

In the airport facility directory.
Reference AIM, paragraph 7-2

En Route Weather Services

7. *What is an en route weather advisory service?*

EFAS is a service specifically designed to provide en route aircraft with timely and meaningful weather advisories pertinent to the type of flight intended, route of flight, and altitude. In conjunction with this service EFAS is also a central collection and distribution point for pilot-reported weather information.
Reference AIM, paragraph 7-4, p. 587

8. *What is the purpose of inflight weather advisories?*

Inflight advisories serve to notify en route pilots of the possibility of encountering hazardous flying conditions that might not have been forecast at the time of the preflight briefing. Whether or not the condition described is potentially hazardous to a particular flight is for the pilot to evaluate on the basis of experience and the operational limits of the aircraft.
Reference AIM, paragraph 7-5, p. 587

9. *What is a SIGMET?*

Significant meteorological information—an inflight advisory forecast of weather hazardous to all aircraft.
Reference Aviation Weather Services, p. 14-7

10. *What is an AIRMET?*

Airman's meteorological information—an inflight advisory forecast of conditions possibly hazardous to light aircraft or inexperienced pilots.
Reference Aviation Weather Services, p. 14-7

11. *What is a convective SIGMET?*

Convective SIGMETs are issued for the following phenomena:

1. Tornadoes.
2. Lines of thunderstorms.
3. Embedded thunderstorms.
4. Thunderstorm areas greater than or equal to thunderstorm intensity level 4 with an area coverage of $\frac{4}{10}$ (40 percent) or more.
5. Hail greater than or equal to ¾ inch in diameter and/or wind gusts to 50 knots or greater.

Reference AIM, paragraph 7-5, p. 588

12. *What is a TWEB?*

Transcribed weather broadcasts are recorded on tapes and broadcast continuously over selected low-frequency navigational aids and/or VORs. Generally the broadcast contains route-oriented data with specially prepared NWS forecasts, inflight advisories, and winds aloft, plus preselected current information such as weather reports, NOTAMs, and special notices.
Reference AIM, paragraph 7-8, p. 590

13. *During flight, ATC advises you of a convective SIGMET. If you are unsure if it pertains to your route of flight, what should you do?*

Pilots, upon hearing the alert notice, if they have not received the advisory or are in doubt, should contact the nearest FSS and ascertain whether the advisory is pertinent to their flight.
Reference AIM, paragraph 7-9, p. 590

14. *What is AWOS?*

Automated weather observing systems are automated weather reporting systems being installed at airports. These systems consist of various sensors, a processor, a computer-generated voice subsystem, and a transmitter to broadcast local, minute-by-minute weather data directly to the pilot.
Reference AIM, paragraph 7-10, p. 594

15. *Can ATC provide you with inflight weather avoidance assistance?*

To the extent possible, controllers will issue pertinent information on weather and assist pilots in avoiding such area when requested. It should be remembered that the controller's primary function is to provide safe separation between aircraft. Any additional service, such as weather avoidance assistance, can only be provided to the extent that it does not interfere with their primary function. It's also worth noting that the separation workload is generally greater than normal when weather disrupts the usual flow of traffic. ATC radar limitations and frequency congestion may also be a factor in limiting the controller's capability to provide additional service.
Reference AIM, paragraph 7-12, p. 603

16. *What is the definition of a ceiling?*

Ceiling is the height above ground (or water) level of the lowest layer of clouds or obscuring phenomenon that is reported as broken, overcast, or obscuration, and not classified as thin or partial.
Reference AIM, paragraph 7-14, p. 604.

17. *When estimating the intensity of snowfall, what would be considered light, moderate, and heavy?*

Light—visibility ⅝ statute mile or more.

Moderate—visibility less than ⅝ statute mile, but not less than ⁵⁄₁₆ statute mile.

Heavy—visibility less than ⁵⁄₁₆ statute mile.
Reference AIM, paragraph 7-18, p. 605

18. *What is a PIREP?*

Pilot weather report. FAA air traffic facilities are required to solicit PIREPs when the following conditions are reported or forecast: ceilings at or below 5000 ft, visibility at or below 5 miles, thunderstorms and related phenomena, icing of light degree or greater, turbulence of moderate degree or greater, and windshear. Pilots are urged to cooperate and promptly volunteer reports of these conditions and other atmospheric data such as cloud bases, tops, and layers; flight visibility; precipitation; visibility restrictions such as haze, smoke, and dust; wind at altitude; and temperature aloft.
Reference AIM, paragraph 7-19, p. 605

19. *What is the correct method of reporting icing conditions?*

The following describes how to report icing conditions:

1. Trace—ice becomes perceptible. Rate of accumulation is slightly greater than the rate of sublimation.
2. Light—rate of accumulation may create a problem if flight is prolonged in this environment.
3. Moderate—rate of accumulation is such that even short encounters become potentially hazardous and use of deicing/anti-icing equipment or flight diversion is necessary.
4. Severe—rate of accumulation is such that deicing/anti-icing equipment fails to reduce or control the hazard. Immediate flight diversion is necessary.

Reference AIM, paragraph 7-20, p. 607

20. *What is windshear?*

Windshear is an unexpected change in wind speed and direction that can be hazardous to aircraft operations.
Reference AIM, paragraph 7-22, p. 608

21. *What is a microburst?*

Microbursts are small-scale intense downdrafts that, on reaching the surface, spread outward in all directions from the downdraft center. This causes the presence of both vertical and horizontal windshears that can be extremely hazardous to all types and categories of aircraft, especially at low altitudes.
Reference AIM, paragraph 7-24, p. 609

Weather Reports and Forecasts

22. *What does a surface aviation weather report contain?*

A surface aviation weather report contains some or all of the following elements:

1. Station designator
2. Type and time of report
3. Sky condition and ceiling
4. Visibility
5. Weather and obstructions to vision
6. Sea level pressure
7. Temperature and dew point
8. Wind direction, speed, and character
9. Altimeter setting
10. Remarks and coded data

Reference Aviation Weather Services, p. 2-1

23. *What are the two types of surface aviation weather reports?*

The two basic types of reports are record observation (SA)—reports taken on the hour—and special reports (RS or SP)—observations taken when needed to report significant changes in weather.
Reference Aviation Weather Services, p. 2-1

24. *Read the following SA:*

BOI SA 1854 150 SCT 30 181/62/42/1304/015

Boise, 1854 Greenwich, one five thousand scattered, visibility three zero, pressure 1018.1 millibars, temperature six two, dew point four two, wind one three zero degrees at four, altimeter three zero one five.
Reference Aviation Weather Services, p. 2-16

25. *Read the following RD:*

JFK RS 1853 W5 X 1/4F 180/68/64/1804/006/RO4RVR22V30 SFC VSBY 1/2

New York Kennedy, record special, 1853 Greenwich, indefinite ceiling five hundred sky obscured, visibility one-quarter, fog, pressure 1018.0 millibars, temperature six eight, dew point six four, wind one eight zero degrees at four altimeter three zero zero six, runway four right visual range variable between two thousand two hundred ft and three thousand ft, surface visibility one half.
Reference Aviation Weather Services, p. 2-16

26. *What do the letters UA or UUA identify?*

The letters UA identify the message as a pilot report. The letters UUA identify an urgent PIREP.
Reference Aviation Weather Services, p. 3-1

27. *Read the following UA:*

UA/OV/TOL/TM2200/FL310/TP B707/TB MDT CAT 350-390

Over Toledo at 2200 GMT and flight level 31,000, a Boeing 707 reported moderate clear air turbulence from 35,000 to 39,000.
Reference Aviation Weather Services, p. 3-2

28. *What is a radar weather report?*

Thunderstorms and general areas of precipitation can be observed by radar. The report includes location of precipitation along with type, intensity, and intensity trend.
Reference Aviation Weather Services, p. 3-2

29. *Read the following radar weather report:*

JAN 1935 SPL LN 10TRWX/NC 86/40 164/60 199/115 12W
C2430 MT 440 AT 159/65 D10

Jackson, MS, special radar report at 1935 GMT. Line of echoes, ten-tenths coverage, thunderstorm, intense rain showers, no change in intensity. Center of the line extends from 86 degrees, 40 nautical miles; 164 degrees, 60 nautical miles to 199 degrees, 115 nautical miles. The line is 12 nautical miles wide (12W). (To display graphically, plot the center points on a map and connect the points with a straight line; since the thunderstorm line is 12 miles wide, it extends 6 miles either side of your plotted line.) Thunderstorm cells are moving from 240 degrees at 30 knots. Maximum top is 44,000 ft msl centered at 159 degrees, 65 nautical miles from JAN. Diameter of this cell is 10 nautical miles (D10).
Reference Aviation Weather Services, p. 3-4

30. *What is a terminal forecast?*

The terminal forecast (FT) is a description of the surface weather expected to occur at an airport. The forecast includes cloud heights and amounts, visibility, weather, and wind related to flight operations within 5 nautical miles of the center of the runway complex.
Reference Aviation Weather Services, p. 4-1

31. *What does the absence of a visibility entry mean on a terminal forecast?*

The absence of a visibility entry specifically implies visibility more than 6 statute miles.
Reference Aviation Weather Services, p. 4-1

32. *What is an area forecast?*

An area forecast (FA) is a forecast of general weather conditions over an area the size of several states. It is used to determine forecast en route weather and to interpolate conditions at airports that do not have FTs issued.
Reference Aviation Weather Services, p. 4-10

33. *How often are area forecasts issued?*

Each FA consists of a 12-hour forecast plus a 6-hour outlook.
Reference Aviation Weather Services, p. 4-10

Charts

34. *What is the purpose of the surface analysis chart?*

The surface analysis chart provides you with a ready means of locating pressure systems and fronts. It also gives you an overview of winds, temperatures, and dew point temperatures as of chart time.
Reference Aviation Weather Services, p. 5-4

35. *What is the weather depiction chart used for?*

The weather depiction chart is a choice place to begin your weather briefing and flight planning. From it you can determine general weather conditions more readily than any other source.
Reference Aviation Weather Services, p. 6-3

36. *How often are the weather depiction charts issued?*

Beginning at 01Z each day, charts are transmitted at 3 hour intervals.
Reference Aviation Weather Services, p. 6-1

37. *What is the purpose of a radar summary chart?*

The radar summary chart aids in preflight planning by identifying general areas and movement of precipitation and/or thunderstorms.
Reference Aviation Weather Services, p. 7-5

38. *What is a good rule of thumb on avoiding thunderstorm echoes?*

Avoid the most intense echoes by at least 20 miles; that is, echoes should be separated by at least 40 miles before you fly between them.
Reference Aviation Weather, p. 121

39. *PROG charts or significant weather prognostic charts are primarily used for what purpose?*

The charts show conditions as they are forecast to be at the valid time of the chart. The 36 and 48 hour surface PROG should only be used for outlook purposes, that is, to get a very generalized weather picture of conditions that are in the relatively distant future.
Reference Aviation Weather Services, p. 8-1

40. *The high-altitude significant weather prognostic chart is valid for what altitudes?*

It encompasses airspace from 24,000- to 63,000-ft pressure altitude.
References Aviation Weather Services, p. 8-7

41. *The winds aloft chart is prepared for what altitudes?*

Forecast winds and temperatures aloft charts are prepared for eight levels on eight separate panels:

6000, 9000, 12,000, 18,000, 24,000, 30,000, 34,000, and 39,000 ft msl.

42. *What does a large K index indicate?*

During the thunderstorm season, a large K index indicates conditions favorable for air mass thunderstorms.
Reference Aviation Weather Services, p. 10-3

NOTAMs

43. *What is a NOTAM?*

Notice to airmen information is that aeronautical information that could affect a pilot's decision to make a flight. It includes such information as airport or primary runway closures, changes in the status of navigational aids, ILSs, radar service availability, and other information essential to planned en route, terminal, or landing operations.
Reference AIM, paragraph 5-3, p. 516

44. *What are the different categories of NOTAMs?*

NOTAM information is classified into three categories: NOTAM(D) or distant, NOTAM(L) or local, and flight data center (FDC) NOTAMs.
Reference AIM, paragraph 5-3, p. 516

45. *Explain the different categories of NOTAMs.*

NOTAM(D) information is disseminated for all navigational facilities that are part of the National Airspace System (NAS), all public use airports, seaplane bases, and heliports listed in the Airport/Facility Directory (A/FS).

NOTAM(L) information includes such data as taxiway closures, personnel and equipment near or crossing runways, airport rotating beacon outages, and airport lighting aids that do no affect instrument approach criteria, such as VASI.

FDC NOTAMs contain such things as amendments to published IAPs and other current aeronautical charts. They are also used to advertise temporary flight restrictions caused by such things as natural disasters or large-scale public events that may generate a congestion of air traffic over a site.
Reference AIM, paragraph 5-3, p. 516

46. *How are the different NOTAMs distributed?*

The complete file of all NOTAM(D) information is maintained in a computer database at the National Communications Center (NATCOM) located in Kansas City, Missouri. This category of information is distributed automatically, appended to the hourly telecommunications system. Air traffic facilities, primarily FSSs, with service A capability have access to the entire NATCOM database of NOTAMS.

NOTAM(L) information is distributed locally only and is not attached to the hourly weather reports.

FDC NOTAMs are transmitted via service A only once and are kept on file at the FSS until published or canceled.

Reference AIM, paragraph 5-3, p. 516

Weather Avoidance Go/No Go Decisions

47. *If you inadvertently enter a thunderstorm, is it a good idea to execute a 180-degree turn?*

Don't turn back once you are in a thunderstorm. A straight course through the storm most likely will get you out of the hazard most quickly. In addition, turning maneuvers increase stresses on the aircraft.

Reference Aviation Weather, p. 123

48. *What, if any, is the significance of a temperature/dewpoint spread of 3° or less?*

Surface temperature/dewpoint spread is important in anticipating fog.

Reference Aviation Weather, p. 38

49. *Explain the different types of icing that might be encountered while flying?*

Clear ice forms when, after initial impact, the remaining liquid portion of the drop flows out over the aircraft surface gradually freezing as a smooth sheet of solid ice. This type of ice forms when drops are large, as in rain or in cumuliform clouds.

Rime ice forms when drops are small, such as those in stratified clouds or light drizzle. The liquid portion remaining after initial impact freezes rapidly before the drop has time to spread over the aircraft surface.

Mixed clear and rime icing forms when drops vary in size or when liquid drops are intermingled with snow or ice particles. It can form rapidly.

Reference Aviation Weather, pp. 92–93

50. *What two conditions are necessary for structural icing to occur?*

Two conditions are necessary for structural icing in flight: (1) the aircraft must be flying through visible water such as rain or cloud droplets, and (2) the temperature at the point where the moisture strikes the aircraft must be 0°C or colder.

Reference Aviation Weather, p. 92

51. *Why should you always remove any frost prior to takeoff?*

A heavy coat of hard frost will cause a 5 to 10 percent increase in stall speed. Even a small amount of frost on airfoils may prevent an aircraft from becoming airborne at normal takeoff speed. Also possible is that once airborne, an aircraft could have insufficient margin of airspeed above stall so that moderate gusts or turning flight could produce incipient or complete stalling.

Reference Aviation Weather, p. 102

52. *For a thunderstorm to form, what three things must be present?*

For a thunderstorm to form, the air must have sufficient water vapor, an unstable lapse rate, and an initial upward boost (lifting) to start the storm process in motion.

Reference Aviation Weather, p. 111

53. *Explain the life cycle of a thunderstorm.*

A thunderstorm cell during its life cycle progresses through three stages: the cumulus, the mature, and the dissipating.

Reference Aviation Weather, p. 111

54. *Discuss each stage of a thunderstorm's life.*

Cumulus stage—Although most cumulus clouds do not grow into thunderstorms, every thunderstorm begins as a cumulus. The key feature of the cumulus stage is an updraft. The updraft varies in strength and extends from very near the surface to the cloud top. Growth rate of the cloud may exceed 3000 ft per minute, so it is inadvisable to attempt to climb over rapidly building cumulus clouds.

Mature stage—Precipitation beginning to fall from the cloud base is the signal that a downdraft has developed and a cell has entered the mature stage.

Dissipating stage—Downdrafts characterize the dissipating stage of the thunderstorm cell and the storm dies rapidly.

Reference Aviation Weather Services, p. 111

55. *Why is hail one of the greatest hazards during a thunderstorm?*

Hail competes with turbulence as the greatest thunderstorm hazard to aircraft. Large hail occurs with severe thunderstorms usually built to great heights. Eventually the hailstones fall, possibly some dis-

tance from the storm core. Hail has been observed in clear air several miles from the parent thunderstorm.
Reference Aviation Weather, p. 115

56. Is frequent lightning a sign of a dissipating thunderstorm?

No, the more frequent the lightning the more severe the thunderstorm.
Reference Aviation Weather, p. 116

Performance

1. What makes your airplane climb?

Climb depends on the reserve power or thrust. Reserve power is the available power over and above that required to maintain horizontal flight at a given speed.
Reference Flight Training Handbook

2. What determines the angle of climb?

The maximum angle of climb would occur where there exists the greatest difference between thrust available and thrust required. The maximum excess thrust and angle of climb will occur at some speed just above the stall speed. Thus, if it is necessary to clear an obstacle after takeoff, the propeller-powered airplane will attain maximum angle of climb at an airspeed close to, if not at, the takeoff speed.
Reference Flight Training Handbook

3. What determines rate of climb?

The rate of climb depends on the difference between the power available and the power required, or the excess power.
Reference Flight Training Handbook

4. What is the absolute ceiling?

The absolute ceiling of the airplane produces zero rate of climb.
Reference Flight Training Handbook

5. What is the service ceiling?

The service ceiling is the altitude at which the airplane is unable to climb at a rate greater than 100 ft per minute.
Reference Flight Training Handbook

6. What is power loading?

Power loading is expressed in pounds per horsepower and is obtained by dividing the total weight of the airplane by the rated horsepower of the engine. It is a significant factor in the airplane's takeoff and climb capabilities.
Reference Flight Training Handbook

7. What is wing loading?

Wing loading is expressed in pounds per square foot and is obtained by dividing the total weight of the airplane in pounds by the wing area (including ailerons) in square feet. It is the airplane's wing loading that determines the landing speed.
Reference Flight Training Handbook

8. How do you achieve maximum range in your airplane?

The maximum range condition is obtained at the maximum lift/drag ratio (L/D_{max}), and it is important to note that for a given airplane configuration, the maximum lift/drag ratio occurs at a particular angle of attack and lift coefficient and is unaffected by weight or altitude.
Reference Flight Training Handbook

9. Why is using the published takeoff speeds in the aircraft flight manual so important?

The effect of proper takeoff speed is especially important when runway lengths and takeoff distances are critical. The takeoff speeds specified in the airplane's flight handbook are generally the minimum safe speed at which the airplane can become airborne. Any attempt to take off below the recommended speed could mean that the airplane may stall, be difficult to control, or have a very low initial rate of climb. An excessive airspeed at takeoff may improve the initial rate of climb and "feel" of the airplane, but will produce an undesirable increase in takeoff distance.
Reference Flight Training Handbook

10. How does an increase in density altitude affect takeoff performance?

An increase in density altitude can produce a twofold effect on takeoff performance: greater takeoff speed and decreased thrust, and reduced net accelerating force.
Reference Flight Training Handbook

11. During a short-field maximum braking effort, how important is aerodynamic drag in helping you slow down?

The use of aerodynamic drag is applicable only for deceleration to 60 or 70 percent of the touchdown speed. At speeds less than 60 to 70 percent of the

touchdown speed, aerodynamic drag is so slight as to be of little use, and braking must be utilized to produce continued deceleration of the airplane.
Reference Flight Training Handbook

You should work on several takeoff and landing performance problems using the airplane flight manual of the airplane you plan on using during the checkride. Work them at both maximum gross weight and with the anticipated load during your checkride.

Flight and Navigation Instruments

1. *What is the range of the VOR?*

Because the equipment is VHF, the signals transmitted are subjected to line-of-sight restrictions. Therefore, its range varies in direct proportion to the altitude of the receiving equipment. Generally the reception range of the signals at an altitude of 1000 ft above ground level is about 40 to 45 miles. This distance increases with altitude.
Reference PHOAK

2. *What are the classes of VORs?*

There are three classes: T—terminal; L—low altitude; and H—high altitude.
Reference PHOAK

3. *How often must a VOR check be done for IFR use?*

Every 30 days.
Reference PHOAK

4. *Discuss the pitot-static system.*

There are two major parts of the pitot-static system: the impact pressure chamber and lines, and the static pressure chamber and lines. This system provides the source of air pressure for the operation of the altimeter, vertical speed indicator (vertical velocity indicator), and the airspeed indicator.
Reference PHOAK

5. *How does the altimeter operate?*

The pressure altimeter is simply an aneroid barometer that measures the pressure of the atmosphere at the level where the altimeter is located and presents an altitude indication in feet.
Reference PHOAK

6. *Why must you adjust the altimeter for the effects of nonstandard pressure and temperature?*

If a flight is made from a high-pressure area to a low-pressure area without adjusting the altimeter, the actual altitude of the airplane will be lower than the indicated altitude; and when flying from a low-pressure area to high-pressure area, the actual altitude of the airplane will be higher than the indicated altitude. The adjustment made by the pilot to compensate for nonstandard pressures does not compensate for nonstandard temperatures. Therefore, if terrain or obstacle clearance is a factor in the selection of a cruising altitude, particularly at higher altitudes, remember to anticipate that colder-than-standard temperature will place the aircraft lower than the altimeter indicates.
Reference PHOAK

7. *List the different types of altitude.*

Absolute altitude—The vertical distance of an aircraft above the terrain.

Indicated altitude—That altitude read directly from the altimeter (uncorrected) after it is set to the current altimeter setting.

Pressure altitude—The altitude indicated when the altimeter setting window is adjusted to 29.92 in. Hg. This is the standard datum plane, a theoretical plane where air pressure (corrected to 15°C) is equal to 29.92 in. Hg.

True altitude—The true vertical distance of the aircraft above sea level; the actual altitude.

Density altitude—This altitude is pressure altitude corrected for nonstandard temperature variation. When conditions are standard, pressure altitude and density altitude are the same. This is an important altitude because it is directly related to the aircraft's takeoff and climb performance.
Reference PHOAK

8. *What is pressure altitude used for?*

Pressure altitude is used for computer solutions to determine density altitude, true altitude, true airspeed, etc.
Reference PHOAK

9. *How does the airspeed indicator operate?*

When the aircraft moves through the air, the pressure on the pitot line becomes greater than the pressure in the static lines. This difference in pressure is registered by the airspeed pointer on the face of the instrument, which is calibrated in miles per hour, knots, or both.
Reference PHOAK

10. *Name the different kinds of airspeed.*

There are three kinds of airspeed that the pilot should understand: indicated airspeed, calibrated airspeed, and true airspeed.

Indicated airspeed—The direct instrument reading obtained from the airspeed indicator, uncorrected for variations in atmospheric density, installation error, or instrument error.

Calibrated airspeed (CAS)—The indicated airspeed corrected for installation error and instrument error.

True airspeed—The airspeed indicator is calibrated to indicate true airspeed under standard sea level conditions—that is, 29.92 in. Hg and 15°C.
Reference PHOAK

11. *Discuss the turn and slip indicator.*

The turn and slip indicator is actually a combination of two instruments: the turn needle and the ball or inclinometer. The needle is gyro-operated to show rate of turn, and the ball reacts to gravity and/or centrifugal force to indicate the need for directional trim.

The turn needle indicates the rate at which the aircraft is turning about its vertical axis.

The ball is actually a balance indicator, and is used as a visual aid to determine coordinated use of the aileron and rudder control. It indicates the "quality" of the turn or whether the aircraft has the correct angle of bank for the rate of turn.
Reference PHOAK

12. *What principle does the heading indicator operate on?*

The operation of the heading indicator depends on the principle of rigidity in space.
Reference PHOAK

13. *What are the limits of the attitude indicator?*

The pitch and bank limits depend on the make and model of the instrument. Limits in the banking plane are usually from 100 degrees to 110 degrees, and the pitch limits are usually from 60 degrees to 70 degrees.

14. *What is a DF steer and when is it used?*

A DF steer provides directional guidance to a pilot who is lost. It is provided by an FSS or tower equipped with VHF homing capability.
Reference Flight Training Manual

15. *Explain the use of the transponder codes 7700, 7600, and 7500.*

7700 is used in an emergency; 7600 is used for lost communications; and 7500 is the hijack code.
Reference Flight Training Manual

Sectional Charts

1. *What is the scale of a sectional chart?*

8 statute miles per inch or 7 nautical miles per inch.
Reference Flight Training Manual

2. *Where are changes to published charts found?*

You can find changes in FDC NOTAMs and the Airport Facilities Directory.
Reference Flight Training Manual

3. *Prior to your checkride, plan a long VFR cross-country flight. This will help you during your checkride, especially if it has been a while since you have done any cross-country work.*

Medical Facts for Pilots

1. *Discuss the regulation concerning the use of oxygen.*

FAR 91.21(a) requires that the flightcrew be provided with and use oxygen at cabin pressure altitudes above 12,500 ft msl up to and including 14,000 ft msl for that portion of the flight that is at those altitudes for more than 30 minutes. The crew must use oxygen continuously above 14,000 ft msl. Also, above cabin altitudes of 15,000 ft msl, all occupants must be provided with oxygen.
Reference FAR 91.211

2. *Discuss some physiological hazards or problems associated with high-altitude flight.*

By far, hypoxia is one of the greatest threats to pilots operating at high altitudes. Hypoxia is the lack of sufficient oxygen in the body cells and tissues. Symptoms of hypoxia vary from individual to individual, but the most dangerous and earliest effect of hypoxia is impairment of judgment. Some other symptoms include behavioral changes, poor coordination, cyanosis, sweating, poor vision, dizziness, and tingling or warm sensations. Additionally, there are four major types of hypoxia:

1. *Hypoxic hypoxia* is caused by insufficient partial pressure of oxygen in the inhaled air resulting from the reduced oxygen pressure at altitude.

2. *Histotoxic hypoxia* is the inability of the body cells to use oxygen because of impaired

cellular respiration. This type of hypoxia cannot be cured by supplemental oxygen because oxygen absorption is impaired at the tissue level. This type of hypoxia is caused by alcohol or drug use and is another excellent reason to abstain from alcohol or drug use prior to flight.

3. *Hypemic hypoxia* is a reduction in the oxygen-carrying capacity of the blood. This may be caused by a contamination of the blood with other gases besides oxygen as a result of anemia, carbon monoxide poisoning, or excessive smoking.

4. *Stagnant hypoxia* is an oxygen deficiency resulting from poor circulation because of the failure of the circulatory system to pump blood to the tissues. This is basically a coronary artery disease and the pilot should be grounded.

Reference AC 61-107

3. *Discuss pressurized airplane characteristics.*

Pressurization in most light airplanes is taken from the turbocharger's compressor or from an engine-driven pneumatic pump. The flow of air into the cabin is controlled by an outflow valve, which maintains a constant pressure (or cabin altitude) by dumping excess pressure overboard.
Reference AC 61-107

4. *Discuss oxygen systems in nonpressurized aircraft.*

Most high-altitude airplanes come equipped with a built-in oxygen system. Another option is the portable system, which normally contains a tank, regulator, masks, outlets, and a pressure gauge.
Reference AC 61-107

5. *Why should a pilot only use aviation oxygen and not medical oxygen or another type of oxygen?*

Aviation oxygen is 100 percent pure oxygen and does not contain impurities. Medical oxygen contains water vapor, which could freeze in the regulator when flying at high altitudes.
Reference AC 61-107

6. *Discuss rapid decompression.*

Decompression is defined as the inability of the airplane's pressurization system to maintain its designed pressure schedule. A rapid decompression normally results in cabin fog because of the fast drop in temperature and the change in relative humidity.

Exposure to windblast and very cold temperatures are also hazardous.
Reference AC 61-107

7. *Discuss the recovery techniques of a rapid decompression.*

Oxygen masks should be placed on immediately, followed by a rapid descent to a safe altitude.
Reference AC 61-107

8. *Explain autokinesis.*

It is an illusion caused by staring at a fixed light on a dark night. It may cause you to think the light is moving.
Reference Flight Training Manual

9. *Explain an elevator illusion.*

It is an abrupt upward vertical acceleration, such as an updraft, that creates the illusion of being in a climb.
Reference Flight Training Manual

10. *What is a false horizon?*

It is an illusion of not being correctly aligned with the horizon due to sloping cloud layers.
Reference Flight Training Manual

11. *How does runway slope affect a pilot's visual perception during an approach to a landing?*

An upsloping runway makes the pilot think that he is higher than he actually is, causing a lower approach.
Reference Flight Training Manual

Federal Aviation Administration Subject Matter Knowledge Codes

To determine the knowledge area in which a particular question was incorrectly answered, compare the subject matter code(s) on AC Form 8080-2, Airmen Written Test Report, to the subject matter outline that follows. The total number of test items missed may differ from the number of subject matter codes shown on AC Form 8080-2, since you may have missed more than one question in a certain subject matter code.

FAR 1   **Definitions and Abbreviations**

A01   General Definitions
A02   Abbreviations and Symbols

FAR 25   **Airworthiness Standards: Transport Category Airplanes**

A03   General
A04   Flight
A05   Structure
A06   Design and Construction
A07   Powerplant
A08   Equipment
A09   Operating Limitations and Information

FAR 23   **Airworthiness Standards: Normal, Utility, and Acrobatic Category Aircraft**

A10   General

FAR 21   **Certification Procedures for Products and Parts**

A11   General

FAR 39   **Airworthiness Directives**

A13   General
A14   Subpart B—Airworthiness Directives

FAR 43   **Maintenance, Preventive Maintenance, Rebuilding, and Alteration**

A15   General
A16   Appendixes

FAR 61   **Certification: Pilots and Flight Instructors**

A20   General
A21   Aircraft Ratings and Special Certificates
A22   Student Pilots
A23   Private Pilots
A24   Commercial Pilots
A25   Airline Transport Pilots
A26   Flight Instructors
A27   Appendix A: Practical Test Requirements for Airline Transport Pilot Certificates and Associated Class and Type Ratings
A28   Appendix B: Practical Test Requirements for Rotorcraft Airline Transport Pilot Certificates with a Helicopter Class Rating and Associated Type Ratings
A29   Recreational Pilot

FAR 63   **Certification: Flight Crewmembers Other Than Pilots**

A30   General
A31   Flight Engineers
A32   Flight Navigators

FAR 65   **Certification: Airmen Other Than Flight Crewmembers**

A40   General
A41   Aircraft Dispatchers
A44   Parachute Riggers

L53   AC 91-14D, Altimeter Setting Sources

L57   AC 91-43, Unreliable Airspeed Indications

L59   AC 91-46, Gyroscopic Instruments—Good Operating Practices

L61   AC 91-50, Importance of Transponder Operation and Altitude Reporting

L62   AC 91-51, Airplane Deice and Anti-Ice Systems

L70   AC 91-67, Minimum Equipment Requirements for General Aviation Operations Under FAR Part 91

L80   AC 103-4, Hazard Associated with Sublimation of Solid Carbon Dioxide (Dry Ice) Aboard Aircraft

L90   AC 105-2C, Sport Parachute Jumping

M01   AC 120-12A, Private Carriage Versus Common Carriage of Persons or Property

M02   AC 120-27B, Aircraft Weight and Balance Control

M08   AC 120-58, Large Aircraft Ground Deicing

M13   AC 121-195-1A, Operational Landing Distances for Wet Runways; Transport Category Airplanes

M51   AC 20-117, Hazards Following Ground Deicing and Ground Operations in Conditions Conducive to Aircraft Icing

M52   AC 00-2.5, Advisory Circular Checklist

American Soaring Handbook—Soaring Society of America

N01   A History of American Soaring

N02   Training

N03   Ground Launch

N04   Airplane Tow

N05   Meteorology

N06   Cross-Country and Wave Soaring

N07   Instruments and Oxygen

N08   Radio, Rope, and Wire

N09   Aerodynamics

N10   Maintenance and Repair

Soaring Flight Manual—Jeppesen-Sanderson, Inc.

N20   Sailplane Aerodynamics

N21   Performance Considerations

N22   Flight Instruments

N23   Weather for Soaring

N24   Medical Factors

N25   Flight Publications and Airspace

N26   Aeronautical Charts and Navigation

N27   Computations for Soaring

N28   Personal Equipment

N29   Preflight and Ground Operations

N30   Aerotow Launch Procedures

N31   Ground Launch Procedures

N32   Basic Flight Maneuvers and Traffic

N33   Soaring Techniques

N34   Cross-Country Soaring

Taming The Gentle Giant—Taylor Publishing

O01   Design and Construction of Balloons

O02   Fuel Source and Supply

O03   Weight and Temperature

O04   Flight Instruments

O05   Balloon Flight Tips

O06   Glossary

Flight Instructor Manual—Balloon Federation of America

O10   Flight Instruction Aids

O11   Human Behavior and Pilot Proficiency

O12   The Flight Check and the Designated Examiner

Propane Systems—Balloon Federation of America, 1991

O20   Propane Glossary

O21   Tanks

O22   Burners, Valves, and Hoses

O23   Refueling, Contamination, and Fuel Management

O24   Repair and Maintenance

Powerline Excerpts—Balloon Federation of America

O30   Excerpts

Balloon Ground School—Balloon Publishing Company

O46   Balloon Operations

Goodyear Airship Operations Manual

P01   Buoyancy

P02   Aerodynamics

P03   Free Ballooning

P04   Aerostatics

P05　Envelope
P06　Car
P07　Powerplant
P08　Airship Ground Handling
P11　Operating Instructions
P12　History
P13　Training

The Parachute Manual, Para Publishing

P31　Regulations
P32　The Parachute Rigger Certificate
P33　The Parachute Loft
P34　Parachute Materials
P35　Personnel Parachute Assemblies
P36　Parachute Component Parts
P37　Maintenance, Alteration, and Manufacturing Procedures
P38　Design and Construction
P39　Parachute Inspecting and Packing
P40　Glossary/Index

The Parachute Manual, Vol. II, Para Publishing

P51　Parachute Regulations
P52　The Parachute Rigger's Certificate
P53　The Parachute Loft
P54　Parachute Materials
P55　Personnel Parachute Assemblies
P56　Parachute Component Parts
P57　Maintenance, Alteration, and Manufacturing
P58　Parachute Design and Construction
P59　Parachute Inspection and Packing
P60　Appendix
P61　Conversion Tables
P62　Product/Manufacturer-Index
P63　Name and Manufacturer Index
P64　Glossary-Index

AC 65-9A　Airframe and Powerplant Mechanics General Handbook

S01　Mathematics
S02　Aircraft Drawings
S03　Aircraft Weight and Balance
S04　Fuels and Fuel Systems
S05　Fluid Lines and Fittings
S06　Aircraft Hardware, Materials, and Processes
S07　Physics
S08　Basic Electricity
S09　Aircraft Generators and Motors
S10　Inspection Fundamentals
S11　Ground Handling, Safety, and Support Equipment

AC 65-12A　Airframe and Powerplant Mechanics Powerplant Handbook

S12　Theory and Construction of Aircraft Engines
S13　Induction and Exhaust Systems
S14　Engine Fuel and Metering Systems
S15　Engine Ignition and Electrical Systems
S16　Engine Starting Systems
S17　Lubrication and Cooling Systems
S18　Propellers
S19　Engine Fire Protection Systems
S20　Engine Maintenance and Operation

AC 65-15A　Airframe and Powerplant Mechanics Airframe Handbook

S21　Aircraft Structures
S22　Assembly and Rigging
S23　Aircraft Structural Repairs
S24　Ice and Rain Protection
S25　Hydraulic and Pneumatic Power Systems
S26　Landing Gear Systems
S27　Fire Protection Systems
S28　Aircraft Electrical Systems
S29　Aircraft Instrument Systems
S30　Communications and Navigation Systems
S31　Cabin Atmosphere Control Systems

EA-ITP-G[2]　A and P Technician General Textbook—International Aviation Publishers (IAP), Inc., Second Edition

S32　Mathematics
S33　Physics
S34　Basic Electricity
S35　Electrical Generators and Motors
S36　Aircraft Drawings
S37　Weight and Balance
S38　Fluid Lines and Fittings
S39　Aircraft Hardware
S40　Corrosion and Its Control
S41　Nondestructive Inspection
S42　Ground Handling and Servicing
S43　Maintenance Forms and Records
S44　Maintenance Publications

EA-ITP-P[2]　A and P Technician Powerplant Textbook—IAP, Inc., Second Edition

S45　Reciprocating Engines
S46　Turbine Engines

S47 Engine Removal and Replacement
S48 Engine Maintenance and Operation
S49 Induction and Exhaust Systems
S50 Engine Fuel and Fuel Metering
S51 Engine Ignition and Electrical Systems
S52 Engine Lubrication and Cooling Systems
S53 Engine Fire Protection Systems
S54 Propellers

EA-ITP-A[2] **A and P Technician Airframe Textbook—IAP, Inc., Second Edition**

S55 Aircraft Structures
S56 Assembly and Rigging
S57 Aircraft Fabric Covering
S58 Aircraft Painting and Finishing
S59 Aircraft Metal Structural Repair
S60 Aircraft Wood and Composite Structural Repair
S61 Aircraft Welding
S62 Ice and Rain Control Systems
S63 Hydraulic and Pneumatic Power Systems
S64 Aircraft Landing Gear Systems
S65 Fire Protection Systems
S66 Aircraft Electrical Systems
S67 Aircraft Instrument Systems
S68 Aircraft Fuel Systems
S69 Aircraft Cabin Atmosphere Control Systems

EA-TEP-2 **Aircraft Gas Turbine Powerplants—IAP, Inc.**

S70 History of Turbine Engine Development
S71 Jet Propulsion Theory
S72 Turbine Engine Design and Construction
S73 Engine Familiarization
S74 Inspection and Maintenance
S75 Lubrication Systems
S76 Fuel Systems
S77 Compressor Anti-Stall Systems
S78 Anti-Icing Systems
S79 Starter Systems
S80 Ignition Systems
S81 Engine Instrument Systems
S82 Fire/Overheat Detection and Extinguishing Systems for Turbine Engines
S83 Engine Operation

The Aircraft Gas Turbine Engine and Its Operation—United Technologies Corporation, Pratt Whitney, 1988

T01 Gas Turbine Engine Fundamentals
T02 Gas Turbine Engine Terms
T03 Gas Turbine Engine Components
T04 Gas Turbine Engine Operation
T05 Operational Characteristics of Jet Engines
T06 Gas Turbine Engine Performance

Aircraft Powerplants—McGraw-Hill, Sixth Edition

T07 Aircraft Powerplant Classification and Progress
T08 Reciprocating-Engine Construction and Nomenclature
T09 Internal-Combustion Engine Theory and Performance
T10 Lubricants and Lubricating Systems
T11 Induction Systems, Superchargers, Turbochargers, and Exhaust Systems
T12 Basic Fuel Systems and Carburetors
T13 Fuel Injection Systems
T14 Reciprocating-Engine Ignition and Starting Systems
T15 Operation, Inspection, Maintenance and Troubleshooting of Reciprocating Engines
T16 Reciprocating-Engine Overhaul Practices
T17 Gas Turbine Engine: Theory, Construction, and Nomenclature
T18 Gas Turbine Engine: Fuels and Fuel Systems
T19 Turbine-Engine Lubricants and Lubricating Systems
T20 Ignition and Starting Systems of Gas-Turbine Engines
T21 Turbofan Engines
T22 Turboprop Engines
T23 Turboshaft Engines
T24 Gas-Turbine Operation, Inspection, Troubleshooting, Maintenance, and Overhaul
T25 Propeller Theory, Nomenclature, and Operation
T26 Turbopropellers and Control Systems

T27 Propeller Installation, Inspection, and Maintenance

T28 Engine Control System

T29 Engine Indicating and Warning Systems

EA-ATD-2   Aircraft Technical Dictionary— IAP, Inc.

T30 Definitions

Aircraft Basic Science—McGraw-Hill, Sixth Edition

T31 Fundamentals of Mathematics

T32 Science Fundamentals

T33 Basic Aerodynamics

T34 Airfoils and their Applications

T35 Aircraft in Flight

T36 Aircraft Drawings

T37 Weight and Balance

T38 Aircraft Materials

T39 Fabrication Techniques and Processes

T40 Aircraft Hardware

T41 Aircraft Fluid Lines and their Fittings

T42 Federal Aviation Regulations and Publications

T43 Ground Handling and Safety

T44 Aircraft Inspection and Servicing

Aircraft Maintenance and Repair—McGraw-Hill, Fifth Edition

T45 Aircraft Systems

T46 Aircraft Hydraulic and Pneumatic Systems

T47 Aircraft Landing Gear Systems

T48 Aircraft Fuel Systems

T49 Environmental Systems

T50 Aircraft Instruments and Instrument Systems

T51 Auxiliary Systems

T52 Assembly and Rigging

EA-363   Transport Category Aircraft Systems—IAP, Inc.

T53 Types, Design Features and Configurations of Transport Aircraft

T54 Auxiliary Power Units, Pneumatic, and Environmental Control Systems

T55 Anti-Icing Systems and Rain Protection

T56 Electrical Power Systems

T57 Flight Control Systems

T58 Fuel Systems

T59 Hydraulic Systems

T60 Oxygen Systems

T61 Warning and Fire Protection Systems

T62 Communications, Instruments, and Navigational Systems

T63 Miscellaneous Aircraft Systems and Maintenance Information

Aircraft Electricity and Electronics—McGraw-Hill, Fourth Edition

T64 Fundamentals of Electricity

T65 Applications of Ohm's Law

T66 Aircraft Storage Batteries

T67 Alternating Current

T68 Electrical Wire and Wiring Practices

T69 Electrical Control Devices

T70 Electric Measuring Instruments

T71 DC Generators and Related Control Circuits

T72 Alternators, Inverters, and Related Controls

T73 Electric Motors

T74 Power Distribution Systems

T75 Design and Maintenance of Aircraft Electrical Systems

T76 Radio Theory

T77 Communication and Navigation Systems

T78 Weather Warning Systems

T79 Electrical Instruments and Autopilot Systems

T80 Digital Electronics

FAA Accident Prevention Program Bulletins

V01 FAA-P-8740-2, Density Altitude

V02 FAA-P-8740-5, Weight and Balance

V03 FAA-P-8740-12, Thunderstorms

V04 FAA-P-8740-19, Flying Light Twins Safely

V05 FAA-P-8740-23, Planning your Takeoff

V06 FAA-P-8740-24, Tips on Winter Flying

V07 FAA-P-8740-25, Always Leave Yourself an Out

V08 FAA-P-8740-30, How to Obtain a Good Weather Briefing

V09 FAA-P-8740-40, Wind Shear

V10 FAA-P-8740-41, Medical Facts for Pilots

V11   FAA-P-8740-44, Impossible Turns
V12   FAA-P-8740-48, On Landings, Part I
V13   FAA-P-8740-49, On Landings, Part II
V14   FAA-P-8740-50, On Landings, Part III
V15   FAA-P-8740-51, How to Avoid a Midair Collision
V16   FAA-P-8740-52, The Silent Emergency

EA-338   Flight Theory for Pilots—IAP, Inc., Third Edition

W01   Introduction
W02   Air Flow and Airspeed Measurement
W03   Aerodynamic Forces on Airfoils
W04   Lift and Stall
W05   Drag
W06   Jet Aircraft Basic Performance
W07   Jet Aircraft Applied Performance
W08   Prop Aircraft Basic Performance
W09   Prop Aircraft Applied Performance
W10   Helicopter Aerodynamics
W11   Hazards of Low Speed Flight
W12   Takeoff Performance
W13   Landing Performance
W14   Maneuvering Performance
W15   Longitudinal Stability and Control
W16   Directional and Lateral Stability and Control
W17   High Speed Flight

Fly the Wing—Iowa State University/Ames, Second Edition

X01   Basic Aerodynamics
X02   High-Speed Aerodynamics
X03   High-Altitude Machs
X04   Approach Speed Control and Target Landings
X05   Preparation for Flight Training
X06   Basic Instrument Scan
X07   Takeoffs
X08   Rejected Takeoffs
X09   Climb, Cruise, and Descent
X10   Steep Turns
X11   Stalls
X12   Unusual Attitudes
X14   Maneuvers at Minimum Speed
X15   Landings: Approach Technique and Performance
X16   ILS Approaches
X17   Missed Approaches and Rejected Landings
X18   Category II and III Approaches
X19   Nonprecision and Circling Approaches
X20   Weight and Balance
X21   Flight Planning
X22   Icing
X23   Use of Anti-Ice and Deice
X24   Winter Operation
X25   Thunderstorm Flight
X26   Low-Level Wind Shear

Technical Standard Orders

Y60   TSO-C23b, Parachute
Y61   TSO-C23c, Personnel Parachute Assemblies

Practical Test Standards

Z01   FAA-S-8081-6, Flight Instructor Practical Test Standards for Airplane
Z02   FAA-S-8081-7, Flight Instructor Practical Test Standards for Rotorcraft
Z03   FAA-S-8081-8, Flight Instructor Practical Test Standards for Glider

NOTE: AC 00-2, Advisory Circular Checklist, transmits the status of all FAA advisory circulars (ACs), as well as FAA internal publications and miscellaneous flight information such as AIM, Airport/Facility Directory, written test question books, practical test standards, and other material directly related to a certificate or rating. To obtain a free copy of the AC 00-2, send your request to:

U.S. Department of Transportation
Utilization and Storage Section, M-443.2
Washington, DC 20590

Index

Illustrations are indicated in **boldface**.

Figures

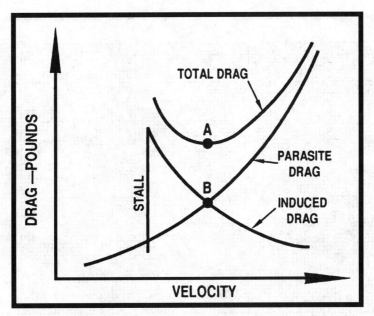

Fig. 1. Drag vs. speed

GROSS WEIGHT 2750 LBS		ANGLE OF BANK			
		LEVEL	30°	45°	60°
POWER		GEAR AND FLAPS UP			
ON	MPH	62	67	74	88
	KTS	54	58	64	76
OFF	MPH	75	81	89	106
	KTS	65	70	77	92
		GEAR AND FLAPS DOWN			
ON	MPH	54	58	64	76
	KTS	47	50	56	66
OFF	MPH	66	71	78	93
	KTS	57	62	68	81

Fig. 2. Stall speeds

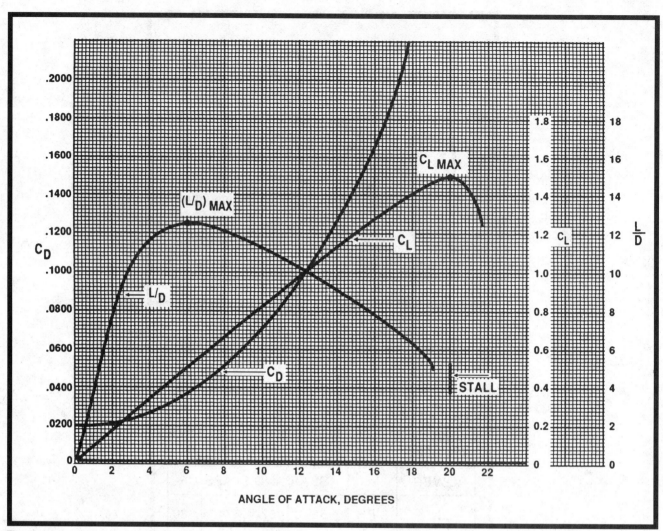

Fig. 3. Angle of attack, degrees

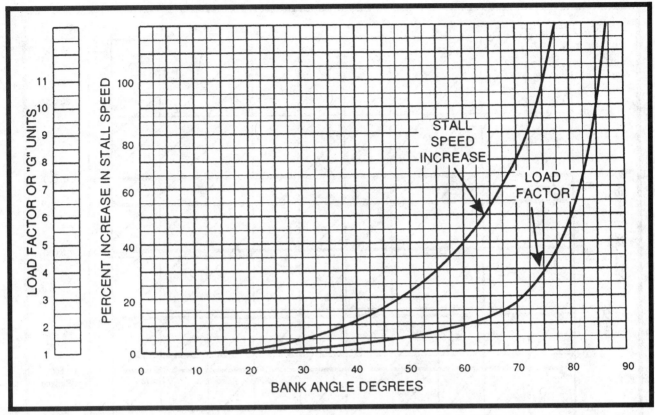

Fig. 4. Stall speed/load factor

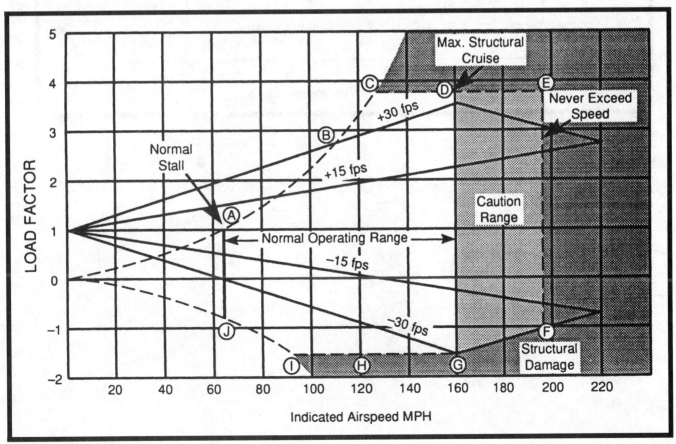

Fig. 5. Velocity vs. G-loads

242

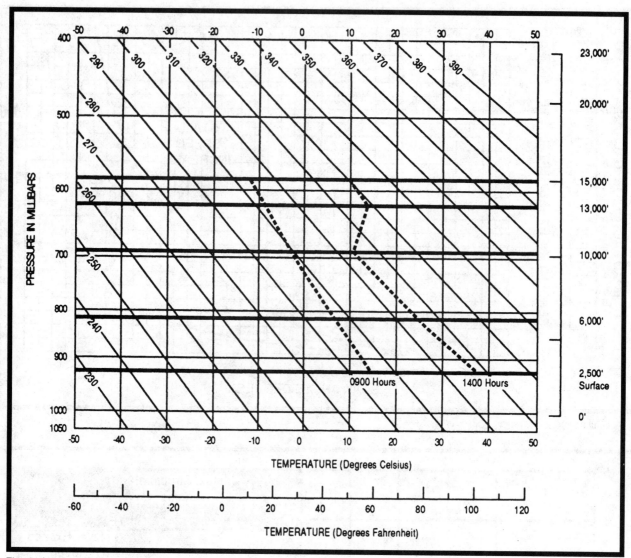

Fig. 6. Adiabatic chart

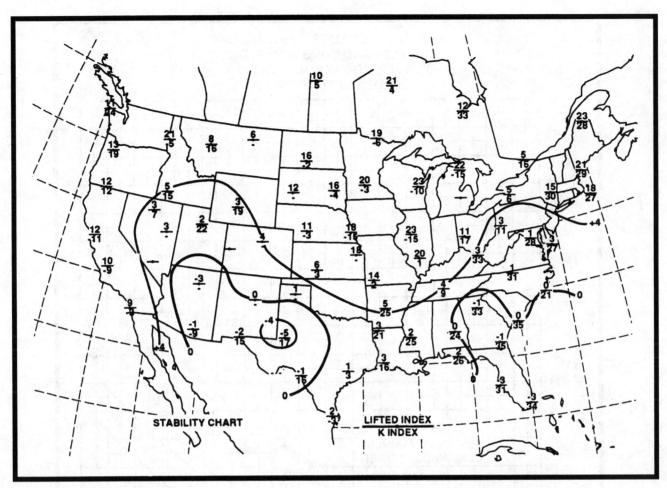

Fig. 7. Stability chart

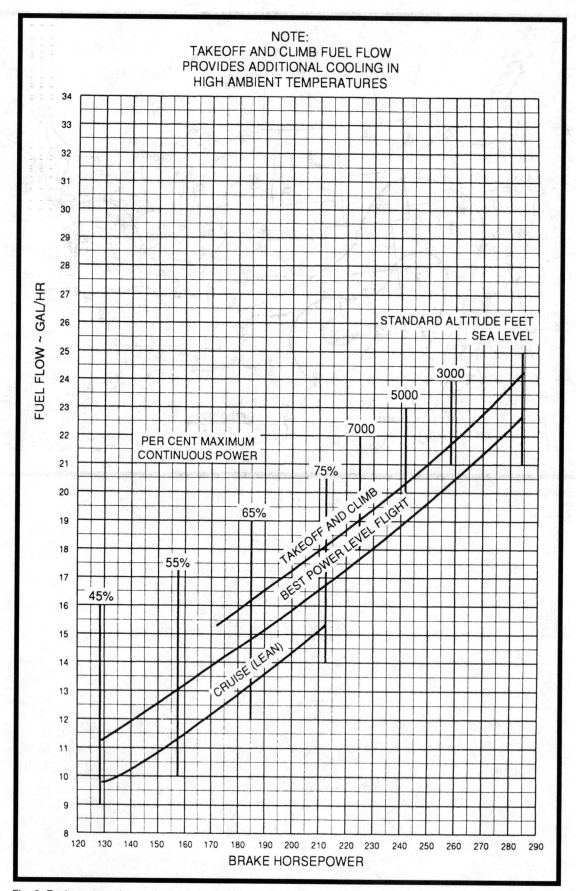

Fig. 8. Fuel consumption vs. brake horsepower

NORMAL CLIMB – 100 KIAS

CONDITIONS:
Flaps Up
Gear Up
2550 RPM
25 Inches MP or Full Throttle
Cowl Flaps Open
Standard Temperature

MIXTURE SETTING	
PRESS ALT	PPH
S.L. to 4000	108
8000	96
12,000	84

NOTES:
1. Add 12 pounds of fuel for engine start, taxi and takeoff allowance.
2. Increase time, fuel and distance by 10% for each 10 °C above standard temperature.
3. Distances shown are based on zero wind.

WEIGHT LBS	PRESS ALT FT	RATE OF CLIMB FPM	FROM SEA LEVEL		
			TIME MIN	FUEL USED POUNDS	DISTANCE NM
3800	S.L.	580	0	0	0
	2000	580	3	6	6
	4000	570	7	12	12
	6000	470	11	19	19
	8000	365	16	27	28
	10,000	265	22	37	40
	12,000	165	32	51	59
3500	S.L.	685	0	0	0
	2000	685	3	5	5
	4000	675	6	11	10
	6000	565	9	16	16
	8000	455	13	23	23
	10,000	350	18	31	33
	12,000	240	25	41	46
3200	S.L.	800	0	0	0
	2000	800	2	4	4
	4000	795	5	9	8
	6000	675	8	14	13
	8000	560	11	19	19
	10,000	445	15	25	27
	12,000	325	20	33	37

Fig. 9. Fuel, time, and distance to climb

MAXIMUM RATE OF CLIMB

CONDITIONS:
Flaps Up
Gear Up
2700 RPM
Full Throttle
Mixture Set at Placard Fuel Flow
Cowl Flaps Open
Standard Temperature

MIXTURE SETTING	
PRESS ALT	PPH
S.L.	138
4000	126
8000	114
12,000	102

NOTES:
1. Add 12 pounds of fuel for engine start, taxi and takeoff allowance.
2. Increase time, fuel and distance by 10% for each 10 °C above standard temperature.
3. Distances shown are based on zero wind.

WEIGHT LBS	PRESS ALT FT	CLIMB SPEED KIAS	RATE OF CLIMB FPM	FROM SEA LEVEL		
				TIME MIN	FUEL USED POUNDS	DISTANCE NM
3800	S.L.	97	860	0	0	0
	2000	95	760	2	6	4
	4000	94	660	5	12	9
	6000	93	565	9	18	14
	8000	91	465	13	26	21
	10,000	90	365	18	35	29
	12,000	89	265	24	47	41
3500	S.L.	95	990	0	0	0
	2000	94	885	2	5	3
	4000	93	780	5	10	7
	6000	91	675	7	16	12
	8000	90	570	11	22	17
	10,000	89	465	15	29	24
	12,000	87	360	20	38	32
3200	S.L.	94	1135	0	0	0
	2000	92	1020	2	4	3
	4000	91	910	4	9	6
	6000	90	800	6	14	10
	8000	88	685	9	19	14
	10,000	87	575	12	25	20
	12,000	86	465	16	32	26

Fig. 10. Fuel, time, and distance to climb

| | | | | | Gross Weight- 2300 Lbs.
Standard Conditions
Zero Wind   Lean Mixture |

NOTE: Maximum cruise is normally limited to 75% power.

ALT.	RPM	% BHP	TAS MPH	GAL / HOUR	38 GAL (NO RESERVE)		48 GAL (NO RESERVE)	
					ENDR. HOURS	RANGE MILES	ENDR. HOURS	RANGE MILES
2500	2700	86	134	9.7	3.9	525	4.9	660
	2600	79	129	8.6	4.4	570	5.6	720
	2500	72	123	7.8	4.9	600	6.2	760
	2400	65	117	7.2	5.3	620	6.7	780
	2300	58	111	6.7	5.7	630	7.2	795
	2200	52	103	6.3	6.1	625	7.7	790
5000	2700	82	134	9.0	4.2	565	5.3	710
	2600	75	128	8.1	4.7	600	5.9	760
	2500	68	122	7.4	5.1	625	6.4	790
	2400	61	116	6.9	5.5	635	6.9	805
	2300	55	108	6.5	5.9	635	7.4	805
	2200	49	100	6.0	6.3	630	7.9	795
7500	2700	78	133	8.4	4.5	600	5.7	755
	2600	71	127	7.7	4.9	625	6.2	790
	2500	64	121	7.1	5.3	645	6.7	810
	2400	58	113	6.7	5.7	645	7.2	820
	2300	52	105	6.2	6.1	640	7.7	810
10,000	2650	70	129	7.6	5.0	640	6.3	810
	2600	67	125	7.3	5.2	650	6.5	820
	2500	61	118	6.9	5.5	655	7.0	830
	2400	55	110	6.4	5.9	650	7.5	825
	2300	49	100	6.0	6.3	635	8.0	800

Fig. 11. Cruise and range performance

PRESSURE ALTITUDE 18,000 FEET

CONDITIONS:
4000 Pounds
Recommended Lean Mixture
Cowl Flaps Closed

NOTE
For best fuel economy at 70% power or less, operate at 6 PPH leaner than shown in this chart or at peak EGT.

RPM	MP	20 °C BELOW STANDARD TEMP -41 °C			STANDARD TEMPERATURE -21 °C			20 °C ABOVE STANDARD TEMP -1 °C		
		% BHP	KTAS	PPH	% BHP	KTAS	PPH	% BHP	KTAS	PPH
2500	30	---	---	---	81	188	106	76	185	100
	28	80	184	105	76	182	99	71	178	93
	26	75	178	99	71	176	93	67	172	88
	24	70	171	91	66	168	86	62	164	81
	22	63	162	84	60	159	79	56	155	75
2400	30	81	185	107	77	183	101	72	180	94
	28	76	179	100	72	177	94	67	173	88
	26	71	172	93	67	170	88	63	166	83
	24	66	165	87	62	163	82	58	159	77
	22	61	158	80	57	155	76	54	150	72
2300	30	79	182	103	74	180	97	70	176	91
	28	74	176	97	70	174	91	65	170	86
	26	69	170	91	65	167	86	61	163	81
	24	64	162	84	60	159	79	56	155	75
	22	58	154	77	55	150	73	51	145	65
2200	26	66	166	87	62	163	82	58	159	77
	24	61	158	80	57	154	76	54	150	72
	22	55	148	73	51	144	69	48	138	66
	20	49	136	66	46	131	63	43	124	59

Fig. 12. Cruise performance

MAXIMUM RATE OF CLIMB

CONDITIONS:
Flaps Up
Gear Up
2600 RPM
Cowl Flaps Open
Standard Temperature

PRESS ALT	MP	PPH
S.L. TO 17,000	35	162
18,000	34	156
20,000	32	144
22,000	30	132
24,000	28	120

NOTES:
1. Add 16 pounds of fuel for engine start, taxi and takeoff allowance.
2. Increase time, fuel and distance by 10% for each 10 °C above standard temperature.
3. Distances shown are based on zero wind.

WEIGHT LBS	PRESS ALT FT	CLIMB SPEED KIAS	RATE OF CLIMB FPM	FROM SEA LEVEL		
				TIME MIN	FUEL USED POUNDS	DISTANCE NM
4000	S.L.	100	930	0	0	0
	4000	100	890	4	12	7
	8000	100	845	9	24	16
	12,000	100	790	14	38	25
	16,000	100	720	19	52	36
	20,000	99	515	26	69	50
	24,000	97	270	37	92	74
3700	S.L.	99	1060	0	0	0
	4000	99	1020	4	10	6
	8000	99	975	8	21	13
	12,000	99	915	12	33	21
	16,000	99	845	17	45	30
	20,000	97	630	22	59	42
	24,000	95	370	30	77	60
3400	S.L.	97	1205	0	0	0
	4000	97	1165	3	9	5
	8000	97	1120	7	19	12
	12,000	97	1060	11	29	18
	16,000	97	985	15	39	26
	20,000	96	760	19	51	36
	24,000	94	485	26	65	50

Fig. 13. Fuel, time, and distance to climb

NORMAL CLIMB – 110 KIAS

CONDITIONS:
Flaps Up
Gear Up
2500 RPM
30 Inches Hg
120 PPH Fuel Flow
Cowl Flaps Open
Standard Temperature

NOTES:
1. Add 16 pounds of fuel for engine start, taxi and takeoff allowance.
2. Increase time, fuel and distance by 10% for each 7 °C above standard temperature.
3. Distances shown are based on zero wind.

WEIGHT LBS	PRESS ALT FT	RATE OF CLIMB FPM	FROM SEA LEVEL		
			TIME MIN	FUEL USED POUNDS	DISTANCE NM
4000	S.L.	605	0	0	0
	4000	570	7	14	13
	8000	530	14	28	27
	12,000	485	22	44	43
	16,000	430	31	62	63
	20,000	365	41	82	87
	S.L.	700	0	0	0
3700	4000	665	6	12	11
	8000	625	12	24	23
	12,000	580	19	37	37
	16,000	525	26	52	53
	20,000	460	34	68	72
	S.L.	810	0	0	0
	4000	775	5	10	9
3400	8000	735	10	21	20
	12,000	690	16	32	31
	16,000	635	22	44	45
	20,000	565	29	57	61

Fig. 14. Fuel, time, and distance to climb

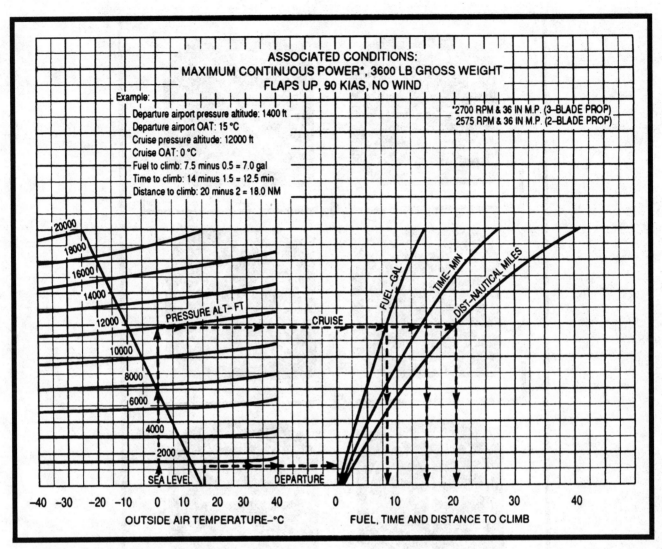

Fig. 15. Fuel, time, and distance to climb

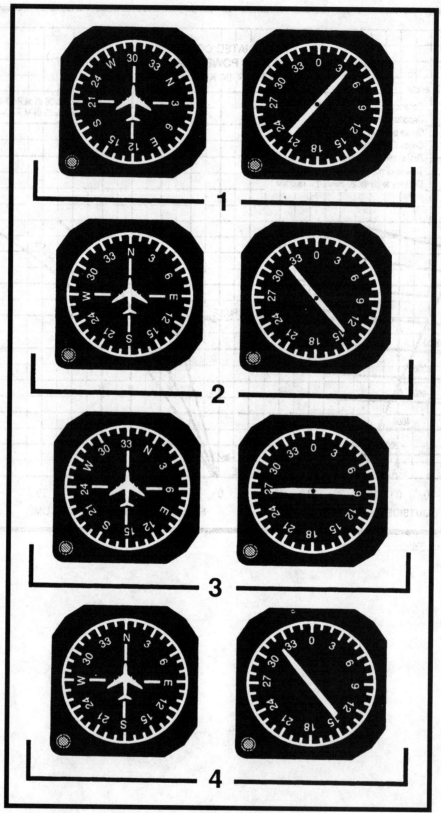

Fig. 16. Magnetic compass/ADF

253

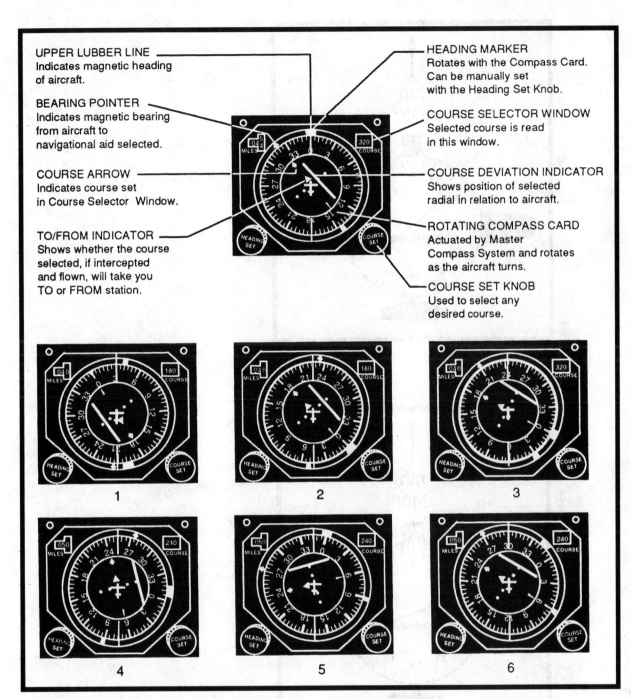

UPPER LUBBER LINE
Indicates magnetic heading
of aircraft.

BEARING POINTER
Indicates magnetic bearing
from aircraft to
navigational aid selected.

COURSE ARROW
Indicates course set
in Course Selector Window.

TO/FROM INDICATOR
Shows whether the course
selected, if intercepted
and flown, will take you
TO or FROM station.

HEADING MARKER
Rotates with the Compass Card.
Can be manually set
with the Heading Set Knob.

COURSE SELECTOR WINDOW
Selected course is read
in this window.

COURSE DEVIATION INDICATOR
Shows position of selected
radial in relation to aircraft.

ROTATING COMPASS CARD
Actuated by Master
Compass System and rotates
as the aircraft turns.

COURSE SET KNOB
Used to select any
desired course.

Fig. 17. Horizontal situation indicator (HSI)

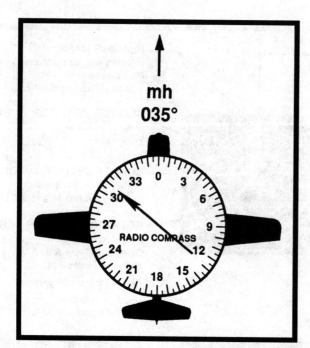

Fig. 18. Magnetic heading/radio compass

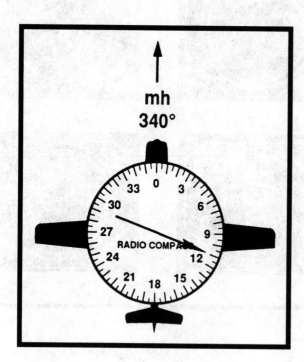

Fig. 19. Magnetic heading/radio compass

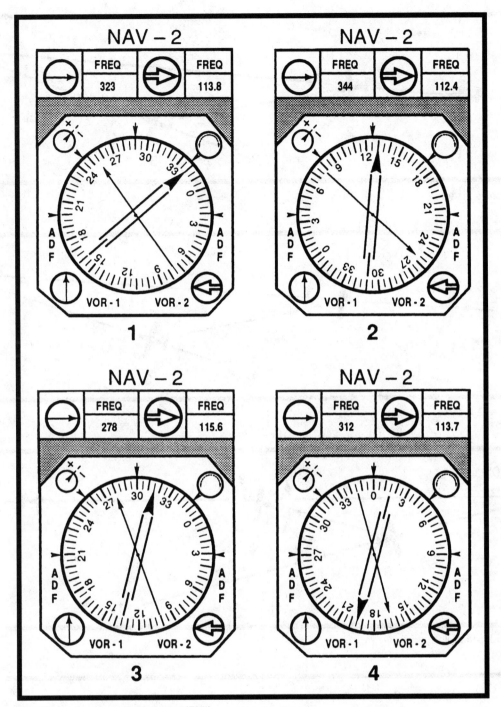

Fig. 20. Radio magnetic indicator (RMI)

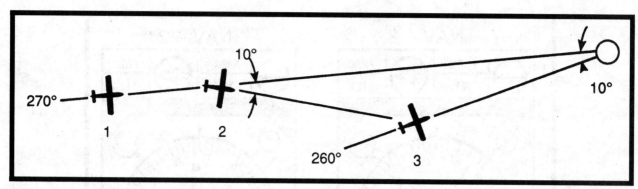

Fig. 21. Isosceles triangle

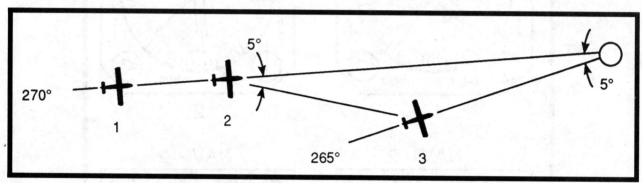

Fig. 22. Isosceles triangle

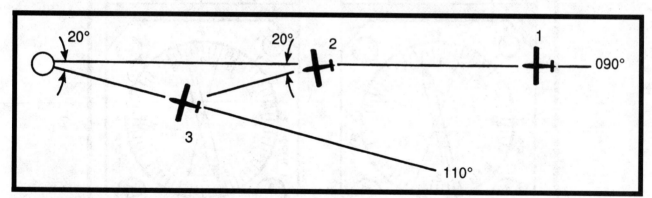

Fig. 23. Isosceles triangle

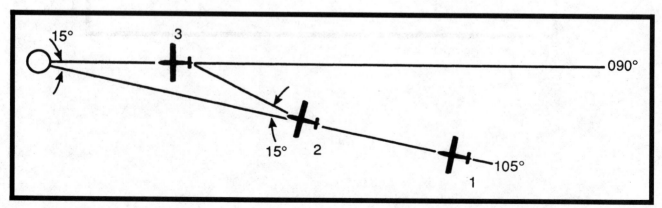

Fig. 24. Isosceles triangle

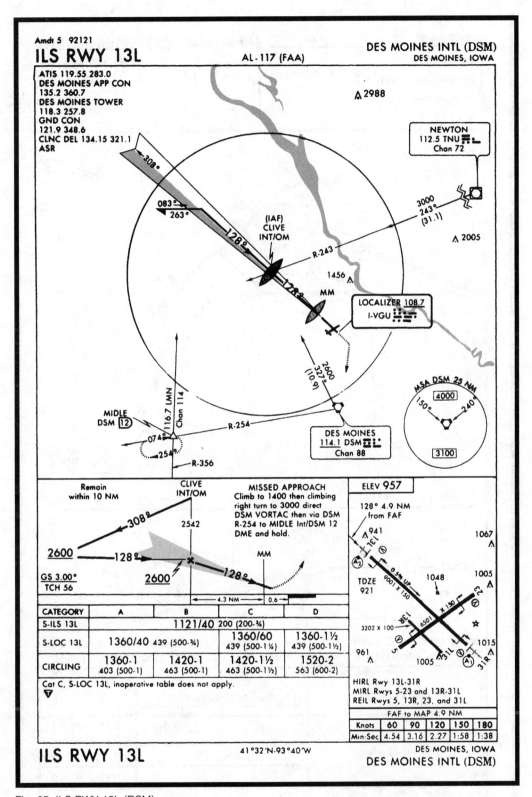

Fig. 25. ILS RWY 13L (DSM)

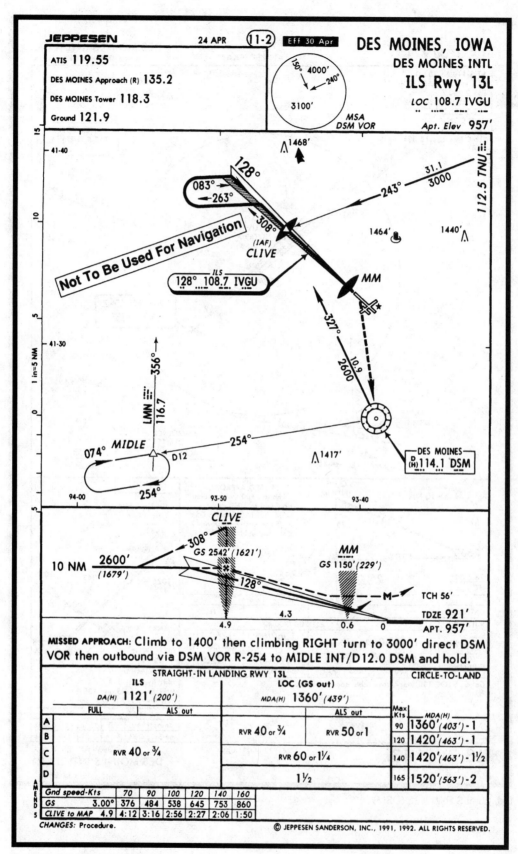

Fig. 25A. ILS RWY 13L (DSM)

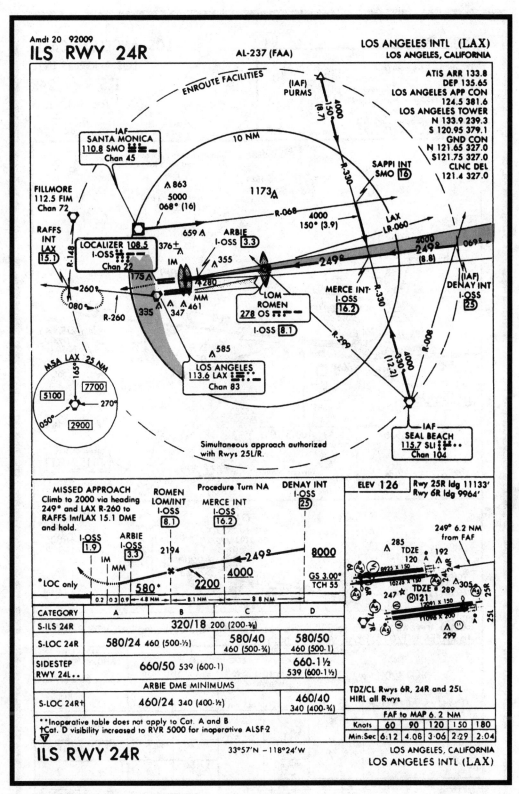

Fig. 26. ILS RWY 24R (LAX)

260

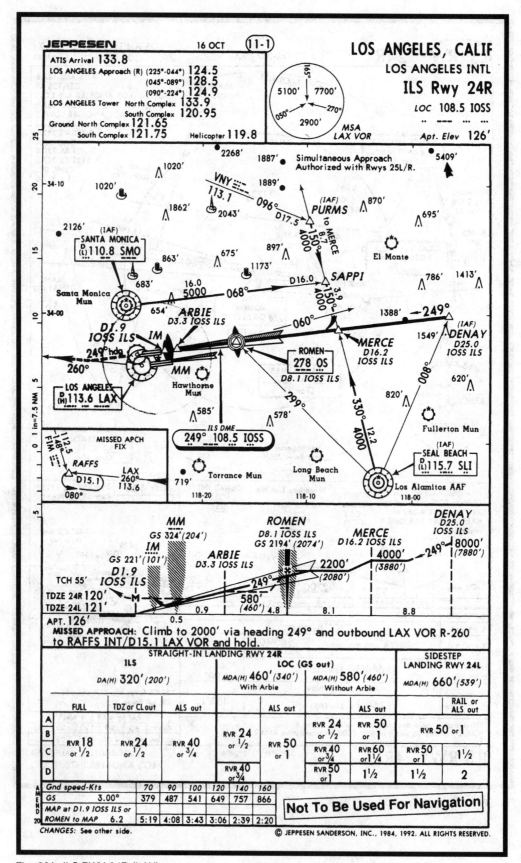

Fig. 26A. ILS RWY 24R (LAX)

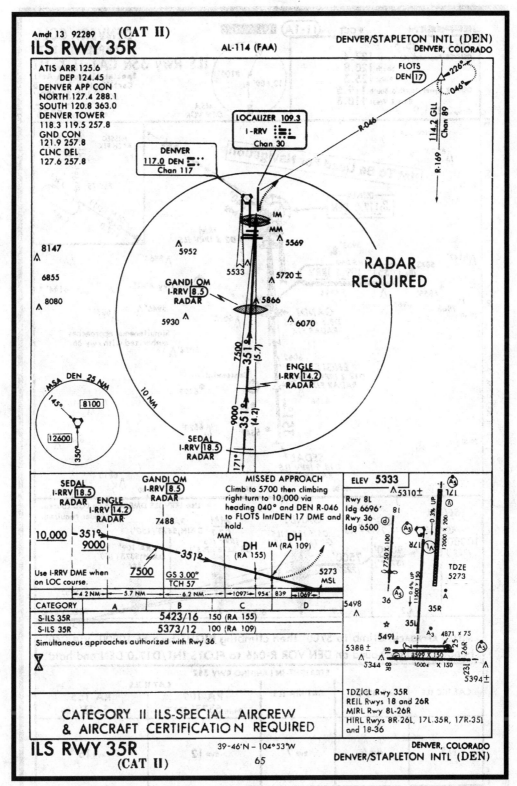

Fig. 27. ILS RWY 35R (CAT II) (DEN)

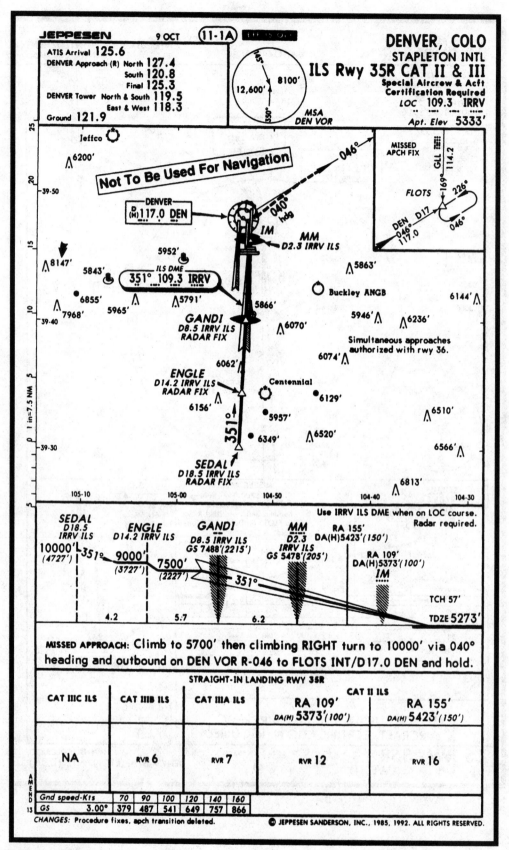

JEPPESEN   9 OCT   (11-1A)   ▊▊ 15 OCT   **DENVER, COLO**
STAPLETON INTL

ATIS Arrival 125.6
DENVER Approach (R) North 127.4
      South 120.8
      Final 125.3
DENVER Tower North & South 119.5
      East & West 118.3
Ground 121.9

ILS Rwy 35R CAT II & III
Special Aircrew & Acft
Certification Required
LOC 109.3 *IRRV*

MSA
DEN VOR

12,600'   8100'
046°
350°

Apt. Elev **5333'**

Not To Be Used For Navigation

Jeffco
△6200'

△8147'
5843'
6855'
7968'
5965'
5952'
△5791'

DENVER
(H) 117.0 DEN
040° hdg
IM
MM
D2.3 IRRV ILS

MISSED APCH FIX
GLL ▦
114.2
FLOTS
226°
169°
DEN D17
046°
117.0
046°

ILS DME
351° 109.3 IRRV

5866'
△5863'
Buckley ANGB
6144'△

GANDI
D8.5 IRRV ILS
RADAR FIX

△6070'
5946'△
△6236'

Simultaneous approaches
authorized with rwy 36.

6062'
6074'△

ENGLE
D14.2 IRRV ILS
RADAR FIX

351°

Centennial
● 6129'
6156'△
5957'
△6510'

6349'
△6520'
6566'△

SEDAL
D18.5 IRRV ILS
RADAR FIX

△6813'

105-10   105-00   104-50   104-40   104-30

Use IRRV ILS DME when on LOC course.
Radar required.

SEDAL D18.5 IRRV ILS	ENGLE D14.2 IRRV ILS	GANDI D8.5 IRRV ILS GS 7488'(2215')	MM D2.3 IRRV ILS GS 5478'(205')	RA 155' DA(H)5423'(150')
10000' (4727')	9000' (3727')	7500' (2227')		RA 109' DA(H)5373'(100') IM

351°   351°   351°

4.2   5.7   6.2

TCH 57'
TDZE 5273'

MISSED APPROACH: Climb to 5700' then climbing RIGHT turn to 10000' via 040°
heading and outbound on DEN VOR R-046 to FLOTS INT/D17.0 DEN and hold.

STRAIGHT-IN LANDING RWY 35R

CAT IIIC ILS	CAT IIIB ILS	CAT IIIA ILS	CAT II ILS	
			RA 109' DA(H) 5373'(100')	RA 155' DA(H) 5423'(150')
NA	RVR 6	RVR 7	RVR 12	RVR 16

Gnd speed-Kts	70	90	100	120	140	160
GS 3.00°	379	487	541	649	757	866

CHANGES: Procedure fixes, apch transition deleted.

© JEPPESEN SANDERSON, INC., 1985, 1992. ALL RIGHTS RESERVED.

Fig. 27A. ILS RWY 35R (CAT II) (DEN)

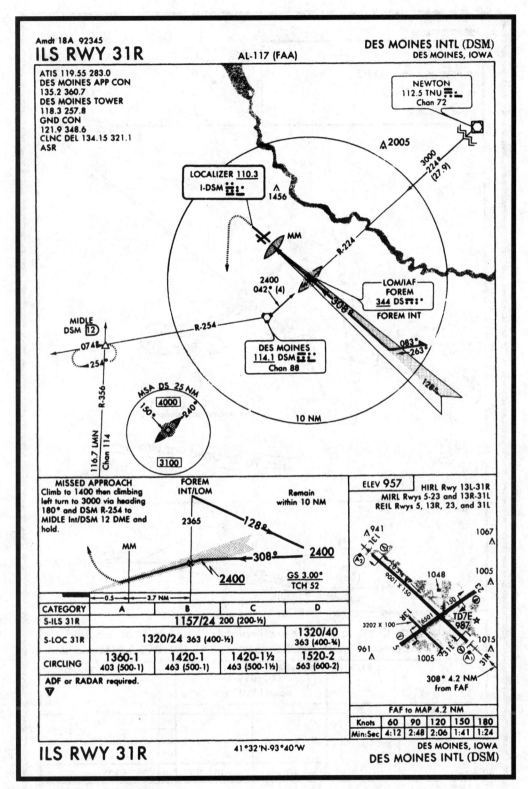

Fig. 28. ILS RWY 31R (DSM)

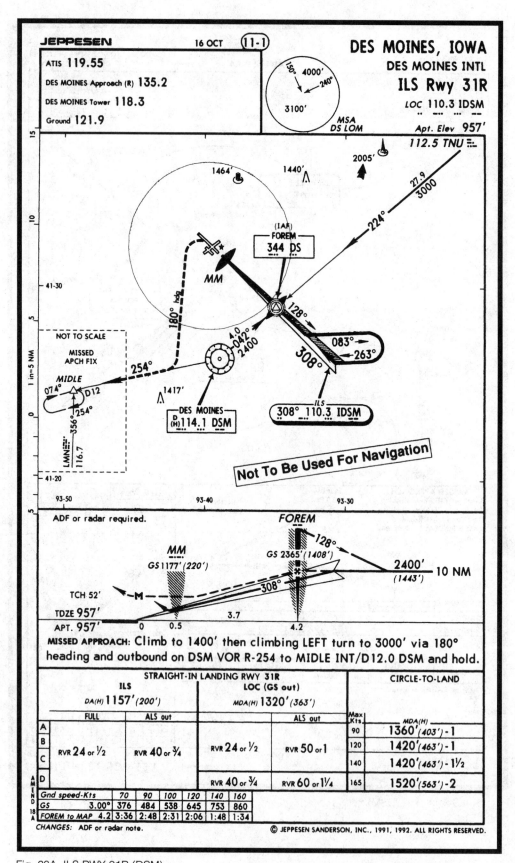

Not To Be Used For Navigation

Fig. 28A. ILS RWY 31R (DSM)

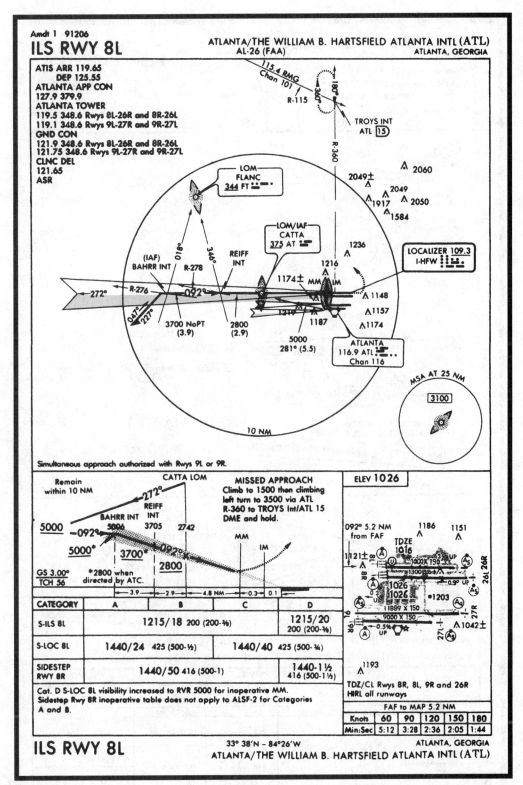

Fig. 29. ILS RWY 8L (ATL)

266

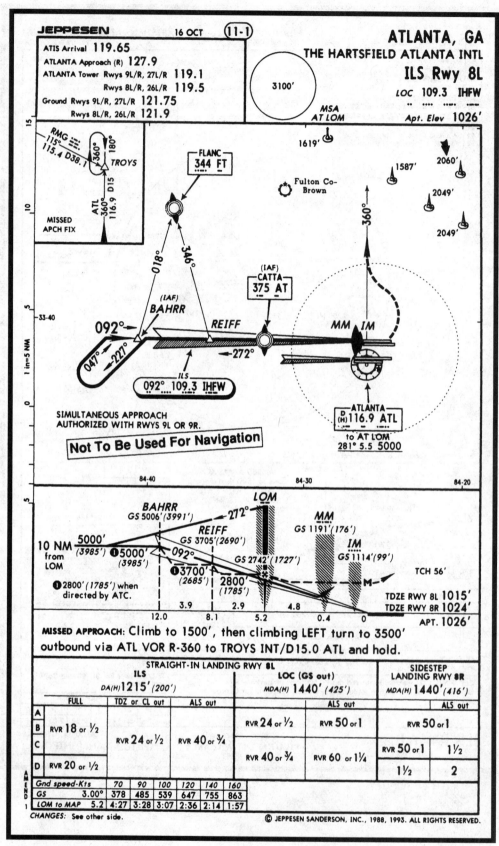

© JEPPESEN SANDERSON, INC., 1988, 1993. ALL RIGHTS RESERVED.

Fig. 29A. ILS RWY 8L (ATL)

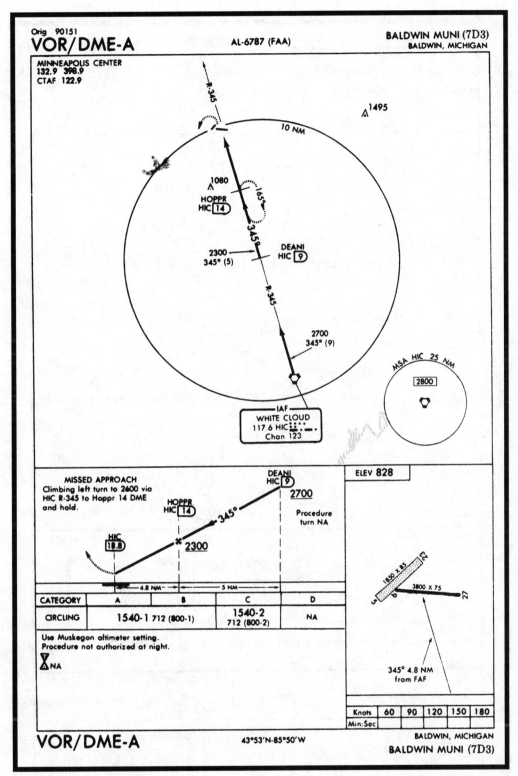

VOR/DME-A   AL-6787 (FAA)   BALDWIN MUNI (7D3) BALDWIN, MICHIGAN

Orig 90151

MINNEAPOLIS CENTER
132.9 398.9
CTAF 122.9

10 NM

∆ 1495

∆ 1080

HOPPR
HIC 14

165°

345°

2300
345° (5)

DEANI
HIC 9

R-345

R-345

2700
345° (9)

MSA HIC 25 NM
2800

IAF
WHITE CLOUD
117.6 HIC
Chan 123

MISSED APPROACH
Climbing left turn to 2600 via
HIC R-345 to Hoppr 14 DME
and hold.

DEANI
HIC 9
2700
Procedure
turn NA

HOPPR
HIC 14
345°
2300

HIC
18.8

ELEV 828

4.8 NM   5 NM

CATEGORY	A	B	C	D
CIRCLING	1540-1 712 (800-1)		1540-2 712 (800-2)	NA

Use Muskegon altimeter setting.
Procedure not authorized at night.

NA

1850 X 85

3800 X 75

27

345° 4.8 NM
from FAF

Knots	60	90	120	150	180
Min:Sec					

VOR/DME-A   43°53'N-85°50'W   BALDWIN, MICHIGAN
BALDWIN MUNI (7D3)

Fig. 30. VOR/DME-A (7D3)

268

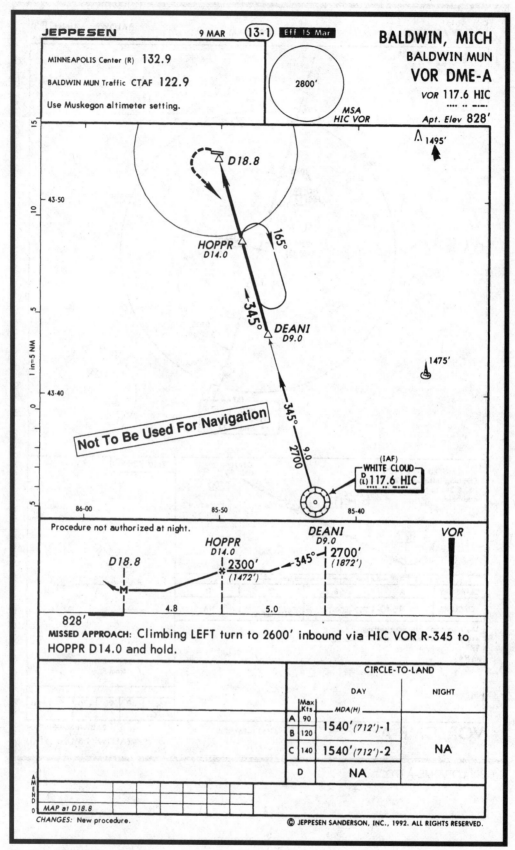

Not To Be Used For Navigation

JEPPESEN 9 MAR (13-1) Eff 15 Mar

BALDWIN, MICH
BALDWIN MUN
VOR DME-A

VOR 117.6 HIC

Apt. Elev 828'

MINNEAPOLIS Center (R) 132.9

BALDWIN MUN Traffic CTAF 122.9

Use Muskegon altimeter setting.

2800'

MSA
HIC VOR

∧ 1495'

D18.8

165°

HOPPR
D14.0

345°

DEANI
D9.0

1475'

345°
9.0
2700

(IAF)
WHITE CLOUD
D
(L) 117.6 HIC

43-50

43-40

1 in=5 NM

86-00 85-50 85-40

Procedure not authorized at night.

HOPPR
D14.0

DEANI
D9.0

VOR

D18.8

2300'
(1472')

345°

2700'
(1872')

828'

4.8 5.0

MISSED APPROACH: Climbing LEFT turn to 2600' inbound via HIC VOR R-345 to
HOPPR D14.0 and hold.

		CIRCLE-TO-LAND	
		DAY	NIGHT
	Max Kts	MDA(H)	
A	90	1540'(712')-1	
B	120		NA
C	140	1540'(712')-2	
D		NA	

AMEND 0

MAP at D18.8

CHANGES: New procedure.

© JEPPESEN SANDERSON, INC., 1992. ALL RIGHTS RESERVED.

Fig. 30A. VOR/DME-A (7D3)

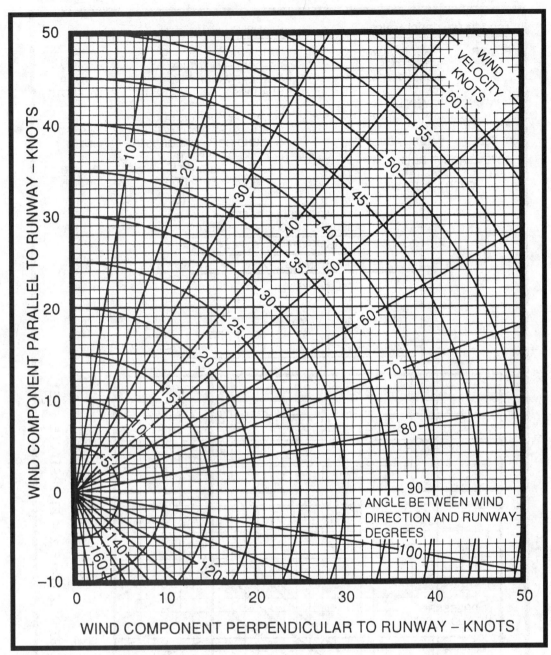

Fig. 31. Wind component chart

ASSOCIATED CONDITIONS:

POWER	TAKEOFF POWER SET BEFORE BRAKE RELEASE
FLAPS	20°
RUNWAY	PAVED, LEVEL, DRY SURFACE
TAKEOFF SPEED	IAS AS TABULATED

NOTE: GROUND ROLL IS APPROX. 73% OF TOTAL TAKEOFF DISTANCE OVER A 50 FT OBSTACLE

EXAMPLE:

OAT	75 °F
PRESSURE ALTITUDE	4000 FT
TAKEOFF WEIGHT	3100 LB
HEADWIND	20 KNOTS
TOTAL TAKEOFF DISTANCE OVER A 50 FT OBSTACLE	1350 FT
GROUND ROLL (73% OF 1350)	986 FT
IAS TAKEOFF SPEED	
LIFT–OFF	74 MPH
AT 50 FT	74 MPH

WEIGHT POUNDS	IAS TAKEOFF SPEED (ASSUMES ZERO INSTR. ERROR)			
	LIFT–OFF		50 FEET	
	MPH	KNOTS	MPH	KNOTS
3400	77	67	77	67
3200	75	65	75	65
3000	72	63	72	63
2800	69	60	69	60
2600	66	57	66	57
2400	63	55	63	55

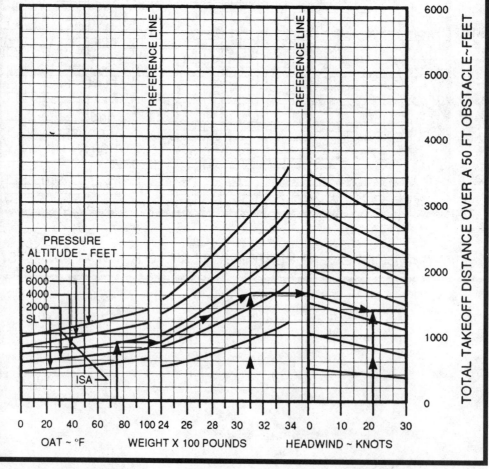

Fig. 32. Obstacle takeoff chart

CONDITIONS:
Flaps Up
Gear Up
2600 RPM
Cowl Flaps Open

PRESS ALT	MP	PPH
S.L. TO 17,000	35	162
18,000	34	156
20,000	32	144
22,000	30	132
24,000	28	120

WEIGHT LBS	PRESS ALT FT	CLIMB SPEED KIAS	RATE OF CLIMB – FPM			
			-20 °C	0 °C	20 °C	40 °C
4000	S.L.	100	1170	1035	895	755
	4000	100	1080	940	800	655
	8000	100	980	840	695	555
	12,000	100	870	730	590	---
	16,000	100	740	605	470	---
	20,000	99	485	355	---	---
	24,000	97	190	70	---	---
3700	S.L.	99	1310	1165	1020	875
	4000	99	1215	1070	925	775
	8000	99	1115	965	815	670
	12,000	99	1000	855	710	---
	16,000	99	865	730	590	---
	20,000	97	600	470	---	---
	24,000	95	295	170	---	---
3400	S.L.	97	1465	1320	1165	1015
	4000	97	1370	1220	1065	910
	8000	97	1265	1110	955	795
	12,000	97	1150	995	845	---
	16,000	97	1010	865	725	---
	20,000	96	730	595	---	---
	24,000	94	405	275	---	---

Fig. 33. Maximum rate-of-climb chart

272

PRESSURE ALTITUDE 6,000 FEET

CONDITIONS:
Recommended Lean Mixture
3800 Pounds
Cowl Flaps Closed

RPM	MP	20 °C BELOW STANDARD TEMP -17 °C			STANDARD TEMPERATURE 3 °C			20 °C ABOVE STANDARD TEMP 23 °C		
		% BHP	KTAS	PPH	% BHP	KTAS	PPH	% BHP	KTAS	PPH
2550	24	---	---	---	78	173	97	75	174	94
	23	76	167	96	74	169	92	71	171	89
	22	72	164	90	69	166	87	67	167	84
	21	68	160	85	65	162	82	63	163	80
2500	24	78	169	98	75	171	95	73	172	91
	23	74	166	93	71	167	90	69	169	87
	22	70	162	88	67	164	85	65	165	82
	21	66	158	83	63	160	80	61	160	77
2400	24	73	165	91	70	166	88	68	167	85
	23	69	161	87	67	163	84	64	164	81
	22	65	158	82	63	159	79	61	160	77
	21	61	154	77	59	155	75	57	155	73
2300	24	68	161	86	66	162	83	64	163	80
	23	65	158	82	62	159	79	60	159	76
	22	61	154	77	59	155	75	57	155	72
	21	57	150	73	55	150	71	53	150	68
2200	24	63	156	80	61	157	77	59	158	75
	23	60	152	76	58	153	73	56	154	71
	22	57	149	72	54	149	70	53	149	67
	21	53	144	68	51	144	66	49	143	64
	20	50	139	64	48	138	62	46	137	60
	19	46	133	60	44	132	58	43	131	57

Fig. 34. Cruise performance chart

ASSOCIATED CONDITIONS:

POWER	AS REQUIRED TO MAINTAIN 800 FT/MIN DESCENT ON APPROACH
FLAPS	DOWN
RUNWAY	PAVED, LEVEL, DRY SURFACE
APPROACH SPEED	IAS A TABULATED

NOTE: GROUND ROLL IS APPROX. 53% OF TOTAL LANDING DISTANCE OVER A 50 FT OBSTACLE.

EXAMPLE:

OAT	75 °F
PRESSURE ALTITUDE	4000 FT
LANDING WEIGHT	3200 LB
HEADWIND	10 KNOTS
TOTAL LANDING DISTANCE OVER A 50 FT OBSTACLE	1475 FT
GROUND ROLL (53% OF 1475)	782 FT
IAS APPROACH SPEED	87 MPH IAS

WEIGHT POUNDS	MPH	KNOTS
3400	90	78
3200	87	76
3000	84	73
2800	81	70
2600	78	68
2400	75	65

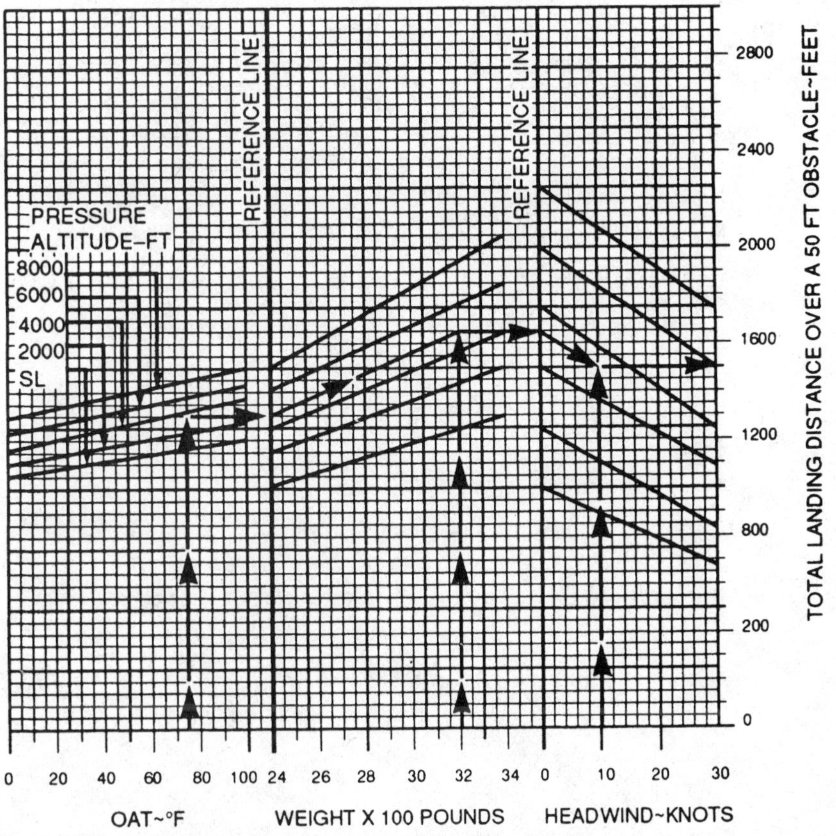

IAS APPROACH SPEED (ASSUMES ZERO INSTR. ERROR)

Fig. 35. Normal landing chart

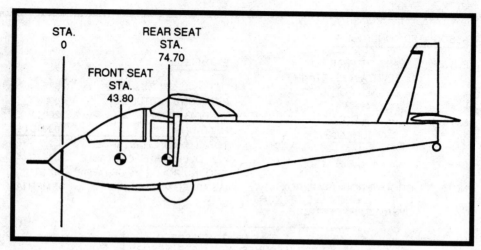

Fig. 36. Stations diagram

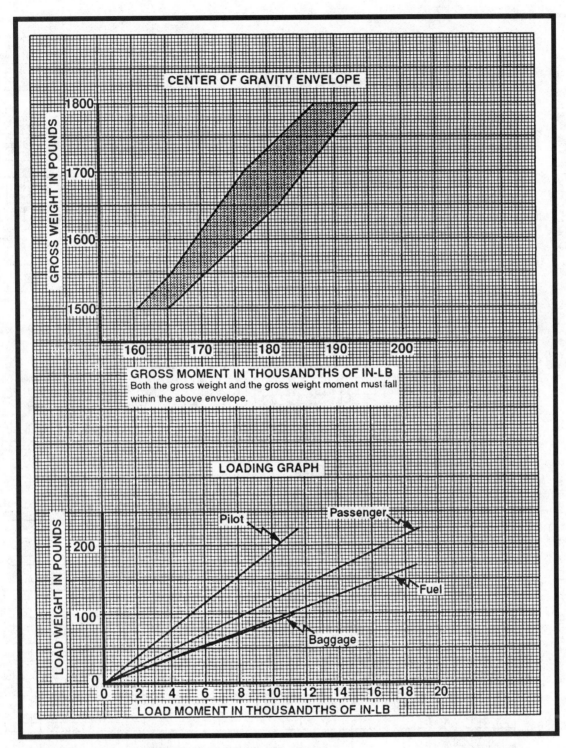

Fig. 37. Center-of-gravity envelope and loading graph

276

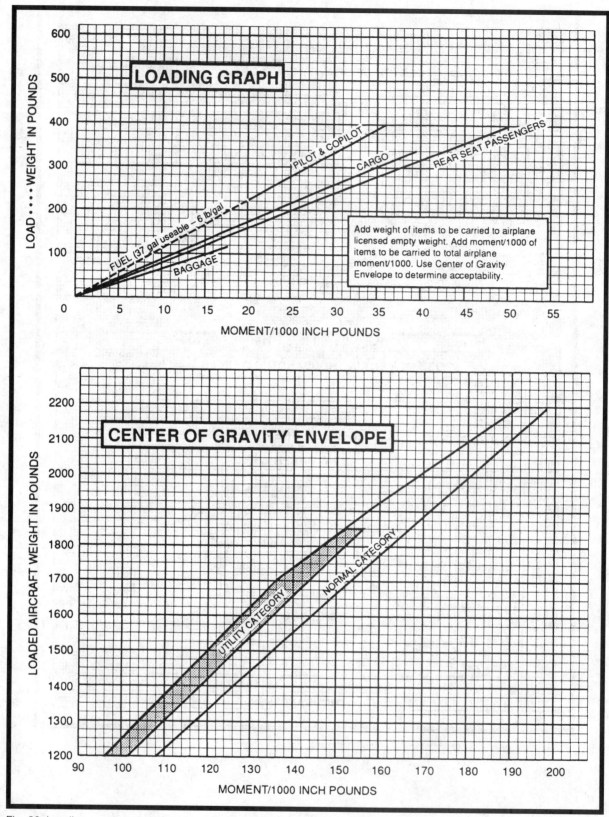

Fig. 38. Loading graph and center-of-gravity envelope

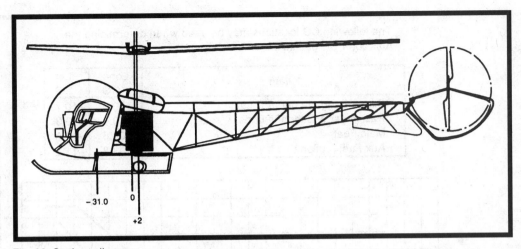

Fig. 39. Stations diagram

The following CG locations may be used when determining the helicopter CG position.

Item	Long CG	Lat CG
Pilot & Baggage under R seat	79.0	+10.7
Passenger & Baggage under L seat	79.0	−9.3
Main Fuel	108.6	−11.0
Aux Fuel (optional)	103.8	+11.2

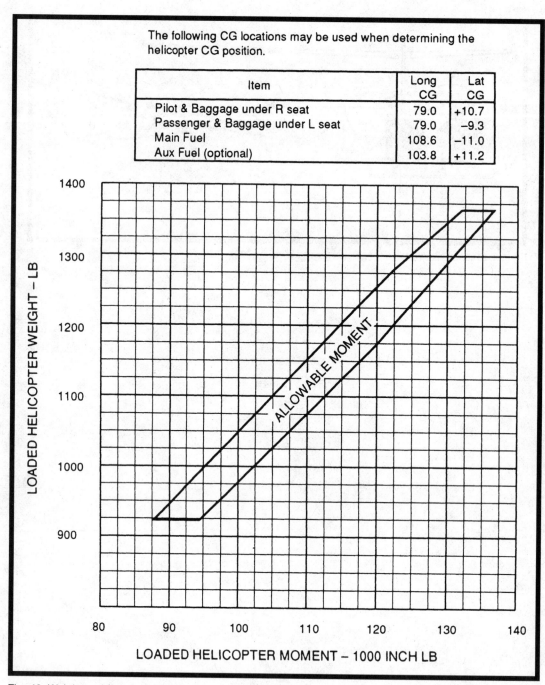

Fig. 40. Weight and balance chart

279

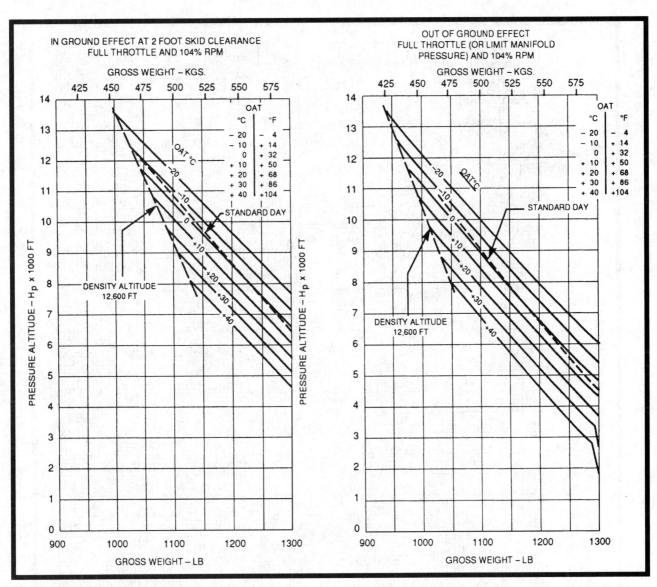

Fig. 41. Hover ceiling vs. gross weight

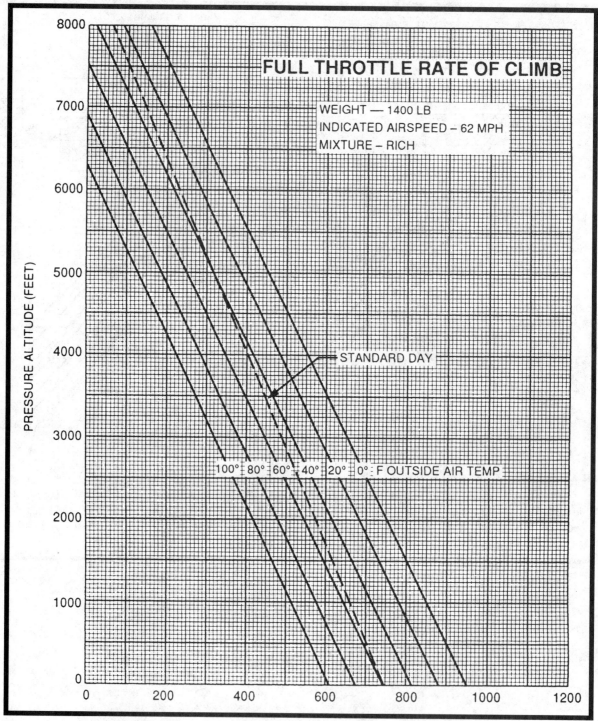

FULL THROTTLE RATE OF CLIMB

WEIGHT — 1400 LB
INDICATED AIRSPEED – 62 MPH
MIXTURE – RICH

STANDARD DAY

100° 80° 60° 40° 20° 0° F OUTSIDE AIR TEMP

PRESSURE ALTITUDE (FEET)

Fig. 42. Rate of climb (ft/min)

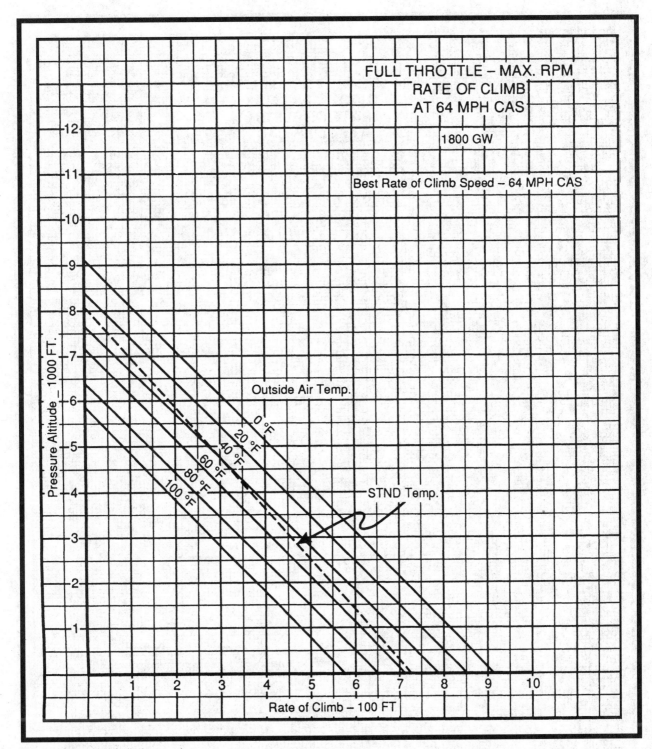

Fig. 43. Best rate-of-climb speed

282

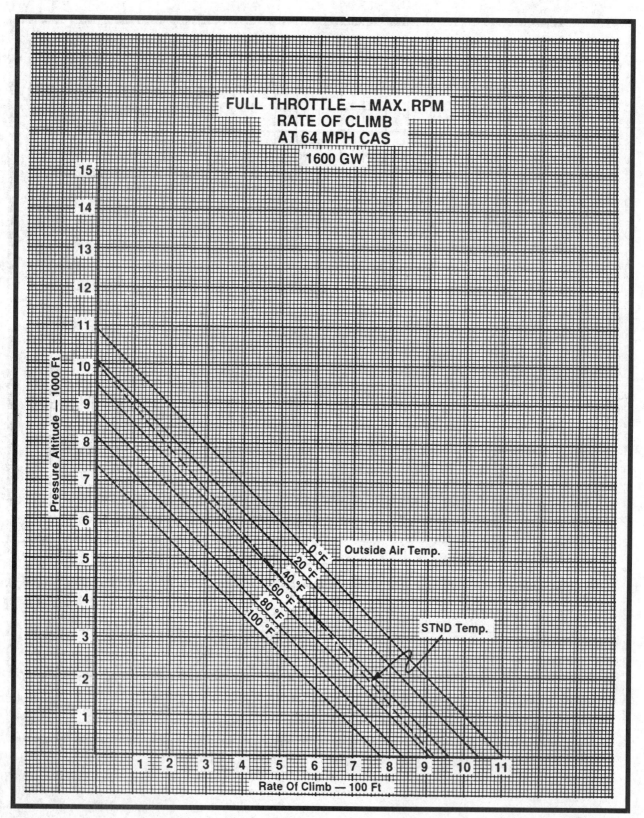

Fig. 44. Rate of climb

283

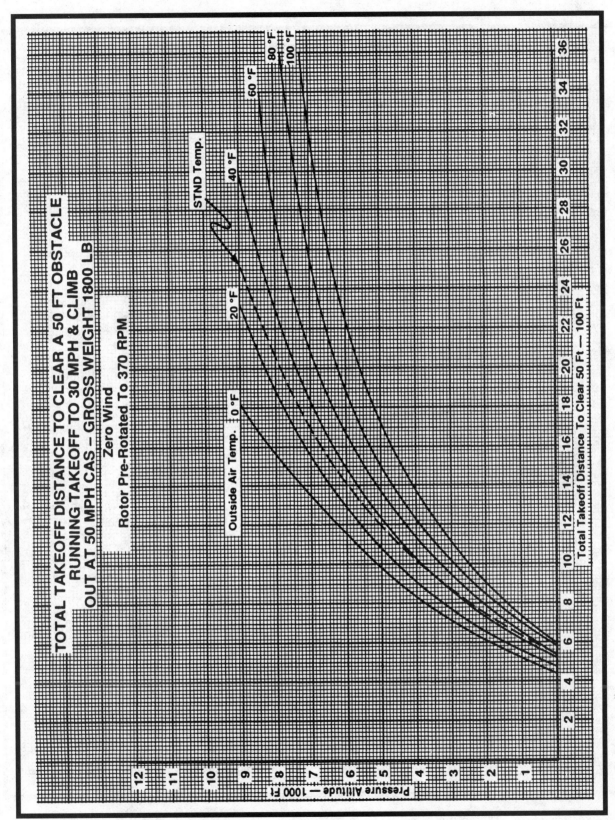

Fig. 45. Running takeoff

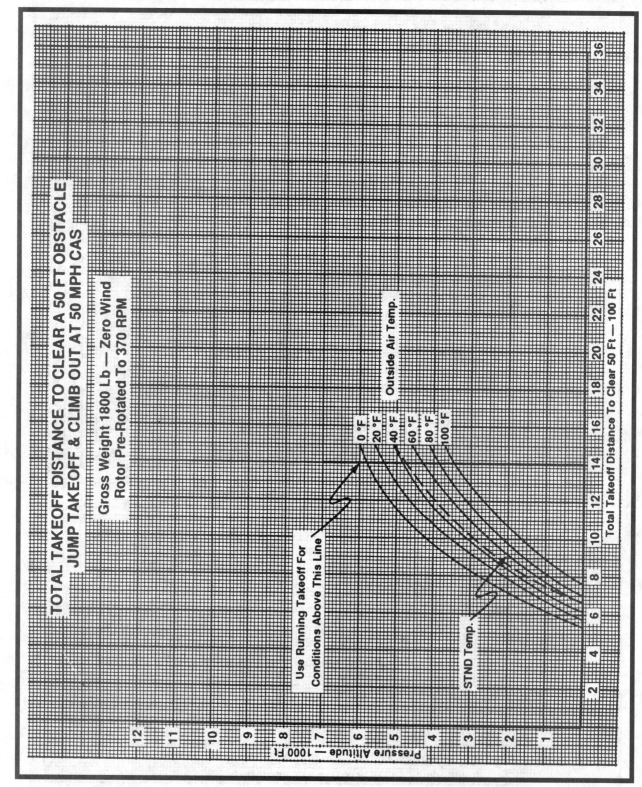

284

Fig. 46. Jump takeoff

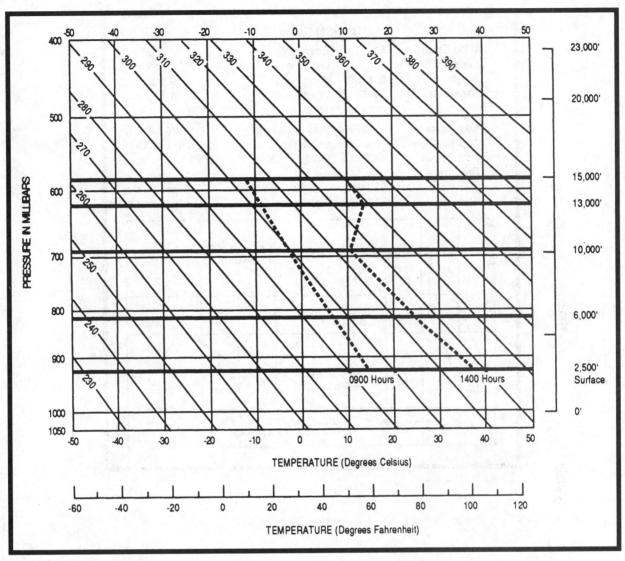

Fig. 47. Adiabatic chart

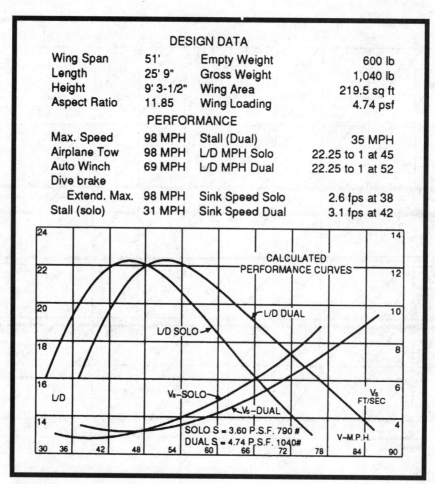

DESIGN DATA

Wing Span	51'	Empty Weight	600 lb
Length	25' 9"	Gross Weight	1,040 lb
Height	9' 3-1/2"	Wing Area	219.5 sq ft
Aspect Ratio	11.85	Wing Loading	4.74 psf

PERFORMANCE

Max. Speed	98 MPH	Stall (Dual)	35 MPH
Airplane Tow	98 MPH	L/D MPH Solo	22.25 to 1 at 45
Auto Winch	69 MPH	L/D MPH Dual	22.25 to 1 at 52
Dive brake			
Extend. Max.	98 MPH	Sink Speed Solo	2.6 fps at 38
Stall (solo)	31 MPH	Sink Speed Dual	3.1 fps at 42

Fig. 48. Performance curves chart

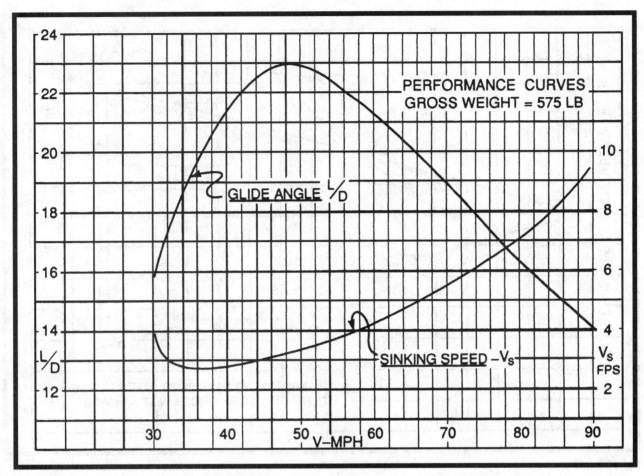

Fig. 49. Performance curves chart

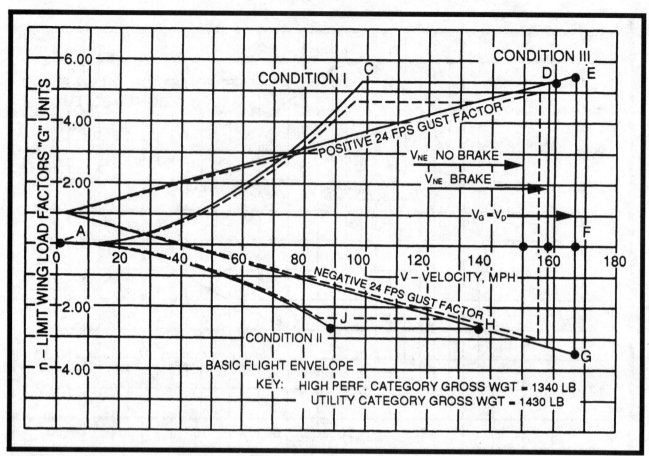

Fig. 50. Flight envelope

Fig. 51. Airport signs

289

Fig. 52. Sectional chart excerpt

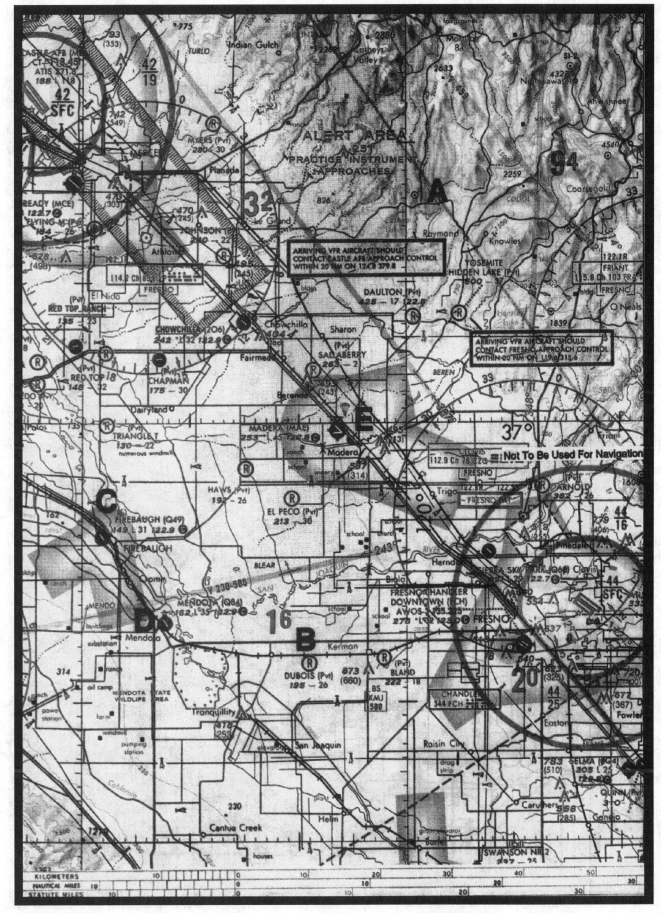

Fig. 53. Sectional chart excerpt

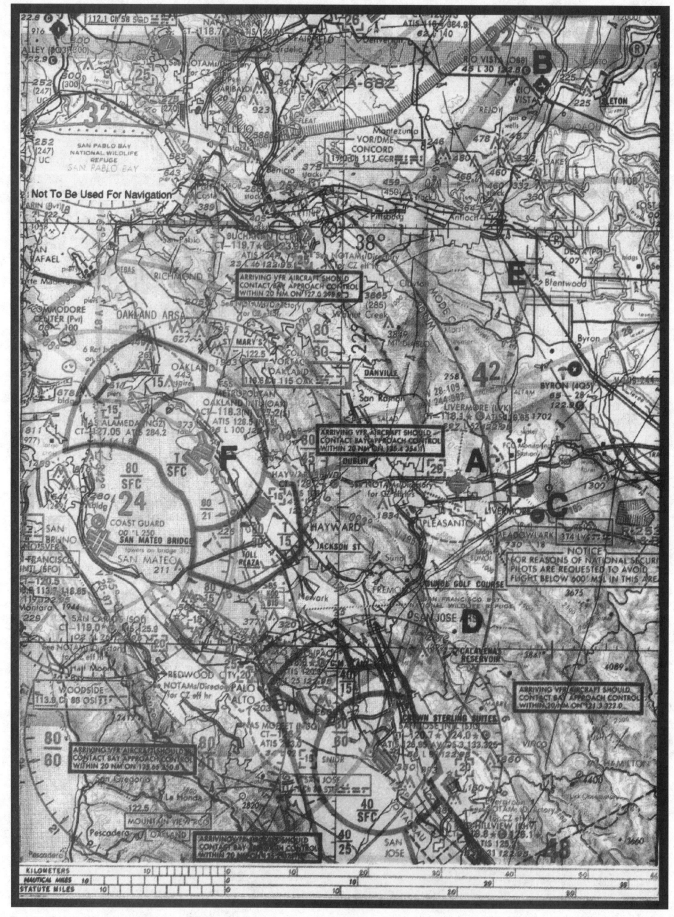

Fig. 54. Sectional chart excerpt

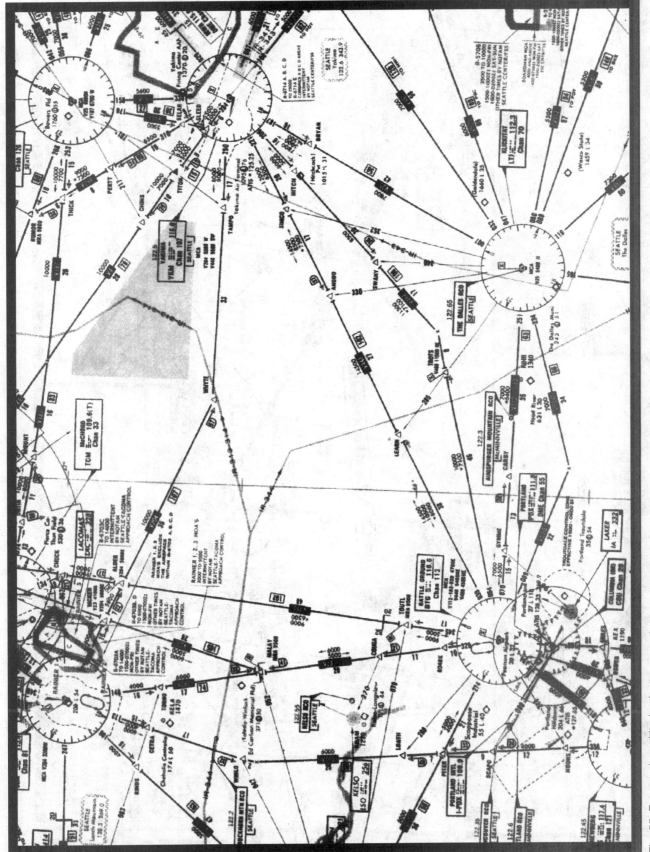

Fig. 55. En route low-altitude chart segment

294

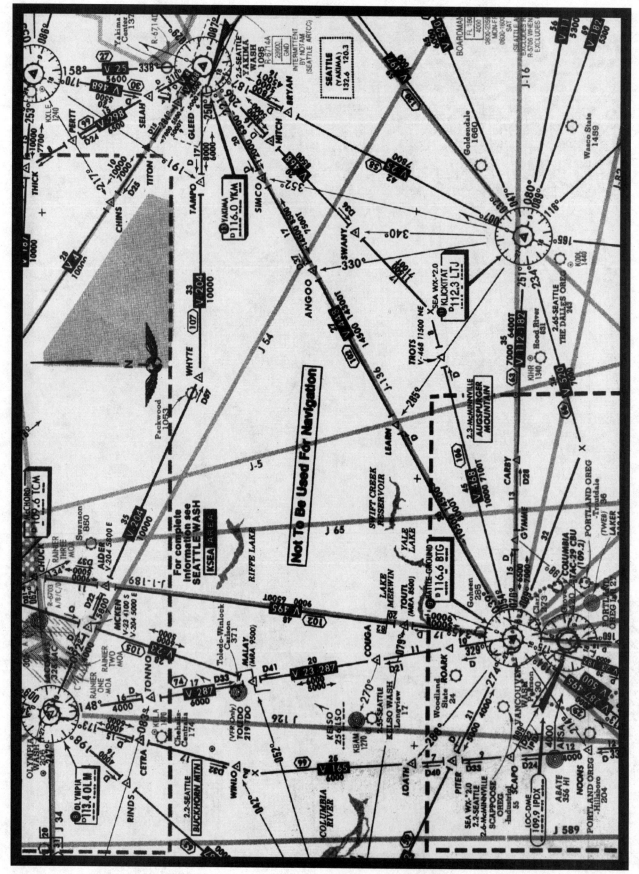

Fig. 55A. En route low-altitude chart segment

About the Author

Douglas S. Carmody, CFII, has been an airline pilot for more than a decade. He currently captains a Fokker F-28 for USAir. A graduate of Embry-Riddle Aeronautical University, he is senior editor of *CFI Magazine* and author of *Private Pilot Test Guide 1996-1998*.

Software Offer

To duplicate the computer-based test-taking experience, order the companion disk for this test guide. The 3 ½" high-density disk contains a program that allows you to take a practice exam presented in a format similar to the actual FAA exam. The program runs on most IBM-compatible computers in either DOS or Windows.

YES, I'm interested. Please send me:

_____ copies 3½" disk (#8705827), $24.95 each . . . . $ _____

Shipping & Handling: $4.00 per disk in U.S./Canada $ _____

Please add applicable state and local sales tax. $ _____

TOTAL $ _____

❑ Check or money order enclosed made payable to McGraw-Hill, Inc.

Charge my ❑ VISA   [VISA]   ❑ MasterCard   [MasterCard]   ❑ American Express   [AMERICAN EXPRESS]

❑ Discover Card   [DISCOVER]

Acct No. _____   Exp. Date _____
Signature _____
Name _____
Address _____
City _____ State _____ Zip _____

TOLL-FREE ORDERING: ☎ **1-800-822-8158**

or write to:
McGraw-Hill, Inc.
Customer Service
P.O. Box 182607
Columbus, OH, 43218-2607

Prices subject to change. Orders outside the U.S. and Canada must be
prepaid in U.S. dollars and include an additional $5.00 for postage and handling.

Key=BC16CPF